Arab Cinema

D1563301

Arab Cinema
History and Cultural Identity
Revised and Updated Edition

Viola Shafik

The American University in Cairo Press
Cairo • New York

To the memory of my mother Elfriede Laux
and with gratitude to my stepmother
Ingrid Offterdinger

Copyright © 1997, 2007, 2016 by
The American University in Cairo Press
113 Sharia Kasr el Aini, Cairo, Egypt
420 Fifth Avenue, New York, NY 10018
www.aucpress.com

All rights reserved. No part of this publication may be reproduced, stored in a retrieval system, or transmitted in any form or by any means, electronic, mechanical, photocopying, recording, or otherwise, without the prior written permission of the publisher.

Exclusive distribution outside Egypt and North America by I.B. Tauris & Co Ltd., 6 Salem Road, London, W2 4BU

Dar el Kutub No. 13776/14
ISBN 978 977 416 690 7

Dar el Kutub Cataloging-in-Publication Data

  Shafik, Viola.
    Arab Cinema: History and Cultural Identity, updated with a new postscript / Viola Shafik.—Cairo: The American University in Cairo Press, 2015
            p.   cm.
              ISBN 978 977 416 690 7
        Motion pictures
              791.43

1 2 3 4 5   19 18 17 16

CONTENTS

PREFACE TO THE
THIRD EDITION

Seventeen years after the appearance of the first edition of *Arab Cinema*, there is a lot to add regarding basic or even comprehensive data on Arab cinemas. Quite a number of dedicated researchers and authors, including Ferid Boughedir, Hady Zaccak, Hamid Dabashi, Gonül Demnez, Josef Gugler, Kevin Dwyer, Mustafa al-Masnaoui, Rasha Salti, Rebecca Hillauer, Roy Armes, Sahar Ali, Lina Khatib, Jamal Bahmad, among others, have worked to fill this gap so that the field of Arab cinema can by no means considered a tabula rasa anymore.

The focus of this book is committed Arab cinema in general and *cinéma d'auteur* in particular, rather than audience and spectatorship, which I examine in my book *Popular Egyptian Cinema: Gender, Class, and Nation*, with regards to Egyptian cinema. At the same time, and without denying the subjectivity of historical accounts, it needs to be underlined that despite my desire to be as comprehensive as possible I did not aim to create an inventory of Arab cinema, but to answer a particular set of research questions tackling the different aspects of film, cultural and national identity, as well as transnationalism in the region.

INTRODUCTION

The Arab world is not, as is often perceived, a monolith, but is made up of different communities, peoples, states, and governmental and societal forms. Neither does it form linguistically, ethnically, or culturally an unchallenged unity. The majority of its inhabitants adhere to Islam, but other religions are represented in the region, including Judaism, Christianity, and Islamic sects such as those of the Alawites and Druze. On the linguistic level little unity exists; in addition to the languages of ethnic minorities like Berbers, Nubians, and Kurds, the Arabic language itself has split into a huge variety of local dialects.

To include such a heterogeneous region in a single study is problematic even when the subject is confined to a relatively clear phenomenon like feature film production. In light of the existing local differences that result, even in the field of cinema, from national character and the political situation of each Arab country, French publications in particular have increasingly tended to speak about Arab cinemas *(les cinémas arabes)* rather than one Arab cinema.

In spite of this, the book touches on more or less all the relevant Arab countries. Although the Arab-Muslim lifestyle and popular culture have developed different local contours, they still possess in many cultural fields a common topography, in particular in so-called high culture—the classical language, science, theology, and the arts of the elites. Furthermore, most Arab countries possess a comparable history regarding colonialism and dependency on foreign powers. Comparisons and juxtapositions may therefore give way to a deeper understanding of cinematic production in each particular country if differences and similarities are taken consciously into consideration.

This book concentrates only on full-length feature film productions. Although it is not confined geographically or temporally, it
cannot deal equally with all Arab countries. Egypt, for example, was
the first Arab country to create a national cinema industry, and its
production still exceeds, at least in quantity, those of other Arab
nations. In the examination of the economic structures of Arab
cinema, Egypt will occupy center place because its commercial
production served partly as a model for Lebanon, Syria, and Iraq. Its
description also serves as a model in other respects; the Lebanese film
industry, for example, functioned until the outbreak of civil war in
1975 in a similar way to the Egyptian industry.

Algerian cinema will be another main focus. With its until recently
exclusively socialist economic structure, it serves on the artistic as
well as the economic level as the counterpart of the Egyptian film
industry, and will therefore also be used as a model.

The extensive inclusion of some film-producing countries,
however, was hampered on a very practical level—not all relevant
films were accessible. During the period of viewing (1990–1992) Iraq
was at war, and life in Lebanon had not yet normalized after the long
civil war. Another difficulty lay in the general distribution system, for
with the exception of commercial Egyptian movies, older works or
films not included in the commercial circuit are rarely available on
tape; a fact that prevented detailed and repeated viewing.

It was not only these obstacles that made it necessary to limit the
number of films under examination. A more positive consideration
was that the reviewing of a smaller number of films allows a more
exact analysis of each. Thus, the films included were chosen from the
works available according to their relevance to the questions of
cultural identity raised by the research.

Theoretical basis

Little attention has so far been paid to the subject of the cultural
identity of Arab cinema. Even among the remarkable number of
Arabic and French publications.[1] I do not know of one work that
deals with this issue in a sufficient and extensive way. The few Arabic
publications dealing, at least according to their titles, with the topic,
such as *Hawiyat al-sinima al-ʿarabiya* (The identity of Arab cinema,
Beirut, 1988) by Samir Farid and *al-Hawiya al-qawmiya fi-l-sinima
al-ʿarabiya* (The national identity of Arab cinema, Beirut, 1986)[2]
edited by ʿAbd al-Munʿim Tulayma, do not offer more than an
anthology of short studies and articles. With few exceptions these are

confined to the question of national identity—meaning the role and effect of nationalism and national liberation movements on Arab cinema—and do not touch on the question of cultural identity. Moreover, the texts are very often dominated by a dichotomy between commercialism and critical social commitment, which leads to a neglect of the influence of popular culture in the form and content of commercial cinema. The film industry's mass production is mainly perceived as alienated: its critics frequently contrast it with the realistic, politically committed cinema that seems to guarantee cultural authenticity. Thus, the socially critical and anti-imperialist attitude of realism is interpreted as a direct expression of true national identity, a concept which needs further verification.

Almost none of the studies deals systematically with the formal means of arrangement alone, or with the rooting of Arab cinema in preceding arts; there is little attempt to define the relation between cinema and music, theater, fine arts, and literature. Examinations of this sort are undertaken only in an anthology edited by Hashim al-Nahas, *al-Insan al-misri ʿala al-shasha* (The Egyptian on screen, Cairo, 1986). It includes texts such as ʿAbd al-Hamid Hawas's "al-Sinima al-misriya wa-l-thaqafa al-shaʿbiya" (Egyptian cinema and popular culture), which touch at least generally on the influence of traditional culture on the audio-visual media.

Some other publications that may serve as an introduction to the subject are included in Georges Sadoul's edition of *The Cinema in the Arab Countries*, published in Beirut in 1966. There are contributions on the relation between the fine arts, language, music, popular theater, and film. In addition, there are some specialized Arab magazines of interest, in particular the Algerian *Les 2 écrans* (The two screens), which offers some valuable studies, like Réda Bensmaïa's article "Cinéma algérien et 'caractère national'" (Algerian cinema and national character), which examines the relation between film and language in Algeria.[3]

The only geographically and historically comprehensive analysis of Arab film making that includes elements of Arab-Muslim culture is presented by Lizbeth Malkmus and Roy Armes in *Arab and African Film Making*. Although cultural identity is not her main subject, Malkmus's treatment of Arab cinema makes the connection between cinematic arrangement and cultural heritage, while trying to describe structural phenomena such as the epic, the comic, the heroic, and the metaphorical. Malkmus's approach is mainly structuralist; she presents specific 'patterns' that she considers most typical of Arab cinema, without clearly specifying historical periods, regional differences, or genres. As a result her study often fails to introduce the film-historical and political context.

It is remarkable that many authors tend to define identity or national affiliation merely by analyzing the story line of a film and its inherent 'message.' While my own research does not completely abandon this method, recognizing as it does the importance of the 'story' to the discourse of a work, it will also consider the film as film, which means examining the technical and artistic methods of *mise en scène*, editing, visual composition, and so on. Extensive examination of these will show the extent to which Arab cinema is rooted in so-called Arab-Muslim culture and what are known as traditional or native arts. This will enable us to address the question of cultural identity on a formal level. An examination of different Arab film genres will also allow an 'intertextual' perspective, as suggested by Robert Stam in his article "Third World Cinema," which proposes that films be compared with other artistic works and means of expression, such as literary movements. At the same time a contextual approach will help to elucidate the connection between cinematic works and historical and political events.[4]

Culture and identity

Film as a medium was invented in the West and is connected to a quasi-industrial form of production that mainly relies on the division of labor and on mass production and distribution. The industrial nations of the northern hemisphere still play the leading role in the technical and artistic development of the medium, and their products have always dominated the Arab market and simultaneously served as a model and rival. In spite of its seventy-year history, and because its existence is based on a Western technique, Arab cinema is frequently criticized as evidence of Westernization and acculturation. Its consideration inevitably touches on the relation between Arab-Muslim culture and the West, and raises questions about notions of authenticity and acculturation, tradition and alienation, and the roots of these relations and ideas.

The history of the West since the end of the Middle Ages may be seen as a continuous journey of discovery to the *terra incognita* of other cultures. Once tracked down, these cultures have been either idealized, dominated, or destroyed. The encounter with the alien entailed its (partly symbolic) incorporation, exclusion, or eradication. Apparently objective scientific disciplines contributed to the 'consumption'—or better the analytic inclusion and exclusion—of recently discovered cultures. Historical and cultural discourses were formulated, based on the construction of the 'Other.'[5] In spite of the actual exchange that took place between the north and south of the Mediterranean over thousands of years, Islam is still perceived in the West as a totally strange culture. Cultural goods from the West, which in the meantime have spread in the so-called Orient, are often unquestioningly referred to as 'imported,' and their adoption as cultural adjustment. What hides behind this notion is the belief in culture as an undivided possession. It serves, as does the term 'intellectual property,' to increase the value of the original over the copy, and to enhance the importance of the original 'proprietor' vis-à-vis the new one.

The idea of the commercial film making of the so-called Third World as an imitation of Western models derives from a comparable concept and is supported by Western as well as Arab film critics. The following description of commercial Egyptian film making, significantly enough published in Arabic and written by the French critic Claude Michel Cluny, author of the *Dictionnaire de cinémas arabes*, serves as evidence:

> Egypt has assumed cinema in the same way as it has assumed other techniques and products. They were offered to it by a mechanized West, which is dominant thanks to its economic power and its ideological and cultural influence. Although the 'cinéastes' from Cairo and Alexandria were the first, they did not approach the real Egypt. For almost half a century they remained strangers to their own culture. Instead they allowed themselves to be dominated by scarcely analyzed European ideas, whose mystery they had not yet solved. In order to develop their 'national' film making they relied on the arrangement of vulgar images (cabaret) or spectacular ones (literature, theater, songs). . .[6]

Arab critics have also perpetuated the idea of unilateral cultural import:

> In these countries—which did not know the era of industrial mechanization, or the painted, animated, or fixed image; or evocative acoustics or movements defined by volume and space; or the alternation of a figurative narration and everything of the life of people, their work, their pain and joy reproduced through this bold visual technique—how was the intrusion of this art apprehended, understood and adopted—an art marking this century on the level of direct contact with, at one and the same time, a worked out and didactic culture and the imaginary and its implied narrative discourse?[7]

The idea of cinema as an alien cultural element, implanted in an 'authentic,' quasi-virgin Arab culture, has to be questioned in the same way as the notion of cultural 'authenticity.' A culture can only be authentic if all its features spring from a particular environment and develop according to its specific conditions. Therefore authenticity can only exist within an impermeable cultural environment, cut off from foreign influences. The countries of North Africa and the Middle East have never formed a closed and secluded cultural environment: "The history of the region is one of polyglot empires, mixing together peoples, cultures, religions, and languages."[8] The popular cultures as well as the high cultures of these countries serve as evidence of this.

The culture of the region must be considered as the result of a dynamic relation of power, formed along several axes: first, the relation between syncretic popular culture and elitist high culture; second, between the different regional 'cultures' of various peoples and ethnic groups, religions, and languages; and third, between the indigenous culture as a whole and the influences that stem from other cultural environments. Even apparently 'authentic' movements like present-day fundamentalism or nationalism do not invalidate this model. Despite the parameters of Arabic language and Islam having, since national independence, been pushed increasingly into the foreground to serve as a starting-point for cultural purification and preservation, the idea of a pure Arab-Muslim culture is a myth. Nationalism and Islamic fundamentalism, which may be considered as movements of purification,[9] are rather the product of modern mass culture and are shaped by mass movements and ideologies.

In the frame of this newly appearing cultural structure, whose development has been decisively supported by the mass media, the cultural model of traditional society has become increasingly invalid, as has the differentiation between high (elitist) and popular culture.[10] Arab culture is penetrated now by a new dynamic, which has invalidated inherited dialectics and exchange processes. Daily life and living conditions in the Arab countries have become increasingly dominated by mass production and mass consumption. Traditional ways of communication and former arts, like oral narration or shadow plays, die out and are substituted by mass media. The products of the culture industry are far removed both from elitist arts, produced and consumed by only a few, and from syncretic and heterogeneous popular arts. Unlike popular arts the mass media are characterized by one-way communication that transforms the human being into a passive recipient who only consumes 'culture.'

The spread of mass media in the Arab countries, necessarily accompanied by the development of 'consumer culture,' is based on a long process. The first Arabic-language newspapers and magazines appeared as early as the middle of the nineteenth century in some Arab countries. Record players, radios, and tape recorders were

introduced from the beginning of this century. The radio in particular has played an important role in altering traditional ways of
organizing leisure time. Not only was it responsible for the spread of
a certain genre of music, but it also replaced in many places the traditional story teller *(hakawati)* of the cafés.

Mass culture is characterized by a tendency to force needs into
line. Its most urgent goal is consumption. Therefore every expression
is transformed into advertising. Means of mass communication
dominate more and more every part of culture and "what matters is
that the mass cultural machine devalues any cultural expression
which is not circulated through it."[11] The leading industrial nations
still form the driving force of this development. They not only
present constantly newer technologies and products, but also create
trends and define new market strategies. An example on the international scale is Hollywood's unchallenged monopoly of cinema.

Some sociopolitical research speaks in this respect of the domination of the developing countries by the so-called First World. The
antagonism between the Third World and the industrial nations,
which initiate development, is described as being between periphery
and center. The same mechanism is seen to dominate representation
on cinema and television screens. In fact, the 'mass mediated
culture' of the West has been disseminated all over the East via the
media. It is dominated by a cultural concept which crystallizes in
what Michael R. Real calls the CWAWMP, the Capitalist, Western,
Adult, White, Male, Print-oriented person.[12] At the same time, the
self-representation of the so-called Third World remains more than
marginal.

Although the described model of acculturation clearly shows the
dependency of the Arab countries and also asserts the view of
passively received and unilateral cultural importation, it would be
wrong to assume that acculturation has the effect of cultural 'brain-
washing.' Western culture, in spite of the consumption of its
products, is by no means adopted completely or without any resistance. Rather, the traditional symbolic order of a society, its goods
and values are confronted with 'consumer culture' and become de-
and revalued. "This process is in some instances actively furthered
by the intellectuals, the new bourgeoisie, and national elites, with the
latter using the media and advertising techniques to package and
repackage traditional symbols—in effect the national tradition is
selectively interpreted and invented to serve the modernizing and
nation-integration aims of controlling national elites."[13]

The same kind of revaluation and 'repackaging' has likewise taken
place in the field of cinema. Imagery, technique, and the 'language' of

the media have been adopted, but transformed according to the regionally prevalent cultural and social system. This book sets out to describe and investigate this dynamic process.

1

THE HISTORY OF ARAB CINEMA

Most Arab countries did not produce films before national independence. In Sudan, Libya, Saudi Arabia, and the United Arab Emirates, production is even now confined to short films or television.[1] Bahrain witnessed the production of its first and only full-length feature film in 1989. At the end of the 1970s the Kuwaiti director Khalid Siddiq shot two full-length features, one of them a coproduction with the Sudan. In Jordan national production has barely exceeded half a dozen feature films.[2] Algeria and Iraq have produced approximately 100 films each, Morocco around seventy, Tunisia around 130, and Syria some 150. Lebanon, owing to an increased production during the 1950s and 1960s, has made some 180 feature films.[3] Only Egypt has far exceeded these countries, with a production of more than 2,500 feature films (all meant for cinema, not for television).

The film medium was invented in the West at the end of the nineteenth century, by which time significant parts of the Middle East and Maghreb were already considered as British and French protectorates. Two decades later the two superpowers had, through the Sykes-Picot agreement, divided almost the whole Arab world between them.[4] The result was long-lasting political and economic dependency, which, except in Egypt, considerably hampered the creation of national film industries and the development of an Arab film culture. The Arab market was flooded by European products, important areas of the economy were dominated by foreign investors, and native entrepreneurs were hardly able to survive.

The Arab countries were also dominated in the cultural realm. Particularly in the French protectorates and colonies the oppression of indigenous culture was enforced with the help of legal restrictions.

At the same time the acculturation of the native population was imposed by a one-sided offer of education.

Encounter with a new medium

In 1896, only a few months after the first screening in Europe had taken place, films by the Lumière brothers were shown to an exclusive Egyptian audience. The screenings took place in the Tousson stock exchange in Alexandria, in the Hamam Schneider (Schneider Baths) in Cairo and elsewhere.[5] Screenings of Lumière films were also organized in the Algerian cities of Algiers and Oran.[6] In Tunis, the Tunisian Albert Shamama (also known as Shemama Chikly) organized a similar event in 1897. In the same year presentations took place at the Moroccan royal palace in Fez.[7] In 1900, films were screened in the Europa Hotel in Jerusalem.[8]

The introduction of special sites for screenings did not take long to follow. In 1896 the first *cinématographe* was established in Algiers.[9] One year later the Cinématographe Lumière in Alexandria was offering regular screenings. It became common in Egypt to present films during theater performances.[10] In 1906 the French company Pathé constructed in Cairo the first regular cinema on Egyptian soil. Apart from this, two more cinématographes were to be run in Cairo and in Alexandria.[11]

In Tunisia the Omnia Pathé started to work in 1907.[12] One year later Egyptian Jews opened a cinema in Jerusalem called the Oracle.[13] In Oran, Algiers, and other Algerian cities in which the European population were concentrated, the first regular cinemas were constructed in 1908.[14]

During the colonial period in Algeria few native Algerians went frequently to the movies. This was not the case in Egypt, however, where cinemas soon offered films with Arabic translations.[15] By 1908 there were already five cinemas in Cairo and Alexandria.[16] Little more than two decades later nearly all the Arab countries had at least a dozen theaters.

The spread of the medium did not proceed smoothly everywhere, however. In Saudi Arabia cinema was not generally accepted until the 1960s and 1970s, after King Faisal had dealt with the objections of Muslim religious scholars.[17] Even so, there are still no movie theaters run in Saudi Arabia.[18] Until 1962 cinemas were also prohibited in North Yemen because of religious suspicions, despite the enthusiasm of the political and religious leader Imam Ahmad, who liked to record his journeys with a movie camera.[19]

Production during the colonial period

In general, the first movie theaters in the Arab countries were owned by foreigners or by immigrant European minorities. In the same way, film production initially remained confined to foreign and non-native investors.

Early in their activities in cinema Louis and Auguste Lumière sought shootings in the so-called Orient—Algeria and Egypt, for example. Palestine—the 'Holy Land'—also attracted many Western cameramen at the turn of the century; not only the Lumière company but also Thomas Edison had films shot in Jerusalem.[20] In 1905 an immigrant Frenchmen, the *pied-noir* Felix Mesguich, shot several short films in Algeria on Lumière's behalf, and in 1906 traveled with his camera to Egypt.[21] A year later he witnessed the French invasion of Morocco.[22]

In Egypt, the only Arab country able to develop a national film industry during the colonial period, native production started with news films. In 1909, for example, an Egyptian is supposed to have filmed the funeral of the Egyptian leader and patriot Mustafa Kamil.[23] In the following years the number of news films and short fiction films produced in Egypt continued to grow.[24] In 1917, with the assistance of the Banca di Roma, Italian investors established a film company in Alexandria. Far from European competition, they considered the period of World War I a good opportunity to exploit the native market as well as the pleasant weather conditions. After the production of three short films, however, the company went bankrupt.[25] The main causes were the poor quality of the films and the producer's lack of knowledge about the host country. One of their films, for example, was banned by the authorities because it showed Quranic verses in Arabic upside down.[26]

Many short fiction films made in the following years by Europeans were shot in cooperation with Egyptian actors. The actor-turned-director Muhammad Karim acted in the films of the Italian company and was the first Egyptian actor to appear on screen.[27] Amin Sidqi and the popular theater actor ʿAli al-Kassar appeared in Bonvelli's film, *The American Aunt* (al-Khala al-amrikaniya), shot in 1920.[28] The next year saw the screening of Victor Rosito's long film, *In the Country of Tutankhamun* (Fi bilad Tut ʿAnkh Amun), shot by the Egyptian cameraman and director Muhammad Bayyumi.[29] In 1923 Bayyumi directed the adaptation of the popular play *The Clerk* (al-Bashkatib) with Amin ʿAttallah and his troupe. Bayyumi had at that time already shot and directed some other short films in Alexandria.

The first short films directed by natives in the other Arab countries were made in the same period. Albert Shamama (Shemama Chikly), who had organized the first screenings in Tunisia, directed the short fiction film *Zuhra* in 1922, and two years later the first Tunisian (silent) full-length feature film, *The Girl from Carthage* (ᶜAin al-ghazal, literally 'the eye of the gazelle'; La fille de Carthage), in which his daughter played the main part.[30]

In Syria the first native full-length feature film, *The Innocent Accused* (al-Muttaham al-bari'), was presented in 1928. It was produced by Ayyub Badri, who also played the main part and directed the film.[31] In Lebanon the first feature film, *The Adventures of Ilyas Mabruk* (Mughamarat Ilyas Mabruk), was directed in 1929 by the immigrant Jordano Pidutti.[32]

One of the first full-length feature films produced (not directed) by a native Egyptian was entitled *Layla* and released in 1927. The Turkish director, Wedad Orfi, had persuaded the theater actress ᶜAziza Amir to produce the film. After a quarrel with Orfi, Amir had Estephane Rosti direct the film in his place. The film was a great success.

In the same year appeared *A Kiss in the Desert* (Qubla fi-l-sahra'), by Ibrahim Lama, a South American of Lebanese origin who had settled in Egypt together with his brother, the actor Badr Lama. In contrast to other Arab countries, where production remained limited to some scattered pioneer works, production in Egypt increased steadily. Starting from 1928 an average of two feature films were shot annually. In 1932 the first two sound films (whose sound still had to be recorded in Paris) appeared almost simultaneously, *Sons of Aristocrats* (Awlad al-dhawat) by Yusuf Wahbi and *The Song of the Heart* (Unshudat al-fu'ad) by Mario Volpi.

The foundation of the Egyptian film industry was laid in 1934/35 when the Misr Bank, under the management of Talaat Harb, established the Studio Misr. The following decade witnessed the rapid development of the film industry. By 1948 six further studios had been built and a total of 345 full-length features produced.[33] In the years after World War II, cinema was the most profitable industrial sector after the textile industry.[34] Between 1945 and 1952 Egyptian production reached an average of 48 films per year, a number comparable to today's production.[35]

The reasons why Egypt alone succeeded in establishing a national film industry are various. Egypt had a dynamic multicultural life in which native Egyptians always played an important role, and which remained relatively undisturbed by colonial authorities. Particularly after the national upheavals of 1919, native Egyptians developed a

Layla the Bedouin (Layla al-badawiya, Egypt, 1937) by Bahiga
Hafiz (*courtesy Cultural Fund, Ministry of Culture, Cairo*)

stronger interest in the medium and combined it with well established
arts like popular musical theater. Numerous theater directors, actors,
and actresses, such as ᶜAziza Amir, Assia Daghir, Fatima Rushdi,
Bahiga Hafiz, Yusuf Wahbi, ᶜAli al-Kassar, and Nagib al-Rihani
worked at the end of the 1920s and in the course of the 1930s as
producers, scriptwriters, or directors. Popular plays like *The Clerk,
Kish Kish Bey* (1931) and *Why Does the Sea Laugh?* (al-Bahr biyid-
hhak lih? 1928) were fixed on celluloid because of their huge success
on the stage. In 1930 the tireless Yusuf Wahbi, actor, producer, and
director all in one, furnished a first, albeit modest, studio, in order to
produce the Muhammad Karim's adaptation of the novel *Zaynab*.[36]

It was not only artists and enthusiasts who invested in cinema.
Beginning in the 1920s, nationalist-oriented entrepreneurs led by
Talaat Harb, founder of the Misr Bank, worked to develop an
independent national industry. In 1925 Talaat Harb decided that

A Robert Scharfenberg set for *I Can't* (Ma'darsh, Egypt, 1946) by Ahmed
Badrakhan (*courtesy Cultural Fund, Ministry of Culture, Cairo*)

cinema was a good investment opportunity and established the
Sharikat Misr li-l-Sinima wa-l-Tamthil (Misr Company for Cinema
and Performance), which was intended to produce advertising and
information films. In 1934 he built the Misr Studio, which was
inaugurated a year later. It was equipped with a laboratory and a
sound studio, and employed several European specialists, among
them German director Fritz Kramp and set designer Robert
Scharfenberg. At the same time the studio sent young Egyptians on
scholarships to Europe—directors Ahmad Badrakhan (Badr Khan)
and Niyazi Mustafa, for example, were among its beneficiaries.

The eager support given to the medium by native capital was neither accidental nor isolated. From 1922 Egypt was formally independent (although British occupation terminated de facto in 1952). An increasing Egyptianization became visible in many fields and was expressed partly in the struggle against foreign dominance in the economy. In 1937 the Egyptian government abolished the Capitulations, which entailed special legal rights for Europeans. In 1942/43, in the context of measures taken to provide work for Egyptians holding high school or university degrees, Arabic was declared obligatory for companies' written communication. From 1946 all company name plates had to be written in Arabic. One year later a law was promulgated fixing the ratio of employed Egyptians to 75 percent of all employees and 90 percent of all blue-collar workers, and the share of Egyptian capital to 51 percent of all capital.[37]

A comparable development would have been unthinkable in the French colonies and protectorates. Even in those countries that were not considered, like Algeria, as an integral part of France, the French authorities forced the acculturation of natives at the expense of indigenous culture. In Algeria—which in 1933 already had 150 theaters,[38] more than Egypt in the same period[39]—not a single feature film was shot by a native director before independence in 1962.[40] The same is true of Morocco before independence in 1954.

Syria's weak economy precluded the existence there of wealthy and powerful entrepreneurs like Talaat Harb who might have initiated an industrial organization for cinema production. Furthermore, the artistic life of the country had been weakened since the end of the nineteenth century, when various talented Syrian artists and intellectuals had emigrated to Egypt because of political and social restrictions at home.[41] Syrian film makers had always to withstand political pressures; in 1928 French authorities hindered the completion of Ayyub Badri's film, *The Innocent Accused* (al-Muttaham al-bari'), because the female protagonist was a Muslim girl. Badri had to change the character and repeat the shooting, and of course suffered considerable financial losses.[42] The presentation of ʿAtta Makka's silent film, *Under the Sky of Damascus* (Taht sama' Dimashq), was blocked in 1932 when the producer was accused of not having paid the fees for the pre-recorded music that accompanied the film.[43]

In the French colonies the hindering of native efforts to produce was part of a general framework of cultural and economic politics. In Algeria indigenous culture was excluded by strict measures and regulations. Already in the middle of the last century authorities prohibited the traditional and popular shadow plays.[44] Arab culture was not furthered in schools. Pupils were taught only in French and the communication of Arab culture was confined to traditional Quran schools. Modern secular Arab institutions for education did not exist. The proportion of Algerian pupils in secondary schools did not exceed 16 percent although the Algerian population of the country was ten times greater than the French.[45] Thus the cultural life of most Algerians, already impoverished by colonialization, was socially marginalized. Their access to cinemas, which were generally concentrated in the Pieds Noirs settlements, remained slight for economic and cultural reasons. Egyptian films, exported to the whole region since the mid-thirties, were only screened in a few remote suburban or provincial cinemas. In the early 1950s they were burdened with immense taxes. In that period only seventy Egyptian films were distributed in Algeria along with 1,400 Western films.[46]

This does not mean that the Maghreb did not see any cinematographic activities before independence. On the contrary, an industrious colonial cinema developed early. From 1919 French directors were shooting films, like *Mektoub* by J. Pinochin and D. Quintin (1919), *Allah's Blood* (Le sang d'Allah)[47] and *In the Shadow of the Harem* (Dans l'ombre du harem, 1928).[48] These works used the Maghreb as an exotic backdrop full of palm trees, camels and belly dancers. They conveyed a heavily distorted image of North Africa as "a sunny land ripe for adventure, where the Arabs are happy monkeys praising Allah for sending them the civilizing influence of French colonialism."[49]

During the 1920s and 1930s France was striving to strengthen its position in Morocco and Tunisia even further. Colonial cinema started to represent fierce fights and battles with "evil Arabs."[50] When national consciousness started spreading throughout North Africa, particularly after the revolt of May 8, 1945, in which thousands of Algerians were killed, colonial films were eager to avoid any contact with social and political realities in the colonies. In this period censorship advised film makers to avoid images of "looting Arabs and armed settlers."[51]

In order to confront the spreading spirit of revolt and at the same time to convey to the natives a positive image of France and of "the role and benefits of France in this country [Algeria] in the cultural, social, economic fields, etc.,"[52] after 1945 the colonial authorities went on the offensive. They started, together with the French army, to use cinema as a means of propaganda. For this reason they established in Morocco the CCM (Centre Cinématographique Marocain) and in Algeria several units like the SAC (Service Algérien du Cinéma), the CNC (Centre National de la Cinématographie) for production and the SDC (Service de Diffusion Cinématographique) for distribution. The short films produced and distributed in Algeria, which were partly furnished with commentaries in the colloquial language, fell into several categories: documentaries on Algeria, on France and its colonies, and on achievements in industry and crafts; information films on the Muslim world and on Islam; films containing medical and pedagogic advice[53] as well as political propaganda. The last, which showed the 'appeasement' of Algeria while presenting the resistance fighters as criminal outlaws[54] had an unintended side-effect. The miserable conditions of life for the native rural population became visible in the images of successful military actions.[55] These propaganda films were distributed through the system of *ciné-buses*, trucks equipped with projectors and sent touring through the countryside, where in 1948 they reached around 465,000 spectators with some 250 screenings.[56]

The French did not confine their aggressive strategies to propaganda films. In 1946 they established the *Studios Africa* in Tunisia as well as the *Studios Souissi*, in a suburb of Rabat in Morocco. The latter was supposed to constitute the basis of a North African 'Hollywood,' whose productions were required to form a counter-weight to Egyptian cinema. Indeed several Arabic-language feature films were produced in 1947 under French direction, particularly in Souissi, among them *Serenade to Maryam* (Ma'zafa muhda illa Maryam; Sérenade à Meryem), *The Cobbler from Cairo* (Iskafi al-Qahira; Savetier du Caire), and *The Seventh Gate* (al-Bab al-sabi'; La septième porte).[57]

Before the studios in Morocco and Tunisia were established, post-production was usually done in Europe. But after World War II a complete technical infrastructure developed, including laboratories. Owned exclusively by Frenchmen, it was of no use to the natives after independence. Shortly before the withdrawal of the French from Tunisia in 1954, the Studios Africa, where hitherto fifty-six films had been produced, were transferred out of the country.[58]

The total number of colonial films produced in the Maghreb is considerable. Until independence in 1956 more than 100 feature films were shot in Morocco. In the same period about eighty films of the same kind were produced in Algeria and more than twenty in Tunisia (not including thousands of folkloric or propaganda documentaries).[59] By contrast, natives had directed only nine feature films.[60]

Nevertheless the European 'orientaleries de bazar,'[61] because they were often marked by a contempt for the conditions of life and aspirations of the Arab population, were not able to compete with Egyptian cinema for the favor of the Arab audience, and Egyptian film witnessed at that time a real boom.[62] This becomes most evident in the insufficient representation of natives. Only six Arab actors played any parts worth mentioning in the 200 feature films that were produced in the Maghreb up to 1954. The Algerian actress Kelthoum,[63] who later played the lead role in Mohamed Lakhdar (Muhammad al-Akhdar) Hamina's *The Wind of the Aurès* (Rih al-Auras, 1966), was one of them. She acted in *The Seventh Gate* (1947) by André Zvoboda, of which two versions were shot in Morocco, an Arabic and a French one.[64]

The cinematographic representation of the indigenous population in North Africa functioned in a similar way to Zionist film making. During the first decades of Zionist film making, which started before the foundation of the state of Israel, Palestinians were pictured above all as barbaric, violent villains, to be met with arms and weapons.[65] Another strategy was simply to deny their existence. Film makers depicted the land alone and its transformation into a blooming paradise at the hands of Jewish settlers.[66] Such films gave weight to the image of a "country without people for a people without a country." A more 'human' representation of Palestinians in Israeli cinema has appeared only since the 1980s in the work of a few liberal film makers.

Cinema and resistance

With the exception of Egypt, Arab nations had almost no opportunity to represent themselves or their culture by means of cinema until national independence. The various national resistance movements were among the first to recognize the latent possibilities of the medium to support and express national self-assertion and liberation. French and Zionist propaganda challenged Algerians and Palestinians to produce counter-representations (partly also counter-propaganda) on the national as well as on an international scale. In 1957, three years after the FLN (Front de la Libération Nationale) had declared the war of liberation in Algeria, a group of Algerians in the Tebessa region founded the first cinema unit, *Groupe Farid*, which was politically linked to the *Wilaya 1* (military district of the Aurès mountains). René Vautier, French director of *Algeria in Flames* (Algérie en flammes, 1957) and *Sakiet Sidi Youcef* (1958), and feature film director Ahmed Rachedi (Ahmad Rashidi) belonged to this group.[67] In 1958 the Tebessan unit was annexed to the Ministry of Information of the provisional Algerian government residing in Tunis, and given the name *Service du Cinéma National*. It aimed at collecting

Dawn of the Damned (Fadjr al-muᶜazabin, Algeria, 1965) by Ahmed Rachedi
(*ONCIC (former)/Ministry of Culture, Algiers*)

the largest possible amount of images and material on the "fight of the
people, the atrocities of colonialism, and the hardships of Algerians,"
and to use them for enlightenment and propaganda.[68] The cinema
service constituted the nucleus of the various public organizations that
were entrusted after independence with the production of films.
Among those who entered cinema through the service was Mohamed
Lakhdar Hamina, the director of *The Chronicle of the Years of Embers*
(Waqa'iᶜ sanawat al-djamr, 1974), and later a prizewinner at Cannes.

In the case of Palestinian film making, cinematographic activities
also developed in connection with armed struggle, started by exiled
Palestinians after the defeat of Egypt, Syria, and Jordan by Israel in
1967, and the subsequent Israeli occupation of further Palestinian
territories. Between 1967 and 1968 Mustapha Abu ᶜAli, Hany
Jawhariya, and Sulafa Jadallah founded in Jordan a film unit that was
annexed to the Palestinian organization Fatah. After the Black
September in 1971—the Jordanian massacre of Palestinian refugees
and resistance fighters—the group moved to Beirut where, in spite of
being equipped with only the most simple means, it continued
producing documentaries about the situation of the Palestinians until
1975. Other Palestinian organizations, like the PFLP (Popular Front

for the Liberation of Palestine), the PDFLP (Popular Democratic Front for the Liberation of Palestine) and the arts and culture section of the PLO began to produce films. Politically and financially, conditions were unfavorable. Cut off from Israel and the occupied territories, they documented military actions and life in the refugee camps. Some film makers even risked their lives; Hany Jawhariya was killed by a bullet in 1976 during the Lebanese Civil War.[69]

The activities of the various cinema departments came to a total halt after the Israeli invasion of Beirut in 1982, and a great part of the Palestinian cinema archive disappeared. Then, after the organization's move to Tunis, the cinema department of the PLO changed its policy and started financing coproductions with Western film makers while drastically limiting its own production.

Unlike the images of the first Algerian unit, the films of the Palestinian *fedayeen (fida'iyyun)* did little to influence world public opinion, though they served the mobilization of Palestinians, Arabs, and leftist Europeans as well as the documentation of Palestinian history and culture.

National film making and the state

Independence represented a sort of catalyst for national film making, even in those Arab countries that did not resist or did little to fight European occupation. In the first ten years after their independence Algeria, Syria, Iraq, and Lebanon each produced one or two feature films a year.[70] By 1965 Iraq was producing up to three films and Lebanon fifteen films a year.

Rapid development in the costly film industry in most countries, with the exceptions of Morocco and Lebanon, was furthered by public investment. On the socialist model, production and distribution were entrusted to a state enterprise. The introduction of the public-sector cinema *(al-qita^c al-^cam)* did not proceed everywhere on the basis of a socialism dictated from above, as happened in Egypt, Iraq, and Algeria. In Syria and Tunisia, for example, film makers and critics themselves demanded state intervention.

The first effective measures the young states took were in distribution. The dominance of Western imports was considered the biggest obstacle to national production; American and European imports prevailed in the film market at the time of the Arab countries' independence, together with a few Egyptian imports. (Not even in Egypt did the Egyptian share of production exceed 20 percent of all distributed films.)

In Syria, from independence in 1946 until 1969, only three or four distribution companies were responsible for the country's import. In 1969 the Syrian film organization *(Mu'assasat al-Sinima)*, which was founded in 1963, assumed the distribution monopoly. Of the some 450 films , imported annually, approximately one third were American, while the rest were mostly Egyptian films along with a few European titles.[71] A similar division also existed in other countries, only in the Maghreb the share of French titles was far larger and the Egyptian smaller. More than ten years after independence, between 1966 and 1969 the share of American and European films was still around 60 percent in Tunisia and Morocco, while the common share of Egyptian and Indian features did not exceed 24 percent.[72]

Two different strategies were developed to undermine the monopoly of Western agencies, which in some countries would dictate films to cinema owners by block-booking. The first strategy consisted in monopolizing importation via public institutions, and the second in nationalizing the distribution network. In Egypt all cinemas were nationalized in 1963, and in Algeria in 1964. Five years later the Algerian ONCIC (Office National pour le Commerce et l'Industrie Cinématographiques; al-Diwan al-Watani li-l-Tidjara wa-l-Sinaᶜa al-Sinima'iya) assumed a total monopoly over distribution. This step resulted in the boycott of the American majors (Metro-Goldwyn Mayer, United Artists, etc.) and the French Gaumont-Pathé. Whereas in the case of Algeria, Western agencies finally gave in in 1974, in Tunisia they were able to ignore for a long time the 1969 decree that had assigned the monopoly to the SATPEC (Société Anonyme Tunisienne de Production et d'Expansion Cinématographique). Besides the SATPEC, seven Tunisian companies and six Western agencies were active until 1972.[73] Not until 1979 could all Western companies be convinced to allow themselves to be represented by the SATPEC on the Tunisian market.[74]

However, it soon became apparent that the monopoly of the state could not change the basic dependence on foreign products. The share of Western films after the monopolization of distribution by the ONCIC in Algeria changed only insignificantly in favor of Arab production. In 1978 the share of Western films was nearly 55.5 percent and thus still the largest, whereas Arab films, including four Algerian works, constituted only 18.8 percent.[75] The annual production in Algeria at that time did not exceed three films, quite insufficient to meet national needs.

Centralized importation has proved to have certain advantages, such as making it possible more effectively to control taxes and other fees from imported films and to reinvest them in home production.

In Syria and Algeria the public sector still uses a proportion of the income from the distribution of foreign films for its national production. However, the monopoly of the state has also caused serious problems: in the long run, owing to insufficient financial means and the incompetence of state officials, the level of imported films decreased considerably, as did the technical standards of projection and movie theaters.[76]

Public investment in production proceeded only sluggishly. Years, sometimes even decades, passed before the public sector met the high costs of constructing and furnishing studios, acquiring technical equipment and laboratories, and training professionals. In Tunisia, it was not until 1968, fully eleven years after its foundation in 1957, that the SATPEC celebrated the completion of its Gammarth studios, which provided production facilities including studios, sound editing, film editing, and a laboratory.[77] During the 1960s the national film organization in Syria started to run a temporary laboratory in rented rooms; the planned studios and technical institutions on specially acquired grounds have never materialized.[78] Until recently, Algerian film makers were forced to develop their color material abroad; it was not until 1991 that the country acquired a modern color laboratory.

Education and know-how

It was not only financial and technical insufficiencies that created problems in founding national film industries, but also the lack of technically qualified professionals. Most of the states made inadequate provision for the training of cineastes; as a result dependence on the West and the former USSR has continued.

In the 1930s Talaat Harb responded to the need for outside expertise by hiring technical consultants from Europe, and this policy was to some extent imitated elsewhere. The Syrian film organization, for instance, followed the Egyptian example during the 1960s, though with much less success. Under the supervision of the Yugoslav director Bosko Vulinich[79] the organization initiated its first production, *The Truck Driver* (Sa'iq al-shahina, 1968). Syrian technicians were thus given some experience, but the results were only moderately successful. The first steps taken by Syrian film makers within the confines of the national film organization did not meet with much success either—the first film directed by the Syrian Muhammad Shahin was never finished. Public sector production improved first during the early 1970s through the employment of several non-

Syrian directors like the Iraqi Kaiss al-Zubaidi, the Lebanese Borhane Alaouié (Burhan ᶜAlawiya) and the Egyptian Taufik Salih, who made the most remarkable Syrian films of that period. It was only during the 1980s that qualified Syrian directors and scriptwriters took over; these included Mohamed Malas, Samir Zikra, Usama Muhammad, Raymond Butrus, and ᶜAbd al-Latif ᶜAbd al-Hamid, all of whom were trained in Moscow.

Algerian cinema today, even after thirty years of existence, still lacks qualified technicians in the fields of sound, camera, lighting, set design, and production management. The country runs no institutions that could teach these professions. A film school established in 1964, the Institut National du Cinéma, was closed down three years later.[80] It is not clear whether this was for bureaucratic reasons or due to the anxiety that its sixty professional graduates would remain jobless.[81] Mouny Berrah states that the real reason was that the school "had become a forum for ideological debate and a site of protest."[82] Algerian film makers and technicians usually receive their training in Europe, mostly in France or Belgium. The same applies to the cineastes of the rest of francophone North Africa.

The Moroccans Ahmed Maanouni and Jilalli Ferhati and the Algerian Merzak Allouache (Mirzaq ᶜAlwash) worked for a while in French film productions. Hamid Benani studied at the French film school IDEC. The Tunisians Mahmoud Ben Mahmoud, Nouri Bouzid, Néjia Ben Mabrouk, and the Algerian Brahim Tsaki studied in Brussels. The Algerian Mohamed Lakhdar Hamina was one of the few directors trained in an East European country, the former Czechoslovakia. Souheil Ben Baraka and the Tunisian producer Ahmed Attia acquired their skills in Italy. Not only inhabitants of the Maghreb studied in Paris; other Arabs, including the Egyptians Taufik Salih and Hussein Kamal and the Lebanese Borhane Alaouié, also studied there. The Palestinian Michel Khleifi received his degree in Brussels and the Iraqi Kaiss al-Zubaidi in Babelsberg, in the former East Germany. The Egyptian director Youssef Chahine (Yusuf Shahin) was one of the very few who were trained in the United States.

Only Egypt and Iraq have solved the problem of training satisfactorily. In Iraq, a cinema department was established in the University of Fine Arts in the late 1970s, and in the 1980s it was furnished with the most up-to-date equipment.[83] Among the teachers was the Egyptian director Taufik Salih.

Already in 1945 a private film school had opened in Cairo,[84] but it survived only a short while. Then, in 1959, the Ministry of Culture established the Higher Film Institute that still provides the country with the necessary young professionals, be they technicians, set designers, scriptwriters, or directors. Almost all Egyptian directors who started working after 1959 have graduated from this school. Together with the limits set by a commercial and industrial orientation, the Film Institute is responsible for the relative homogeneity and continuity of Egyptian film making, both in form and content.

Hollywood or socialism

In spite of nationalizations, Arab film making has constantly been dominated by the mechanisms and standards of the cultural industry introduced by Egyptian producers. With the advent of sound, the Egyptian film industry started the commercial exploitation of popular Egyptian songs and singers whose music had already spread by radio and record all over the Arab world. The appearance of the famous musician Muhammad ʿAbd al-Wahhab or the singer Umm Kulthum gained the first Egyptian sound movies a decisive advantage, and hampered the development of other Arab film industries.[85]

Beside the musical, two other genres, melodrama and farce, joined temporarily by adventure ('bedouin') films, led to the success of the Egyptian film industry. In general, early films contained an accumulation of comic situations and events, fairy tale stories in the style of the Arabian Nights, or sentimental and often unlucky love stories, which were mostly interspersed with music or dance. In the course of the boom that started in the late 1940s with the end of World War II import restrictions, a new popular formula crystallized. It was shaped by an entertaining mixture of genres that borrowed from all kinds of films from farce to melodrama, and had an obligatory happy ending. Dance, in particular belly dance, as well as music and songs were considered indispensable. Elements of the American music hall film moved into Egyptian cinema. The adaptation of successful Hollywood productions was quite common and during the 1950s and 1960s the spectrum widened as new genres like the police film and melodramatic realism made their appearance. During the 1970s and 1980s the latter developed to become 'social drama,' a kind of action film with a tendency to social critique. In the same period, characteristics of the Asian karate film were adopted by some directors while the old genres like farce, melodrama, and musical increasingly retreated.

At the same time Egyptian film was to be used as a vehicle for advertising spots. The so-called entrepreneur cinema (sinima al-muqawalat)[86] developed a special category of films, ordered by international distributors and produced by minor companies within a very

Anwar Wagdi (left) in *The Big Lapse* (al-Zalla al-kubra, Egypt, 1945) by Ibrahim ᶜImara (*courtesy Muhammad Bakr, photogapher, Cairo*)

short time period, on a very low budget, and with second-rate actors. Films of this sort are mainly distributed on video and only exceptionally reach movie theaters.

The nationalization of the Egyptian film industry during the Nasser era could not change its basic commercial structure. In any case, the activity of the public sector in the field of production lasted only a few years and was terminated by the partial reprivatization initiated under Sadat in 1971 (which, however, did not include the studios and laboratories. They have remained state property up to date). Three years later the huge success of *Take Care of Zuzu!* (Khalli balak min Zuzu!) by Hasan al-Imam, the master of Egyptian melodrama, signaled the revival of purely commercial Egyptian cinema.

Publicity poster for *Rebels on the Sea* (al-Mushaghibun fi-l-bahriya, Egypt, 1992) starring Fifi Abdu, directed by Nasser Hussein

The period of state ownership brought about only a partial and temporary rise in technical and artistic standards. In spite of efforts to promote a national film culture, exerted particularly by Tharwat ᶜUkasha during his period in office as minister of culture, production remained dominated by the maxim of rentability. In order to prevent the loss of foreign markets, the products of the national film organization followed the same commercial guidelines as the private sector, which meant that they retained stars and popular features. Although the production of realist and patriotic films also spread among mainstream directors, art films that attempted to develop a specific national film language, like Chadi Abdessalam's (Shadi ᶜAbd al-Salam) *The Mummy* (al-Mumya', 1969; also known as *The Night of Counting the Years*), remained exceptional.

All the popular genres created by Egyptian cinema throughout its history share the absolute determination to entertain and the permanent readiness to compromise in line with the oft-recited motto *al-gumhur ᶜayiz kida* (colloquial: 'the audience wants it like this'). The Egyptian film industry lives like Hollywood on the image of its sometimes very famous stars. With their assistance, particularly that of the popular singers, Egyptian cinema at the beginning was able to overcome an important obstacle hampering the inter-Arab exchange of movies: the distinct dialects of the Mashriq and Maghreb, i.e., the eastern and western part of the so-called Arab world. The continuous consumption of Egyptian mass production caused the audience in many regions to acquire at least a passive knowledge of the Egyptian dialect. This process gained the distribution of Egyptian films an advantage that Arab competitors from Tunisia, Algeria, and Syria could attain only exceptionally.

With the video boom that started in the 1970s the market for Egyptian cinema shifted more to the Arab south-east. Already in 1959, 155 of a total of 222 exported 16-millimeter prints were sent to Saudi Arabia.[87] (These films were of course designed only for private screenings.) The introduction of electronic media in the Gulf states resulted in an increasing consumption of the Egyptian mass product, whereas in the Arab west, demand for Egyptian movies declined rapidly in some places, not least because of increasing home production in these countries. Indeed, between 1980 and 1989 the share of Egyptian films in Morocco did not exceed 3 percent and in some years, like 1988, not even one film was imported from Egypt.[88]

This development forced the Egyptian film industry into an increasing dependency on distribution companies from the Arabian Peninsula. There were discussions in the 1970s about investments by Saudi Arabian businessmen, who wanted through a kind of joint venture to take over the public companies with their studios; such investments have failed to materialize, however, because of protest by cineastes. Yet many Egyptian producers take up production loans offered by distributors from the Gulf states—mainly those who can fix the selling price and thus the budget of a film according to the popularity of the cast.[89] For this reason actors' fees are enormous in comparison to the total budget. The average budget of an Egyptian feature film at present is approximately LE750,000 (LE = Egyptian pounds), i.e., about US$230,000. Up to LE300,000 may have to be spent on fees for the stars, which means that little remains for props, set, costumes, transport, and wages.

The Egyptian model was followed in almost all Arab countries. Immediately after independence, private entrepreneurs were in many cases to make use of Egyptian know-how. In Syria several privately produced films were directed by Egyptians in the 1960s and 1970s, including works by Hilmi Rafla and cAtif Salim. Commercial Syrian cinema still follows Egyptian concepts today; the latest works of the Syrian comic Doureid Laham have been well received by Egyptian audiences, and show the same mixture of social criticism, verbal comedy, musical inserts, and theatrical performances as many Egyptian feature films.

In the first stage of production in Iraq, from 1945 to 1951, private

Iraqi producers undertook various coproductions with Egypt and Lebanon. Successful Egyptian directors, including Ahmed Badrakhan, Niyazi Mustafa, and Ahmad Kamil Mursi directed some of these works.[90] Egyptian melodramas were so acclaimed by audiences that in the first period after independence at least a dozen melodramas were shot there.[91] They scarcely differed from Egyptian products: "It is always love that holds the first place, spiced with mean seductions, rapes, adulteries, prisons, dead persons, suicide, and mental illness, on the background of dark misfortune molding the pleasant victim."[92]

In the Maghreb too, film makers showed much interest in this genre. The Tunisian Omar Khlifi made pointed use of the Egyptian formula in his work, particularly in *Screams* (Surakh; Hurlements, 1972), which dealt with the situation of women in the countryside. His social criticism came wrapped in a rather melodramatic plot, in order to provide the audience with what it was used to.[93] In Morocco, a number of feature films inspired by the Egyptian musical were produced, such as the first full-length Moroccan film *Life Is a Struggle* (al-Hayatu kifah; Vaincre pour vivre, 1968) by Mohamed Ben Abderrahmane Tazi and Ahmed Mesnaoui starring the singer Abdelwahab Doukali and *Silence Is a One Way Street* (al-Samt itidjah mamnuᶜ; Silence, sens interdit; 1973) by Abdallah Mesbahi with Abdelhédi Belkhayat.[94]

Lebanon, however, had the closest relation to the Egyptian center of production. Not only did it export some of its greatest stars to Egypt—including Asmahan, Farid al-Atrash, and Sabah—but it also constituted the most important trade center for commercial Egyptian cinema. Until the 1970s, Lebanese distributors monopolized the export of Egyptian films. The Lebanese film industry was even able to compete with the 'Hollywood on the Nile.'

In the context of the broad economic upswing in Lebanon after World War II, private entrepreneurs became increasingly interested in cinema. They established several studios and shared in film productions. From 1953 until 1962, twenty-four feature films appeared; in the following eight years there were no less than 100.[95] This sudden boom was an indirect result of the nationalization of the Egyptian film industry in 1963, which led Egyptian, Syrian, Lebanese, and Jordanian producers to withdraw from Egypt and invest in Lebanon instead.[96]

Lebanese cinema not only followed the same entertaining formula as its model, but even developed in cooperation with Egyptian film makers and actors. A slim majority of Lebanese feature films (54 out of 100) that were produced between 1963 and 1970 used Egyptian dialect for the dialogue. A further twenty films contained a linguistic mixture allowing each actor to speak his native tongue. Only twenty-two films used the Lebanese dialect exclusively.[97]

The development of a national character for Lebanese cinema started only in 1975 with the eruption of civil war. This, together with the partial reprivatization of the Egyptian film industry, led to a rapid reduction in Lebanese production, and gradually Lebanese cinema came out from under the shadow of its Egyptian mentor.[98]

In the socialist-oriented Arab countries the public sector became the godfather to a politically committed, modernist, 'Third Worldist' cinema[99] that consciously created a distance from the products of the 'dream factory' of commercial cinema. The Egyptian director Salah Abu Seif wrote in 1965:

> Now that the revolution has expressed in the National Charter a global vision of history and of the future in a solid revolutionary context, it is imperative to see how weak our films are on the analytical and political level. It is now the task of the state to create on the basis of the Charter a mature cinematographic world where man's struggle against fatal social conditions and his striving to change his destiny are expressed.[100]

In practice, cineastes and functionaries all too often equated non-commercial cinema with ideological indoctrination, transforming the medium into a basis for political propaganda:

> As socialist cinema sides with the struggle of all progressive powers against the enemies of the people, in particular colonialists, capitalist exploiters, feudal landowners, reactionaries, bureaucrats, arrivistes, and deviators . . ., it should denounce them incessantly and work for their destruction.[101]

Neither distributors nor audiences acclaimed the agitprop of 'socialist' cinema. In Algeria until 1972 almost all feature films dealt with the war of liberation. Scores of works spoke in favor of the agrarian revolution, i.e., the land reform ordered by the Algerian president, Boumedienne. The limited success of this immensely politicized cinema forced functionaries and film makers to change their attitude. Many directors started to give these didactic subjects commercial packaging in order to convince audiences. One of the very few exceptions that succeeded in breaking even was the comedy *Hassan Terro* (Hasan al-tirru, 1968) by Mohamed Lakhdar Hamina, where the popular Algerian comic Ahmed Rouiched portrayed a cowardly resistance fighter. Rouiched's series of Hassan films that followed, among them *The Escape of Hassan Terro* (Hurub Hasan al-tirru, 1974) by Mustapha Badie (Badiᶜ) and *Hassan Taxi* (1982) by Mohamed Slim Riad (Muhammad Salim Riyad) were to use the same farce-like style found in commercial works from the Mashriq.

Publicity poster for *Let Us Climb the Mountains* (Li-nas^cad ila al-djabal, Algeria, 1989) by ^cAbd al-^cAziz b. Mahdjub

Commercialism in state productions was largely imposed by officials of the ONCIC. The director Ahmed Rachedi, who managed this public organization from 1967 to 1973 and shot in the same period his resistance film *The Opium and the Baton* (al-Afyun wa-l-^casa, 1969), made deliberate compromises in order to satisfy the taste of the audience: "I do not support festival films. There is no cinema without a large audience. It is probably for this reason that I made concessions in *The Opium and the Baton*."[102] The substantial battle scene in this film, the French nude in Rachedi's *Ali in Wonderland* (Ard al-sarab, 1978) and the casting of the Egyptian star ᶜIzzat al-ᶜAlayli as the main actor in *Monsieur Fabre's Mill* (Tahunat M. Fabre, 1983) are examples of such concessions to the audience.

Several works on the war of independence borrowed from commercial genres, and thus became a sub-category of the American western. The heroic Algerian resistance fighters *(mudjahidun)* establish law and order; totally alone (one against all) the partisan accepts the challenge of his evil adversaries (Frenchmen and native feudal lords). Like the protagonist of *The Outlaws* (al-Kharidjun ᶜan al-qanun; Les hors la loi, 1969) by Tewfik Fares, he lives the life of a noble outlaw in the wilderness, equipped with a horse, a sombrero, and a hunting rifle.

> The Algerian resistance fighter tries to speak and to roll his shoulders like the outlaw of the American film. He even learns judo; you only ask yourself where. In order to have the actor's studio expression he pulls faces. Denying his own person to the utmost, the peasant in the bush strives to walk like a GI: the way he wears his hat and machine gun, everything is there except the result.[103]

A similar style can also be found in the sole Algerian feature film that deals with the Palestinian question, *We Will Return* (Sanaᶜud, 1971) by Mohamed Slim Riad. This urged Hala Salmane to ask how it was possible to denounce Western imperialism in its Zionist version with such a peculiarly American film language. "I wanted audiences to identify with my heroes. The Americans have succeeded in getting the whole world to admire the heroes of their westerns and their war films. Why should we not do the same?" answered the director.[104]

The crisis of the public sector

Unsurprisingly, the contradictory demands of the public sector's task resulted in crisis. In Syria, Egypt, and Algeria, this was mainly expressed in decreasing production rates. During the 1970s the Syrian public sector produced one or two feature films a year (nineteen in total). In the 1980s there were only eight feature films. The private sector, on the other hand, produced an average of eleven films annually between 1970 and 1979.[105]

In Egypt, the number of productions decreased continuously after the foundation of the National Film Organization and reached its lowest level since the 1940s in 1967 with thirty-two films. The number of feature films then remained at around forty films per year and did not increase until 1974. The film organization never made more than thirteen feature films a year.[106] Corruption and nepotism contributed to the wasting of public money. In 1971, when Sadat started reprivatization, the debts of the film organization are reported to have reached seven million Egyptian pounds. This forced the public sector to withdraw completely from the production of full-length feature films.[107]

In Iraq, where no private production has been carried through since 1977,[108] the Revolutionary Council decided in 1980 to found the semi-private company Babylon in order to stimulate film production.[109] The Iraqi Film and Theater Organization (al-Mu'assasa al-ᶜAmma li-l-Sinima wa-l-Masrah), created in 1959, had produced from 1969 to 1983 only sixteen feature films.[110]

In Algeria, the socialist production model was also caught in a crisis. In 1984 the ONCIC was so indebted that it had to be divided into two organizations with different functions, the ENAPROC (Entreprise Nationale Algérienne de la Production Cinématographique) and the ENADEC (Entreprise Nationale Algérienne de la Distribution Cinématographique). They were connected only loosely under the supervision of the new CAAIC (Centre Algérien pour l'Art et l'Industrie Cinématographique). Although in 1985 the CAAIC started reprivatizing cinemas, its financial troubles were still so great at the end of the 1980s that it had no foreign exchange at its disposal either for imports or for the post production laboratory work abroad. Jean Pierre Lledo's film *Lumière*, for example, shot in 1988, had to wait four years to be completed. In order to surmount the chronic lack of foreign exchange, the organization coproduced five of its seven films shot after 1989 with other countries, including France, Bulgaria, Tunisia, and Burkina Faso. It also produced one film with the help of the Algerian ENPA (Entreprise Nationale de Production Audiovisuelle). This organization, founded in 1986 by the RTA (Radio-Télévision Algérien), has been competing since 1988 with the CAAIC in the field of feature film production. From 1988 until 1992, it produced no less than eighteen feature films meant for broadcasting, which included six coproductions. Only recently have private production companies been allowed to work in Algeria. Film makers such as Merzak Allouache and Malek Lakhdar Hamina, director of *Autumn October in Algiers* (Kharif uktubar al-Djaza'ir, 1992), who were able to find financial partners abroad, started to make use of this opportunity. Moreover, the FDATIC (Fonds de Développement de l'Art et de l'Industrie Cinématographique) awards production subsidies in order to stimulate film economy.

The Tunisian and Moroccan economic system has turned out to be more effective than the socialist model. At no time in either country did the state monopolize production and distribution. During the 1970s the Tunisian SATPEC produced only a few films. In 1974 and 1975 the society fell into deep financial trouble due to its being "torn beween its commercial vocation and the demands of the Ministry of Culture."[111] Since the beginning of the 1980s, the SATPEC has been content to support private production with up to 30 percent of the budget.[112] The subsidies are given mainly as services. In a small country like Tunisia, a feature film can never actually pay for itself, no matter how much public support it receives. Tunisian producers increasingly look for foreign coproducers and buyers, especially in the West. Pursuing this policy, they have in recent years been able to secure at least half of the country's production.

In Morocco a comparable model helped to improve production rates. As in other Arab countries, private distributors prefer not to invest their capital in Moroccan productions. Therefore, the state has tried to further film production through a special film fund supplied by taxes. In 1956, two years before independence, a fund had been created, the Fonds Nationales d'Expansion de la Cinématographie. Its influence remained minor at the beginning. Productions were undertaken only by the Service du Cinéma, founded in 1944 by the colonial authorities and the CCM (Centre Cinématographique Marocain). Their production consisted mainly of short films. Because of bureaucratic obstacles and trade monopolies held by foreign companies, both institutions were for a long time unable to contribute to the development of national cinema. Since the film fund or the Fonds de Soutien à l'Expansion de l'Industrie Cinématographique was restructured and enabled to give awards reaching up to 50 percent of the film budget, the number of Moroccan feature films has increased considerably.[113] While the country had produced only eighteen films from 1968 to 1979, thirty-three films were produced between 1980 and 1986, since the intro-duction of the award.[114]

Censorship

In spite of many Arab states' withdrawal in recent decades from involvement in cinema, official dominance has remained unchallenged in at least one respect. All Arab governments, be they capitalist or socialist, have reduced the medium's freedom of expression through legal restrictions.

In most Arab countries, film projects must first pass a state committee, which grants or denies permission to shoot. Once this permission is obtained, another official license, a so-called visa, is necessary in order to exploit the film commercially. This is normally approved by a committee of the Ministry of Information or a special censorship authority.

The most important taboo areas kept under state surveillance are religion, sex, and politics. A summary of the Egyptian law of censorship issued in 1976 may clarify this:

> 'Heavenly' religions [i.e., Islam, Christianity, and Judaism] should not be criticized. Heresy and magic should not be positively portrayed. Immoral actions and vices are not to be justified and must be punished. Images of naked human bodies or the inordinate emphasis on individual erotic parts, the representation of sexually arousing scenes, and scenes of alcohol consumption and drug use are not allowed. Also prohibited is the use of obscene and indecent speech. The sanctity of marriage, family values, and one's parents must be respected. Beside the prohibition on the excessive use of horror and violence, or inciting their imitation, it is forbidden to represent social problems as hopeless, to upset the mind, or to divide religions, classes, and national unity.[115]

In general, criticism of Islam is not allowed, this being the official state religion in most Arab countries. By extension, a positive representation of atheism is not appropriate. Even the overtly secular Algerian cinema attacks only maraboutism and practices of popular Islam, steering clear of orthodox Muslim conviction. National unity is maintained not through a just representation of different native religions but through the exclusive representation of Muslim conditions of life and convictions. Although there are many Christian directors working in Egypt—including Youssef Chahine, Samir Seif, Khairy Beshara, Daoud Abd El-Sayyed, and Yousry Nasrallah—Christian characters hardly ever appear on the screen, and then mostly in minor roles. The representation of Jews is also frowned upon.[116] In Lebanon, the sole Arab state with a non-Muslim president, the confessional structure of the country found expression on the screen. In order to preserve national unity in 1943 the so-called National Pact (al-wifaq al-watani) fixed an equal division of political posts among Christians and Muslims. Following the same principle, commercial Lebanese film makers during the first period of Civil War at the end of the 1970s and beginning of the 1980s, tried to divide their main roles, positive and negative, as equally as possible among Muslim and Christian actors.[117]

The taboo on sex arises from the moral code of Arab-Muslim culture. In some countries, like Iraq, even the representation of prostitution is prohibited.[118] In other countries, only the exposure of the human body—including the realist representation of sexual intercourse or birth—constitutes a taboo. Transgressions in a few Algerian and Tunisian films are the only exceptions, which thereby emphasize the rule. Algerian cinema in particular, despite its apparently progressive and revolutionary attitude, is profoundly prudish. According to Algerian critic Mouny Berrah, only one Algerian feature film, *Layla and Her Sisters* (Layla wa-akhawatiha; Leila et les autres), shot in 1977 by Sid Ali Mazif, contains a kiss.[119] The few violations of rules occurring in Algerian cinema, like the undressing of the female protagonist in Mohamed Slim Riad's *South Wind* (Rih al-djanub, 1975)[120] are mainly based on pedagogic intentions to challenge and educate the audience, whereas in Tunisia they are the result of Western coproduction. The European market offers to film makers and producers alternative financial and spiritual spaces, which help them to face the pressure of domestic censorship. An example is Ferid Boughedir's *Halfaouine* (Halfawin: ᶜAsfur al-sath, literally, 'the bird on the roof,' 1989). The film contains scenes of a Turkish bath, where almost bare women can be seen bathing. The freedom Boughedir managed to force out of censorship is by no means typical. During the same period, director Nouri Bouzid had to accept several cuts in his film *Golden Horseshoes* (Safa'ih min dhahab, 1989) before it received permission for public screening. The scenes that had to be sacrificed contained images of sexual intercourse and a sequence showing the methods of torture used by Tunisian policemen.[121]

Overt political censorship also occurs, especially of any direct criticism of the political leadership. In Egypt from 1971 to 1973, after Sadat's seizure of power, all films that addressed the 1967 defeat by Israel were prohibited. This affected, among others, *Shadows on the Other Side* (Zilal ᶜala al-djanib al-akhar, 1973) by Ghaleb Chaath and *The Sparrow* (al-ᶜUsfur, 1971) by Youssef Chahine. In 1986 the Egyptian director Atef El-Tayeb had to change the final scene of his film *The Innocent* (al-Bari'). Images of a young man whose military service required him to work in an internment camp of the Central Security Service had to be removed because they showed him, machine gun in hand, rebelling against the authoritarian and inhuman methods used in the camp.

Depending on its ideological orientation, social criticism may also be prohibited. In pre-Nasserist Egypt, and in Morocco during the 1970s, representations of social abuses had to take censorship into account. In Iraq, the glorification of feudalism and capitalism, and negative or racist representations of "the people's struggle against colonialism or imperialism" are prohibited.[122] In Algeria, where censorship was decreed in 1967,[123] a higher commission worked to make the content of films produced by the ONCIC correspond with the socialist orientation and the guidelines of foreign affairs fixed by the National Charter.[124] This commission, appointed by the Ministry of Culture and Information, was the sole arbiter of whether a project could be produced. As no private production companies existed at that time, authors and film makers were automatically forced to use self-censorship. At the beginning of the 1970s some of them lodged a complaint in a common manifesto presented to the Ministry of Information.[125] The same commission also had the task of maintaining 'Arab-Muslim customs.' Vague notions like 'public order' and 'good morals'[126] and the prohibition of 'things that do not correspond to what is commonly accepted' and 'embarrass the audience'[127] have turned the laws of censorship into an unpredictable official weapon.

Non-socialist governments also practice economic censorship. In Morocco, for example, this is exerted by withholding public film awards, which are essential for home productions.[128] This means of censorship is hardly contestable and is perhaps more serious than the direct official censorship exerted in other Arab countries.

Film makers and producers circumvent restrictions in various ways. In the case of Atef El-Tayeb's *The Innocent*, two different versions were made, one for the domestic market and another for export. (In Iraq such a solution would not have been allowed.) Another strategy is to encode a message or action stylistically, for example, through the use of various forms of antiphrasis. In his films, *Alexandria Why?* (Iskandariya lih? 1978) and *Alexandria Now and Forever* (Iskandariya kaman wa kaman, 1991), the Egyptian director Youssef Chahine veils the homoerotic inclination of his protagonist by representing sexual desire as murderous hatred or by replacing a man with a woman with masculine behavior. Hamid Benani's use of the Moroccan flag in *Wechma* (Washma, literally 'tattoo,' 1970), which is placed ironically on the coffin of the protagonist whose death was caused by unjust and authoritarian social conditions, constitutes such an antiphrasis.[129] Another tactic is to distort the representation through distance, irony, and ambiguity, as is common in film satires. In Syrian director Samir Zikra's *The Events of the Coming Year* (Waqa'ic al-cam al-muqbil, 1986), for example, a state official's speech is constantly repeated by a parrot. In Doureid Laham's film, *The Report* (al-Taqrir, Syria, 1986), a balance set up in a court hangs lopsided. The trial, however, is not 'real,' but takes place in the protagonist's dream.

The Report (al-Taqrir, Syria, 1986) by Doureid Laham

Cinéma artisanal and coproduction

Despite these various economic and political restrictions, an artistically ambitious and individualist tendency has emerged in Arab cinema since the 1970s. The works of the 'New Arab Cinema' cannot be assigned to any one category or genre. They range from observant portrayals of social conditions to autobiographical stories and avant-garde art movies. In contrast to commercial or socialist cinema, some currents of the New Cinema employ unconventional stylistic forms and transgress taboos.

This change of direction in Arab cinema resulted in part from an intellectual reorientation following Egypt, Jordan, and Syria's defeat in the 1967 Six Day War. The gradual disillusionment with and subsequent renunciation of nationalist and Pan-Arab ideology led to the alienation of many intellectuals from the national political leadership, whose inefficiency was exposed. Accusations were made of totalitarianism and state paternalism.

Even so, some films made in the new spirit were produced by state enterprises. They are marked not only by an unconventional style but also by a deviation from official ideologies and political discourses, as can be seen in films such as *Omar Gatlato* (ᶜUmar qatlatu al-rudjla, 1976) and *Adventures of a Hero* (Mughamarat

The Events of the Coming Year (Waqa'iᶜ al-ᶜam al-muqbil, Syria, 1986) by Samir Zikra

batal, 1976) by the Algerian Merzak Allouache, or *The Half-Meter Incident* (Hadithat al-nisf mitr, 1981) and *Stars in Broad Daylight* (Nudjum al-nahar, 1988) by the Syrians Samir Zikra and Usama Muhammad. The unconventionally distant and ironic tone of these films was a counter to the prevailing political conformism in public production.

However, artistically ambitious individualist directors were not always able to work within the framework of the public, and even less the commercial, production system. In order to escape economic and political constraints, they adopted various strategies. In some cases they returned to a pre-industrial production mode, avoiding as much as possible the division of labor. This turned the film makers into "truly orchestrated people playing several roles: scriptwriter, dialogue-writer, director, editor, and in some cases even principal actors. By assuming several functions the film maker in the end becomes omnipresent and his way of working that of a craftsman *[artisanal]*."[130]

One characteristic of the craftsman's way of production is the search for financial sources that might allow the film maker greater freedom. In Morocco in the 1970s a film makers' collective, Sigma 3, was formed and produced members' films in rotation, including

Wechma (1970) by Hamid Benani. But financial problems soon led to the group's collapse.[131] Many *auteur* film makers, including the Moroccans Hamid Benani, Jilalli Ferhati, Nabyl Lahlou, the Lebanese Maroun Baghdadi, Borhane Alaouié, Jocelyne Saab (Sacb), Heiny Srour and Randa Chahal (Shahhal), and the Egyptian Youssef Chahine, have founded private production companies and sought foreign coproducers to help finance their projects.

For some film makers who were driven into exile by occupation, political oppression, or civil war, coproductions still represent the sole means of finance. The Palestinians Michel Khleifi, Rashid Masharawi, Elia Suleiman, and the already-cited Lebanese directors would not have been able to realize their works otherwise.

Arab art movies and *auteur* films sometimes attract great interest from the West but are often hardly distributed in their own countries. This was the case, for example, with the Moroccan films *Wechma* by Hamid Benani, *A Thousand and One Hands* (Alf yad wa yad, 1972) by Souheil Ben Baraka, and *El-Chergui* (al-Sharqi, 1975) by Moumen Smihi.[132] In Tunisia, only a few *auteur* films, like Nouri Bouzid's *Man of Ashes* (Rih al-sadd, 1986), gained the favor of their native audience. Néjia Ben Mabrouk's *Sama* (The Trace, 1982), coproduced with the German television channel Zweites Deutsches Fernsehen (ZDF), is a classic of Arab cinema but is still waiting for distribution in Tunisia. The same situation applies to some Lebanese films shot by independent directors during the civil war, including *Encounter in Beirut* (Bayrut al-liqa', 1981) by Borhane Alaouié, *Layla and the Wolves* (Layla wa-l-dhi'ab, 1984) by Heiny Srour, and *The Razor's Edge* (Ghazal al-banat, 1985) by Jocelyne Saab.

For all its artistic qualities and its refusal of mere industrial forms of production, the so-called New Arab Cinema is not at all independent. The system of financing with cultural funds and the support of television channels, which is common in Europe, exists in the Arab countries only to a small degree. Television stations are normally run by the state and serve as an official mouthpiece. With the exception of the Algerian RTA, which produced Assia Djebar's experimental semi-documentary, *The Nuba of the Women of Mont Chenoua* (La nouba des femmes de Mont Chenoua, 1976) and Farouk Beloufa's *Nahla* (1979), which are among the most outstanding examples of Algerian *cinéma d'auteur*, no Arab television station has offered any help to native art-cinema. On the contrary, critical and unconventional films are heavily censored before broadcasting or not accepted at all.

In order to finance their films, independent film makers have only two options: to rely either on public subsidies or on foreign producers. A feature film can hardly pay its own high production costs, primarily because the Arab countries suffer from a considerable lack of cinemas. In 1970 no more then 107 cinemas existed in Iraq.[133] Six years later there were 322 movie-theaters in Algeria,[134] and in 1991 only seventy-seven cinemas were running in Tunisia[135] These numbers greatly surpass the UNESCO ideal of seventy cinemas per one million inhabitants.[136] A comparison between Egypt and former West Germany, which has a comparably large population, provides some context. In 1983 West Germany possessed no less then 3,664 cinemas[137] in contrast to Egypt, where in 1986 there were only 267.[138]

Public film organizations, as well as private producers, increasingly consider coproduction or the advance sale of European rights a good way to lower production costs and save hard currency. Although Pan-Arab cooperation might have been expected in this respect, coproductions between the competing Arab film industries and producers are in fact exceptional. Only Algerian organizations—the former ONCIC, the CAAIC, and the ENPA—turned out to be flexible. They coproduced two politically critical films by the Egyptian Youssef Chahine and various north- and black-African productions, including films by the two Tunisians Brahim Babai and Taieb Louhichi (Tayyib al-Wuhaishi).

The Maghreb states, in particular Morocco, have many years of experience in coproduction. They have offered services mainly to foreign, primarily Western, producers and film makers. Images shot in the country by foreigners are seen as useful advertisements for tourism.[139] In 1977, a new phase of coproduction started in Morocco with *Blood Wedding* (ʿUrs al-damm) by Souheil Ben Baraka, adapted from Garcia Lorca's drama. This introduced the production of Moroccan films with the support of Western capital. Ben Baraka's preceding film, *A Thousand and One Hands* (1972), had been a commercial flop at home,[140] but was highly considered at European festivals, giving Ben Baraka the chance to finance his work through coproduction. His films, however, became increasingly alienated from the Moroccan context, as he started using European actors to satisfy his Western audience. In *The Petroleum War Will Not Take Place* (Harb al-bitrul lan taqaʿ, 1975), he approached the style of an American political thriller. For a while, the film was denied screening permission in Morocco. More recently, Moroccan film makers such as Jilalli Ferhati, Mohamed Ben Abderrahmane Tazi, and Farida Ben Lyazid have managed to remain faithful to Moroccan themes and audiences at the same time as making use of foreign capital.

The Tunisian SATPEC also offered services to foreign projects

Halfaouine (Halfawin: ᶜAsfur al-sath, Tunisia, 1989) by Ferid Boughedir

during the 1970s, but according to Ferid Boughedir, the results were disappointing to the organization. Some European producers embezzled the SATPEC's share in the profit and withheld its name in the credits. Fernando Arrabal's production *Viva la muerte* was one of the few successes. Arrabal paid back four of sixty million (old) francs to the SATPEC. According to Boughedir, who worked as an assistant in Arrabal's film, he did so only because he was planning another coproduction.[141]

As in Morocco, a new phase of coproduction has started in Tunisia, with an improvement of industrial structures and a rise in production. From 1980 to 1992, Tunisians produced twenty-six feature films, twice as many as in the preceding decade. Half of these were financed by coproduction.[142] Only in three cases were the foreign partners Arab companies. Tunisian producers like Hassan Daldoul and Ahmed Attia have increasingly pre-sold rights to European television stations, mainly the German ZDF, French La Sept, and British Channel Four. Films financed in this way include Nouri Bouzid's *Golden Horseshoes*, Ferid Boughedir's *Halfaouine*, the short film sampler, *The Gulf War and After* (Harb al-khalidj wa baᶜd), and *Chichkhan* by Mahmoud Ben Mahmoud and Fadhel Jaibi (Fadil Djuᶜaybi). On a technical level, Tunisian cinema has equaled Western standards. Ferid Boughedir's *Halfaouine* was so successful that it was not only broadcast abroad but released in the cinemas of several European countries.

The Tunisian police film *Chichkhan* (Shish Khan; Poussiére de diamants, 1991) is an example of the negative effects European financing has on style and content. Although the story is set in Tunisia, the Italian mafia is as much present as the protagonist's entirely European way of life. A connection with Tunisia can only be seen in language and setting. The rest is a multicultural assortment that, ironically, was not appreciated by European audiences.

In other coproductions, adapting to consumers outside the Arab countries is more subtle. Although the Tunisian Nacer Khemir works hard to employ elements of classical Arab-Muslim culture in his film *The Lost Necklace of the Dove* (Tauq al-hamama al-mafqud, 1990), by quoting and alluding to Arab visual art and literature, his representation can also be seen as a colorful and exotic Thousand-and-One-Nights picture-book.

Similarly, Boughedir's *Halfaouine* (Halfawin; ʿUsfur al-sath, literally, 'the bird on the roof,' 1989) contains numerous exotic and folkloristic elements. The director uses the awakening sexual curiosity of his adolescent protagonist to introduce the observer into the 'mysterious' world of Arab women, to which, according to the film, men have no access. The images of the Turkish bath in particular are reminiscent of the harem subjects of nineteenth century orientalist painting in Europe.

Buyers' requirements also greatly influence the arrangement of products. Gulf money coming into Egyptian cinema since the 1970s has brought with it a noticeable prudishness. Egyptian film makers and producers have gone to great lengths to satisfy particularly the extremely conservative censorship of Saudi Arabia. While Hussein Kamal's *My Father Is up the Tree* (Abi fauq al-shadjara) drew crowds in 1969 because of its supposedly 100 kisses, today there is hardly a single kiss to be seen.

However, in the 1990s an increasing Egyptian tendency toward European coproductions has also appeared. Apart from Youssef Chahine's most recent spectacles, *The Emigrant* (al-Muhagir, 1994) and *Destiny* (al-Masir, 1997), the projects of young directors such as Yousry Nasrallah, Asma' al-Bakri, Radwan al-Kashif, Khalid al-Haggar, and ʿAtif Hatata have received Western support.

However, European coproductions tend to be less successful at the box office than native commercial films, particularly in Egypt. At the same time, coproduced films have succeeded in representing Arab cinema abroad while marginalizing Arab mainstream cinema, not in quantity but in terms of quality and evaluation. In this way, Western hegemony over regional productions has been reinforced on the financial and on the ideological levels. Today, it is primarily the

Western audience, curators, and producers who are in a position to evaluate and define the international status of Arab films.

Diversification in the satellite era

In Egypt, the interest in coproductions is related to the most recent crisis of a film industry whose production rates have fallen dangerously: eighteen full-length feature films in 1994, twenty-five in 1995 and twenty-two in 1996, from an average of around sixty a year at the end of the 1980s. The industry's chronic lack of investment has been exacerbated by a sudden growth in the electronic entertainment industry. In 1994 alone, five television productions were released in movie theaters, competing heavily with film industry products. This boom, which also affects the advertisement sector, has caused a serious shortage of studios, equipment, and technicians. In 1995, 80 percent of cinema studios were rented to television and advertisement productions.

One reason behind this situation is the advent of satellite television in the early 1990s. Two dozen Arab channels, including those of the Egyptian ERTU (Egyptian Radio and TV Union), are run in the Arab world and Europe and in the last few years have multiplied the need for new Arab programs. The film industry, however, is unable to profit from this development. Due to insufficient trade regulations, Egyptian movies are sold and aired for ridiculous prices, mostly just a few hundred US dollars, thus seriously undermining future production.

Not only Egyptian cinema is struck by a deep crisis. Because of the persisting trade boycott on Iraq, it has become almost impossible for Iraqis to obtain raw stock in order to shoot films. The last Algerian full-length feature film, *Bab El-Oued City* (Bab al-Wad Huma) by Merzak Allouache, was made in 1994, and its shooting in Algiers took place under very difficult security conditions. Since then, with most Algerian cineastes sentenced to death by the Islamists and voluntarily exiled, local production has come to an almost complete halt.

However, the 1990s have also been characterized by an immense diversification of the social groups represented. In 1995, one of the first Berber-language films, *Machaho* (Once upon a time, 1995) by the Algerian Belkacem Hadjadj, was released in France. Two years earlier, *A Silent Traveler* (1993) by the Iraqi-Kurd Ibrahim Salman, was produced in the Netherlands and shot in Greece. This is the first full-length fiction film by an Iraqi director to use Kurdish for its dialogue and to address Arab-Iraqi repression in northern Iraq. New

The Mountain (al-Djabal, Palestine, 1991) by Hanna Elias
(*courtesy Institut du Monde Arabe, Paris*)

directors also appeared in Israel and the occupied territories, including Hanna Elias, Nizar Hassan, Norma Morcos, and Omar al-Qattan, most of whom are working on documentaries. Rashid Masharawi, however, gives a fictional insight into life in the refugee camps in *The Curfew* (Hatta ish^car akhar, 1993) and *Haifa* (1995). Elia Suleiman attempts in his short fiction *Homage by Assassination* (1992) and his full-length feature *Chronicle of a Disappearance* (1997) to deconstruct Western and Arab discourses related to Palestinians.

In Egypt since 1987, Coptic directors have started to direct religious feature films, most of which are produced by the Coptic Orthodox Church and a few by Protestant institutions. The majority of the sixteen such films made by the end of 1996 portray the lives and ordeals of Egyptian saints and martyrs. They are supposed to be distributed only within the churches, thus creating a sort of confessional counter public.

In terms of diversification, Lebanon has undergone the most extraordinary development. Several feature film coproductions and dozens of short films have been shot, mostly on video, by young directors from various religious and ethnic backgrounds, including Lebanese-

Armenians. Examples are the documentary portrayals by Mohamed Soueid and Jayce Salloum's film essays such as *This Is Not Beirut* (Hadha laysat Bayrut, 1994). Most recent features are characterized by visual and narrative experimentation, such as Dima al-Joundi's *Between You and Me, Beirut* (Bayni wa baynik Bayrut, 1992), Jean Claude Codsi's (Qudsi) *The Time Has Come* (An al-awan, 1994), and Samir Habashi's *The Tornado* (al-Iᶜsar, 1994). They are all inspired by painful experiences of civil war and returning to a destroyed Lebanon.

This diversification and the appearance of directors representing hitherto marginalized ethnic or religious groups indicates on the ideological level a further disintegration of the common notion of nationhood and unitarian nationalism. It does not necessarily signify greater pluralism or democracy, for in part it accompanies emergence of counter-nationalisms, i.e., sectarian, confessional, or ethnic identities engendered by the exclusive and at times violent nationalist politics of some Arab governments.[143]

2

ARTISTIC ROOTS OF ARAB CINEMA

Image and symbolic arrangement

Image and Islam

"A day you don't set eyes on a photograph is as rare as a day you don't get sight of something written," states Victor Burgin.[1] The statement is certainly true of any Arab country. Where in former times images of man and beast were regarded as taboo, all sorts of reproductions are now common in daily life. Walking through any large Arab city, you see huge posters and advertising hoardings. Products and packages carry all sorts of images. Even the rulers of the most conservative Arab states allow themselves to be photographed and their image to be widely distributed. Today in the Arab world the audio-visual media represent the most important means of leisure, even though the first Arab television programs were broadcast only in the 1960s.[2] Images from around the world penetrate private spheres that were once carefully hidden from the public. Many women of the Arab peninsula, still living in the secluded world of their ancestors, are confronted today with the celluloid copies of screen goddesses from Cairo and Hollywood, and probably make comparisons.

Clearly, as Mohamed Aziza puts it, the "process of modernization amounts to the process of acquiring new images."[3] But how, to take up a formulation of Mostefa Lacheraf, was visual technical reproduction with all its effects absorbed and digested in a culture that knew neither the modern painting, the animated, nor the fixed image?[4]

Unlike the Western tradition of painting, Islamic art did not attach much importance to spatial illustration and reproduction,[5] and preferred abstract representation.[6] Religiously motivated Islamic iconoclasm, prohibiting the depiction of creatures—man and beast, who, unlike plants, carry a 'soul'[7]—was in principal made responsible for this preference. The Quran itself does not contain unequivocal instructions on the subject. The few verses Muslim legal scholars refer to in their interpretation (*sura* 34, verses 12–13 and *sura* 3, verse 43) mainly emphasize God's creative ability *(musawwar)*. In sura 5, verse 92, the faithful are advised to keep away from images, which are works of Satan. However, the images referred to here are literally graven images and idols *(asnam)*, and the reference is therefore to the practices of pre-Islamic paganism.

It seems that there are social and political factors behind the prohibition. As Oleg Grabar indicates, the explicit prohibition of images expressed in some sayings of the Prophet (*hadith*s) was finally established only in the middle of the eighth century, after the Muslim conquests.[8] This was a period when the new faith was fighting for its cultural recognition and to avoid being assimilated into the culture of the recently conquered regions of the former Byzantine empire. The Muslim encounter with the imposing monuments and art of the countries of the Fertile Crescent seems to have produced first admiration and imitation (for example the construction of the Dome in Jerusalem), then an ideologically motivated refusal. As Grabar puts it, "to a Muslim of the early eighth century, images were one of the most characteristic, and in part hateful aspects of Christianity."[9] In the time that followed, the illustrative artist was defamed as one who competes with God. One hadith speaks of a heavy punishment awaiting the producer of images. Another one says that no angel will enter a house where images are kept (or where dogs live).[10]

The existence of a prohibition against images does not mean that no figurative illustrations were in fact made.[11] The representation of living beings was common in some secular art, including book illustration, the decoration of private rooms, and arrangements of basic commodities such as textiles and carpets, and in some products of popular art. (Some examples of the latter are the Egyptian sugar dolls sold on the Prophet's birthday as well as wall paintings on the façades of farmhouses, painted on the occasion of its inhabitants' pilgrimage to Mecca.) The prohibition was also circumvented by showing corpses as shadows or by weaving them into a dense landscape or other scenery.[12] Similarly, holes were pierced in the figurative dolls of shadow plays to destroy their corporality.

It remains true, however, that figurative illustrations in Islamic culture did not form such an influential tradition as was the case in the West. Miniatures and wall paintings were not accessible to every-body, but confined to the private use of wealthy people. Unlike in medieval Europe, where paintings reached the people through churches and had a definite pedagogic and indoctrinating function, mosques and Quran schools, until today, use only decorative ornaments and calligraphy.[13]

Given this state of affairs, it is remarkable that the photographic image was so easily accepted in the Muslim countries. Religious objections were minor, with the exception of those put forward in Saudi Arabia. The legal scholars (ʿulamaʾ) of al-Azhar University in Egypt protested in 1927 when the actor and director Yusuf Wahbi announced his intention to assume the role of the Prophet on screen.[14] In 1930 they objected again for similar reasons,[15] resulting in a general and still valid prohibition against portraying the Prophet and the four righteous caliphs.[16] Religious resistance was, however, far more concerned with moral issues and was directed largely against the moral contents of films and their representations. Subjected to particular criticism were erotic love and the consumption of alcohol. In Syria and Lebanon, Muslim organizations temporarily called for keeping women away from screenings. A pan-Islamic congress held in Karachi in 1952 even demanded that all Muslim states close down their cinemas, but no one followed the call.[17] Only in Saudi Arabia are public screenings still forbidden, although television is allowed.[18]

That photographic illustration has not aroused any serious official religiously motivated disapproval is founded on two common religious justifications. One declares the photographic image to be a sign similar to a formula without any spatial characteristics, based on the following hadith: "Angels do not enter a house where an image is stored except if it is a sign on fabric" (inna al-malaʾika la tadkhulu baytan fih suratun illa raqamun fi thaubin).[19] In analogy to a pattern, photography is considered a sign and not a creation.

The second justification also does not perceive photography as creating anew or giving a soul to things. It declares photography, and in the same way, 'moving images,' as a shadow, reinforcing the power of God, the creator, rather than competing with it.[20] These were the arguments the Saudi Arabian King Ibn Saud (d. 1953) used in order to break the resistance of the culamaʾ against photography. He told them photography is "nothing else than a combination of light and shadow presenting God's creation, without changing it."[21] As the Saudi Arabian culamaʾ could not find anything wrong with light or shadow, they finally gave in and allowed the use of photography.

Cinematic conversion of indigenous fine arts

Traditional Islamic principles of representation have rarely been applied to Arab cinema. The colorful non-spatial painting of miniatures and the ornamental rhythms of the arabesque, basically structured by light and shadow, almost never found their way to the screen. Nearly all Arab film makers stuck to classical rules of Western art instead. The rules of conventional Western composition were adhered to, even though the encounter with European art had started comparatively late. In Egypt, for example, the first modern art school opened only in 1908,[22] a time when cinema was already on the advance.

The twentieth century saw not only the spread of three-dimensional realist plastic art and central perspective, but also a confrontation with a new idea of art, based on the dichotomy between fine arts on the one hand and arts and crafts on the other. This conception promoted the artist as an individual genius, and further undermined the position of traditional arts and crafts genres, like miniatures in Algeria and calligraphy in Syria. Increasingly, these were either cultivated on the margins or completely integrated into modern art.

The traditionally subdued position of art in the Arab countries may have contributed to the replacement of Islamic types of illustration. As traditional art was mainly supposed to serve decorative ends, it was, unlike poetry and music, seen as a craft. As such, it did not become a subject of theory and research.[23] By becoming connected to an artistic elite, Arab fine arts came into conflict with native cinema, which was closer to popular than to elitist art, particularly in its early days. Probably for this reason, modern Arab art did not show any interest in the media and, conversely, film makers were not particularly preoccupied with refined visual aesthetics—unlike in Europe, where artists such as Hans Richter, Man Ray, and Fernand Léger introduced an artistic experimental cinema and helped to enlarge the aesthetic possibilities of the medium. Artistic directions, such as surrealism, futurism, and expressionism were expressed in cinema, and helped create a consciousness among European film makers of problems of visual representation.

The first serious efforts in Arab cinema to pay particular attention to visual representation came at the end of the 1960s. The Egyptian set-designer and director Chadi Abdessalam decided that the preoccupation of the short-lived department of experimental film (Wahdat al-Film al-Tadjribi) should be the image. This department, of which he was appointed head in 1968, constituted an under-section of the public documentary film center. Abdessalam is still considered one of the most extraordinary Egyptian set- and costume-designers. He worked not only on native costume-films, like *Saladin* (al-Nasir Salah al-Din, 1963) by Youssef Chahine and *Wa Islamah* (O, Islam, 1961) by Andrew Marton, but also designed costumes for the Polish film *Pharao* and an episode of Rossellini's serial *Mankind's Fight for Survival*, among others.

The short films produced by Abdessalam's department were, with few exceptions, documentaries. Their most important innovation was that they did not comment on the images, a practice that until then had been considered obligatory in Egyptian documentaries. Now the image was supposed to carry the crucial information. Therefore, film makers of the department to whom ᶜAtif al-Bakri, Samir ᶜUf and Ibrahim al-Mugi belonged were submitted to fewer restrictions than usual in their consumption of raw stock for experiments at the Center. Abdessalam's short film, *Horizons* (Afaq, 1973), depicting without commentary a panorama of contemporary artistic activities in the country, is an example of this production mode.

Abdessalam's first and only full-length feature, *The Mummy* (al-Mumya', also known as *The Night of Counting the Years*, 1969), applies indigenous principles of representation. These are drawn, however, from ancient Egyptian art, not Islamic.

The film is set in the time of the archaeological discovery of the royal tombs near Thebes in 1881. Following the death of the chief of the Hurrabat tribe, his son Wanis learns that his tribe has been living for generations on robbing tombs. Wanis's older brother refuses to take part in the violation and is soon murdered on the orders of the tribe's elders. The younger brother is left helpless, torn between a sense of shame on the one hand and loyalty to his kinship on the other. He starts asking questions about his pharaonic ancestors. He does not know their history, nor is he able to decipher the signs that they have left on the walls of the old temples. When he discovers that the archaeologists investigating the area do have this knowledge, he decides to betray to them the whereabouts of the tombs.

The Mummy treats the relation between contemporary Egyptians and their ancient culture allegorically. The protagonist's wish to take up the challenge of his past is met on the level of visual representation as on other levels. The clear and strict composition of images refers to the monumental statics of old Egyptian sculptures and paintings. The same effect is achieved by the spare, dignified movements of the actors, their relief-like arrangement in front of the rocks, the desert, or in buildings. The use of classical Arabic, which is unusual in Egyptian cinema, reinforces on the linguistic level the impression of monumentalism. However, the visual allusion to past

The Mummy (al-Mumya', also known as *The Night of Counting the Years*, 1969) by Chadi Abdessalam

greatness is not shallow glorification, for it is starkly contradicted on the level of the narration by the painful loss of that very past.

By using pre-Islamic artistic traditions for cinema, Abdessalam's work corresponds, on the ideological level, to the pharaonism movement of the 1920s and 1930s, represented among others by the writer Taha Husain and the sculptor Mahmud Mukhtar.[24] Abdessalam's artistic starting-point, however, found no successor in Egypt. His next project, on the pharaonic heretic and philosopher Akhenaten, was never realized despite many years of intensive preparation and research. After the partial reprivatization of the film industry and up to the director's death in 1986, no Egyptian producer was ready to finance Chadi Abdessalam's expensive project.

An attempt to make use of the Islamic heritage in visual representation in cinema has so far been made only by the Tunisian Nacer Khemir. In his films *Wanderers in the Desert* (al-Ha'imun fi-l-sahra'; Les baliseurs du desert, 1984) and *The Lost Necklace of the Dove* (1990), Khemir revives the legendary Moorish Andalusia. The images he chooses reflect a decisive characteristic of parts of Arab-Islamic representation: while the world outside, the landscape and the external appearance of Muslim cities, is characterized by the monotony of the desert and the omnipresence of dust, the interiors and objects of daily life are colorfully decorated.[25] Khemir contrasts the clay architecture of an old city in the south of Tunisia with the rich and nuanced colors of the costumes and the tastefully decorated furniture.

Particularly in *The Lost Necklace of the Dove*, Khemir draws on the rich colors of Islamic miniatures, whose variety is enormous. The colored inks of this art form possessed "a range far surpassing our own usual supply of black, blue, or red, and extending to the color of peacocks, of the rose, pistachio and apricot; also ruby red, purple, green, yellow, and white, in addition to many mysterious inks of special qualities whose colors cannot be easily surmised."[26]

Apart from this careful use of colors, Khemir also exploits the non-spatial qualities of the miniature in his arrangement of film images. This is true for *The Lost Necklace of the Dove* and for *Wanderers in the Desert*. According to Khemir, the latter "breaks with traditional Arab cinema, because it is fabricated like a miniature and does not represent a copy of reality."[27] In fact Khemir uses miniature paintings as models for set, costumes, and even for the narration, just as miniatures were used to illustrate fictional stories and to depict mythical creatures. This vein of fantasy is translated by the director into fairy-tale like stories.

Wanderers in the Desert (al-Ha'imun fi-l-sahra'; Les baliseurs du desert, Tunisia, 1984) by Nacer Khemir *(courtesy Institut du Monde Arabe, Paris)*

In his two feature films, Khemir pays special attention to the correlation between image and language, by questioning the functionalization of the image by language, so common in Arab cinema. Instead of doing a visual 'translation' of political or daily-life linguistic usage, he searches for images that might change linguistic meaning, that could alter the connotations of certain notions. "If we speak of a garden or a palace, it is translated mentally into park and castle."[28] Saying the words 'palace' and 'garden' today, most Arabic speakers will hardly imagine the architecture of an Arab palace or the arrangement of an Andalusian garden, but will rather imagine European parks and castles. Khemir's films aim to provide the audience with these lost visual images, to be "a sort of real mirror for what certain texts can say."[29]

Reality and film image

With its preference for abstraction, Islamic art does not equate art and reality, as the ornament shows. The ornament or 'arabesque,' as it was first called during the Renaissance,[30] is regarded as the most 'authentic' of all Islamic art genres. The application of the abstract principle of geometry and the work with contrasts, light and shadow, as well as the arbitrariness of the decorated object, give way to rhythmicality and infinite growth of forms.[31] In the rhythmic ornament, space rests unrestricted, beginning and ending are intertwined, the contradictions between light and shadow, up and down, are indissolubly connected. Rather than the ornament being bound to a finite vanishing point, the transition to the infinite seems open.

The ornament is neither meant to symbolize reality nor to express a concrete metaphysical conclusion. Even during the early days of Islam, Islamic art neglected iconographic significance and chose the peripheral to become the main focus of its artistic representation.[32] Thus, the abstraction of the Islamic ornament "is not like a chemical formula, the simplified symbolization of some reality; like certain mathematical abstractions, it is a reality in itself."[33]

It is because of Islamic art's distance from reality and its refusal of figurative spatial representation that its principles were hardly applied in cinema. Unlike the mechanical photographic image, they are not related to the real. A photograph "presents a pattern of light and shadow . . . showing a strong analogy to the structure of objects that were situated in front of the camera while photographing."[34] The 'figurative code'[35] resulting from the analogy to the real contributes to 'naturalize' the represented and seduces the audience to equate reality and image.

The discovery of the central perspective is one of the most important achievements of the European Renaissance and is generally
regarded as the first step toward the principle of photography. It
constitutes the basis of the figurative code and contributes decisively
to the spatial impression of an illustration. Central perspective creates
a precisely defined relation between observer and the subject of an
image. It helps the observer to assume the represented distances and
proportions correctly and at the same time suggests the existence of
only one possible point of view. The vanishing point of the image
bundles the view of the observer and ties it to a standpoint outside
the represented. Hence, one might say that the idea of a space
defined by perspective promotes the analytical, 'objective' view and
asserts the division between subject and object. "It creates for the—in
a way egocentric—observer, who has to fend for himself, an environment that is apparently independent of him. It confronts him with
appearances that seem like inanimate objects."[36] It gives him not only
the feeling that he comprehends reality completely, but also a sense
that he is able to control it.

The analogy between reality and photography gives the false
impression that film images have no significances deviating from the
original. Thus, the symbolic potential hiding behind this apparently
objective figurative procedure of representation is neglected. The
'rhetorics of the image' formulated by Roland Barthes clarify that not
only paintings, but also cinema and photography are equipped with a
variety of signs that may be connotated or read. Significance of
meaning is produced already by choosing a certain part for an image
or a particular time for photographing or shooting.[37]

The significance of space

A beautiful young woman wearing a rural dress escapes through a
night landscape. In a great hurry, she storms through fields and
meadows, forges ahead in the brushwood. The wind brushes through
leaves and branches flickering in the moonlight. Their rustling startles
the fugitive. The strong movement of the trees seems menacing, as if
someone might step out of their shadow at any moment and block
the way of the defenseless woman.

The peculiar life of its own that space develops here in Youssef
Chahine's Carmen adaptation *Lovers' Call* (Nida' al-ᶜushshaq, 1960)
is a rarity in commercial Arab cinema. More characteristic of many
mainstream directors is the conception of photographic image as a
pure analogy of the real, bare of any specific significance. Expressive
spatial arrangements are exceptional, as are still lives of landscapes,

inner rooms, or objects. Space, in the sense of milieu or environment, is often used as a simple sign indicating historical or geographic conditions or the social status of characters. Its application as a carrier of atmosphere is restricted to superficial expression without symbolic depth. Love scenes in Egyptian cinema are a good example. Ever since the musicals of singer and musician Muhammad ᶜAbd al-Wahhab, romantic rendezvous take place on a boat on the Nile, in a park, or in a garden café close to the water.

One of the most successful Egyptian works of 1991, *al-Kitkat*, directed by the New Realist Daoud Abd El-Sayyed, an adaptation of Ibrahim Aslan's novel *Malik al-hazin*, is set in the alleys of al-Kitkat in the poor Cairo neighborhood of Imbaba. The blind Shaykh Husni owns an old house there in which several people show economic interest. Yusuf, Husni's son for example, wants to finance his emigration by selling it, whereas the neighbor, a wealthy butcher, dreams of pulling it down and putting up a more profitable building in its place. But to everybody's displeasure, it turns out that Shaykh Husni has pawned his house to a drug-dealer in exchange for a daily supply of hashish. In spite of, or just because of, his handicap, Shaykh Husni succeeds in playing off all parties against each other and denounces their selfish intentions to the whole neighborhood.

The alley, with its houses, cafés and shops—which, incidentally, were entirely built in the studio—is closely connected to the action. Its cramped, overpopulated dwellings, its dirty, narrow passages used by the women as kitchen and laundry, the ruins where men drink away their grief at night, and the small garage in which Shaykh Husni and his friends meet secretly to smoke hashish, define the social roles and behavior of the protagonists. Space first of all reflects social conditions, but is never related to a character's psychology. The protagonists' relation to their spatial environment depends mainly on 'objective' measurement and does not go beyond the usage of functional daily life. Space has no life of its own, and nowhere corresponds to the protagonists' subjective perceptions.

A slightly different understanding of space is found in films directed by the Algerian Mohamed Lakhdar Hamina. In *Chronicle of the Years of Embers* (Waqa'iᶜ sanawat al-djamr, 1974), shot in cinemascope, the relation between characters and space is also socially defined, but is marked by a much more intensive correlation than in *al-Kitkat*. The film opens with ragged peasants standing on their dusty barren land waiting for the rain. The long takes of the cracked and parched earth in the glaring sunlight, of cattle dying of thirst, and of the strained faces of a peasant and his child create deep tension. In one of the next sequences, a peasant's large family is

Chronicle of the Years of Embers (Waqa'ic sanawat al-djamr, Algeria, 1974) by Mohamed Lakhdar Hamina (*ONCIC (former)/Ministry of Culture, Algiers*)

gathered at night in its poor clay hut. The only sound is that of the father whetting a tool, while the others crouch silently on the floor. A child gets up and approaches the water bag, wanting to open it. But the heavy bag slips away. Its precious contents pour out on the floor. The depressing atmosphere created by the images of the silent family reaches its peak in losing the water. It is further stressed by the meager furnishings and the dark colors. In *Chronicle of the Years of Embers* man's environment is not merely a shallow backdrop; rather the film dramatizes the social and environmental conditions of its characters in a highly visual manner.

Another, unconventional, use of space, can be observed in *Golden Horseshoes* (Safa'ih min dhahab, 1989) by the Tunisian Nouri Bouzid. A political prisoner returns to his parents' house after several years of detention. During his night walk through the barely lit rooms and inner yards, he meets its former inhabitants. The homecomer tries to speak to them, to take up common reminiscences. But the

Sama (The Trace, Tunisia, 1982) by Néjia Ben Mabrouk

figures soon vanish again. They are not flesh and blood, but visions emanating from his memory.

The domestic setting of this film embodies a deeper and far more multi-layered meaning than exists, for example, in *al-Kitkat* or in *Chronicle of the Years of Embers*. The deserted building visited by the protagonist immediately after his release from prison signifies more than a past home. It rather corresponds to his feelings. His walk through its rooms stands for an attempted return to himself and to his life before his imprisonment.

The use of space as an expression of the psychological condition of characters is well known in Western literature and film art. Symbols of this sort are said to be metonymically motivated. The use of the beautiful but eery city of Venice as a symbol of death belongs to this sort of symbolic creation, as in Visconti's *Death in Venice* (1971) among others.[38] The inclusion of metonymically motivated symbolism proves a differentiated comprehension of the image and the *mise en scène*. In Arab film making it appears mainly in the *cinéma d'auteur*, for example in *Sama* (The Trace, 1982) by the Tunisian director Néjia Ben Mabrouk.

Ben Mabrouk's film tells the story of a young girl, Sabra, who tries to escape the restriction of her family. Sabra spends her childhood in a small provincial house where she has to stay most of the day because she is not allowed to play on the street. The openings of the house define Sabra's relation to the world outside. They open the view onto the world of her father and brothers outdoors and at the same time, protect her from the looks of strangers that could intrude into the family's intimate (female) realm. Thus, the house is always dark. The shuttered windows allow sunlight in as a small, unobtrusive spot at the most. Darkness inside contrasts sharply with the exterior dominated by glaring sunlight that almost blinds Sabra on the rare occasions when she goes out.

Time passes and Sabra is about to take her school leaving exam and has therefore to move to the capital. After much effort, her mother manages to find some poor accommodation for her. The room she rents in the Casbah (old city) is a dark and gloomy dungeon without windows or electric lights. Locked up with her books in this depressing room and constantly observed by her suspicious landlady the young woman almost suffocates. In this way, the spatial environment corresponds to the inner feelings of the protagonist.

The power of symbols

Like figurative illustration, the use of symbols is not common in traditional Arab Islamic art. Symbolic representation, though not allegory, is uncommon not only in the fine arts but also in literary genres like classical poetry. Although Arab poetry is rich with 'images' and metaphors—for a long time it was expected that each verse should contain a complete image[39]—poets rarely created any meaningful symbolism. Sufi poetry is the only exception, symbolically transferring topics and images of ordinary love poetry to the believer's love toward the Almighty.[40]

Only Arab fiction and poetry that evolved at the beginning of this century opened up to symbols and mythologies, European, ancient, and indigenous, and integrated them into literary creations.[41] In the course of the 1950s, a further development took place,[42] touching genres like the realist novel, which started to make intensive use of the myth in particular.[43] Via the realist novel various symbols flowed into Arab cinema, as in the Syrian adaptations of the work of the Palestinian realist Ghassan Kanafani, *The Knife* (al-Sikkin, 1972) by Khaled Hamada, and *The Duped* (al-Makhduʿun) by Taufik Salih.

The functional spatial arrangement of Arab cinema is juxtaposed with a similarly functional symbolism. Most of its symbols belong either to the metaphorical or the synecdochic type. In the first, an image or an action represents something else, whereas in the latter, one single part represents the whole, as one peasant stands as a representative for his entire class.[44] Moreover, in cinema as in literature, the symbolic meaning of an action or an image emerges from the total context. "All filmic connotations result from appropriate associations between different elements of the film . . ., whether they are elements contained in different images (montage), or whether they figure the same 'shot' but succeed one another (camera movement), or whether finally they are in the same shot simultaneously (sometimes called 'editing in the camera')."[45]

Muhammad ᶜAbd al-Wahhab in *The White Rose* (al-Warda al-bayda', Egypt, 1933/34) by Muhammad Karim (*courtesy Cultural Fund, Ministry of Culture, Cairo*)

Many Arab films connect different elements in a rather unequivocal way in order to fix the symbol's meaning to an unambiguous statement. Such metaphorical symbolism can be observed in an early Egyptian work, the first musical starring Muhammad ᶜAbd al-Wahhab, *The White Rose* (al-Warda al-bayda', 1933/34) by Muhammad Karim. The young protagonist (ᶜAbd al-Wahhab) is presented a rose by the daughter of his wealthy employer after he helps her in the garden to collect the pearls of her torn necklace. In the following scene, the young man returns home holding the white rose in his hands and starts to sing, while the girl is shown stringing the white pearls. The objects, i.e., their images, white rose and bright pearls, are thus connected to the protagonists. Moreover, the relation of the characters is defined, as the course of the action shows, through the image of the white rose. In spite of the immense love he feels and even after his ascent as an acclaimed singer, the poor employee relinquishes his desire to ask for his beloved's hand in marriage because of his own inferior social position. Thus, the white rose evokes (in contrast to the red rose) the idea of pure love, innocent of selfish (sexual) intentions. In order to express this meaning, director Muhammad Karim is not satisfied to connect images alone, but calls in an additional and even more unambiguous means of expression, the words of the song "Ya wardat al-hubb al-safi" (Oh, rose of pure love), sung by ᶜAbd al-Wahhab while holding the rose in his hands.

There is a huge number of films with such unambiguous symbolism. In Youssef Chahine's *The Sparrow* (al-ᶜUsfur, 1971), set a short while before and during the Six Day War in June 1967, the protagonist, Bahiya, makes several friends, including a young police officer and a journalist. They use Bahiya's house as meeting point, and together they try to uncover a circle of black marketeers who are responsible for the theft of machines from public companies. The trail begins to lead to the highest official levels. During the inquiries, war starts. The friends worriedly follow developments. When, after the defeat, Nasser announces his resignation, Bahiya is the first to hurry out into the street, leading the crowds of demonstrators pleading for their leader to stay.

Bahiya is characterized as a kind and upright mother figure who surrounds her friends with care. As the leader of the masses protesting against Nasser's resignation, she collects the few patriots, offers them shelter, and demands a strong national leadership. Bahiya is an ideal figure, a symbol of motherly Egypt. The image of Egypt as a generous, nourishing mother is widespread—"Misr umm al-dunya" ('Egypt is the mother of the world'). Yet, the film also makes it clear that Bahiya represents Egypt in a metaphorical sense: "Masr, ya amma ya bahiya" (colloquial: 'oh, beautiful mother Egypt') are the words of a patriotic song by Sayyid Darwish that introduces the whole film.

In *Sejnane* (1974), the Tunisian director Abdellatif Ben Ammar draws a symbolic connection between the oppression of women in patriarchal society and political colonialism. The story is set in 1952 on the eve of national independence and tells of Kamil, a young highschool student, whose father has become the victim of a politically motivated murder. His father's death leads Kamil to take part in the resistance against French occupation. As a result he is expelled from school, and starts working in a printshop, where he becomes acquainted with Anissa, his employer's daughter. She is drawn to Kamil but is promised by her parents to a man twice her age. Unused to questioning her parents' authority, she accepts her fate. Kamil intensifies his involvement with the workers and the resistance movement, and the film ends with Anissa's wedding shown simultaneously with a scene in which Kamil and his comrades are killed by a hail of bullets from the French army. The bride's defloration is undercut with images of dying rebels. The synecdochic symbolisms of the two strings of action combine to equate patriarchal family structure with murderous colonialism and vice versa.

The Knife (al-Sikkin, Syria, 1972) by Khaled Hamada (*courtesy National Film Organization, Damascus*)

Synecdochic and metaphorical symbols reduced to clear statements, as in *The Sparrow* and *Sejnane*, are found in the film production of most Arab countries after independence. They often take political or religious themes. In Khaled Hamada's film *The Knife*, an Arab informer forces a Palestinian girl to become his lover, while her brother decides to escape from Israeli occupation and leave his defenseless sister to the 'rapist.' The discourse of 'raped' Palestine stems from nationalist Pan-Arab rhetorics.

In the Egyptian films *Give My Heart Back!* (Rudd qalbi, 1957) by ⁀Izz al-Din zul-Fiqar and *A Man in Our House* (Fi baytina radjul, 1961) by Henri Barakat, a young officer from a poor family and a young resistance fighter respectively represent the new order. In *Men under the Sun* (Ridjal taht al-shams, Syria, 1970), an episode film by, among others, Nabil Maleh, a Palestinian child born in difficult conditions during the flight from the occupiers symbolizes the persistence and decisiveness of his parents, who synecdochically represent his nation as a whole. In Lakhdar Hamina's *Chronicle of the Years of Embers*, a poor rural family represents the Algerian nation as it lives through the different periods of French colonialism.

The juxtaposition of symbols and literal meaning and their subordination to political metaphorism prevailing in the rhetorics of nationalist and socialist leaderships is a clear characteristic of some mainstream and most realist anti-colonial cinema. This tendency may be partly rooted in the lack of symbolic representation in pre-colonial Islamic culture but has certainly been strengthened by the authoritarian and didactic concepts of nationalist and revolutionary film making.

However, these concepts have been challenged over the last two decades by some critical representatives of the emerging *cinéma d'auteur*, most notably in the work of intellectual Maghrebi directors whose skepticism of the dominating authoritarian and patriarchal system is expressed in the release of symbols into a multitude of meanings. Accordingly, the relation of the individual to image and space is no longer functionally defined but rather subjective and non-conformist, and feeds into a partly deconstructive individualism hostile to any political unitarianism.

The theater

The shadow play

A plane crashes in the desert; survivors appear from behind the dunes. A tiny uninhabited oasis lies in front of them. What follows is *The Beginning* (al-Bidaya, 1986), a twelve character piece on capitalism and stalled democracy. The new beginning that the passengers have in this isolated oasis ends with a one-man dictatorship. The businessman skillfully manipulates his companions, and has soon seized possession of the whole oasis with all its food supplies. From now on, the passengers have to serve only his interests. The resistance of a young rebel is soon broken, and only the rescue helicopter that finally succeeds in finding the victims brings salvation from this nightmare.

The Beginning, a satire by the early master of realist cinema, the Egyptian Salah Abu Seif, unfolds a good deal of its comedy in the theatrical performance of its protagonists. Costumes, as well as the actors' exaggerated gestures and facial expressions bring out, in a caricatural manner, the major characteristics of their personalities: the greedy businessman with his attaché case, the simple peasant in his traditional *galabiya*, the poor rebellious young man dressed in blue jeans, and the opportunist female doctor wearing thick glasses. They are supposed to represent a cross-section of Egyptian society. Their acting is not intended to portray their psychological states, but to underline their social roles. The plot is only superficially integrated with the oasis setting. At no point does it reflect the inner life of the characters. They are like puppets moving against a colored backdrop.

The Beginning (al-Bidaya, Egypt, 1986) by Salah Abu Seif

The viewer looking for cinematic variety achieved by movement, rhythm, complex spatiality, or atmospheric visual arrangements, will be disappointed. *The Beginning* presents itself as a piece of illustrated speech theater. Salah Abu Seif's way of handling film is nothing unusual, as it has occurred repeatedly in many Arab films of a commercial cut.

In one of his earlier realist films, *The Second Wife* (al-Zaudja al-thaniya, 1967), Salah Abu Seif himself pointed out the tradition from which his style is drawn. In the prologue of the film, a traveling entertainer sets up his *sunduq al-dunya*,[46] inviting bystanders to hear his performance, a folk tale, and to watch the accompanying pictures in the box. In the following sequence, Abu Seif introduces his characters first in an animation before shifting to the performance of real actors, thus clearly juxtaposing his film style with the schematized repertory of folk tales.

The film goes on to tell the story of an old village mayor, married but childless, who wishes to have an heir to his fortune. He falls in love with the pretty young wife of a poor peasant, who has already given birth to several children and seems to suit the mayor's plans to remarry. When she does not bow to his wishes voluntarily, he tries to blackmail her. He accuses her husband of theft and demands as a

The Second Wife (al-Zaudja al-thaniya, Egypt, 1967) by Salah Abu Seif (*courtesy Muhammad Bakr, photogapher, Cairo*)

service in return for his exoneration the divorce of the couple. After a failed escape together, husband and wife accept their fate. The young peasant's wife is married to the mayor against her will, and looks for revenge. She uses the jealousy of his first wife skillfully in order to prevent him from consummating and enjoying his new marriage. When she becomes pregnant by her former husband, the mayor has to recognize that he has lost the game. Inwardly broken, he falls ill and dies. The young peasant woman is reunited with her family, and her child inherits the old man's fortune.

Just as in a folk tale, the clever poor outwit the influential and self-righteous wealthy. The characterization of the figures is similar to that of *The Beginning*, with stereotyped models defined mainly by their social affiliations. In style and construction, the film refers clearly to the popular narrative scheme set up in its prologue.

Sunduq al-dunya relies on schematized, visually abstracted figures, and partly improvised dialogues. It is closely related to the much older and formerly widespread shadow play *(khayal al-zil)*, which is one of the oldest predecessors of theater in the region. Performances were generally accompanied by music[47] and presented at private celebrations, on religious holidays and in cafés.[48] Normally, the figures were made of slightly transparent pieces of leather fixed to long sticks, whose silhouettes were reflected on an illuminated screen. As marionettes and three-dimensional puppets were almost unknown in the Middle East and North Africa,[49] the shadow play must be considered the nearest native equivalent to 'puppet' theater.

Since shadow play figures, like puppets, cannot make facial expressions or use mimesis, there is little individuality or ambiguity in these performances. The figures are largely prototypes, through which general experiences and knowledge are more easily conveyed than individual ones. Their grotesque characteristics are intensified by their stereotyped, frozen facial expression and by the obvious contradiction between constant movement and actual inanimation.[50]

Originating in India, shadow play probably first came to the Middle East via Iraq,[51] and from there spread to other Arab countries. The earliest written records we have of popular shadow plays, such as the "Crocodile Play" (Licbat al-timsah) and "Alien and Strange" (Gharib wa cadjib), are from fourteenth century Egypt and are very expressive of that environment.[52] The form of "Alien and Strange" shows similarities to a classical literary genre, the *maqama*. During the Ottoman period, Arab shadow play received a new impetus from Turkish Karagöz (Arabic: *karakuz* or *karadjuz*), although the Turkish shadow play is probably itself based on the Arab model. Karagöz, which in Turkish literally means 'black eye,' presumably comes from the Arabic Qaraqush, the name of a dreaded comrade-in-arms of Saladin. Qaraqush soon became the subject of Egyptian shadow plays and to this day remains a synonym for arbitrary, unjust despotism.[53] From the beginning of the twentieth century, with the introduction of modern theater and cinema, the traditional shadow play has been increasingly threatened with oblivion. Shadow plays may however have contributed greatly to the easy acceptance and spread of cinema in the region.

Elements of popular theater are still present in mainstream cinema. Even very recent films like *The Cock of the Walk* (Dik al-barabir, 1993) by the Egyptian Hussein Kamal relate to puppet theater by using popular proverbs, plays-upon-words, suggestive remarks, and stereotypical overacting.

This predilection for caricatural theatrical performances is not limited to Egypt and can be observed particularly in commercial comedies such as the films of Algerian comedian Rouiched or the Syrian Doureid Laham. Similar tendencies appear even in works that may be assigned to so-called New Arab cinema, including *Halfaouine* by the Tunisian Ferid Boughedir or *The Search for My Wife's Husband* (al-Bahth can zawdj imra'ati, 1994) by the Moroccan Mohamed Ben Abderrahmane Tazi.

To some extent this persistence reflects the needs of a partly still illiterate mass audience. However, at least in Egypt, the exaggerated cliché-like style of performance and representation is also rooted in the commercial stardom system and the conditions of production connected to it. Successful films often shape a role, which the star then adopts in following narratives. The industry's exploitation and reproduction of certain topics and story-types lead to frequent repetitions and uniform performances. Stereotypes are often strengthened by characterizing figures by their social roles. This is not confined to farce and comedy, but is used also in realist cinema. It is a tendency that reflects the increasing loss of individuality in modern society.

Beginnings of Arab theater

The influence of popular theater genres on cinema was first felt in Egypt, introducing elements of Karagöz, shadow play and *fasl mudhik* (comic scenes). Some of these genres, like the *fasl mudhik*, a sort of improvised sketch, were further influenced by European forms of theater, like commedia dell'arte and speech theater.

No real dramatic theater developed in the Arab countries before the encounter with European theater. Simpler forms of mimesis were common, including the Shi'ite passion plays *(taᶜziya)*, storytelling *(al-haki)*, praising *(madh)*, the Maghrebi round theater *(masrah al-halaqa)* performed at market places,[54] and the reciting of *maqama* poetry. These genres involved the basics of mimicry[55] and, with the exception of the *maqama*, are examples of popular art.[56]

The comic scene or *fasl mudhik* in particular, which is closely related to farce, is an important popular predecessor of modern Arab theater. In the middle of the eighteenth century, European travelers reported the existence in Egypt of small troupes, called *muhabbazun*, who performed the genre in public places and during private festivities. One of the plays observed in 1815 dealt with the exposing of a deceitful camel merchant, another told the story of a foolish European traveler who was led to believe in the generous hospitality of an Arab.[57] At the end of the nineteenth century, the *fasl mudhik* assumed elements of the commedia dell'arte, which was introduced to the country by visiting Italian troupes.[58]

This means that until the nineteenth century the Arabic-speaking world did not possess a theater in the Western sense. Although Arab scholars and writers of the early Islamic age had access to the records of Greek drama, they did not make any use of it. The reason for this is most probably Greek drama's huge pantheon of gods, goddesses, and half-gods, which cannot easily be reconciled with Islamic monotheism. Another important factor may have been the incompatibility of Greek drama with the Islamic philosophy of life. Islam's conviction that man's fate is completely dependent on the will of the Creator, who is the source of all things, made the conflict between human beings and heavenly powers, an element so essential to Greek drama, seem irrelevant.[59]

The hero of the classic Western drama is an individualist. Spiritual conflicts and involvements with fate constitute his nature. He stands in eternal opposition to divine arbitrariness, to a hostile environment, or to other restrictions. This idea of a dramatic hero is not familiar to the Arab art of narration. Instead of conjuring up conflict between good and evil, known and unknown—indispensable elements in the structuring of drama—Arab poets took just one side, either extolling the pleasures of life or accepting death as an unalterable fate.[60] Only rarely did Muslim authors arrange popular, but in their essence dramatic topics (sometimes originated in the pre-Islamic period), according to the principles of drama. An example is *Madjnun and Layla*, whose story line resembles that of *Romeo and Juliet*.

However, this does not mean that Arabic-Islamic literature did not engender any dramatic structures at all. It created, for example, the *maqama*, a fictional genre showing formal similarities to drama. The *maqama*, literally 'situation,' is considered the most important form of prose in classical Arabic literature and was often written in rhymes. Through the eyes of a fictive narrator, the author described different situations and adventures in the life of his hero.[61] Certain scenes involve mimicry, where the protagonists are given monologues and dialogues that express their specific character.[62] The *maqama*, though, had no strict construction like Greek drama and was not performed by actors.

The development of a European-style theater in the Arab region started in the middle of the nineteenth century. In 1848 the Maronite Marun al-Naqqash presented the first Arab play in Beirut. It was an adaptation of *The Miser* by Molière. Various Syrian and Lebanese writers and directors, who emigrated to Egypt, followed in his footsteps and Arabized a large number of French plays. Genuine Arab dramas, like the original and popular plays by the 'Egyptian Molière,' Ya'qub Sanu', appeared at the beginning of the twentieth century.

Egypt soon became the center of Arab theater. For decades it attracted many talented Syrian and Lebanese artists, leading to the fast growth of various troupes at the turn of the century. Without any state support, they remained largely dependent on the preferences of the audience, who, as quickly became apparent, had not much

interest in a merely classical European repertoire. Similarly unsuccessful were the dramas of intellectual Egyptian writers such as
Ahmad Shauqi, Taufiq al-Hakim, and Mahmud Taymur, published
during World War I. By contrast the melodramas and comedies of
Yusuf Wahbi, and the vaudevilles of actors Nagib al-Rihani and ⁽Ali
al-Kassar were saturated with popular elements, and found a ready
audience. They were usually accompanied by music, contained
suggestive comic dialogues and a more scenic composition. Their
characters were drawn from different sources, including the *fasl
mudhik*, commedia dell'arte, shadow play, and Karagöz.[63] "The
popular theater in Egypt," wrote Landau in 1953, "remains to our
day a mixture of the tradition of local humor and showmanship, with
a strong flavor of West-European means of enlivening this local tradition. The result is somewhat suggestive of modern burlesque."[64]

Theater and cinema

In most Arab countries, modern native theater developed much later
than in Egypt. Syria and Lebanon, in spite of their achievements in
translating and Arabizing Western dramas, took some time to recover
from the continuous loss of talented artists. In Jordan and Iraq, the
development of theater was considerably delayed by British occupation.[65] In North Africa, interest in Arabic-language theater was
expressed only after World War I, mainly because of French efforts
to marginalize indigenous culture.[66] Guest performances by Egyptian
companies, like those of George Abyad in the 1930s, impelled native
endeavors. Rashid Ksentini, for example, presented more then 100
sketches and plays and contributed decisively to the foundation of
popular musical theater in Algeria.[67] During the 1950s, the comedies
and dramas of the Algerian Muhi'l-Din (Muhi al-Din Bash Tarzi)
achieved great success,[68] while in Tunisia the number of troupes
increased drastically after independence, leading to the presentation
of more than 500 plays between 1966 and 1971.[69]

In Egypt, the close relation between popular theater and native film
making dates back to the 1920s. The first genuinely Egyptian
production resulted from the activities of actors, actresses, and directors of theater. Muhammad Bayyumi's short film *The Clerk* (al-
Bashkatib) was shot in 1922 and starred Amin ⁽Attallah and his
troupe. *Layla*, the first widely acknowledged full-length feature film,
was made on the initiative of the theater actress ⁽Aziza Amir. In
1930, the actor Yusuf Wahbi established the first small studio in
Egypt. Plays with public appeal, like Nagib al-Rihani's *Kish Kish Bey*,
were adapted for the screen, and in the course of the 1930s the stars

Nagib al-Rihani (*courtesy Muhammad Bakr, photographer, Cairo*)   ᶜAli al-Kassar (*courtesy Muhammad Bakr, photographer, Cairo*)

of popular Egyptian theater, Nagib al-Rihani, ᶜAli al-Kassar, and Yusuf Wahbi, had a great influence on the developing art of film making. During the pre-World War II era and shortly after the war they appeared in a large number of feature films, but their work was not confined to acting. They also contributed in writing the screenplays and dialogues of their films and, in the case of Wahbi, directed and produced as well.

The closeness of some of these artists to folk art is illustrated by the example of ᶜAli al-Kassar. "Continuing the activity of the farce performers and *fasl mudhik* enactors, al-Kassar had no regular theater of his own, but wandered about in various towns and villages, tuning the audiences' ears to the fine, sharp tongue of the Barbarin."[70] In films like *Seven o'Clock* (al-Saᶜa sabᶜa, 1937) or *Lend me Three Pounds!* (Salifni talata gini, 1938), both directed by Togo Mizrahi, ᶜAli al-Kassar appears in the role of a black Nubian, ᶜUthman ᶜAbd al-Basit, the *barbari*.[71] ᶜUthman is a real Karagöz, a notoriously unlucky person, who gets off lightly only at the end of the film.

In *Seven o'Clock* ᶜUthman works as a messenger for a bank in Alexandria. One night, burglars break into his bedroom and steal a sum of money belonging to the bank. When, next morning, ᶜUthman confesses the theft to his employer, he himself is suspected of having committed the crime. Clandestinely, he travels to Aswan in order to pawn a piece of land, but the police are already on his trail. Disguised as a peasant woman, ᶜUthman drives back to Alexandria. On the train, he is hired as a servant to a lecherous old gentleman. ᶜUthman is eventually exposed in his employer's house. On his way to the police station, the alarm clock rings. It is seven o'clock: it was all a dream.

Several dramatically closed scenes decompose the whole, rather simple and point-oriented, narration. At the beginning of the film ᶜUthman loses his bicycle while running an errand. A young *khawaga*[72] disappears with the bicycle, which ᶜUthman had parked in front of the bank. ᶜUthman finally finds his bicycle in front of another bank. He starts to recover it, but is stopped by a policeman who accuses him of theft. After some comings and goings, the real thief gets away and the Nubian start his errands again.

Another sequence, no less extensive, follows a short while later. ᶜUthman gets drunk in a pub together with his friend George, a rather corpulent *khawaga*. The two set off tipsily for home, and manage to confuse the doors of their houses several times. When George eventually settles in his bed, ᶜUthman enters the room and convinces him that he is actually in ᶜUthman's bed. As ᶜUthman is undressing, he hears his wife and mother-in-law screaming in the opposite building. In his underwear, he leaves the bedroom and walks into the neighboring house. There, he finds George in his apartment. But ᶜUthman wonders what the women are doing in his friend's house. When the confusion is finally cleared up, George leaves ᶜUthman's flat, but gets lost on his way home. Although these events are supposed to prepare the ground for ᶜUthman's dream of the burglars' break-in, the context is almost totally subverted because of the internal dynamics of the scene. The representation of the comic sketches seems more important than the preservation of a complete context.

The character of the Nubian ᶜUthman is comic, not only because of his naivety and the absurd situations he gets involved in, but also because of his ethnic description. His major characteristics are a specific dress and a strong Nubian-Sudanese accent. The same applies to some other secondary characters, who are also defined by religious or ethnic affiliation. In *Seven o'Clock*, the gigantic but kind-hearted George and a thieving *khawaga* appear beside ᶜUthman. Their appearance may be explained by the film's location, the cosmopolitan seaport of Alexandria, but comparable characters are found in other films shot in Cairo.

In Niyazi Mustafa's *Salama Is Fine* (Salama fi khayr, 1937), Nagib al-Rihani plays a simple errand boy who slips, for a short while, into the role of a foreign prince. Unlike *Seven o'Clock*, this charming confusion comedy does not get lost in a number of sketches. The main plot is strictly subordinated to the theme of 'getting into trouble and out again.' But the film does contain elements of popular theater, including a distinctive overtone of verbal comedy. For this reason, some scenes make use of the language and the behavior of foreigners and native minorities. A Christian colleague of Salama works as a bookkeeper. Asked for invoices, he replies in melodious tones reminiscent of Coptic liturgy. Salama answers mockingly using the same intonation.[73] Again, Salama's neighbors, who live in the same building, are a European family with many children. The young mother is forever trying, in broken Arabic, to tame her horde of children.

Comic characters with distinctive accents, such as the loyally devoted Nubian servants or the naive, clumsy, upper Egyptian *fellaheen* (peasants) formed for decades a stereotype repertoire constantly repeated in Egyptian cinema. *Fasl mudhik* and shadow plays also presented these figures. Shadow plays possessed a stable group of figures, including a *muqaddim* or moderator, the cumbersome Rikhim, a Maghrebi, and a Nubian or Sudanese *barbari*.[74] In some Egyptian *fasl mudhik* sketches at the beginning of the last century, a foolish European traveler[75] and a Coptic bookkeeper[76] contributed to the audience's amusement. These characters also belonged to the often repeated repertoire of modern popular Egyptian theater.[77]

In the construction of films, in particular those of ᶜAli al-Kassar, parallels to popular forms of theater are easily recognized. The shadow play, for example, is structured by an introduction that contains religious praises presented by the *muqaddim* and is followed by a variety of sketches presenting the rest of the characters improvising prose dialogues. The overall plot seems weak in comparison to the sometimes wild and lewd dialogues.[78]

Karagöz

Some Syrian films of the 1960s featuring the comic duo Doureid Laham and Nihad al-Qalᶜi contain elements similar to Egyptian farce. The duo first came to be known through the television sketch *The Pearl Necklace* (ᶜIqd al-lulu), which was so successful that the two performers adapted it for theater, and also to cinema in a film directed in 1964 by Yusuf al-Maᶜluf. The popular humor of the two comedians was characterized, according to the Syrian film critic and director Salah Dehni, by a certain anarchism. He describes Doureid, in particular, as being in his very core cynical and destructive. "Doureid never reaches the point of trusting others, or of having an

Doureid Laham (left) and Nihad Qal^ci in *The Millionaire* (al-Milyunira, Syria and Lebanon, 1966) by Yusuf al-Ma^cluf

honest relationship. He is always skeptical, ready to give back or even to anticipate a blow that could hit him."[79]

Laham and Qal^ci made more than a dozen comedies in this spirit, including *The Two Homeless* (al-Sharidan, 1965), *Love in Istanbul* (Gharam fi Istanbul, 1967), *The Nice Thief* (al-Liss al-zarif, 1968), *The Ladies' Taylor* (Khayyat al-sayyidat, 1969), and *The Suitable Man* (al-Radjul al-munasib, 1970).

In *The Vagabonds* (al-Sa^calik, 1967)[80] by Yusuf al-Ma^cluf, Doureid and Nihad appear as a pair of many-sided crooks. Nihad is a swindler working in the way of a conscientious businessman, who invests a lot of money to realize his projects. But, following his plan to swindle a Turkish aristocrat out of a huge sum of donation money meant for a dogs' nursing home, the smart Doureid crosses his path. Through his diverse disguises and good connections with waiters, Doureid manages to cheat people as fast as his wealthy competitor does. Nihad finally has no choice but to cooperate with his adversary. Together, they try to get their hands on an Egyptian widow's fortune. In order to gain the woman's confidence, Nihad buys a Greek freighter. Soon, however, he discovers that he himself has been taken for a ride. Before the clever widow can escape with the money, everyone involved is reunited in police custody.

Apart from the widowed businesswoman, played by the Egyptian actress Miryam Fakhr al-Din, a Turkish lady, a Greek businessman, an Egyptian traveler, and a Persian astrologer appear in *The Vagabonds*. The last two characters are played by Doureid Laham, who uses fancy dress and the appropriate conspicuous accent to get his fellow citizens to part with their money. It is true, given the popularity of Egyptian movies, that the use of the Egyptian vernacular may have been based on commercial considerations, but all the other accents are certainly introduced for the sake of amusement.

In early Arab drama, dialects were used in order to differentiate its characters socially, as in Marun al-Naqqash's adaptation of *The Miser* by Molière. But this was certainly not the intention of *The Vagabonds*, which aims principally for comic effect. This raises the possibility of a connection between the film and the formerly widespread traditional Syrian shadow plays, which, unlike the Egyptian variety, were more or less identical to the Turkish Karagöz.

Doureid Laham himself denies any links to the popular Karagöz, which has almost entirely died out. He points, instead, to the American comedians Stan Laurel and Oliver Hardy.[81] Indeed, there is at least a physical similarity between the Arab and the American duo. Nihad al-Qalᶜi's corpulence recalls Hardy, while Laham's frailness comes close to that of Laurel. But, unlike "Fat and Stupid," as Laurel and Hardy were known in Germany, Doureid and Nihad are both, each in his own specific way, clever and cunning. This makes them first opponents, then turns them into friends who are eventually outwitted by someone else—and, last not least, lines them up as successors of the popular Syrian Karagöz and his partner Hiwaz.

The main parts of most Syrian shadow plays known today are taken by Karagöz and his friend and mentor Hiwaz (Hagivad in Turkish). In *The Bath House* (Fasl al-hamam), Karagöz and Hiwaz, being swindlers and deceived at the same time, rent a faulty bath house and ask its customers to provide the facilities, including the water. In another play, the pleasant good-for-nothings are at loggerheads with their quarrelsome wives and with the Turk who is in charge of keeping law and order.

Other 'foreigners,' such as the European doctor, appear in Karagöz plays, all speaking broken Arabic, so that language again constitutes an essential source of comedy.[82] For example, in *The Beggars* Hiwaz teaches Karagöz to beg in different languages. Eventually, he inadvertently asks his own wife for charity.[83]

Farce

Arab film farce might then be seen as the descendant of the traditional shadow play and the *fasl mudhik*. It differs from comedy by
lacking 'production of meaning.' While comedy puts events in a
causal context by introducing a conflict and resolving it later, farce
largely consists of a loose combination of individual sketches. It uses
stereotypical characters and is marked by its irrealism and imaginative freedom. In principle, farce tends to transgress limits and to
break taboos.[84] Its affinity to commedia dell'arte is obvious,
supported by the aesthetics of carnival as defined by Bakhtin.[85] As in
commedia dell'arte, and medieval carnival in Europe, performances
draw on exceptional social situations. The high-ranking in society,
the king or pope, is degraded to the status of a beggar and vice-versa.
The hidden body, the normally intimate, is exposed. Sexual allusions
are expressed by plays on words or by phallic objects, such as the
huge nose or the pointed cap.[86] The cathartic and at the same time
socially stabilizing function of such performances is evident.

Obscenities in language and actions are characteristic of Egyptian
fasl mudhik and all other Arab shadow plays. They run so much
counter to today's sense of propriety, however, that a contemporary
Arab author felt himself obliged, while editing *The Bath House*, to
eliminate the excesses of the original text.[87] The lewd character of
Karagöz performances becomes obvious in a report about the
Tunisian shadow plays of the last century: "Karagöz . . . was generally pictured as a man-about-town who annoyed and deceived others,
relieved them of their possessions and beat them for good measure. .
. . The Madame or European Lady often had a hard time, for her
broad crinoline usually excited Karagöz's curiosity; however, he
never paid her seduction fees. Other characters who suffered at his
hands were the Moroccan and the Arab yokel whom Karagöz
defeated not by his wit, but by his unending store of obscenities and
by fistcuffing or whipping. In short, Karagöz had a moral code of his
own, which was the punishment by force of all and sundry who tried
to deceive or rob him."[88]

The preponderance of Europeans among Karagöz's victims
suggests that the performances conveyed a political message, which
at times became a thorn in the rulers' flesh. In Algeria in 1843, the
French authorities banned the native shadow plays for being subversive; they were thus condemned to extinction.[89] According to Nouri,
similar prohibitions were applied in Tunisia.[90]

Modern Arab film farce, however, developed in the framework of
politically and religiously controlled mass production. Eschewing the

Sexual transgression in *Seven o'Clock* (al-Sa°a sab°a, Egypt, 1937) by Togo Mizrahi

tearing speed and excessive physical violence of its American counterpart,[91] it relies more on language. However, the transgression of taboos characteristic of traditional performances is highly restricted in Arab film farce. Political allusions and sexual suggestiveness fall victim to censorship. Only traces of the genre's potential subversiveness are found in Arab films. In the already cited *Seven o'Clock*, °Ali al-Kassar hurls a barrage of abuse at a deaf and dumb acquaintance, who misunderstands it as expressions of friendship. In *Lend me Three Pounds!* the actor's language is certainly colorful, but he does not use any insults with sexual connotations. °Uthman appears in the film dressed as a woman. As such he attracts lecherous looks from his admirer, and at one point a suspicious servant grabs his stuffed bosom, but these incidents only hint at the genre's possibilities. Actions that would normally be considered taboo are tolerated in this case because °Uthman is not really a woman.

Ever mindful of the interests of influential social and political groups and its massive consumption, Egyptian cinema in the 1930s and 1940s generally adopted the role of an upholder of moral standards. There is, however, some breaking of taboos, and some social inversion, even if their cathartic function is limited. In Anwar Wagdi's *Girls' Flirtation* (Ghazal al-banat, 1949), a pasha is mocked by a simple employee. Wearing a straw hat and an apron, and carrying garden scissors in his hands, he is taken for a gardener. His 'degradation' does not last long, however. Soon after, real conditions

Salama Is Fine (Salama fi khayr, Egypt, 1937) by Niyazi Mustafa (*courtesy Muhammad Bakr, photographer, Cairo*)

are restored and the genuine 'little man' is himself regimented and accused of being a thief by the pasha's daughter.

Another film, *Salama Is Fine*, starring Nagib al-Rihani, derives a great deal of its comedy from the tension between Salama's real identity as an errand boy and his adopted role as a prince. He gets into a number of dangerous situations because of his disguise, but his adventures pay off in the end with a financial reward.

Only in one film, *The Second Wife*, where the mayor is outwitted, are the former conditions of power not restored. This is no wonder, because in the period between the appearance of this work in 1967 and the preceding examples, several profound and radical social changes had taken place. Land reform and the nationalization of private property had, in reality, deprived the old ruling class of its power base.

New Arab theater in cinema

During the 1970s and 1980s, a new theatrical movement attracted attention in several Arab countries. The New Theater *(al-masrah al-djadid)* in Tunisia and *al-hakawati* (the storyteller) in Lebanon, for example, tried to connect their avantgardist endeavor to consciously chosen elements of native narrative and theatrical forms. Their work also found expression in cinema.

The Tunisian New Theater was founded in 1975 and, until 1980, comprised five members: Jelila Baccar, Mohammed Driss, Fadhel Jaibi (Fadil Dju^caybi), Fadhel Jaziri, and Habib Masrouki. Usually, these five shared in the writing and directing of their plays and their two films, *The Marriage* (al-^cUrs, 1978) and *Arabs* (^cArab, 1988).

The Marriage, which was shot in black and white, is characterized by immense emotional density and deep dramatic tension. Organized like a studio theater play, it is centered around two actors whose performance is confined to one simple location. The protagonists, a newly married couple on their wedding night, have a fierce quarrel, which reveals their weakness and social opportunism. The surrounding space is completely included in the performance. The barely furnished room and its insufficient structural substance, the crumbling mortar softened by a downpour, intensify the conflict's drama and underline the morbid character of their failed intersexual relation. "In the cinematic version, space has become more realistic, more sensuous, and thus more concrete. This brings the characters into contact with the objects, the light, and a room with a special ground resonance, etc., leading to another sensuality and therefore to another impact."[92]

By applying the spatial-temporal structure of theater to film, an impressive symbiosis of both forms of performance is created. Real time is not undermined by montage nor are wide angle shots of the space cut by close-ups. Thus, the relationship between character and space acquires a deeper intensity. "The duration of a shot is an essential and basic idea. If you had to show a close-up of a face or hands, the time of the plot would vanish, the time of the character-body and the audience would function alone."[93]

Plot and characters are loosely based on "The petty bourgeois wedding" *(Die Kleinbürgerhochzeit)* by Bertolt Brecht, but the protagonists of the Tunisian play own "a biography, a history and a consciousness,"[94] rooted in Tunisian reality. Yet the figures' relation to society is not expressed in stereotypical characterizations such as social roles, nor does space contribute to their definition. In this respect *The Marriage*'s idea of the hero differs essentially from that of commercial Arab cinema. The characters' relation to each other and their attitude toward space and objects are, in its cinematic translation, antagonistic, and in a state of conflict.

Although the members of the New Theater studied in Europe, they reject the self-reflexive nature of Western intellectual cinema. In their films they want to come into direct contact with their audience by reflecting its daily life, its alienation, and mechanisms.[95] They set their work consciously apart from production schemes applied by Hollywood. "We are our own producers, which means economic use of means and an extremely reduced staff."[96] Tunisian audiences, however, did not appreciate this concept.[97] The group's work differed too much from the schemes and conventions of popular cinema.

Another example of a symbiosis of experimental Arab theater and cinema is the semi-fictional film *Maarakeh* (Ma^{c}raka; literally, 'battle,' 1985), by the Lebanese theater director Roger Asaaf (^{c}Asaf). This is a common work by a group of actors and performers, whose script was developed by Asaaf together with his troupe, al-Hakawati. According to the Lebanese critic Mohamed Soueid, groups like al-Hakawati, who started working during the civil war, succeeded much better then native film making in reflecting Lebanese reality. In their plays, they dealt with the complicated situation of the civil war and tried to express the daily suffering of the population.[98] Unlike the New Theater in Tunisia, al-Hakawati were eager to include popular elements and traditional narrative structures in their plays, and as a result their concept of theater was highly acclaimed by audiences.

In *Maarakeh*, the actors, together with the inhabitants of the Shi'ite village Maarakeh in the south of Lebanon, reconstruct the birth of native resistance to the Israelis. Parallel to the images of the Israeli invasion and the actions taken against it by women, men, and children, documentary sections portray the daily life of the Shi'ite population, including the celebration of the feast of ^{c}Ashura and the accompanying *ta^{c}ziya*, a Shi'ite 'passion play' held annually in memory of the assassination of Husain, the Prophet's grandson. Apart from ritual castigation, the *ta^{c}ziya* comprise the enactment of Husain's suffering. By setting this popular Islamic mimetic tradition in a topical context, the film represents the cultural background of Shi'ite confessionalism developing in the course of the Lebanese civil war. It makes clear how war and resistance served as a catalyst for a confessionally defined cultural identity.

Maarakeh is evidence of an emancipating comprehension of theater. Performance does not serve as a mass product reinforcing social conditions, but as an artistic means of expression that, if required, the audience may develop further.[99]

This conceptual comprehension of theater can also be observed in other, more recent experimental theater projects, such as the work of the Egyptian al-Warsha (literally, 'the workshop') led by Hassan El-Geretli (Hasan Giritly). This sort of experimental theater stresses neither the idea of a 'problematic hero' caught in conflict with his environment, nor of a creature steered only by fate or society. Its 'intellectual' reappropriation of so-called popular and traditional culture sets it apart from the rather unconscious use of these elements in mainstream cinema.

Language and the art of narration

Language as a "social battleground"[100]

The so-called high culture of the Arab countries has been dominated by classical Arabic *(al-fusha)*, while popular culture has made use of the numerous dialects *(al-ᶜamiya)*, which in some cases differ considerably from the classical language. Because of cinema's 'realistic' capabilities, film makers from the very beginning preferred to use colloquial dialects for dialogue. The classical language, or its more recent form, modern standard Arabic, has been confined to genres such as the news, or educational, historical, and religious films.

The Egyptian musical *Dananir*[101] by Ahmed Badrakhan, released in the season 1940/1, is one of the few works in Arab film history to use classical Arabic in the dialogue. The story is set in the ninth century during the reign of the Abbassid caliph Harun al-Rashid, and relates an historical incident, the discord between the caliph and his vizier Djaᶜfar al-Barmaki, which ends with Djaᶜfar being put to death. Both the caliph and his vizier later appear in *The Thousand and One Nights*.

Umm Kulthum in *Dananir* (Egypt, 1940/41) by Ahmed Badrakhan

The reign of the caliph Harun al-Rashid was one of the most splendid epochs in the history of Islam, and Dananir evokes in numerous scenes the greatness of classical Arab culture. In one the film's final sequences, the slave-girl heroine Dananir walks singing and lamenting through the ruins of Djaᶜfar's former palace. This motif is reminiscent of the conventions of the pre-Islamic and classical Arabic poem *(al-qasida)*, which begins with the poet walking through ruins lamenting the loss of the beloved.

The extravagant sets and the musical score, supported by the appearance of the famous singer Umm Kulthum as Dananir, contributes to the impression of classical grandeur. The majesty of Arab-Muslim history is further evoked by the musical genre of *al-ghina' al-ᶜarabi* (Arab singing) presented by Umm Kulthum. Classical and modern standard Arabic are used in the songs and in the dialogue, which is embroidered with quotations from the great poet Abu Nuwas, a contemporary of Harun al-Rashid. The classical language is transformed into a "mythical language that functions as a last refuge, verbal magic, whose incomprehensibility is understood as the irrefutable proof of the sacred"[102] and serves as a bridge to a mythically transfigured past.

The 'mythical' qualities of classical Arabic derive from its role as a transmitter of divine revelation. The revelation of the Quran marks in every respect, politically as well as culturally, the beginning of Arab-Muslim culture. In the regions conquered by Islam, Arabic also became the instrument of spiritual and scientific knowledge and superseded or marginalized other native languages. In modern times, with the introduction of new Western ideas and technology, it has become necessary to adapt classical Arabic to these new ideas and to social changes in the Arab region.

Writers from non-Muslim minorities, in particular Lebanese and Syrian Christians, tried to modernize language by translating Western literature as well as through their own literary creations.[103] Their endeavors contributed to the separation of language from the context of religion and paved the way for its use as a basis of national, non-confessional identity.

During the twentieth century, journalistic use forced the development of what is called Modern Standard Arabic. Like classical Arabic it differs considerably from colloquial Arabic and remains, in principal, reserved for official or intellectual use. As it is used in the media and serves as a *lingua franca* between the different Arab countries, it represents today a sort of functional language *(véhiculaire)* in the public field.[104]

Apart from this *lingua franca*, innumerable local vernacular languages have spread in the Arab world: the languages of minorities, such as Armenians, Turks, Circassians, Kurds, Berbers, and Nubians exist alongside numerous Arabic dialects, some of which differ immensely in vocabulary and grammar from classical Arabic. They can be assigned to different regions as follows: the dialects of the Mashriq, meaning Egypt and the Levant; those of the Gulf states and the countries of the Fertile Crescent including Iraq; and the dialects of northwest Africa, the Maghreb, where the influence of the Berber languages and French has rendered the contemporary colloquials almost incomprehensible to Eastern Arabs.

Regional vernaculars can also be counted as local languages or 'mother tongues.' They are in general confined to the communication of a relatively small group and correspond to the needs of their daily life. The Algerian Reda Bensmaïa has observed in his native country "a language that is made of 'bric-a-brac,' that lives on 'stolen, moved words,' 'emigrating' from one language to another: a bizarre mixture of 'good' French, colloquial Arabic, and the Kabyle used in the cities. 'Ouach rak bian?'(So, how are you doing?)"[105]

In the Maghreb, mainly in Algeria, the divergence between classical and colloquial Arabic, and the long lasting, intensive colonization, encouraged the spread of French, which seemed then to meet the needs of modern times much better. Representing modern science and technology, it functioned as a *lingua franca* and hampered the diffusion of Modern Standard Arabic. "Every colonized people—which means every people that has developed an inferiority complex, because its cultural specificity has been buried— is situated with regard to the language of the civilisatory nation, which means the culture of the metropolis."[106] This situation persists until today. The laborious campaign, undertaken for years in Algeria, to Arabize the systems of education and public administration, has not really succeeded. On the contrary, it has contributed to widening the gap between the elite, educated in French private schools, and the masses graduating from public Arabic-speaking schools.[107]

Consequently, in post-colonial Algeria the question of which language Algerian cinema should use is subject to fierce ideological dispute. For example:

> It would be much more useful to take as a starting-point a spoken Arabic that has been cleansed from all imperfections and foreign words. In purifying and enriching it with a simple vocabulary we would turn it into a comprehensible language. The other advantage cinema would draw from this formula is that it would offer the viewer the opportunity of varying his vocabulary by adopting new words.[108]

Omar Gatlato (Algeria, 1976) by Merzak Allouache

Armed with intentions of this kind, Algerian cinema nevertheless did not aim at an authentic representation of different native social groups but to merge different tribes and ethnic groups into a nation. Thus, the first films dealing with Berber identity, such as *The Birds of Summer* (Les oiseaux de l'été, 1978) by Abderrahmane Bouguermouh, had to wait until the late 1970s. Bouguermouh's early short film on the subject, *Like a Soul* (Comme une âme, 1965) had been banned for a long time.[109] One of the few more recent films actually using Berber language, such as *Machaho* (1995) by Belkacem Hadjadj, was coproduced and released in France. In general, most Algerian fiction films have used a cleansed colloquial Arabic, without taking local dialects and vernaculars into account. They particularly avoid French vocabulary, although in urbanized regions a French-Arabic mixture prevails in daily life.

Only a few Algerian films have dissociated themselves from "the cinema of the great abstract syntheses; one sole 'language', one sole 'territory', one sole 'religion.'"[110] *Omar Gatlato* (1976) by Merzak Allouache was the first of these few exceptions. Its young protagonists speak a slang typical of the capital's youth, "with its sophistication, its imagery, its humor, and its philosophy. The sophistication and the plays on words, certain tics and intonations transferred to cinema 'speak' directly to the audience."[111] In this film the authenticity of language corresponds to an unpretentious plot, the psychological credibility of the characters, and a faithful representation of a specific local environment.

Egyptian film making from the beginning gave priority to dialect.

There was no doubt that dialogue was best formulated in the language of daily life. This of course served commercial purposes: directed at a partly illiterate mass audience, the use of classical Arabic in cinema would have caused financial losses. Unlike the classical language, dialect offers an additional advantage in its ability to convey elements of popular culture via linguistic expression and metaphor. Representatives of popular Egyptian theater used the colloquial in an imaginative way, particularly in farce, introducing a popular, sometimes burlesque verbal comedy to early cinema.

In the farce *Girls' Flirtation* (Ghazal al-banat, 1949) by Anwar Wagdi, with dialogues written by Badi[c] Khayri and the popular comedian Nagib al-Rihani, verbal comedy is central to the plot. In order to amuse the audience, the main character confronts and undermines elegant classical language with comparatively crude dialect. Arabic teacher Hamam (Nagib al-Rihani) tries to explain to his uninterested pupil Layla the literary phrase *man fak* (incessantly). Layla confuses the expression with a phonetically almost identical vernacular formulation (*sa[c]it ma infak*, when it came loose) and asks: "May I say, when the button of the jacket came loose?"[112] Hamam shakes his head: "No, no, what button? When you say, Zayd walked incessantly, that means, he walked so long that his feet became bare, or [c]Umar was eating incessantly, that means, [c]Umar liked the food so much that he piled it in front of him and wiped out the bowl until he couldn't get out of the chair."[113]

Nagib al-Rihani noted people's talk exactly. The vivid illustrations, mainly concerning bodily functions, which are given by the teacher Hamam as an explanation for the classical literary phrase, show clearly the gap that opens up between the two forms of language. This fissure is used in a burlesque, carnivalesque manner to overthrow and parody the elitist language, the language of religion, politics, and intellect.[114]

However, the popular and sometimes subversive use of language in farce was not able to prevent dialect from being used as an instrument of power. Egyptian cinema relies mainly on Cairo's colloquial. Other local vernaculars, such as those of Upper Egypt or Alexandria, are largely excluded or must endure bowdlerization by the actors of the capital. The two Nubian languages have not been used in a single film. Even visually the Nubian minority has been misrepresented. Since [c]Ali al-Kassar's simple and comic [c]Uthman, Egyptian cinema has with few exceptions shown Nubians as ever-smiling, simple servants who speak only broken Arabic.

Cairo's vernacular also dominates the screens beyond Egypt. The success of Egyptian cinema in neighboring countries has made its

language the *lingua franca* of commercial Arab cinema. Imitators of
the Egyptian film industry in Lebanon and Syria produced scores of
Egyptian-speaking films. Films for television and serials currently
produced by the Gulf states use the dialect in the same way. The
widespread commercial use of this cinematographic *lingua franca* on
the one hand cuts off its connection to the Egyptian street, and on the
other prevents the representation and circulation of other local
dialects and their exchange among the Arab countries. Thus, the
colloquial of the Egyptian capital has been juxtaposed to the
dominating and centralized culture of its 'white' and Arab inhabitants, while marginalizing all the speakers of other dialects.

Language and cinema

The question of language usage in cinema seems even more important when we consider the close connection of the medium to
language in its broadest sense. "Films are saturated by language from
the beginning to the end of their existence; they come from language
and ultimately return to it."[115] All stages of fictional film making are
dominated by language. The plot is first developed as a written script
to be presented to a producer. On the basis of the script preparations
for production and shooting start. Director and film team communicate during shooting by means of language. Then, after completion, a
film is retold, summarized, discussed, and criticized.

In dialogue and comment film also offers space for verbal linguistic
expression, and also includes written language in titles, subtitles,
headlines, signs, and so on. In addition, film contains some other, less
evident linguistic "tracks"[116]—literary references of images, sound
effects, and film music, as well as the stream of thoughts, the "inner
speech" of the audience,[117] induced during the screening and
sometimes expressed in loud comments. With these numerous
language tracks, the whole existence of a film takes place "within the
powerful gravitational field of what Bakhtin calls 'the word.'"[118]

An analysis of the relation of Arabic language and cinema therefore
cannot only be confined to easily accessible tracks like dialogue and
the narrative structures connected to, it but has to include other
aspects such as linguistic imagery and metaphor. Closer examination
of these tracks is needed; Arab cinema has often been characterized
as being dominated by language,[119] but no in-depth research has
been carried out to prove it.

Linguistic images

Clearly then, many Arab directors and authors trust the signifying power of words much more than visual arrangements. Consequently, they prefer to fix the meaning of symbols by giving clear linguistic indications. Some even 'translate' literary metaphors, images and expressions without further ado into the visual.

In *The Thug* (al-Futuwwa, 1957) by the Egyptian Salah Abu Seif, a young peasant finds an unskilled job at the Cairo vegetable market. He is to sell a cart full of water melons, and as he does not possess a donkey, he pulls the fruit cart himself through the streets. While selling the first melon he discovers that he has been cheated. All day long he tries to sell the low quality merchandise but receives only derision and mockery.

The image of the peasant laboriously pulling the cart instead of a donkey represents a direct illustration of the colloquial expression 'working like a donkey' (*yishtaghal zayy il-humar*), which means doing very hard work. The further metaphorical meaning of the image goes beyond the analogy with the quoted linguistic expression; that the peasant is stupid enough to do the work of a donkey also equates him with the animal. The word 'donkey' has undergone, in

Farid Shauqi in *The Thug* (al-Futuwwa, Egypt, 1957) by Salah Abu Seif (*courtesy Muhammad Bakr, photographer, Cairo*)

The South Wind (Rih al-djanub, Algeria, 1975) by Mohamed Slim Riad

the same way as the image of the man in the film, a transfer of meaning, a change of place, as linguistic metaphors do.[120] Thus, the visually metaphorical derives in every respect from language.

Numerous literary metaphors can be found in Abu Seif's films. In *Cairo 30* (al-Qahira 30, 1966) the director portrays a deceived husband by placing him in front of a hunting trophy in a way that the horns seem to come out of his head. This image seeks to make the audience understand, that the man has been 'given horns' by his wife *(rakibitlu urun)*, a colloquial way of saying betrayed. In *Youth of a Woman* (Shabab imra'a, 1956) a young man cannot resist the seduction of a wealthy miller's wife and becomes her lover. His emotional dependence is expressed by the following sequence: a donkey, owned by the woman, which has to work the millstone day by day, approaches the camera with his eyes covered with black blinkers. The next image presents the miller's wife standing behind her lover covering his eyes with her hands: metaphorically he too is blinkered.

The metaphorical final scene of the Algerian film *South Wind* (Rih al-djanub, 1975) by Mohamed Slim Riad demonstrates how little the image is trusted and how much language is preferred as a tool of expression, by simply translating linguistic expressions into visual metaphors. The shepherd Rabah and the student Nafisa escape their native village in the mountains. He wants to get away from poverty and illiteracy; she is escaping from a marriage her parents are planning for her. The girl's father climbs on his horse and follows them. Once they have reached the highway the two runaways wait for a bus, while the horseman is rapidly catching up. At the last moment the girl's father is overtaken by the bus. The young people get on and disappear into the distance. In this scene progress has literally 'overtaken' tradition.

Conventions of dialogue

The interplay between language and other carriers of meaning is rarely consciously arranged in Arab films. The production of meaning by spoken words, i.e., by dialogue, is preferably given the dominant position. In the already mentioned *South Wind*, based on a novel of the same title by Abdelhamid Benhadouga (ᶜAbd al-Hamid b. Haduqa), monologue and dialogue are the main carriers of information. The introduction of the film is simply a longish monologue by the protagonist, Nafisa, who is seen lying on the bed in her room, staring at the ceiling, and pondering her situation: she is eighteen years old, goes to school in the capital Algiers, and says that she wants to decide her life for herself, including the choice of her husband. This prologue anticipates the course of the film. Nafisa, as we soon learn, is spending her holidays with her family in the village and is not supposed to return to Algiers. Her father, one of the village notables, wants to marry her to the powerful functionary Malik. Nafisa decides to flee.

Several times in the course of the action Nafisa expresses her thoughts out loud. The introduction of almost every character is carried out linguistically via monologue or dialogue. They describe their own attitudes and personalities in words that often sound like declarations of their, in part, politically oriented intentions. Changes in life as well as reactions to events are communicated verbally. Rabah, for example, wants to escape his demeaning work as a shepherd and therefore gives it up. He returns very early in the morning to his deaf and dumb mother, telling her about his decision in sign language. Then he speaks an audible phrase that is apparently meant for the audience: "How long haven't I seen my mother?" he says. "I walk out before dawn and come back only in the dark." The director and scriptwriter, Slim Riad, might have represented this state of affairs visually, but obviously wanted to stress the deplorable situation of the young man. For this reason, the scene is accompanied by a melancholic tremolo of violins.

The structuring of a plot by dialogue and monologue is a tradition created in the theater. Its use here, however, is less connected to the generally powerful influence of theater on Arab film making. The intention is much more to reach an illiterate audience who are accustomed to oral narrative forms, and arises from the didactic aims of this state-produced film. The message is supposed to reach the audience directly and clearly. The fixation on verbal utterances helps submit the narration to political doctrine and to rid it of ambiguous subtexts. Its aim is to revolutionize culturally the 'backward' and 'conservative' rural population. In other Algerian films, like *El-Moufid* (The useful man, 1978) and *The Nomads* (Masirat al-ru^{c}a, 1975) produced during the same period, the protagonists repeat almost word-for-word official speeches about the benefits of the agrarian revolution. The use of classical Arabic in these parts of the dialogue further stress its message.

The use of monologue is also common in less politically motivated films. Flashbacks into the characters' stories are preferably presented in speech and not visually, so that they are rather like anecdotes. In *al-Kitkat* (1991) by the Egyptian Daoud Abd El-Sayyed, several characters give verbal details of their lives. Yusuf tells his girlfriend Saniya about his childhood and his relationship with his father, Sheikh Husni. Saniya delivers a monologue about the various stages of her failed marriage. Sheikh Husni amuses a circle of friends with a fantastic story about how he went blind as a child. He woke up one morning with a red spot on his chest that made him get up and walk to the riverside. There he discovered a fairy-like female form, taking off her clothes and sprinkling herself with water. He stared at her so intensely that he lost his sight.

The special interest in monologue and dialogue is based on a long tradition in Arab cinema. Some dialogues, like those from Nagib al-Rihani, are extremely imaginative and funny. The already mentioned farce *Girls' Flirtation* exemplifies their peculiarities: play upon words, metaphor, verses, and anecdotes. Relative to the importance of these, the story of the film seems rather trite: Layla (performed by the singer Layla Murad), the daughter of a pasha, prefers singing and dancing with her friends to her education. When she fails once again to pass her exams—she is particularly weak in Arabic grammar—the teacher Hamam (Nagib al-Rihani) is hired to give her lessons. To divert the teaching, Layla starts to flirt with the good-natured and naive Hamam, who promptly falls in love with her. But Layla's heart beats for the owner of a nightclub. In what follows the teacher suffers badly to save his protégé from the greedy and cunning nightclub owner, who is of course only interested in Layla's money.

From the outset the teacher's name Hamam (literally, 'pigeon') offers the possibility for ambiguous play upon words. The absent-minded pasha on several occasions calls the teacher 'firakh' (chicken). When Hamam indicates to him the misunderstanding, the pasha replies angry, "Do you think I want to eat you?" (*huwwa ana haklak?*).

Colloquial rhymes also provide amusement. The pasha's employees quarrel over who is going to tell him that his daughter has failed her exams. The bookkeeper says to the governess, "(The last time) he threw me out with a glass, this time do you want it to be the refrigerator?"[121] The governess, Mrs. Masha' Allah (God's will) replies: "God beware, Mr. Ghadab Allah (God's anger), stay away from Mrs. Masha' Allah!"[122] Then someone else tries to persuade her with a rhyme: "Your coffee delights him / your smile relaxes him / you have to tell him!"[123]

The dialogue of *Girls' Flirtation* is constantly enriched by little jokes and funny anecdotes. For example, Hamam tells the pasha's servants what happened to him once in a restaurant. The waiter served him a dish of pigeon saying the following words: "Please, eat yourself up." *(itfaddal kul baᶜdak!)* This way Hamam is mocked twice. The request to 'eat himself up' is not only an allusion to his name, but also refers to a metaphor used in Egyptian colloquial meaning 'to get cross.'

The careful arrangement of the "track" of the dialogue in some of the early Egyptian talkies points back to the strong influence of popular theater. Many films of the 1930s and 1940s, in which popular theater actors like ᶜAli al-Kassar, George Abyad, Nagib al-Rihani, and Yusuf Wahbi participated, resemble theater productions. Typical of Yusuf Wahbi's melodramas, for example, were particular 'verbal' gestures and facial expressions. the plot of al-Kassar's films comprise a number of loosely connected sketches, which maintain their tension mainly through verbal comedy.

Forms of narration

The anecdotal speech in some Arab films shows parallels to classical structures. 'Secretaries' school,' a literary school of 'general culture' that was created for court use during the eighth and ninth century and served to educate administrators and state officials, developed a special form of prose. The students used "anthologies containing pieces of prose, extracts from speeches, memorable sayings of the great names of Islamic thought, quotations from Greek or Iranian works translated into Arabic, anecdotes, and above all poems and fragments of verse. The whole was intended to be memorized and used when the occasion arose in distinguished conversation."[124] In the classical Islamic Age, the use of anecdotes and verses was an important feature of refined speech. In Arab countries today the same features can be heard to an extent in discussions and debates. Even political (non-official) discussions are spiced with funny, sometimes brisant anecdotes.

The narration of anecdotes is not only one of the conventions of elite Arabic literature, but is also part of folk art, where *A Thousand*

and One Nights may serve as an example. This is particularly true of its intertwined stories within stories, which are aptly described in the words of Hugo von Hoffmannsthal concerning the traditional Islamic town: "How much and how fast you enter it, how quickly it surrounds you; so closed, with so many cores and no exit, as if you have entered the interior of a pomegranate."[125]

The Arabian Nights assumed fixed written form in several stages and drew from different narrative sources. They use an Indian-Persian background frame story, parts of classic belles lettres (*adab* literature),[126] folk and adventure novellas, as well as popular stories originally handed down orally from medieval Egypt.[127] The nested structure of some stories looks back to the stage of oral transmission. Stories of this sort were among those recited publicly by the *hakawati* (storyteller) and were structured in a spiral of episodes and prolonged by narrative inserts. This structure helped to postpone the end of the story in order to create tension and to encourage the audience to stay or to come back.

The inclination to anecdote and narrative inserts continues in Arabic cinema on the level of the dialogue as well as in the plot. In several sequences of his film *al-Kitkat*, the Egyptian director Daoud Abd El-Sayyed describes the friendship of two blind men, Sheikh Husni and Sheikh ʿUbayd. At their first encounter, Husni succeeds in convincing ʿUbayd that he is dealing with a sighted man. During their walks and visits to cafés together he impressively describes for him the surroundings, the beauty of the women, and the danger of deep potholes and high curbstones. He even invites his new friend to the movies and tells him the story of the film—a completely different story, of course, to that on the screen. Inevitably, his tricks also lead to misunderstandings. At one point Sheikh Husni takes the arm of a stranger instead of his friend's and walks away. On another occasion the two blind men fall into the river during a ride—simulated by Sheikh Husni—on a boat that is in fact moored to the bank. The scenes with the two sheikhs each form a closed anecdotal insert that is not directly connected to the main narration, and could be removed without damage to the plot.

Anecdotal narration is particularly characteristic of early Egyptian cinema. Short sketches were inserted, for example, in *Ali Baba and the Forty Thieves* (ʿAli Baba wa-l-arbaʿin harami, 1942) by Togo Mizrahi, starring the comedian ʿAli al-Kassar. These sketches do not belong to the literary original, a tale from *A Thousand and One Nights*. In one such scene, Ali Baba is on his way to the place where he usually cuts his wood, pulling his donkey behind him with a rope. Two robbers approach him unnoticed. One of them takes the donkey

al-Kitkat (Egypt, 1991) by Daoud Abd El-Sayyed

and the other puts his own head into the loop. Ali Baba notices the metamorphosis of his pack animal only once he arrives at his destination, and can find no explanation for what has happened. But the robber puts one forward: he tells him that he had been transformed into a donkey because of an evil curse. Ali Baba believes him and lets him go. Then he goes to the market to buy a new donkey, where he is offered at a high price his own stolen animal! As in other films with ᶜAli al-Kassar the dramatic course of the narration is weak. Individual scenes seem to be more important than causal relations or a logical plot.

Traditional narrative forms left unmistakable traces in early Arab films, but were gradually replaced .by the conventional 'Western' drama, or at least dominated by it. Even subjects that are based on long tradition and fixed in a literary form, like the story of Antar and Abla, filmed by Salah Abu Seif in 1948 in *Antar and Abla's Adventures* (Mughamarat ᶜAntar wa ᶜAbla), were molded to it.

In the Egyptian film, *Hasan and Naima* (Hasan wa Naᶜima, 1959) by Henri Barakat, based on the well-known *mawwal* (colloquial ballad set to music) of the same title, the story that had been orally passed down is deformed by dramatization to become almost unrecognizable. In the film Naima, the daughter of a wealthy peasant, falls in love with the singer Hasan. He asks to marry her, but is refused by her father because Naima's greedy and choleric cousin Atwa has designs on the estates of his uncle and wants therefore to keep her for himself. Naima decides to flee and to join Hasan, but is brought back the very next day by her father, who promises the couple will celebrate their wedding in a short while. This does not happen, because Atwa ambushes Hasan and seriously injures him. He then celebrates his own engagement to his cousin. Hasan, however, survives the attack and comes back to call Naima's father to account. The affair culminates in a showdown between Hasan and Atwa, who has in the meantime enraged the whole village. Finally the wrongdoer receives a just punishment, while Hasan and Naima happily celebrate their wedding.

The film follows in all its stages the classic dramatic structure, with a beginning, middle, and end. The opening introduces the 'who, how, what, when'; Naima, her father, Hasan, Atwa, and the village are presented. In the next stage conflict arises: Hasan and Naima's spontaneous love is brought into question by Hasan's low social status and the intriguing cousin. Naima escapes and the crisis develops until Hasan's life is threatened. Then comes the turning point, when the inhabitants of the village back the lovers and support Hasan's fight against Atwa. But Atwa threatens Hasan's life until the very end, and the situation is only finally resolved with the death of the villain.[128]

Barakat's work is a typical Egyptian melodrama. In spite of the happy ending it sticks completely to the conventions of the genre, with its "triangle stories and its double morality," and its subjects, "the conflict between generations and social ascent."[129] Thus it forms a sort of vulgarized drama, "the bourgeois form of tragedy."[130]

Barakat's *Hasan and Naᶜima* deviates on several levels from the traditional version. Unlike the film the *mawwal* starts with a prologue that anticipates the end of the story. It is followed by a rather linear chronological narration, which as a whole is structured by a division into scenes and does not possess the logical solidity of the drama.

The *mawwal* of Hasan and Naima also differs substantially in content. It ends tragically. The best known version, sung by Muhammad Taha, who incidentally appears in the film, tells how Hasan was trapped by Naima's family. After bringing him to the house with the promise of celebrating the wedding, the men surround him and cut off his head. Naima, who witnesses the crime, hides the head in a basket, to reveal all later. Hasan's body is thrown into the river, but floats to the village of his mother, who recognizes him in spite of his mutilation. Then a police officer, disguised as a woman in order to solve the case, meets Naima, who tells him what happened. There is no malicious cousin in this version.

During the 1950s, neither the audience nor professionals would have appreciated an adaptation that remained close to the original. All genres, ranging from melodrama, comedy, and thriller to realism, were dominated during this period by the structure of conventional drama, precisely the dramatic conflict of two antagonistic powers, which all events contribute to resolve. Similarly, socialist realism, which was driven by the idea of class struggle, was structured by binary antagonisms. It seems that social and political tensions that resulted from colonialism, the temporary division of the world into two political blocs and the formation of a modern mass society had engendered a more and more conflict-oriented evaluation of human existence.[131]

Farewell to drama

Since the 1970s a certain turning away from the principles of conventional drama can be observed in Egyptian Middle Cinema,[132] for example in the committed commercial cinema of the New Realists, as well as in Arab *cinéma d'auteur*. Some representatives of the latter intentionally fall back upon traditional popular or elitist forms of narration. This movement occurs on a conscious and rather intellectual level and is far away from the much more spontaneous adoption of traditional narrative structures in early commercial cinema. In particular, film makers from the Maghreb, in a sort of return-to-the-roots movement, have been eager to tap the wealth of the indigenous art of narration. Moroccan films such as *Wechma* by Hamid Benani, *El-Chergui* (al-Sharqi, 1975)[133] by Moumen Smihi, and *Miracle* (Sarab; Mirage, 1980) by Ahmed Bouanani are considered the most important experiments, attempting—with varying success—to integrate folk fables, stories, and popular symbols in the plot.[134]

Elsewhere, comparable efforts have been made. The Algerian director Merzak Allouache tried to copy the narrative structure of *A Thousand and One Nights*. His *Adventures of a Hero* (Mughamarat batal, 1978) is set in an imaginary desert state. Mahdi, the son of a poor oasis dweller, is considered a chosen person by his tribe and receives all possible privileges, including an excellent education. When he attains the necessary maturity, the heads of the tribe equip Mahdi with a motorbike and send him on a journey that will allow him to fulfill his destiny. But before leaving, a companion of his youth initiates him into a secret: it was Mahdi's own father who gave

Wechma (Tatoo, Morocco, 1970) by Hamid Benani

him as a newborn the sign of the chosen. Mahdi does not want to hear the unpleasant truth and leaves in spite of it. On his journey he meets not only strange border guards, guerrillas, and dangerous death squads, but also petrified human beings, princesses threatened by dragons, and other beauties in distress. Mahdi is not looking for personal happiness with some princess however; he wants to save the world. When he arrives in a great town, he tries to preach revolution, but no one listens; no one wants to struggle against bar owners or stop extravagant parties. Indeed, no one even shows much interest in fighting for lower restaurant prices. After a long series of failures, Mahdi gives up his solo run and joins a democratic (!) movement.

Adventures of a Hero has an epic fairy tale-like narrative structure that is based on the various, partly closed, 'adventures' of the main character. Nevertheless the plot is again divided into beginning, central crisis, turning point, and resolution. This conventional dramatic arrangement is undermined by the epic structure. The not very skillful mixture of two narrative forms obstructs the narrative flow and is partly responsible for an overly long exposition. In addition, the allegorical character of the story places the quasi-fairy tale quite deliberately in a contemporary political (leftist) context.

In contrast, some works only pretend to use popular or traditional narrative structures. *The Lost Necklace of the Dove*, by the Tunisian

Nacer Khemir, is set in Andalusia during the eleventh century. The young calligraphy student Hasan is a friend of the boy Zayn, an orphan who works in town as an errand boy and furtively delivers the messages of lovers. Zayn is waiting impatiently for the return of his imaginary father. He confesses his worries and hopes to the cursed prince Harun, a small ape who lives in an abandoned well. During the public burning of forbidden books, Hasan finds a page torn out of a mysterious book that is believed to contain sixty different synonyms for the word 'love.' On the paper Hasan finds the image of the princess of Samarkand, with whom he immediately falls in love. Hasan recruits Zayn to help him look for the book. Together they decide to search a bookseller's, but a fire breaks out in the shop, and Zayn disappears. The young go-between meets his father outside the gates of the city under a pomegranate tree, and is invited to visit his father's subterranean empire. Meanwhile Hasan is looking for Zayn but his intentions are thwarted by a siege of the city, which forces him to flee. On the road he meets a mysterious rider who is looking for the same book and whose feature seems familiar to him. The very moment the calligraphy student recognizes the rider as the princess of Samarkand they lose sight of each other in the turmoil of war.

The title *The Lost Necklace of the Dove* alludes to the classical Arab literary work *Tauq al-hamama* (The necklace of the dove) by the scholar Ibn Hazm al-Andalusi (b. 994). The texts include theoretical treaties and many short, partly autobiographical, stories and anecdotes. The structure of Nacer Khemir's film has nothing in common with the book, and it uses only a few of its characters, like the unobtrusive go-between.

Although Khemir's film is fantastic and fairy tale-like, the structure of the plot is by no means as traditional as the content might suggest. The director does not develop conflict and then resolve it climactically, but instead intertwines two linear strings of action that are both dominated by the epic motif of search. Such a combination is a characteristic not of traditional narrative forms, but of modern literature and cinema. The film's allusion to tradition, however, is further underlined by its use of classical Arabic. Together with its quasi-traditional narration, its visual aestheticism confirms the existence of a glorious Islamic past.

A much more successful use of popular narrative forms can be found in the Tunisian film, *Khalifa the Bald* (Khalifa al-aqrac, 1969), an adaptation of a novel of the same name by Bechir Khraief (Bashir Khurayyif). In his film the director Hamouda Ben Halima tries to combine an anecdotal narrative structure with spontaneity and powerful improvisation on the lines of the French *nouvelle vague*.

The story is set in the old part of Tunis at the turn of this century. Bald Khalifa works as a messenger and is therefore allowed to enter all the houses in the neighborhood, including the female domain. But he is deprived of this privilege after he is ordered to get a dream interpreted by the fortune teller Bu Bakr. In Bu Bakr's eyes Khalifa has committed several offenses, among others the theft of a cock and the seduction of a young widow, for which the fortune teller now exposes him.

The plot is structured as an intertwined narration. Khalifa's offenses represent closed inserts, which interrupt the spatial and temporal logic of the background story. The characters are schematically stylized, and the acting seems similar to the spontaneously improvised *mise en scène*. The choice of 16mm black and white film (probably largely for economic reasons) reinforces the impression of improvisation. Ben Halima succeeds much more than Nacer Khemir and Merzak Allouache in capturing the off-the-cuff character of the art of oral narration.

Polyphone narrations

Several Arab directors have made comparable efforts to separate from conventional drama without explicitly resorting to native traditions. The Egyptian director Youssef Chahine, who since *The Sparrow* has been able to create his own individual style, must be considered in this respect a pioneer. In the semi-autobiographical film, *An Egyptian Fairy Tale* (Hadduta misriya, 1982), the protagonist, film director Yahia, suffers from a heart attack, which forces him to travel to London to undergo open heart surgery. Once he is anaesthetized he notices a small guest in his blood vessels: Yahia, the child. Other visions from the past join him: his frustrated mother and her liaisons, the death of his older brother, the stony path of his career, problems with producers, and so on. The story switches back and forth in time, mixing past and present. An imaginary tribunal of the family, calling the protagonist to account, alternates with flashbacks, actual events, and documentary sequences. The linearity of the plot is interrupted on several occasions. The conflict has no clear features.

The Syrian film *Dreams of the City* (Ahlam al-madina, 1984) by Mohamed Malas contains numerous scenes of daily life that describe the situation of the adolescent Dib. It is set in the early 1950s against the background of the dictatorship of Chichakli, which is terminated at the end of the film. After his father's death, Dib comes with his beautiful, young mother and a younger brother to live in Damascus. They seek lodging at the house of their old and

Yasmin Khlat (left) as Dib's mother in *Dreams of the City* (Ahlam al-madina, Syria, 1984) by Mohamed Malas

embittered grandfather, who only reluctantly puts a small room at their disposal. Considering his grandchildren a burden, he sends the younger boy to an orphanage, while Dib has to work as an errand boy in a laundry. Trying to escape the harassment of the grandfather, Dib's mother gives in to the attempts of a marriage broker to arrange a new marriage for her. But she soon comes back disillusioned, and Dib later attempts, without success, to take revenge for his mother's humiliation.

In the course of the film Dib only ages a few months. Events have neither changed his life nor resolved the conflicts he lives. The situation at the end of the film does not differ dramatically from the beginning. A comparable epic structure can also be found in other films of Arab *cinéma d'auteur* from the same period, for example in *The Events of the Coming Year* (Waqa'i^c al-^cam al-muqbil, 1986) by the Syrian Samir Zikra and *Man of Ashes* (Rih al-sadd, 1986) by the Tunisian Nouri Bouzid.

In his film *Nahla* (1979) the Algerian director Farouk Beloufa goes a step further. He abandons a clear narrative perspective connected to one central hero. Instead, Beloufa's film unfolds a panorama of Beirut from January to April 1975. Among the most important characters are the Algerian journalist Larbi, the Palestinian woman Hind, and two Lebanese sisters, the self-conscious and ambitious journalist Maha and the singer Nahla. Some other figures appear, like

Nahla's business-minded uncle Sulayman, the Palestinian Michel, who together with Hind joins the Palestinian resistance, Maha's self-pitying Egyptian husband, and Maha's opportunist and anti-Palestinian colleague Nasri. They all are tied together by their admiration for Nahla's voice. Nahla's uncle wants to commercialize her abilities, particularly because—like Nahla's friends—an increasingly large audience identifies with her committed songs. But during her first large public appearance, while singing the word 'I' Nahla suddenly loses her voice.

Nahla's story forms only one string in the network of the plot, which consists of a huge number of unspectacular scenes that cannot be connected by a conventional linear structure. Debates and discussion between different protagonists, walks and drives through the streets, letters, articles, radio transmissions, press conferences, songs, concerts, feasts, assassinations, street battles, together make up the film.

The numerous scenes and scraps of action carry their own lives. The following scene demonstrates this clearly: Larbi, the Algerian journalist, walks apparently aimlessly through the streets one night. A radio is on, music can be heard. There are cars, neon signs, shops, people. Larbi watches two nuns passing by. He follows them, for no obvious reason, then walks back again. He wanders further through the streets, then enters a café. Then we see Nahla during a television transmission. Her movements and reactions are fidgety, as is the movement of the camera. The impression is created of an uncontrolled stream of consciousness, as it is used in contemporary literature. Farouk Beloufa's camera technique is to a very large extent responsible: frequent changes of views, angles, and images, a constantly moving camera and the continuous movement of objects create an almost documentary character and capture plenty of incidental details that are not functionalized in the working of a fixed plot.

Beloufa's mosaic narration corresponds with the literary style of the Algerian novelist Rachid Boudjedra, who wrote the script of *Nahla*, and who also experiments in his writing with the traditional story in a story narration. Although Boudjedra's script was modified by the director and changed during the shooting, the film develops through the visual capabilities of the medium a hallucinatory tone that is typical of Boudjedra's work. In the film, political events form the narration's only linearity. They range from Kissinger's mission in the Middle East, the formation of Palestinian organizations in Lebanon, the disagreements between the different Lebanese fronts leading up to the massacre in a Palestinian camp on April 13, 1975, and the escalation to the point of armed struggle in the streets. The plot spirals to a climax via numerous observational and dramatic scenes, which hang like small shoots and continuously multiply perspectives and levels of action.

The introduction to the *cinéma d'auteur* of the narrative means of modern literature, including epic narrative forms, and the transfer of techniques like the stream of consciousness, combined with ruptures in temporal and spatial linearity, break up the conventional dramatic tension building. The shattering of a clear narrative perspective allows a rather subjective, multi-layered, 'decentralized' representation.

To date, these narrative forms have primarily been applied by the *cinéma d'auteur*. They reflect the stylistic and intellectual individualism of its representatives and seem, partially, to express a conscious cultural reorientation and self-confirmation vis-à-vis the West, which is the main financial backer of Arab *cinéma d'auteur*. Due to the reflexive and intellectual aspirations of the genre, however, its reference to native traditions lacks the spontaneity of early cinema. Linguistically, like most of the popular mainstream genres this cinema neglects the mythical and 'purified' language of nationalist film making applied in the historical and realist genre, and prefers the use of the syncretistic regional vernaculars that stress a regional and hybrid identity.

Music

Music in daily life

In the last twenty years no film has described the ordinary relation of Arabs to music better than *Omar Gatlato*[135] (ʿUmar qatlatu al-rudjla, 1976), by the Algerian Merzak Allouache. The director presents his main character in an unusual way. Omar is a young, but not quite handsome man. He introduces himself to the audience while sitting in his room in his parent's flat. Facing the camera, he talks about his life and work situation. He shares the tiny flat in Algiers with his large family, comprising his mother, grandfather, and his brothers and sisters, including one divorced sister and her numerous children. There is not much room, even to sleep. Unlike many other young men from the same neighborhood, Omar is at least employed, but his small income as a clerk has to support the whole family. His dearest possessions are a small cassette recorder that helps him pass his leisure time and a microphone that a friend obtained for him on the black market. With these he records Indian music during screenings at the cinema. Other cultural events open to Omar and his friends are a third-class amateur theater and the rare performances of a popular Algerian singer. Otherwise, the young men can only sit in the café or go out to the street. Women do not figure in these activities. The only female they meet is an unnerved usherette at the cinema, who has to defend herself constantly against harassment from members of the all-male audience.

Omar would have remained in an exclusively male world, were it not for the mysterious voice of a young woman resounding from an old cassette given to him by a friend. The voice speaks about the ordinary impressions of its owner's home, but Omar cannot help feeling that it is directed to him personally. Through his friend, he tries to find the girl. When he finally succeeds in wringing a date out of her, his friends make fun of him. Omar has to decide whether to remain faithful to his familiar male world with all its small highlights or to get to know the woman.

Omar, as depicted by Merzak Allouache, is a typical young and impoverished Algerian man, whose circumstances reflect those of many young men in other Arab countries. Imprisoned in disastrous working and living conditions, secluded from the world of women, their leisure options are severely limited. Therefore, cinema, music, and the street play a decisive role in their life. Although not its principal subject, *Omar Gatlato* does feature the main occasions for musical performances, namely private and religious feasts, and their modern supplements, radio, concert, and cinema. The film also describes the psychological effect of music. The songs of a *chaabi* singer[136] whom Omar admires offer him a rare opportunity to forget about himself and his situation. As his enthusiasm and his anticipation before the performances show, the music gives him a peculiar mental excitement. When his tape recorder is stolen in a mugging, Omar feels it as a disastrous loss

The tape with the young girl's monologue opens up another important level in the psychology of the male protagonist. Omar is fascinated by the female voice and wakes up suddenly in the world of yearning love. This love, however, as can be seen in the classical motif of Arab poetry *Layla and Madjnun* (Layla wa Madjnun), is based on female absence. Only the prohibition on meeting Layla throws Qaiss into his love mania. There is almost no contemporary Arab song that does not deal with love or the pain of separation. Thus, the sight of the real woman arouses in Omar first of all confusion. For Omar, unable to cope with the opposite sex face to face, the voice (equated in the film with music) takes the place of the real beloved, thus forming one of the mightiest psychological obstacles to real exchange between the sexes.

Music as a guarantee for box office hits

Music played a decisive role in the development of Arab film making. The first sound film, *Song of the Heart* (Unshudat al-fu'ad, Egypt, 1931/32), by Mario Volpi, was already furnished with music and songs. Muhammad Karim's musical *The White Rose* (1933/34), starring the singer and composer Muhammad ᶜAbd al-Wahhab, was the first Egyptian feature film to be exported on a large scale to the neighboring Arab countries.[137]

It is no accident that Egyptian producers from the 1930s were obsessed by the idea of producing musicals.[138] Of the 918 feature films produced between 1931 and 1961, 370—i.e., more than a third—were musicals. In some years, as between 1944 and 1946, 50 percent of all films belonged to this genre.[139] Beside the two most distinguished stars of Arab music, Umm Kulthum and ᶜAbd al-Wahhab, whose popularity remained relatively independent of their success in cinema, more than forty-six male and female singers appeared in Egyptian film musicals. Some of them, like Shadya, participated in as many as thirty films.[140] Only a few, however, such as Muhammad ᶜAbd al-Wahhab, Farid al-Atrash, ᶜAbd al-ᶜAziz Mahmud, or the specialist in 'Bedouin' rhythms,[141] Kahlawi, left a peculiar musical mark on their films.[142] The Lebanese Farid al-Atrash combined all sorts of music in his works, ranging from Lebanese folklore to Viennese waltz, as can be heard, for example, in *The Victory of Youth* (Intisar al-shabab, 1941) and *Love and Revenge* (Gharam wa intiqam, 1944). The Egyptian musician Muhammad ᶜAbd al-Wahhab was even more inventive than Farid al-Atrash. He acted in only seven films, between 1933 and 1946, but enriched for decades the musical arrangements of innumerable other works with new ideas and rhythmic combinations.[143]

Most musicals contain at least one dance, most often a belly dance. As early as 1935/36, a film introduced the dancer Badiᶜa Masabni, who owned a well-known variety theater where several prominent belly dancers were trained. Some of the dancers who subsequently appeared, such as Samya Gamal and Tahiya Carioca, borrowed their music from the cabaret or nightclub and folklore.[144] Samya Gamal developed a sort of expressive dance as an individual characteristic in her performances, as can be seen in *ᶜAfrita Hanim* (literally, 'Lady Demon,' 1949) and *Cigarette and Wineglass* (Sigara wa ka's, 1955). Naᶜima ᶜAkif, on the other hand, presented a colorful mixture of belly dancing, flamenco, and tap dancing.

In contrast to these developments, the historical films tried to reconstruct the dance of the *djawari* (singing girls) of former

Naᶜima ᶜAkif (*courtesy Muhammad Bakr, photographer, Cairo*)

times,[145] combining elements from the ballet and the oriental dance, as in *Dananir* (1940/41) and *Sallama* (1945). In the course of the 1940s, group dances inspired by the music hall appeared. As with the films that focused only on songs, the action was matched to the various musical performances. Their stories usually dealt either with the figure of a singer or a dancer or were set in locations such as nightclubs or theaters. Another option was to build into the plot occasions like weddings, celebrations, or parties, that provided opportunities for musical performances.

Since the beginning of Arab cinema, the production of musicals has remained very largely confined to the Egyptian film industry. Other Arab countries' attempts to enter this field were always overshadowed by the big Egyptian brother. The musicals shot in Morocco in the early 1970s imitated the Egyptian model (*Life Is a Struggle* by Mohamed Ben Abderrahmane Tazi and *Silence Is a One Way Street* by Abdallah Mesbahi). The same is true of the latest films of the Syrian comedian, Doureid Laham. *The Frontiers* (al-Hudud, 1984) and *Kafrun* (1990) each contain several songs, but they do not differ much in style or presentation from Egyptian musicals shot during the same period. Lebanese cinema, Egypt's closest rival in the

Fayruz (center) in *The Seller of the Rings* (Baya^c al-khawatim, Egypt, 1965) by Youssef Chahine

1950s and 1960s, lost its most talented interpreters, Farid al-Atrash, his sister Asmahan, and Sabah, to the 'Hollywood on the Nile.' It was only during the 1960s that genuinely Lebanese musicals were produced, including the films starring the Rahbani brothers, who became famous through their music theater. The Egyptian director Youssef Chahine directed their first film, *The Seller of the Rings* (Baya^c al-khawatim, 1965), which was an adaptation of an operetta by the Rahbani brothers. The Rahbani films, in which the singer Fayruz always played the main character, were governed by patriotism and traditionalism. They used the Mont Liban dialect, and their stories were set in the mountains, in the traditional Maronite (Lebanese Christian) region. More highly acclaimed than Chahine's adaptation were the two subsequent Rahbani musicals, *Safar Barlak* (1967) and *The Daughter of the Guardian* (Bint al-haris, 1968), both directed by the Egyptian Henri Barakat.[146]

In Egypt, musicals have very often achieved the biggest commercial successes. The revue film and musical, *My Father Is up the Tree* (1969) by Hussein Kamal, with the singer ^{c}Abd al-Halim Hafiz, ran in Cairo alone for more than five months.[147] During the 1970s, the musical's importance declined. In his tragic musical *The Return of the*

ᶜAmr Diyab (center) in *Ice Cream in Glim* (Egypt, 1992) by Khairy Beshara
(*courtesy Cultural Fund, Ministry of Culture, Cairo*)

Prodigal Son (ᶜAudat al-ibn al-dal, 1976), introducing the Lebanese
singer, Magda al-Rumi, Chahine attempted to provide the genre with
a political message and bring it closer to Epic Theater, but the film
met with little approval and was not imitated. In the course of the
1980s, the singer stars disappeared altogether from the screen with
no new generation to follow.

However, the musical has not completely lost its attraction for
audience and film makers. The New Realist Khairy Beshara used
songs by the Nubian pop singer Muhammad Munir in his *Necklace
And Bracelet* (al-Tauq wa-l-iswira, 1986). Other films, for example,
Silence, Listen! (Samaᶜ huss, 1990) and *Ya Mahalabiya Ya* (1991) by
Sherif ᶜArafa, revive the music hall film. Two of the greatest hits of
1991, *The Crabs* (Kaburya) by Khairy Beshara and *al-Kitkat* by
Daoud Abd El-Sayyed (which ran for more than fifteen weeks in
Cairo cinemas) contained several musical inserts. Khairy Beshara
tried to revive the tradition of the local music hall and musical film by
using young pop stars like ᶜAmr Diyab and Muhammad Fu'ad in his
Ice Cream in Glim and *Abracadabra America* (Amrika shika bika,
1993). Their musical qualities do not reach the standards of the
earlier Egyptian musical.

The reasons for the tremendous success of musicals in the Arab countries, in particular in the early decades of Arab cinema, are to be found in prevailing social conditions as well as in traditional culture: "The social formation itself turned the Arab world first into an audience of listeners before becoming an audience of spectators."[148] In the case of the Maghreb states, whose own musical tradition of 'Andalusian' music was far away from the tear-jerking sentimentality of the Egyptian song,[149] political reasons were decisive too. There was a vacuum in the national culture, which had been deeply weakened by colonialism and the subsequent profound social changes, which Egyptian culture could easily fill.

The culturally and politically mobilizing effect of Egyptian and Arab music is clearly described in Moufida Tlatli's film *Silence of the Palaces* (Samt al-qusur, Tunisia, 1994) set in Tunis at the eve of independence. The adolescent heroine, the illegitimate daughter of a maid, finds an outlet from her restricted personal situation in singing Umm Kulthum songs, and at the end of the film rebels by singing a nationalist Tunisian song at a wedding party of her mother's pro-French masters.

From the turn of the century, songs by popular Egyptian interpreters such as Salama Higazi and the nationalist Sayyid Darwish were distributed on record. Their massive spread had its point of departure in the cafés of Arab towns, where record-players were installed to entertain the patrons. Then, during the 1930s, other powerful distribution channels were added, radio and cinema, which underlined the precursor position of the Egyptians.[150]

In spite of all the commercial mechanisms that determined the development of the Egyptian musical and the introduction of Western elements, it would be inappropriate to label it as a variation on Hollywood—a form of plagiarism—as is sometimes suggested by Western film theory.[151] This view ignores the specific needs of the Arab audience and their rootedness in native culture. The combination of music and acting was by no means only introduced with the spread of sound in cinema. Music and dance were already important elements in the traditional shadow plays and in the *fasl mudhik*.[152] Moreover, the success of modern theater in the Arab region, especially in Egypt, would have been impossible without the use of musical interpretations. The survival of a theatrical troupe playing a solely classical (in the beginning mainly European) repertoire was therefore not guaranteed. At the turn of the century, the Syrian Iskandar Farah introduced musical performances in his often changing classical plays. His Egyptian star singer, Salama Higazi, was gifted with such an extraordinary voice that he was declared the Caruso of the East. In 1905, Higazi formed his own independent troupe, the Dar al-Tamthil al-ᶜArabi.[153] In his theater, music became the main element of the performance.

Of the two greatest representatives of Egyptian theater between the two world wars, George Abyad and Yusuf Wahbi, the former offered mere speech theater. Wahbi was the more successful because he used music in his adaptations of foreign pieces and in his own creations, which ranged from social drama to comedy. The same applies to ᶜAli al-Kassar and Nagib al-Rihani. Musical forms of theater also developed in other Arab countries, such as Lebanon and Algeria. It is true that the Western operetta and the French vaudeville theater inspired these musical practices more often than the shadow play, but they certainly met the needs of the audience, which had been shaped by native quasi-theatrical practices.[154]

Music and language

In Europe, incidental music was employed in the age of silent movies. It was used to create sound effects and, in places, anticipated the synchronized sound.[155] Music also helped to compensate for missing dialogue. The reinforcement of movements with a specific musical rhythm, so-called mickey mousing, further developed in the talkies, and the comments made on action by using an emotionally explicit musical interpretation (for instance the tremolo of instruments to create tension and suspense) has for the most part retained until today the character of a linguistic statement. Thus, the incidental music to some love scenes seems like a direct 'translation' of the German expression *der Himmel hängt voller Geigen* ('the sky hangs full of violins').[156]

Comparable musical comments were also used in Arab cinema. Muhammad Karim's *A Happy Day* (Yaum saᶜid, 1940) contains a part of the operetta *Madjnun wa Layla*, composed by ᶜAbd al-Wahhab, performed by ᶜAbd al-Wahhab and Asmahan. In one instance, the music evokes desert scenery through a melody played on an oboe. Elsewhere, when the song "The wind and the youth" (al-Hawa' wa-l-shabab) speaks of drinking wine, the voice moves suddenly from a leisurely speed to a lively rhythm in order to mimic the holding of the wine glass.[157]

The song or vocal interpretation is doubtless the heart of Arab musicals. The close connection of music to language is based on a long tradition in Arab culture. Vocal interpretation formed, in most secular music genres that developed over the centuries in the Arabic-speaking region, the most important element of the performance. The *nuba* in the Maghreb and the *qasida, muwashshah,* and *mawwal* in the

Mashreq all rely basically on singing. The *qasida* and the *mawwal* even carry the names of poetic genres. Typically enough, the genesis of Arab singing *(ghina')* is closely connected to poetry.[158] Already in the pre-Islamic period, famous female singers used to recite and interpret verses of the great poets with musical accompaniment.[159] This tradition was continued later by singing slave girls *(djawari)*. The intonation of a poem, similar to the strictly regulated but nevertheless melodic recitation of the Quran, served as mnemonic, in particular as long as the preservation and spread of the text proceeded orally. Singing was held to increase the enjoyment of the poetic text.

Modern musicals included not only classical forms like the *qasida*, but also lighter ones like the *taqtuqa* (light popular song), the *unshuda* or *nashid* (hymn), and *ughniya* (song). Another genre, very much dominated by language, that spread in cinema during the 1950s, is the so-called monologue, half song, half speech, accompanied by explicit gestures and facial expressions and often by dance. The monologue was not generally used by singers, but performed by actors. Naᶜima ᶜAkif, for example, and the comedians Shukuku and Ismaᶜil Yasin, made use of it.[160]

The song texts in musicals are often closely related to the narration. In Muhammad Karim's *The White Rose* the text of the song "Oh, rose of pure love" (Ya wardat al-hubb al-safi), constitutes title and summary in one. Although this song is not performed in the first scene of the film, it forms a sort of leitmotif of the story, which deals with the unselfish and self-sacrificing love of a minor employee for the daughter of his wealthy boss.

Not all songs in musicals perform such a clear dramatic function as "Oh, rose of pure love." Sometimes they just mark the start or the end of a certain section of narration, and are irrelevant to the development of the plot as such. Instead, they offer a sort of retrospective on events. In *Dananir* (1940/41) by Ahmed Badrakhan, Umm Kulthum plays the role of a young bedouin called Dananir. During a hunting excursion, Djaᶜfar, vizier of the Caliph Harun al-Rashid, accidentally hears her singing. Djaᶜfar is so fascinated that he decides to take the girl to Baghdad and have her trained by a famous singing master. Dananir makes fast progress and soon she is entertaining the caliph as well as Djaᶜfar. At the same time, the other members of the ruling house, envious of Djaᶜfar's privileged position, start to hatch a plot that costs him the confidence of the ruler and eventually his life. Harun's anger at his former favorite is so immense that he even forbids his lamentation. Dananir, however, keeps the memory of her master. She walks through the ruins of Djaᶜfar's former palace and sings about the loss of the beloved. When she is finally taken to the caliph for this offense, he recognizes her as a symbol of fidelity and allows her to return to her homeland in the desert.

The first song in the film is in praise of water and is sung by Umm Kulthum, in the desert, beside a spring. At this point, Dananir is still an entirely nature-bound nomad. The following song, "Unshudat Baghdad," is a sort of march song, performed on the way to Baghdad, heralding the basic change in the protagonist's life. Then, two rather solemn pieces follow, both part of the *qasida* "Quli li-taifiki" (Tell your shadow!), one of them dealing with love. The *qasida* is performed in the palaces of the Caliph and of Dja^cfar. It is addressed to Dja^cfar and indicates, parallel to the action, an intensification of Dananir's relationship with him—a relationship that is however never explicitly characterized as an intimate love relationship. At this point in the film Dananir is at the height of her career.

Umm Kulthum's fifth song is a cheerful *taqtuqa*,[161] "Bukra al-safar" (The voyage is tomorrow). This song is the only one in the Egyptian dialect. Dramatically, it functions as a retarding moment, because the positive change predicted by the lively rhythm does not occur. In fact, the journey is prevented by the plot and Dja^cfar is sentenced to death in the next scene. The last song, "al-Qasr al-mahdjur" (The deserted palace) formulates a sad lamentation on the loss of the beloved[162] and signals the tragic end of the story. Dananir walks through Dja^cfar's destroyed palace and sings a classical Arabic poem consisting of eighteen verses by the poet Ahmad Rami, starting with the following words:

> "The birds' rhymes escaped you,
> so did the ripeness of roses.
> Oh, palace, life seems like lines
> [...]
> The wind died in [your rooms],
> the hope ceased,
> nicer than the smile of roses."[163]

Particularly with the *qasida*s, *Dananir* introduces the so-called *ghina' ^carabi* (Arabic singing), an intonated classical Arabic poetry that has no real tradition in Egypt itself,[164] but was known in the pre- and early Islamic age. This revived form of singing corresponds profoundly with the explicit historicism of the film.

Music of emotions

"Since its emergence, Egyptian cinema has preferred to produce (or reproduce) emotions rather than the real," writes Abbas Fadhil

Ibrahim.[165] This is particularly true of the musical. Music has always been deeply connected to the emotional life of the different Arab people—only the Sufis used it as a means of spiritual recognition. According to legend, Lamak created the first lute with the bone of his deceased son, in order to lament his loss.[166] A large part of traditional Arab music is connected to producing certain moods and emotions. Responsible for their realization is the basic formula of Arab music, the *maqam*,[167] which is formed by a certain melodic mode with fixed intervals. Each *maqam* is said to express a certain mood and to possess its own "ethic content."[168] A *maqam* is able to create strong emotion in listeners, be it pride, power, joy, longing, love, sadness, or pain.[169] An Arab musician and singer, by additionally using unforeseen variations or specific intervals and stressing them slightly, is able to arouse such an emotional fervor that listeners will interrupt the performance with spontaneous shouts of appreciation.

In many of the early Arab musicals, vocal performances were directly related to the exterior or inner situation of the protagonist. According to Ahmed Badrakhan, who made a name for himself with romances and musical melodramas, working with some of Egypt's most important musical stars, including Farid al-Atrash and Nagat al-Saghira,[170] "Music in cinema must be turned into film music, expressing exactly the emotions as well as everything else of nature or psychological conditions that can be seen on the screen."[171]

Muhammad Karim seems to have followed a similar conviction. The *mise en scène* in *The White Rose* clearly aims to transmit moods and feelings. In one of the most visually attractive scenes of the film, Karim succeeds in creating an atmosphere of happiness and lively joy by presenting idyllic images of nature edited in time with the music. The protagonist meets his beloved in the countryside after a long separation. Early in the morning, the couple stroll together. The water wheels are humming, the water draws circles, fields and trees reflect the bright sunlight, while the hero praises both love and the beauty of the world.

The emotional functions of music suggested that the musical was to become the domain of melodrama. No other genre offers such potential for emotionally charged situations, no other dramatic form—as can be seen in the etymology of the word (Greek: *melos* = song, *drama* = plot)—is so fond of music. The early works of the genres, like those resulting from the cooperation of Muhammad Karim and ᶜAbd al-Wahhab, for example *Tears of Love* (Dumuᶜ al-hubb, 1935/36) and *Long Live Love* (Yahya al-hubb, 1937/38), already developed as a main subject love that does not befit one's rank. A comparable topic is found in films with Umm Kulthum, who

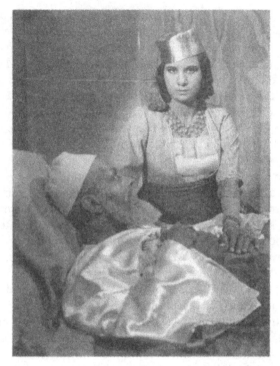

Umm Kulthum in *Widad* (Egypt, 1936) by Fritz
Kramp *(courtesy Muhammad Bakr, photographer,
Cairo)*

appeared in three of her six films as a poor servant or slave who falls
in love with her master. The same orientation continues in many
Egyptian melodramas, even in the time after independence in 1952.
The basic conflict between love and patriarchism, woman and
authoritarian father, individual and social order, was rarely won by
liberty or sentiment.

Yet, upon closer examination, the stylized sentimentality of
melodrama has not much to do with the moods and feelings of the
traditional Arab song. On the contrary, the director Ahmed
Badrakhan became convinced that an essential part of traditional
music, the *tarab*, the joyful excitement that normally builds up in the
audience during the performance, was detrimental to film viewing.
"The composition of a song must match with the poetic meaning and
emphasize it. Yet, emotions should be aroused only in a way that they
do not reach the border of delight *(tarab)*. *Tarab* needs the repetition
of the moving piece *(al-maqtaᶜ al-hazzaz)*, which arouses the pleasure
of the audience, but a film is not able to repeat such a piece."[172]

The primacy of time

In the course of the years in cinema the Arab song has been increasingly submitted to the dictates of time. Not only was *tarab* sacrificed to temporal continuity, but several other drastic changes had to be made in order to adapt traditional Arab music to the rhythm of film. Muhammad Karim, for example, was able to convince ᶜAbd al-Wahhab to give up the long instrumental introduction in his compositions for *The White Rose*. He also prevented him from running over six minutes in any song.[173] As the traditional *maqam*, unlike melody in European songs, is not submitted to a specific temporal rhythmic organization and its performance may last for hours, this change can be considered as a rather decisive intervention. But ᶜAbd al-Wahhab went even further. He introduced various dance rhythms, like tango, rumba, samba, and foxtrot,[174] and was the first to use sung duets *(thuna'i ghina'i)*.[175] The Egyptian duet is a song that alternates between man and woman, accompanied by an instrumental ensemble. It is derived from the conventions of the operetta. ᶜAbd al-Wahhab also enlarged the traditional ensemble *(takht)*, normally consisting of only six instruments, to an orchestra and added instru-

Muhammad ᶜAbd al-Wahhab and his orchestra in *Girls' Flirtation* (Ghazl al-banat, Egypt, 1949) by Anwar Wagdi *(courtesy Muhammad Bakr, photographer, Cairo)*

Farid al-Atrash in *Song of Eternity* (Lahn al-khulud, Egypt, 1952) by Henri Barakat *(courtesy Muhammad Bakr, photographer, Cairo)*

ments including piano, timpani, and double bass. The number of Arab instruments was increased, resulting in a completely different sound volume than that of the traditional *takht*.[176] All this made the songs very popular.

In spite of these innovations, some of the early musicals seem rather slow by today's standards. In *Dananir*, musical performances are felt to be far too long, although the length of each is between four and seven minutes only. One reason for this is that the singer's movements and actions are very slight—most often she simply stands facing the audience. The six songs in *Dananir* occupy thirty-four from a total of ninety-six minutes, about a third of the screening time; there are also sequences with distinct Western-style background music. (Egyptian musicals in general use only Western music for the background.) Some films with ᶜAbd al-Wahhab contain as many as eleven songs.[177] Inevitably, this hampers the flow of action, in particular when songs are only superficially integrated into the narration.

Directors like Henri Barakat and Niyazi Mustafa, who left Egyptian cinema more than 100 works, among them many music-hall films, subsequently tried hard to achieve a more successful fusion of musical interpretation with the plot. In *Song of Eternity* (Lahn al-khulud, 1952) by Barakat, one of the most distinctive musical melodramas, the musical scenes with Farid al-Atrash are much more organically linked to other parts than in *Dananir*, for example, where songs and action are almost independent. This is partly due to the reduction of songs to three minutes, and also to the cutting and multiplication of different shots during the performance. At the same time, several little technical tricks, like the introduction of a radio transmission or the playing of records, allows the start of a parallel action during the singing, resulting in a much more varied visual arrangement.

The initial attachment of the musical to melodrama loosened in the course of the years and time was given to cheerful comedies, as well as music hall films inspired by the American model. From the formal point of view, many of these films cannot be categorized, but represent rather a melange of genres. Thus, publicity of this sort was common: "a dramatic comedy love story with songs and dances."[178] *Girls' Flirtation* by Anwar Wagdi and his revue film *Gold* (Dhahab, 1951) are prime examples of this type of cinema.

In *Gold*, a young bourgeois woman is forced by her family to abandon her baby, which a poor traveling entertainer then finds in front of a mosque and takes with him. The baby grows to become a cheeky little girl who stands by her foster father's side when he is doing his tracks. Then, by accident, they meet the young mother, who recognizes the girl as her abandoned child, falls in love with the entertainer, and this time stands up resolutely to her family.

With the star Fayruz, a talented little girl who dances and sings, Wagdi succeeded, in certain respects, in creating a pendant to Charlie Chaplin's *The Kid*. The partly comic, partly melodramatic plot is seasoned with Fayruz's performances. Unlike in early musicals, the songs of this film do not reflect the feelings of the protagonists, but are intended simply to entertain. The dances range from belly dancing to flamenco and American music hall.

In the words of Salah Ezz Eddine:

> The musical genre in these films attained an almost childlike ease. It seduced less by its simplicity than by its novelty. Its principal aim was passing diversion corresponding exactly to the current humor. . . . The easy new style helped make the exaggerated melodramatic character that had belonged to Arab cinema at that time disappear. It forced Arab cinema to renew itself and to give up its pretended seriousness."[179]

This childlike speed also characterizes the musicals of the 1960s, mainly driven forward by the pace of contemporary, fashionable music. In Hussein Kamal's box office hit *My Father Is up the Tree*, with songs by ᶜAbd al-Halim Hafiz, this tendency is further reinforced by show inserts and group dances. These developments

Love in the dark (Hubb fi-l-zalam, 1953) by Hasan al-Imam (*courtesy Muhammad Bakr, photographer, Cairo*)

ᶜAbd al-Halim Hafiz and Nadia Lutfi in *My Father Is up the Tree* (Egypt, 1969) by Hussein Kamal (*courtesy Muhammad Bakr, photographer, Cairo*)

correspond to the permissiveness of the young characters and their liberal dress, including skimpy bathing suits and miniskirts.

During the late Nasserist era, the musical was gradually overtaken by other genres, including police films and social drama. At the same time, musicals shed the classical Arab music forms. The increasing popularity of beat and pop music replaced the stately measures of former times. The tendency to accelerate can be noted also in other parts of Egyptian cinema. Already during the 1950s, with films like *The Beast* (al-Wahsh, 1953) by Abu Seif or Chahine's *Mortal Revenge* (Sira͑ fi-l-wadi; literally, 'struggle in the valley'; French, Ciel d'enfer, 1954), the directors tried to compensate for the lack of music through adventure and suspense, or precisely a cinematic rhythm decisively accelerated by movement and editing. Thus, they also submitted to the primacy of time.

This development culminates temporarily in one of the latest Egyptian music hall films, which paradoxically criticizes the selling out of Arab music and at the same time carries it even further. The actor Mamduh ͑Abd al-͑Alim and the actress Layla ͑Ilwi appear in *Silence, Listen!* as Hummus and Halawa, who make their living by working as traveling entertainers at popular feasts. On several occasions in the film, the couple sings their song "Hummus wa halawa" (Chickpea and sesame butter), while Halawa presents a second-rate belly dance. On one of these occasions, an organ-grinder steals the melody of their song and passes it on to Ghandur, a wealthy, established singer. Ghandur turns the melody into a pompous patriotic song, with which he appears in front of high society and on television. When Hummus and Halawa finally get the chance to perform their song in a real nightclub, they are charged with having disparaged a patriotic song. The couple's endeavor to get the melody back fails as Ghandur uses all his influence, from material seduction to violence, in order to keep it for himself. A dream sequence is a decisive scene in this respect, in which Hummus and Halawa are confronted with Ghandur's Western pop music and take part in a group dance, including jazz, break dance, disco, waltz, and even ballet. The performance is called 'money'—Hummus and Halawa are supposed to be bribed—and symbolizes the attempt to capture humane and original 'popular' culture by the dominating, inhumane, modern 'capitalist' culture.

Yet the rather overt message of the film's director, Sherif Arafa, and its author, Mahir ͑Awad, contains a considerable immanent contradiction. The melody and harmonies of the song "Hummus wa halawa", which is characterized by surrounding, arrangement, and instruments as a popular Arab song, is in fact identical with the supposedly alienated music. The putative authentic turns out to be itself only an imitation. Thus, the film's message is reduced to a mere ideological reproach, sweepingly charging the establishment of being Westernized. The music, like the shine of costumes and decoration, is fake.

Silence, Listen! is a good example of the syncretistic musical melange that is the dominant sound track of cinema in recent decades, little more than a local form of modern, international music. The "disarticulated and impersonal language" now dominating the "completely undermined and mixed up genres," must be seen as a result of the increasing mass mediation of culture.[180] However, in *Silence, Listen!* this syncretistic music has been linked to so-called traditional and native culture, thus switching its signs, so to speak, in order to function as a means of cultural identification. In this case it is not that the 'traditional' content has been repackaged and modernized, but that the modern itself has been declared as original and authentic.

Music and film structure

The commercial exploitation of the Egyptian musical and its development, being ruled only by supply and demand, prevented any new orientation in the relation of musical and cinematographic form. Only a few film makers have reconsidered the relation of native traditional music and cultural identity. Michel Khleifi did so by placing quasi-traditional music in the context of national (Palestinian) liberation. In his documentary *Fertile Memory* (al-Dhakira al-khisba, 1980) and the semi-documentary *Canticle of the Stones* (Nashid al-hadjar, 1990) he undercuts documentary images and the drama with songs and footage of the music group Sabrin, whose quasi-traditional music was inextricably linked with the intifada and the new resistance from within the occupied territories.

Almost no Arab film maker, however, explores the essence of traditional music and tries to apply its rules to cinematic rhythm and dramatic structure. The exception is the Algerian writer Assia Djebar, who lives in France and writes in French. In the 1970s, she interrupted her literary work and turned temporarily to cinema. Working with the audio-visual media offered her a way out of the linguistic dilemma she felt as an Algerian using French in her writing.[181] Both films Assia Djebar directed at this time alluded to music in their titles: *The Nuba of the Women of Mont Chenoua* (La nouba des femmes de Mont Chenoua, 1976) and *Zerda and the Songs of Oblivion* (La zerda et les chants de l'oubli, 1982). Since, according to Djebar, Arab culture lacks suitable visual traditions, she decided to borrow from music, which was "the only thing in Algeria that was not destroyed by colonialism."[182] During her search for an authentic means of arrangement, she came across the music of her childhood, the Andalusian *nuba*, whose structure she took over for her first film.[183]

Nuba is a traditional genre of music, comparable to a cantata or suite. It has a western and an eastern form—the latter is supposed to have originated in Arab Spain during the eighth and ninth century and has spread mainly in the Maghreb. It consists of an interaction between voice and instruments in a fixed course and key. After a metrically free instrumental and vocal introduction, elegiac singing follows, turning then into two lively, but rhythmically different, final sections. The most popular form of *nuba* in Algeria, the *nuba gharnati*, usually consists of eight movements: three introductory movements, *da'ira*, *mustakhbir*, and *tushiya* (also *taushiha*); three vocal movements, *masdar*, *bataih*, and *daradj*, which are preceded by an instrumental part. They are followed by a further vocal movement, the *insiraf* with its introductory *tushiya* and finally the *khalas*, the finale.[184] Assia Djebar seems to consider only four or five movements relevant for her work.

The subject of *The Nuba of the Women of Mont Chenoua* is introduced in a fictional part. Layla, an educated woman, returns from abroad with her child and her paralyzed husband to her home village in the mountains. During her expeditions through the region, she visits several (real) women and listens to them talk about daily life, the war of independence, and the history of the tribe, reaching back to the last century. The stories told by these women, of whom only those over fifty and under twelve appear on screen, form the core of the film. They are further framed by the memories of the fictive protagonist, containing elements of the film maker's biography.

The expected structure of the film was schematically summed up during the shooting of the film as follows:

- Present I: Layla, the second return.
- Present II: Layla, the first return and the search for the disappeared brother.
- History I: memories of the women peasants from 1954–62.
- History II: memories of the grandparents.

These elements are presented in three or a maximum of four movements, each of them possessing its own rhythm. First an istikhbar *(mustakhbir)*[185] or prelude takes place, in which all themes, instrumental or vocal, are announced. The khlass *(khalas)* forms the finale, in which the fusion of

collective and individual memories of a reconciled Layla are effected in a
fast rhythm. . . . The core of the film lies between them, either with a piece
that is arranged like a rather slow meceder *(masdar)* or as a faster btaihi
(bataih) and is finally concluded with a melancholic dreamy nesraf
(insiraf)."[186]

The division of the film similar to that of an Andalusian *nuba* not
only has consequences for the temporal course, but also comprises
the interaction of other elements. As in the original *nuba*, in which
instruments and voice take turns, and then come together again, so in
the film image and sound, as well as the protagonist and her
surroundings, are combined.

However, Assia Djebar applies the *nuba*'s forming parts and
principles of arrangement to cinema without using it as background
music. Instead, she dedicates her film to Bèla Bartok and uses pieces
he composed during his stay in Algeria in 1913. Thus, the author
indicates her direction unequivocally: she is not interested in a
folkloric imitation of her own cultural heritage, but in reconditioning
it according to the present. Accordingly, it is not a local resident who
draws out the memories, but an emigrated, quasi-alienated member
of the tribe. With the instruments of her Western education, she
uncovers her own submerged roots, thus making them accessible to
herself and others.

3

CULTURAL IDENTITY AND GENRE

Having described the arts that have flourished in Arab cinema, and the degree of their rooting in Arab-Islamic culture, it is now necessary to analyse certain common genres and their relation to prevailing sociopolitical and cultural conditions in the Arab countries. From the conventions and subjects of the respective film genres, it is possible to gather information about the refusal or rehabilitation of indigenous culture, about myths and symbols contributing to the formation of identity, as well as about attitudes toward Western ideology and ideas such as socialism, materialism, laicism, and individualism. For this purpose some of the genres—precisely, literary adaptations, realist and historical films, and *cinéma d'auteur*—that seem to contribute notably to the construction, or deconstruction, of certain effective political discourses will be examined.

The literary adaptation

The close relation between literature and cinema is not an Arab peculiarity, but an international phenomenon. In the West, as well as in the East, cinema borrowed very early on from other artistic forms, mainly from literature, in order to secure its further development. Although in Western countries, moving images had formed in the beginning a part of the funfair and vaudeville theater entertainment, after a while they lost some of their attraction. Hence, to become a form of bourgeois entertainment was one of its strategies for survival.[1] Thus, soon after its invention, cinema started to bow to bourgeois narrative traditions and to tell stories that were respectable and rich in content. In doing so, it drew on the immense treasury of realist feature novels *(Feuilletonroman).*[2]

In the Arab world the early perception of cinema went in a different direction. After being introduced first into the most elevated strata of society it became increasingly a means of popular entertainment, primarily consumed by the middle and lower urban classes. Like Western cinema, Arab cinema developed a strong interaction between literature and cinema, as we will further ascertain in the examination of realism. This is most evident in the genre of literary adaptation.

However, the number of literary adaptations varies considerably among the different Arab countries. About a dozen novels and novelettes by native authors have been adapted in the Maghreb countries. Adaptations of foreign works have also been undertaken. Among the most important are Souheil Ben Baraka's *Amok* (1982), an adaptation of *Cry the Beloved Country* by the South African Alan Paton, *Blood Wedding* (ʿUrs al-damm, 1977) based on Garcia Lorca's drama of the same title, and the Tunisian Taieb Louhichi's *Layla's Madman* (Madjnun Layla, 1988), adapted from a novel by André Miquel.[3] In Egypt, and in Syria, realist cinema during the 1950s and 1960s created a boom in literary adaptations. Some outstanding works by realist authors such as Ghassan Kanafani, Hanna Mina, Naguib Mahfouz, and Yusuf Idris were transferred to the screen. In Egypt, about 260 literary adaptations out of a total feature film production of approximately 2,500 films are supposed to have been realized between 1930 and 1993.[4]

During the first decades of Egyptian cinema, various famous novels and narratives from Western literature have found their way onto the screen, including some of the most distinguished works of early European realism—*La dame aux camélias* by Alexandre Dumas fils, *Thérèse Raquin* by Emile Zola, Victor Hugo's *Les Misérables*, and Dostoevsky's *Crime and Punishment.*

At first sight, adapting subjects originated in another culture seems to be clear evidence of cultural alienation and invites charges of imitation and plagiarism. However, notions of the 'original' and the 'copy' overshadow an analysis whose terminology draws from a hierarchic idea of culture and derives from an obligation to originality that is in no way natural. In fact, the notion of intellectual property attained real importance to European culture only with the appearance of the Sturm und Drang literary school in the second half of the eighteenth century.[5] Until then Western writers appropriated the subjects of other authors without inhibition, and rewrote and rearranged them. Famous works like *Don Quixote, Simplicissimus,*

Werther, and *Robinson Crusoe* may be considered as such 'plagiarisms.' Decisive for the evaluation of these works was the How and not the What of their arrangement.[6] As Elisabeth Frenzel demonstrates, the migration of subjects and the appropriation and rearrangement of topics is a worldwide phenomenon. Topics migrate from one cultural environment to another, and from one genre to another, adapting to particular social conditions.[7]

La dame aux camélias: *an example of cultural repackaging*

La dame aux camélias is a nineteenth-century novel by the French author Alexandre Dumas *fils,* and shows early realist tendencies in its preoccupation with social conditions. In Egypt, its subject has been adapted for screen twice: in *Layla* (1942) by Togo Mizrahi and in *Promise of Love* (ᶜAhd al-hawa, 1955) by Ahmed Badrakhan after a script by ᶜAli al-Zurqani. Themes of the story also appear in many other films, for example in Hussein Kamal's *My Father Is up the Tree* (1969). It is no surprise that all three works are musicals—Verdi had already adapted the story in his opera *La Traviata,* attracted no doubt by the melodramatic nature of the story.

In the Egyptian films, *La dame aux camélias* was thoroughly Arabized. Only the story-line was taken over from the original version: Armand Duval is a young man with a bourgeois background who falls in love with the much sought-after courtesan, Marguerite Gautier. Marguerite feels similarly toward Armand, which soon hampers her from carrying on her trade. When Armand decides to sell his inheritance in order to pay his beloved's debts, his father intervenes. He asks Marguerite to give up his son, pretending that the marriage of Armand's respectable sister is endangered by the scandal. Marguerite, who in the meantime has become critically ill, convinces her lover of her faithlessness and dies a short while later, deeply in debt.

The theme of the selfless courtesan reached a high point with *La dame aux camélias.* As Dumas himself points out in his novel, the subject stems from an older text written by Abbé Prévost,[8] and indeed the persona of the noble courtesan reaches back to antiquity.[9] Its rediscovery by French realism is connected to a change in the intellectual attitudes of the time. The new literary genre became the critic of social abuses and of bourgeois morals and snobbery, although it never completely liberated itself from either. Some similarities can be observed in Egyptian melodrama. During the 1940s and 1950s the theme of the noble woman either seduced or failed became increasingly popular. As a list set up by Galal al-

Charkawi shows, in the twenty-three films screened in the season of 1945/46 alone, nine girls were seduced and two raped.[10]

The two Egyptian adaptations of *La dame aux camélias*, *Layla* (1942) and *Promise of Love* (1955), schematize the plot considerably in accordance with the conventions of Egyptian melodrama. The poor become poorer and the rich richer, and they do without the background story of the literary model. In Dumas's version, the first-person narrator in the novel comes to know the miserable Armand after Marguerite's demise. The novel unfolds the story from the end using several perspectives expressed in letters, parts of a diary, and reports of various involved persons, a technique that the films also forego.

The Egyptian characters representing the young lover, Farid in *Layla* and Wahid in *Promise of Love*, stem from a much wealthier home than their French counterpart. Their fathers are not civil servants but prosperous landowners. Unlike Armand, who takes part freely and easily in the night-life of Paris, the Egyptian heroes seem naive and inexperienced in dealing with the demimonde. They wish to marry the courtesan in order to rescue her, an attitude Armand never shares. The existence of a sexual relationship is almost hidden. In *Layla*, there is some suspicion of it, but in the later adaptation, *Promise of Love*, there is no trace of it.

The main female character has likewise undergone decisive changes. The French *dame aux camélias* loves her independence and chooses her lovers consciously. Layla is much closer to this than Amal in *The Promise of Love*. Like Marguerite, Layla self-confidently mocks the clumsy overtures of her admirer. Yet overall, she is represented as a victim of circumstances. This trait is stressed even more in Amal, who appears completely passive and helpless. In both Egyptian versions, the women are encouraged into prostitution by a friend. In the literary model, Marguerite has a close friend, Prudence, who profits from Marguerite's work, but seems unable to influence her in any way. Marguerite lets herself be kept by men because of her love of luxury and her disturbed relation with her unloving mother. Her Egyptian counterparts are motivated only by material poverty. Amal, for example, has to take care of a blind mother and two younger brothers and sisters.

By reinforcing the contradictions in both Egyptian melodramas, the conflict is carried to the utmost. Individual happiness and love stand on the one side while tradition and family are on the other. The main contenders are the loving woman and the authoritarian father.[11] Furthermore, both films succeed, in comparison with the Western model, in achieving an important shift of meaning, by means of their

Farid al-Atrash and Maryam Fakhr al-Din in *Promise of Love* (ᶜAhd al-hawa, Egypt, 1955) by Ahmed Badrakhan *(courtesy Muhammad Bakr, photographer, Cairo)*

representation of native and Western cultures. Layla ends up in a poor room, taken care of only by her old lady's maid, who, in costume and manners, is explicitly Egyptian. Amal in *The Promise of Love* dies in the poorly furnished house of her clearly destitute mother. She wears traditional clothes and a veil. (Amal's four-poster bed with shining bed linen forms the sole comfort and seems as much out of place as her elegant and fashionable Western wardrobe.) Servants and maids in both films are faithful and kind and are assigned, through their behavior and clothing, to the traditional Egyptian, in part rural, milieu. The protagonists, who wear Western costumes, are for the most part permissive and immoral. Wahid in *The Promise of Love* is at first presented as a righteous young man, although, unlike his father, he is not interested in the Friday prayers. Even though his family is dressed in almost Western-style clothes, its members are clearly characterized as traditional and Muslim, through their surrounding, the rural environment, and their morals (Wahid's father wears an Arab cloak *(ᶜabaya)* and is preparing for his pilgrimage). Both films represent Western lifestyle as a potential moral danger.

In these various ways, then, the Egyptian adaptations of *La dame aux camélias* Arabize the subject essentially, even though they are set in the milieu of Western influenced Egyptian *haute bourgeoisie*. The ethical content of the narration is adapted and reformulated according to the moral code of Arab-Islamic culture and is furnished with an indirect critique of Western lifestyle. Adaptation here is not simply wholesale appropriation nor a simple alienated imitation, but is rather a repackaging of 'traditional' values in a 'modern' form.

Realism

Starting with national independence in the 1950s and 1960s, film making in the Arab countries increasingly avoided fictive entertainment and examined social reality instead. Situated against the background of nationalist and marxist ideology, cinematic realism *(al-waqiʿiya)* aimed to reflect the world and daily life of the indigenous population. It denounced colonial oppression and social abuse. The genre spread throughout the Arab countries and developed various regional forms. Apart from Egyptian realism, there was revolutionary Algerian cinema, sometimes called *al-sinima al-djidid* (New Cinema),[12] and Alternative Cinema *(al-sinima al-badila)*[13] in Syria. The films of the Lebanese directors George Nasr and George Qaʿi at the end of the 1950s showed realistic tendencies[14] as did the works of the Iraqi directors Mohamed Choukri Jamil, Sahib Hadad, and Fayçal al-Yasseri during the 1970s.[15] In Tunisia and Morocco a similar tendency can be seen in *Under the Autumn Rain* (Taht matar al-kharif, 1966) by the Tunisian Ahmed Kechine and *Spring Sun* (Shams al-rabiʿ, 1970) by the Moroccan Latif Lahlou. *The Cruel Sea* (Bass ya bahr; literally 'Stop, sea!'; La mer cruelle, 1971) by the Kuwaiti Khalid Siddiq belongs in the same category.

Western film theory has provided a number of categories derived from the confrontation with different realist trends in occidental film making since the beginning of the century: poetic realism in France, Italian neorealism, and socialist realism in the former USSR, for example. The various theoretical approaches cover a vast spectrum of cinematic arrangements and range from the analysis of narrative structures to technical and topical characterizations.

Regarding narration, Colin MacCabe's notion of classic realist text,[16] which he derives from the narrative structures of nineteenth-century classic realist literature, seems helpful. According to MacCabe, the classic realist text is based on a dominant discourse, that of the all-knowing narrator, who does not admit his subjectivity at any point in the text. This discourse produces realist illusion by denying itself as an utterance: "The real is not articulated—it is."[17] This "discourse of knowledge" suggests one sole perspective to which all other discourses (including those of the characters) are subordinate. Several competing perspectives with equal weight cannot exist in this kind of narration, for they would reduce the identification of the observer. Therefore realist conventions convey the impression of a closed universe, a 'panopticon' in which reality and fiction are the same.[18]

However, MacCabe's definition alone does not suffice to circumscribe realism. Genres that are non-realist regarding their content— for example, modern science fiction—apply the same discourse of knowledge as classic realism. Hence, to classify a film as realist, other characteristics have to be taken into consideration. In his analysis of Italian neorealism, André Bazin pointed to features like quasi-documentary style, refusal of the star system, the occasional employment of amateur actors, and shooting in original locations to give the impression of an authentic environment.[19]

No less important are those characteristics that in Raymond Williams's view are common to all literary and cinematic realisms— contemporaneity, secularism, and social inclusiveness.[20] "Realism focused . . . upon the external social reality, which it saw as a human construct, the result of human intervention. This led to stress upon the determining action of people upon their environment rather than their passive molding by it."[21] Realism that is oriented toward the past or the next world is scarcely imaginable. Instead, realism describes the visible appearances and experiences of reality that are (apparently) accessible to everybody and thus form a common denominator of daily life experience. The representation of human fate on the background of an entire social context forms the essence of the realist genre.

In particular the notion of social inclusiveness, which is probably better paraphrased as balanced social representation, attains significance because what counts is not the representation of only certain social strata (like the working class or bourgeoisie), but an equal representation of all social groups and their interaction. This maxim contradicts the ideas of socialist realism, where ideally the whole narration should be subordinated to the perspective of the proletariat.[22]

However, realist conventions against all pretense do not guarantee that "things are shown as they are." This has already been stated by the dramatist and scriptwriter Bertolt Brecht. His concept of realism was based on a completely contrasting approach, namely the alienation of the discourse of knowledge that dominates the classic realist text. In Brecht's view, true insight into reality can only be achieved when the unconditional identification of the audience with the narration is abolished.[23]

Brecht's concept of realism has only slightly influenced the field of cinema in general and in the Arab countries in particular, although his plays aroused strong interest during the 1960s and 1970s. Instead Arab cinema stayed faithful to the principles of conventional realism, which is, like all film genres, no more or less than a fictional discourse on reality.

Egyptian realism

Egyptian realism is the only Arab realism that has entered film history under the name 'realism.' This is not to say that Egyptian realism was more 'realistic' or more adequate to reality than other comparable trends in Arab cinema. Its name only expresses the changed attitude of a part of commercial Egyptian film making toward social reality. Its essential characteristics are description that attempted to be faithful to the environment and the choice of the simple man from the lower social strata as protagonist. As such, Egyptian realism differs remarkably in its themes and narration from the other genres of the Egyptian film industry—farce, melodrama, or musical.

Egyptian realism started in the early 1950s, before all other Arab countries except Lebanon. Yet its qualitative importance is constantly confused in film history with its actual marginality. Between 1951 and 1971 the film industry in Egypt produced a total of 1,012 works.[24] Apart from a dozen patriotic films, about thirty-two realist films were shot,[25] i.e., one and a half films per year over the whole period. After nationalization the annual average increased only slightly. Between 1963 and 1971 only two realist films appeared per year. In general, realism was confined to three directors, Salah Abu Seif, Taufik Salih, and Youssef Chahine, whose works, with the exception of Salih, had a strong commercial element. Only for a short while during the 1960s were they joined by a few mainstream directors, among them Henri Barakat, Kamal El-Cheikh, and Hussein Kamal.

In spite of the state's openness after the coup d'état of the Free Officers in 1952 to the interests of the underprivileged classes and thus to realist representations (though not representations of topical politics), the genre remained at the mercy of the market. The nationalization of the film industry came rather late (in 1963) and initiated no basic changes in its economic structure. As a result, most realist works were produced by the private sector and commercial interests were taken into consideration during their making.

Fatin Hamama (center) in *Bitter Day, Sweet Day* (Yaum hulw, yaum murr, Egypt, 1988) by Khairy Beshara

In the early 1980s, after a slack period during the 1970s, realism was revived with the help of the generation of 'New Realists,' Atef El-Tayeb, Mohamed Khan, Khairy Beshara, Bashir El-Dik, and Daoud Abd El-Sayyed, whose works were dominated by very much the same commercial interests as the preceding wave of the 1960s.[26]

In the shadow of censorship and commerce

The first Egyptian feature film that was considered realist by Egyptian film critics was *Determination* (al-ᶜAzima) by Kamal Selim, made in 1939. It is set almost exclusively in the environment of the petty bourgeoisie. Muhammad lives with his parents in a traditional neighborhood. Although his father is only a simple barber, the young man has received a good education that should allow him to start a career as a civil servant. But Muhammad cannot find a job, although he needs one desperately in order to marry the neighbor's daughter, Fatima, who is also the object of the wealthy butcher's attention. With the assistance of a pasha, Muhammad is finally able to find a job and marry his beloved. But his luck lasts only a short while; because of a misunderstanding Muhammad loses his job, which makes his wife's family urge her to separate from him. All ends well though, as together with the son of the pasha the protagonist is able to set up his own company, and nothing can prevent his marital happiness.

As this short summary demonstrates, the realism of *Determination* does not consist in the construction of the plot, which is arranged according to conventional drama, but in the 'setting,' the environment of the protagonist. The director's original intention was to call the film 'The Alley' (*al-Hara*), but this was rejected by the producer of the film, since Studio Misr did not consider it suitable for advertising.[27]

The peculiarity of *Determination* lies in the alley and its inhabitants. This was in sharp contrast to other films of that time. The familiar surroundings of ordinary people were not pictured at all or only briefly and without details, even if those people were represented main characters. In Selim's film the vivid life of the alley is a main element of the plot. Passers-by, traders, visitors to the café, and inhabitants of the small houses, all take part in the action and show deep interest in what happens to the protagonist and his bride.

In spite of its interest in expressing a social critique—two keenly-felt problems of the time are represented, arranged marriage and the missing contribution of the native bourgeoisie in building a national economy—*Determination* also contains various non-realistic elements. The narrative structure, which introduces the pasha as *deus ex machina*, indicates this clearly. Muhammad cannot alter his situation alone. The decisive and positive changes in his career are initiated by the pasha or his son. Thus, his story is lifted into a fabulous, fairy tale-like realm, for in reality not every minor employee maintains a friendly relationship with an influential pasha and family.

Selim's difficulties with his producer and his concessions to the system on the level of the narration can be seen as a result of the increasingly unfavorable attitude of the industry toward realist representation. The musical director Ahmed Badrakhan, for example, was convinced that realist narration in feature films was totally unsuitable:

> It is noteworthy that a plot or script that is set in a simple environment, like that of the workers or peasants, has only limited success, for cinema relies first of all on images. The middle class, which forms the majority of the audience, does not wish to see the world in which they live, but on the contrary are eager to have an insight into circles they do not know but read about in novels. . . . Here are some places that are suitable to appear in a film: the theater, the music hall, the editorial office of a newspaper, a big hotel, the stock exchange, the summer holiday, the horse race, a gambling casino.[28]

Despite such attitudes, in 1945, six years after *Determination*, a work appeared that was far less willing to compromise. This was *The Black Market* (al-Suq al-sauda') by Kamil al-Tilmissani. The main part is again taken by a young employee, Hamid, who is living during World War II in a small attic room. He loves Nagya, whose father and another unscrupulous trader are hoarding merchandise. Because of the shortage of goods, the two merchants are able to raise prices extortionately and in spite of his modest origins Nagya's father becomes extremely rich. The defenseless inhabitants of the alley are dependent on his goods, and cannot fight back. Only Hamid cannot give in. He tries to uncover the wheelings and dealings of the speculators, even at the risk of losing Nagya's love.

Not least because of its analytical approach, *The Black Market* did not achieve the same success as *Determination*. Without any melodramatic tear-jerking al-Tilmissani demonstrates the problems that Hamid has to overcome while trying to uncover the blackmarketeers. His realism unfolds not so much in the details of his environmental description but in reference to the entire social context.

Selim's and al-Tilmissani's achievements can only be appraised in the knowledge that during the 1930s and 1940s a phenomenon appeared in Egyptian cinema similar to the 'classic separation of style' *(Stiltrennung)* that prevailed for a long time in Western literature. In antiquity as well as in the Middle Ages, references to the popular environment and characters were allowed in low literature, for example in merry tales *(Schwank)* and burlesque stories *(Burleske)*, but not in texts of elevated style.[29] During the 1930s and 40s, representatives of lower social classes appeared in Egyptian cinema primarily in farce. In romance and melodrama persons of lower social status, despite poverty being essential to the genre, were reduced to stylized signs. Although the fellah (Egyptian peasant) in these films was granted his typical, indigenous costume, he was not characterized realistically but served mostly for amusement. The dresses of 'poor' main characters were often adapted to the Western clothing of the upper strata. Their original environment was not at all or only schematically represented.

The contempt for the native culture of the underprivileged classes found in many films of this time was accompanied with some moral qualifications by a relatively positive representation of Western lifestyle (though not Western morals). Togo Mizrahi's film *Layla from the Countryside* (Layla bint al-rif, 1941) characterizes life in the countryside as provincial, since it lacks institutions like sporting clubs and nightclubs. In spite of her wealth the protagonist, daughter of a farmer, is ridiculed because of her dress and manners and presented as socially unacceptable. She finally appears attractive to the hero only when she shows some fashion consciousness and knowledge of the French language.

The only traditional elements that in this film remain exempt from the accusation of backwardness are those norms that maintain patri-

archal order, that is first of all those that affect the position of women
and family. The protagonist approves his peasant wife's adaptation to
the lifestyle of the city, he even supports it, but he is not willing to
grant her emotional or sexual freedom, although he himself refuses
for a long time to consummate their marriage. He justifies this
attitude by his male honor *(karama / sharaf)*.

The obstacles to a more realistic presentation of the poor, as well
as of native culture, were not only put up by the commercial system
but also by legislative restrictions. The censorship law, the so-called
Faruq Code issued in 1949 by the Ministry of Social Affairs,[30]
excluded realism by equating it with subversive leftist trends. Thus it
prohibited among others the following representations:

- Images of apparently soiled alleys, of hand and donkey carts, itinerant
  traders, copper cleaners *(mubayyad al-nahas)*, poor farm houses and
  their furnishings, and women wearing enveloping gowns *(al-mila'a al-
  laf)*.
- The shaking of the social order by revolutions, demonstrations, and
  strikes.
- The approval of crimes or the proliferation of the spirit of revolt as a
  means of demanding rights.
- Everything touching Eastern habits and traditions.[31]

These regulations could be wholly ignored by Egyptian cinema
only after the coup in 1952 and the abolition of the monarchy.

Literature as catalyst

Realist literature played a decisive role in establishing realist cinema
in Egypt. The first long Egyptian feature film, *Zaynab* (1930) by
Muhammad Karim, which included some social critique, was
adapted from a novel by Muhammad Husain Haikal published for
the first time in 1914 under the same title.[32] Zaynab, the sensitive
daughter of a peasant, experiences a harmless flirtation with the
educated son of a landowner, Hamid. Then Zaynab falls in love with
Ibrahim, but her parents marry her to Hasan, one of his friends. The
girl has no opportunity to object. As a result of the conflict between
marital faithfulness and her actual feelings, Zaynab's health is so
damaged that she falls ill and dies.

Haikal's work is considered as the first real Egyptian novel[33] and is
described in form and content as a didactic novel *(Bildungsroman)*.[34]
The adaptation of *Zaynab*, which stayed close to the literary original,
assumed not only its critique of traditional family structure, the
position of women and arranged marriage, but also Haikal's romanti-
cizing and aestheticizing style, which resulted in comprehensive and
rather nostalgic descriptions of life in the countryside. The director of

the film, Muhammad Karim, made the same effort to present as beautiful and clean an image as possible of his native country. For this reason he ordered all animals to be washed before the shooting.[35] The resulting aesthetic stood of course in contrast to the socially critical elements of the story.

The realist wave of the 1950s owes a great deal to the influence of the Egyptian novelist Naguib Mahfouz, who left deep traces particularly in the work of Salah Abu Seif, the most popular representative of cinematographic realism in Egypt. From 1951 to 1952 with his films *Master Hasan* (al-Usta Hasan) and *Your Day Is Coming* (Lak yaum ya zalim), Abu Seif introduced Egyptian realism of the postcolonial period. He was to complete in the following two decades fifteen realist (or quasi-realist) feature films, out of his total of forty films.

The cooperation between Salah Abu Seif and Naguib Mahfouz started with the film *The Avenger* (al-Muntaqim, 1947), whose script they wrote together. This was Naguib Mahfouz's first experience of scriptwriting.[36] In the following years Mahfouz contributed to nine scripts of Abu Seif, including *Raya and Sakina* (Raya wa Sakina), *The Beast* (al-Wahsh), *Youth of a Woman* (Shabab imra'a) and *Between Sky and Earth* (Bayn al-sama' wa-l-ard).[37] These served as drafts for Abu Seif's most outstanding works. Two adaptations of novels by Mahfouz, directed by Abu Seif—*Beginning and End* (Bidaya wa nihaya) and *Cairo 30* from al-Qahira al-djadida (The new Cairo)—count among the most important films of Egyptian realism.

During the 1960s Mahfouz held important positions in the world of cinema. He was at various times in charge of censorship, of the film fund, and of a department of the film organization, and worked for the ministry of culture as a consultant for cinema.[38] From 1947 until 1959 he contributed to no less than eighteen scripts,[39] most of which belong to the realist category. Up to 1978, fifteen adaptations of his novels were produced, primarily works from his first, pre-revolution, period.[40]

Abu Seif states that realist literature had a major influence on his own work. He admired in particular the work of Russian realists including Chekov.[41] French authors of the last century also aroused his interest. Indeed his first realist film, *Your Day Is Coming*, was, in environment and characters, an adaptation of Zola's *Thérèse Raquin*.

The close connection between literature and realism is not only observed in the work of Salah Abu Seif. Taufik Salih, for example, adapted *Diary of a Country Prosecutor* (Yaumiyat na'ib fi-l-aryaf) by Taufik al-Hakim. The script for his first film, *Alley of Fools* (Darb al-

Publicity poster for *Diary of a Country Prosecutor* (Yaumiyat na'ib fi-l-aryaf, Egypt, 1968) by Taufik Salih

mahabil, 1955), stems from Naguib Mahfouz. Another realist, Youssef Chahine, adapted the novel *The Earth* (al-Ard) by ᶜAbd al-Rahman al-Sharqawi, to produce one of the most notable examples of Egyptian realism (*al-Ard*, 1968).[42] Other directors owe their few realist films to adaptations of literary texts: Henri Barakat's *The Sin* (al-Haram, 1965) is from a novel by Yusuf Idris; Kamal El-Cheikh made *Miramar* (1968) and *The Thief and the Dogs* (al-Liss wa-l-kilab, 1962), both by Mahfouz; and Hussein Kamal adapted Mahfouz's *Adrift on the Nile* (Tharthara fauq al-Nil; literally, 'babbling on the Nile,' 1971).

The interest of the realist directors in literature is not purely spiritual. Novels constitute an easily accessible reservoir of ideas. Their adaptation also seems advisable from the commercial point of view, for the success of a novel might be repeated in the cinema. Also, the background of the directors themselves may have contributed to this tendency. Youssef Chahine and Taufik Salih come from the bourgeoisie, as does Henri Barakat. The only exception is Salah Abu Seif, who grew up in the rather popular and poor Cairo neighborhood of Bulaq. With the help of literary texts most directors were able to compensate for their insufficient knowledge of the living circumstances of the lower classes. Taufik Salih, for example, before making *Alley of Fools*, received an introduction from Naguib Mahfouz. According to the director, the novelist took him to Old

Cairo (al-Gamaliya neighborhood) and described for him the life of his friends and relatives there.[43]

Commercial realism

Realists portraying the lives of ordinary workers and peasants on the screen chose their subjects from real life as well as from literature. The stories of *The Beast* (1953), *Raya and Sakina* (1953) and *The Thug* (1957) by Abu Seif go back to actual events, although these are out of the ordinary (in the first two films the activities of criminal bands provide the action), and immersion in the popular environment creates a realist impression.

A similar combination of the commercial and the realist (spectacular event plus observation of daily life) is found in *Cairo Main Station* (Bab al-hadid, 1958) by Youssef Chahine. Poverty in his native village has driven the ragged and crippled Qinawi to the metropolis. The main railway station (in colloquial *bab al-hadid*, 'the iron gate') means to him the center of the world. He lives here in a shabby old wagon, which he decorates with pin-up girls. Qinawi is a silent voyeur, who is allowed to participate in life only by watching. So it is no wonder that the woman for whom his heart longs has not shown any interest in him. The sexy and decisive soft-drink seller, Hanuma, only has eyes for the gallant porter Abu Siri[c]. After a failed attempt to approach Hanuma, Qinawi decides to kill her. But another girl falls victim of his murderous attempt. When Qinawi goes after Hanuma's blood again, he finishes up in a straitjacket.

With motifs of criminality like murder and chase, *Cairo Main Station* produces considerable suspense. At the same time, several parallel stories unfolding within the station break the dramatic structure of the background story: the porters try to set up a trade union; a panicked peasant family wander through the crowd; a feminist gives a speech; two young lovers keep their secret appointments. These inserts are mainly observations made by Qinawi and allow the audience to participate in his voyeurism, thereby helping to reinforce the realism of the film. Thus the narrative structure, which follows the conventions of the police film with the introduction of conflict, climax, and resolution, is broken by a series of other scenes. This kind of structure appears only in a few Egyptian realist films, as most directors and scriptwriters followed the principles of conventional drama and avoided epic narrative forms.

The Thug (1957), whose script was co-written by Naguib Mahfouz, was one of the most successful of Salah Abu Seif's realist films and is a typical example of Egyptian realism. Its theme came from a report in the newspapers. The young peasant Haridi, starting out as an unskilled worker at the vegetable market in Cairo, gets into a quarrel with some influential traders who are monopolizing the market. Although without any means, the peasant is received warmly and supported by other traders, in particular by a beautiful female trader. Together they develop a plan to put a stop to the game of the 'king of the market.' However, the example of Haridi is soon to prove that solidarity does not last for long: the former unskilled worker changes into an unscrupulous speculator, who himself threatens the position of the king of the market. The struggle that starts between the two is only terminated by the intervention of the police. An epilogue follows, showing the arrival of another peasant at the market who, like Haridi, is slapped early on, and will try his luck in the same way.

The protagonists of *The Thug* are exclusively peasants, workers, and traders, who live and work in the area of the market. Members of higher social classes appear only as negative, marginal figures. The identification of the characters is made through morality alone, the antagonism between good and evil. Zayd, the influential king of the market, is unscrupulous and authoritarian. His appearance, his facial expressions, and his physique are unattractive, whereas Haridi and his friends are presented in a very positive way, humorous, helpful, and showing solidarity.

The film does not attempt a psychological study of the characters. Immediately upon his arrival Haridi seems naive and foolish, but as soon as he is established in the city, his behavior becomes unscrupulous and devious. None of the protagonists possess real individual features. The heroes are characterized in principle by their professional and social affiliations and can be, as the epilogue clearly indicates, substituted for at any time.

The main parts of the film are acted by the two stars Farid Shauqi and Tahiya Carioca. Their acting reinforces the stylization of the characters even further and makes the influence of farce and theater apparent. But the employment of amateur actors, who probably could have given the characters greater authenticity, would have been unthinkable. Cooperation with star actors was a tribute that the realists had to pay to the film industry.

Similar considerations apply to the treatment of the environment in Egyptian realism. Contrary to Italian neorealism, which at times exchanged the studio entirely for filming on location,[44] Egyptian realism remained a child of the studios, with all that this meant for faithfulness to detail and creating an appropriate atmosphere.[45] However directors like Salah Abu Seif tried to compensate for this by an exact study of the environment: "For 'Le Costaud' *[The Thug]* for example I went every day to the [market], after I had studied the economic background, the power structures in the market. We rebuilt the in the studio in such a way that even the people who go there every day could not notice any difference in the film."[46]

Hampered socialism

Analyses simply oriented toward materialist or socialist realism are an exception in Egyptian realism. In *Struggle of the Heroes* (Sira^c al-abtal, 1962), directed and written by Taufik Salih, the socialist discourse appears clearly in the course of the narration and in characterization. A young doctor who starts working in the countryside wants to contribute to improving the villager's lives. But this only brings him enemies: the midwife who is anxious about losing her income, the peasants who trust neither his medical advice nor his suggestions for reform, and the landowner who needs obedient and passive villagers to maintain his personal interests. With the assistance of his wife, the doctor succeeds in uncovering the intrigues of the landowner and the midwife and encourages the peasants to show solidarity and convinces them to follow the path of progress.

During the making of his films, Taufik Salih often came up against censorship and bureaucracy. His films produced by the film organi- zation, *Mister Bulti* (al-Sayyid Bulti, 1967) and *The Rebels* (al- Mutamarridun, 1966), both had to wait two years until their release. In the case of *Mister Bulti,* which deals with the struggle of fishermen at work against a monopolist, the censor used a scene of two young women shaving their legs as a pretext for postponing the release of the film.[47]

Due to the inconsistencies and contradictions of cultural politics in Egypt, Taufik Salih constantly suffered from bureaucratic obstacles. Finally in the early 1970s he was forced to search for producers abroad. As the example of Salih shows, in spite of socialist planning, governmental endeavor in no way furthered socialist realism.

Outside of Salih's work, other examples of socialist realism are few. *The Earth* (al-Ard, 1968), by Youssef Chahine, deals with the struggle of small farmers against the tyranny of the big landowners. The representation of class struggle is largely due to the literary basis of the film. The author, ^cAbd al-Rahman al-Sharqawi, is one of the few Egyptian writers who expressed an uncompromising Marxism.[48]

Apart from *The Earth, Mister Bulti,* and *Struggle of the Heroes,* Egyptian realists did not normally glorify the working or peasant class. Some of them, like Abu Seif in *The Thug* and *Youth of a Woman* even depicted peasants with mockery and condescension. This is not so strange in view of the often contradictory attitude of the film makers, not least that of Salah Abu Seif. In spite of his work as an influential civil servant—he was head of the governmental production company *Film Intadj*—Abu Seif continued to pay tribute to commercial forms of production. Even after the nationalization of the film industry, he directed commercial films, although he spoke in favor of the socialist film and made theoretical efforts to develop a popular and at the same time socially critical cinema.

> The artist, and in particular the film maker, has the most effective means of speaking to the masses. Of all artists, the film maker is most capable of describing the struggle of man in an accessible and elevated style. . . . Cinema aims to educate the people's sense of beauty. Therefore it has to respond to two important factors: entertainment and dealing with social problems. On this basis, no contradiction exists between socialism and comedy. If we are able to produce films making the people laugh at their enemies and their allies and about their own faults in order to correct them, we know that we have succeeded in making a valuable socialist cinema.[49]

However, it seems that in his practical work the director was not always able to combine socialism and entertainment. Between 1963 and 1971 during his work at the film organization, Abu Seif directed only three realist films, while in the same period he shot one religious and two mainstream works.

Melodrama and ideological potpourri

Egyptian realism does not constitute a coherent ideological movement. It displays secular tendencies as well as traditional moral and religious concepts. Fatalist convictions are juxtaposed with materialist approaches. Its level of political consciousness was also in general low and confined to harmless social critique concurring with the system. Nasserism and the new regime were conceived positively and in part glorified, as in *Dawn of a New Day* (Fadjr yaum djadid, 1964) by Youssef Chahine. Through the figure of a young student the director characterizes the new system as dynamic and progressive, while the pre-revolutionary bourgeoisie is shown as parasitic and unable to share in bearing the ideals of progress and social justice.

Only a few were critical. Taufik Salih, who made an optimistic appeal for the construction of a new social order in *Struggle of the Heroes*, soon took a considerably more skeptical position. His critical and highly allegorical film *The Rebels* was produced one year before the disaster of 1967, the military defeat by Israel that clearly demonstrated the weaknesses of the regime. In a sanatorium far off in the desert, first-class patients enjoy various privileges while third-class patients are even deprived of fresh water. After the arrival of a young

Shukri Sarhan (right) in *The Rebels* (al-Mutamarridun, 1966) by Taufik Salih

doctor, himself a victim of lung disease, the underprivileged decide to protest. For a short while the rebels take over the sanatorium and create just conditions. But they soon fall into a trap and become corrupted. A last attempt to create solidarity among the dissidents ends tragically, and the revolt is shattered by force. The censor and state functionaries understood Taufik Salih's narrative as an allegory on Nasser's reign, and consequently the film was banned for two years.

In Egyptian realism, analysis of the totality of societal conditions is often undertaken only superficially and reflects the diffuse political convictions of its producers. In *The Thug*, for example, Mahfouz and Abu Seif equate the rules of the free market economy, which they see as leading to trade monopolies and illegal speculation, with the pre-Nasserist political system. As becomes clear, the influential 'king of the market' has friends at the very top (pashas and ministers) who support him and at the same time make profit out of him. But this system breaks down violently, and during a police raid the picture of the king falls from a wall, signifying the coup d'état.

In spite of the positive change that the intervention of the police promises, the film's epilogue is skeptical. A new 'Haridi' enters the market, indicating that the story can repeat itself at any time.

Although the film was shot in 1956, four years after the overthrow of the old and corrupted system, the makers seem convinced that the people remain victims of unjust social circumstances.

Taufik Salih and Naguib Mahfouz in *Alley of Fools* (1955) castigate greed and profiteering (i.e., materialism) and contrast it with a Muslim ethos. The film tells of a conflict that starts among the inhabitants of an alley over a lottery ticket. A young worker buys a ticket for his fiancée, which wins the first prize a short while later. The couple need the money desperately, as the young man's job in a bicycle workshop brings in far too little to finance the marriage. However, the fiancée's religious father tells her that games of chance are prohibited by Islam, and the young woman throws the ticket away in the street. Thus the ticket falls into the hands of the fool who sits with his goat on the edge of the street. Several inhabitants of the alley try in various ways to get hold of the money. The efforts of the imam (Muslim cleric) to initiate peace fail. No one wants to believe his admonitions that only God is able to reduce poverty and that working is the best way to material success. Only the young couple follow his advice and decide to strive to meet their basic needs alone.

Very often ideas influenced by socialism were not much more than moral interpretations. Following the conventions of classical drama, directors gave class struggle the form of a fight between good and evil. Yet in many works the struggle does not take place between classes. Poverty itself opposes the protagonist, as an abstract but invincible enemy. The reasons for his or her social decline are merely personal or dictated by fate. The film *Beginning and End* by Salah Abu Seif follows this scheme, according to which a petty bourgeois family is driven into misery because of the loss of the father. The attempt to escape poverty leads to the decline of the entire family.

The adaptation of a novel by Yusuf Idris, *The Sin* (al-Haram, 1965), directed by Henri Barakat, follows a similar principle. Under a tree in the fields a dead infant is found. The village notables start to investigate the case. As inquiries in the village remain fruitless their suspicion is directed toward the women of the itinerant workers camped outside the village. They soon conclude that ᶜAziza, who has been suffering from fever for days, must be the murderer. Slowly the notables uncover the background of the crime. ᶜAziza, who has to support a handicapped husband and two children, was raped in the fields, and attempting to hide the child after her delivery, she unintentionally suffocated it. Everybody is now sympathetic toward ᶜAziza's fate and no one thinks of taking her to court. Still her condition deteriorates progressively, until she dies.

One might then describe the attitude to social conditions of many

The Sin (al-Haram, Egypt, 1965) by Henri Barakat

realist works as fatalist. Mostly, the individual is rendered helpless to circumstances, awarding society an omnipotence similar to fate.[50] Nearly all Salah Abu Seif's heroes, from Master Hasan to the family of *Beginning and End,* are driven into irrevocable social isolation by their poverty. Apart from in films like *The Sin, The Earth,* and *Struggle of the Heroes,* solidarity and common action are treated with skepticism or are not even taken into consideration. The isolated individual, be it the uprooted and emotionally and sexually deprived Qinawi in *Cairo Main Station* or the child murderer in *The Sin,* has no choice. This socio-economic determinism of Egyptian realism, which also marks many works of Naguib Mahfouz,[51] prevents the adoption of real secularism. Although realism excludes normally obvious utterances concerning divine omnipotence and providence, and demonstrates in the choice of its topics a connection to the present and this world, its protagonists only exceptionally reach the stage of a human being deliberately acting to decide their fate. The mostly tragic circumstances of the hero align the genre with melodrama and make its description as 'melodramatic realism' seem suitable.

New realism

After the start of reprivatization in 1971, production of realist films decreased rapidly and did not flourish again until after the death of Sadat in 1982 with the work of a second generation. The new realism, whose representatives include Atef El-Tayeb, Bashir El-Dik, Mohamed Khan, Khairy Beshara, ʿAli Badrakhan, and Daoud Abd El-Sayyed has also now declined.

New realism appeared, at least regarding its subjects, to be much more pragmatic than the old version, although it functioned according to the same mechanisms. It similarly borrowed from commercial genres, but rather than melodrama it used elements of action and police film. Like the old realism, it could not do without stars and was also based on the commercial system of production, which quickly dampened the new wave. New realism differed externally in its choice of environment, mainly that of the urban petty bourgeoisie, and a stronger integration of original locations that meant a further (but still partial) renunciation of the studio.

The Bus Driver (Sawwaq al-utubis, 1982) by Atef El-Tayeb is a typical example of new realism. Its narrative is based on an idea of

Nur al-Sharif (far left) as *The Bus Driver* (Sawwaq al-utubis, 1982) by Atef El-Tayeb

the director and his colleagues Mohamed Khan and Bashir El-Dik,[52] and is considered by some critics as the start of new realism.[53] Hasan is confronted with a serious problem: a corrupt brother-in-law who was managing his father's carpentry workshop turns out to have evaded taxes for many years. As a result, the workshop is in danger of being expropriated by the government. Although they have profited from the economic Open Door Policy, none of his brothers and sisters is ready to invest in their father's business. Instead they consider the place as a suitable object for their own speculations. Hasan himself does not earn enough money in his job as bus and taxi driver to help out. But shortly before the expropriation he finds a solution. He decides to sell the taxi and accepts the offer of some friends to lend him money. But when Hasan finally gets hold of the money it is already too late. His father suffers a heart attack and dies.

However, Atef El-Tayeb does not end his film with the tragic death of the father. Instead he allows his protagonist a further scene. Echoing the opening scene, Hasan drives his overcrowded public bus and once again the passengers discover a pickpocket, who escapes through the window. But this time Hasan does not let the thief get away. He stops the bus, catches the man, and knocks him down.

The realism of the 1980s has discovered new enemies. Instead of the old landowners, it is unscrupulous businessmen, corrupt nouveaux riches, and thieves that have made it good. It is not poverty that is reproached now but uncontrolled materialism, which started, according to many films, during the period of the economic Open Door Policy (infitah) initiated by Sadat. The new materialism endangers even the unity of families. In *The Flood* (al-Tufan, 1985) by Bashir El-Dik, as in *The Bus Driver*, the grown-up children risk or even actively contribute to the death of their parents in order to enlarge their profit. Conflicts and rivalries that start between relatives and friends are terminated in many cases by a bloody showdown, as for example in *The Vagabonds* (al-Saᶜalik, 1983) by Daoud Abd El-Sayyed, in which two former urban tramps who have managed to get rich together, end up killing each other.

The concept of humanity in new realism differs essentially from that of the 1950s and 1960s. With the possibilities for social mobility during the period of *infitah*, the earlier determinism seems to have become outdated. The new heroes take the initiative, defend themselves, and are not afraid to use violence against the crooks, even though their personal aspirations to wealth are not fulfilled. Their moral struggle against materialism, egotism, and corruption makes them guardians of the family and traditional social norms.

Cinema of revolution in Algeria

The prerequisites for the development of Algerian realism differ considerably from those for Egyptian realism. Algerian film making started only in 1964, at a time when Egyptian realism had almost passed its first peak. The only audio-visual traditions that existed until then in Algeria were colonial propaganda and Pieds Noirs cinema. As a child of the war of independence,[54] Algerian cinema was characterized from the start by a considerable politicization, forming the basis of its revolutionary and didactic character and its constant endeavor to reshape society.

Like Egyptian realism, revolutionary cinema in Algeria developed schemes for representing reality. The often conventional and stereotyped dramatization of social and political conditions led to the appearance of clichés that contradicted the 'authenticity' of representation. While historical films on the war of independence became to some extent a variation of the American western, realism degenerated in part into a sort of political instruction and propaganda film.

During the first decade after independence, Algerian film making mainly concentrated on the period of the war of liberation. Until 1972, the majority of films dealt with the resistance against colonialism. In 1979, works like this still formed two thirds of the total production completed until then.[55] After the agrarian revolution (or land reform) in 1971, a so-called New Cinema *(sinima djidid)*[56] began gradually to open up to other subjects. Among the problems that film makers became increasingly occupied with were the social injustices of post-colonial society, emigration and foreign labor, in France in particular, as well as bureaucracy and female emancipation. With these topics, daily life started to gain importance over the exceptional situation of the war of liberation. This new orientation was to define the notion of *sinima djidid*. However, this new notion did not differentiate sufficiently between genres, as for example between realism and *cinéma d'auteur*, and hence, because of its partly agitating character, many works of Algerian realism could be described as a cinema of revolution rather than as New Cinema.

Naturalism

Like Italian neorealism, Algerian cinema was at first aided by the economic situation in attaining realist aesthetics. The lack of studios led automatically to a preference for authentic sets. In addition, the choice of the environment of the underprivileged classes as a subject and the absence of a star system allowed the use of amateur actors.

Wind From the Aurès (Rih al-Auras, 1966) by Mohamed Lakhdar

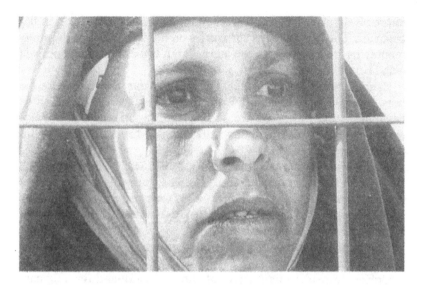

Kelthoum in *Wind From the Aurès* (Rih al-Auras, Algeria, 1966) by Mohamed Lakhdar Hamina (*courtesy Institut du Monde Arabe, Paris*)

Hamina, which is the second Algerian-directed full-length feature film (the first was in 1965), derives much of its realist quality from these two factors. Apart from the main character, most roles in the film are performed by amateurs. The story itself is set among the poorest of the poor: a village in the Aurès mountains is submitted to violent French bombardment, killing several of its inhabitants. A young man who loses his father in this attack decides to support the resistance against the occupiers. A short while later, French soldiers come to his home to arrest him. His mother waits in vain for him to return and finally sets out to search for him. Carrying two chickens and a food basket, she walks from one internment camp to another, until she reaches the place where her son has been detained. Everyday she comes to the barbed-wire fence in order to see him, defying the French guards' attempts to intimidate her. One day, the woman cannot find her son among the prisoners. Her long wait is useless, and in desperation she throws herself against the charged electric fence.

   The perspective of the film narration coincides completely with the confined horizon of the simple peasant woman. There is little treatment of the larger political context. The bombardment, the death of the husband, and the disappearance of the son happen suddenly with little preparation. An egg bursting in hot ashes or a dead chicken appear as signs of impending disaster. The naivety of the mother, impressively played by the actress Kelthoum, finds expression in her behavior. The two chickens she carries on her walk through the stony mountains are not food for the journey, but bribes that she hopes will help liberate her son.

Hamina barely misses a detail in his shots: the poor fittings of the huts, the mats, the earthen pots, the fireplace, and the chicken in its hatch in the wall. They are accorded no less importance than the face of the protagonist and her daily work, ranging from cleaning the hut to baking bread.

This faithfulness to the smallest details is a result of the director's close connection to his subject. Hamina himself comes from a peasant family and his narration is based on a real event. "*The Aurès Wind* represents, in a way, my grandmother's search, looking in vain for my father from one camp to another. . . . Without becoming biographical, nevertheless, I draw from my memory in order to find the right tone."[57]

Unlike most subsequent works of anti-colonialist and revolutionary Algerian cinema, *Wind From the Aurès* is not structured by the narrative principle of dramatic increase that gradually dissolves. The strong presence of objects and of human labor give the film an intensity that replaces the tension of 'drama' and places it in the tradition of naturalism. Events occur in a steady monotony, while characters are at the mercy of events, such as the French bombardment, for example. The film retains a "commitment to continuity, to the unfolding of a scene,"[58] creating the impression of a quasi-documentary observation. The characters are not the object of identification, but of distanced contemplation. The stream of action is mainly defined by the epic topic of search and barely reveals anything of the background, the social and political conflicts responsible for the hero's fate. The narrative structure of *Wind from the Aurès* is rather exceptional in Algerian film making, but its naturalist attitude in describing environment and characters has been adopted by many films.

Class struggle

The socialist orientation of Boumedienne's government after the declaration of the agrarian revolution in 1971 became visible in cinema, in form and in content. It resulted in an increased reference to the present, with more stress on internal Algerian social contradictions and hence stronger antagonisms in film plots. Apart from the peasants who dominated the films on the war of independence, other social groups were now represented, including industrial workers (*The Good Families*, al-Usar al-tayyiba, 1972), fishermen (*The Net*, al-

Shabaka, 1976) and Bedouins (*The Nomads*, Masirat al-ruᶜa, 1976). Controversial subjects were increasingly raised, like emigration (*Ali in Wonderland*, Ard al-sarab, 1978) and female emancipation (*The South Wind*, 1975; *Layla and her Sisters*, Layla wa akhawatiha, 1977; *A Wife for My Son*; Une femme pour mon fils, 1982). The introduction of a socialist economic order was dealt with most intensively in (*The Good Families, Barriers* (al-Hawadjiz, 1977), *El-Moufid* (al-Mufid), and *The Charcoal Maker* (al-Fahham). The antagonisms between different competing social interest groups dominated the plots of these films.

Noua (Nuwwa), shot in 1972 by Abdelaziz Tolbi, is set in 1954 and describes, by means of the inhuman conditions that the Algerian rural population was condemned to live under, the reasons leading to the armed struggle. Although the film carries the name of the village's beauty, Noua, her story forms only one episode in the network of often merely observant scenes. The local dignitaries, Qadi and Hadj (the native feudal landowner), and the French authorities—or better, their executive, the police—treat agricultural workers and lease-holders (*khammas* farmers)[59] at their own discretion. *Khammas* farmers who are in debt are mercilessly driven off their small plots of land, while their starving women and children try to get jobs as day laborers on the vast estates of French colons. The young girls are harassed by the native landlords. When Noua's father dares defend his daughter against the Hadj's sons, he is put in detention. Threatened with kidnapping and being sold to a brothel, Noua decides to escape. Together with a young agricultural worker whom she loves, she joins the resistance.

Tolbi's *Noua*, whose story is based on a novelette by Tahar Ouatar, presents a panorama of impoverishment and exploitation. It clearly illustrates how poor social conditions provoked the resistance against the French. Unlike the idealist films featuring resistance fighters that had prevailed until then in Algerian film making, this film, which was produced one year after land reform, refers consciously to the present. In Tolbi's words, "Even though the film is supposed to be set in 1954, the script is based on the life of the people and their daily reality that I saw in front of me. Those are the people who act in the film. All the parts, whether main or secondary parts, are acted by people who themselves live in this situation. . . . There is a text at the beginning of the film saying that the film was shot in 1972 without any embellishment or make-up. Nineteen fifty-four and 1972 are alike."[60]

In his film, Tolbi creates the impression of realism by doing without professional actors and by courageous camera work that does not shy away from dirt or poverty. Long sequences in the film are dedicated to the peasants' miserable housing and to images of emaciated, badly nourished people. Accompanied by symphonic music, these black and white shots pay tribute to Eisenstein and Pudowkin, who during the 1920s and 1930s described the poverty of the people with similarly impressive images. The essential stylistic feature of their films was the principle of montage based on juxtaposition and collision (also possible within one take) that is also partly followed in *Noua*. This method of editing is not meant so much to create temporal or spatial continuity as to uncover social antagonisms. The national struggle for liberation is linked, in *Noua*, in such a way, to the idea of class struggle. By visually confronting the privileged elite on the one hand, and the suppressed classes on the other, Abdelaziz Tolbi tries to make social injustice visible. For example, he shows a long line of bare feet belonging to men, women, and children queuing for work in front of the colons' elegant, white manor house. In the next sequence, an agricultural worker whose request has just been turned down walks along a road at the lower edge of the image. The angle slowly opens up and gives way to a view of a hill, above which the estate of the colons stands, surrounded by huge fields.

The Charcoal Maker (al-Fahham; Le Charbonnier, 1972) by Mohamed Bouamari follows the same editing principle as *Noua*, even though it is set in the time after independence. The charcoal maker and his family dwell in great poverty on a dilapidated farm. Without permission the head of the family cuts trees in the woods and works it to charcoal. But his goods do not find any buyers on the market since bottled gas has replaced them. No longer able to feed his family, the man vents his frustration on his wife and children. However he categorically rejects his wife's suggestion that she participate in supporting the family. Instead, he thinks of seeking work with the local landowner or even in the capital. Eventually, the charcoal maker travels to Algiers, hoping that a former co-fighter in the liberation war, who has become the director of a public company, may help him. But the functionary offers him only empty promises. Now, the charcoal maker realizes that the agrarian revolution abolishing traditional taboos and unjust property conditions is the only way out of his dilemma. In front of the village's dignitaries, he orders his wife to take off her veil and gives her permission to go to work.

Particularly in its second part, the structure of *The Charcoal Maker* is based on several antagonisms: rich and poor, traditional and modern, urban and rural, educated and uneducated. After the charcoal maker leaves his former comrade's office, he compares his deprived life in the countryside with the elegant comfort of the

The Charcoal Maker (al-Fahham; Le Charbonnier, Algeria, 1972) by Mohamed Bouamari (*courtesy Institut du Monde Arabe, Paris*)

capital. Then he contrasts his present situation with images of a better future. Although he himself is illiterate he imagines calling for his children when they come back from school, while he is wearing a suit. Images of his wife crouching on the mud floor, combing wool, are followed by shots of her standing in a factory hall observing a modern weaving machine. After her arduous attempts to set a wood fire—while the radio broadcasts an almond cake recipe—we see her handling clean pots on a gas stove.

The agrarian revolution: between tradition and modernity

In the period after the declaration of the agrarian revolution, the antagonism between progress and tradition, which had already been expressed in *The Charcoal Maker*, manifested itself parallel to class contradictions. Amar Laskri (ᶜAmmar al-ᶜAskari) for example, in his film *El-Moufid* (The Useful Man, 1978) mixes documentary and fictional images from the countryside and uses a large variety of opposites, including rich and poor, progressive and conservative. Shots of the procession of a religious brotherhood precede images of brand new combine harvesters and trucks, carrying young activists, who cheer for the agrarian revolution.

While many films of this sort idealized the aims of the agrarian revolution, the traditional social order characterized by feudalism, maraboutism, and sexual segregation, formed one of its main targets. *South Wind* (Rih al-djanub, 1975) by Mohamed Slim Riad presents an impoverished village in the mountains as a microcosm of rural Algerian society. The traditional order is represented through al-Qadir, a wealthy farmer. The progressive, influential mayor Malik, a former resistance fighter, is his opponent. An opportunistic school teacher tries to mediate between the two parties, while the poor farmers, day laborers, women, and children have little or no influence.

In order to use the mayor, al-Qadir wants to marry his daughter Nafisa to him. But it soon becomes clear that Malik, who represents the generation that, by resisting colonialism, paved the path to progress, is not at all interested in an alliance with the big landowner. The real holders of the future, however, are the youth. Nafisa and a young shepherd both leave the village with its entrenched structures, Nafisa to continue her studies, and the man to join a cooperative and educate himself.

The film's message is clear: it upholds the socialist economic model vis-à-vis rural misery, manifested in poverty, superstition, and the lack of medical care. Traditional culture, unable to contribute to the creation of a better society, is perceived as an obstacle to development. Religion also, represented in the film only through superstitious customs, constitutes an obstacle. The sole religious authority appearing in *South Wind* is an old marabout, to whom al-Qadir turns for help when his daughter breaks down while protesting against the arranged marriage planned by her father. The old man's attempt to 'cure' the girl with magic formulas seems anachronistic and ridiculous, given her real situation.

Discrediting traditional culture by means of Marxist social analysis is also a feature of works of the 1980s, such as Mohamed Chouikh's *The Citadel* (al-Qalᶜa, 1988). Qaddur is a servant living in the stable of an affluent fabric merchant. He takes care of the animals, the shop and looks after his master's four wives. Qaddur himself cannot afford to marry, but has to be satisfied trying to catch a glimpse of the neighbor's beautiful wife, who hangs out her linen in the sun everyday. In an effort to gain her attention, he steals a small piece of fabric from the shop in order to pay the marabout for a love potion. But the magician orders him to bring a strand of the woman's hair. Qaddur succeeds in entering the neighbor's house and tries to cut off a curl of the woman's hair, which causes her to panic. When the fabric merchant learns about the incident, he swears to marry Qaddur off that very day. The fulfillment of his vow, however, turns out to be far more complicated then he had expected. All the women of the village are taken. Even in the local brothel, none can be found. In order to save face, the merchant decides to prepare the wedding nonetheless. When the unsuspecting Qaddur enters the bride's room, he finds only a rigid display dummy. In front of the assembled guests Qaddur throws himself from a cliff.

The Citadel discredits so-called traditional culture in part by its negative representation of religious authority. The marabouts are dismissed as hypocritical magicians and avaricious swindlers, supporting an unjust and inhuman system. Moreover, Chouikh represents institutionalized polygamy and arranged marriages as a result of unjust property conditions. The traditionally described social and family order seems deprived of any positive aspects. And, as Qaddur's example proves, it cannot be escaped except by flight or self-destruction. By presenting a completely negative example, the film argues for a modern, 'humane,' and progressive social order.

However, the appeal to cultural revolution in Algerian cinema sometimes hides, in its core, a conservative morality. In *The Net* (1976) by Ghouti Bendeddouche, Mu^cammar is hardly able to support himself and his wife through his work on a fishing boat. One day on his way home he meets a beautiful town-dweller who has had a car accident on the mountainous road. Seduced by the idea of wealth and comfort, Mu^cammar decides to try his luck in the city. But he cannot find the beautiful woman again or get an adequate job. After a while, he returns home disillusioned. Here he is confronted with new problems, for the wealthy Si Khalifa wants to monopolize fishing and fish processing in the region. Together with some friends, Mu^cammar mobilizes the fishermen and workers of the fish factory, incites them to strike, and initiates the foundation of a cooperative.

The double standards of *The Net* emerge clearly in its portrayal of women. Although at the end of the film, Mu^cammar's wife Laliya leads the female workers of Si Khalifa's fish factory to strike, she never appears as a self-motivated, active personality. Her gestures and facial expressions signify, without exception, her timidity and resignation. Laliya's decision to work in the factory was not based on her personal desires, but was forced by Mu^cammar's absence—he had left her for three years without any financial support. Laliya's anger against her husband does not lead to real independence however. On the contrary, in the course of the strike, she gets closer to her husband again because of their common political interest. Thus, Laliya's emancipation seems attainable only in the framework of a greater social plan of agrarian or socialist revolution, and is not based on an individual, internally motivated act. Indeed, the man's

desires are also subordinated to the same ideal. Muᶜammar's escape
does not lead to individual freedom but to social and political
responsibility.

Ṣinima djidid

The Net has a plot structure that is repeated in many Algerian films
dealing with the agrarian revolution. Only two options are given to
the miserable peasants and workers. They can either surrender to the
good will of local entrepreneurs (big landowners and industrials)
who, as a rule, do not shrink from criminal actions, or they can adopt
the ideas of the agrarian revolution and join a cooperative. The
conflict developing between the two parties is most often resolved by
use of force, for example in a violent brawl.

The stereotypical cut of subjects is due to a functionalization of
narration, serving two different ends. Entertainment is supposed to
achieve economic success, and simultaneously a political message is
to be transmitted. This specific commercialism, spreading in state-
produced films, was furthered by several film makers who held
important posts in the field of cinema, including Ahmed Rachedi.

Only a few Algerian directors were able to combine their didactic
and socially critical intentions in an unusual form.[61] *Tahya ya Didou*
(literally, 'Long live Didou!,' 1971) by Mohamed Zinet is a conglom-
erate of documentary and fictional shots commented on by the poet
Didou. Scenes of the streets of the now independent Algiers mix with
Didou's poetic impressions. Narrative scenes are set in between,
including a group of rebellious children who tease a policeman, and a
French tourist couple leading a conversation about changes in the
country since independence. In the course of events, the husband
turns out to have worked for French state security forces. In a restaurant, he unexpectedly meets one of his victims, whom he had
tortured. But his fear of exposure is unnecessary. The man is blind
and cannot recognize his former tormentor.

Mohamed Bouamari's (Muhammad Buᶜammari) film *First Step*
(Awwal khutwa, 1978) also combines an unusual narrative form with
a realist attitude. To get in the mood, the actors present themselves
and their characters at the beginning. The background story as such
is undercut with the protagonists' fantasies and with flashbacks to
their personal histories, in addition to a line of action that is set in a
past historical age. The different, indirectly connected stories center
around a female teacher, who is the first woman to be elected mayor
in a small Algerian provincial town. The marital crisis in which she
and her husband find themselves after her election forms the
background story. Although the self-aware teacher has married her

husband out of love and he himself theoretically approves women's equality, he in fact has difficulties accepting her influential position.

The female scriptwriter, Fatiha Nadjar, uses the marital disagreement as an opportunity to examine the difficulties of a relationship based on partnership in a patriarchal society. Scenes imagined by the protagonists, in which they go through different possible forms of gender relations, award the narration the character of a model. The unfamiliarity that is created by the introduction of competing narrative levels underlines this impression. Accordingly, the individuality of the characters is neutralized. Conflicts resulting from gender relations seem to be socially defined.

A totally different tone is introduced in Merzak Allouache's film *Omar Gatlato*, which can be classified formally as *cinéma d'auteur*. It is one of the first Algerian feature films to immerse itself in the daily life of urban youth. Instead of forcing social antagonisms into an omnipresent dramatic structure, *Omar Gatlato* draws its tension from the regularity of a young employee's daily life. Allouache breaks realist conventions by replacing the omniscient realist discourse with subjective narration. The protagonist addresses the spectator directly in his monologues and thus makes uncritical identification impossible.

Official Algerian cinema's preoccupation with social and political subjects has persisted into the early 1990s, when many films started addressing either issues of women's liberation or the question of Muslim fundamentalism or both. These films include *Sahara Blues* (1992) by Rabah Bouberas, *Radhia* (1992) by Mohamed Lamine Merbah, *Touchia* (Taushiha, 1993) by Rashid bin Hadj, *Youssef or the Legend of the Seventh Sleeper* (Yusuf aw usturat al-na'im al-sabiᶜ, 1993) by Mohamed Chouikh, and *Female Demon* (Démon au feminin, 1993) by Hafsa Zinat-Koudil. Some of these films are marked by a slight departure from official political discourses and, more importantly, increasingly place the individual in conflict with his social surroundings.

However, in general, Algerian 'cinema of revolution' hardly managed to link social critique with an adequate representation of different social groups for being burdened with 'political commission.' Largely dictated by official policy, the majority of films do not realize the authenticity demanded by the Algerian philosopher Mostefa Lacheraf by transmitting "a vision of itself or of the world implicating a way to live, taste, choices, a collective memory, familiar gestures, or even a language whose words stem from immediate experience or from a far and inherited mysterious practice."[62] Instead, Algerian realism has devoted itself to presenting a clear cut, often negative, reality while demanding the realization of utopia, thus imprinting its 'revolutionary' political ideals on reality.

The Alternative Cinema in Syria

Like the Algerian revolutionary cinema, Syrian state production has been highly politicized. In 1972, during the First Damascus Festival for Young Arab Cinema *(Mihradjan Dimashq al-Awal li-Sinima al-Shabab al-ʿArabi)*, organized by the National Film Organization, it started to manifest its orientation.[63] The works of committed film makers, including a representative of the Egyptian New Cinema Society, Ali Abd El-Khalek, the Egyptian Taufik Salih, the Kuwaiti Khalid al-Siddiq, the Syrians Nabil Maleh and Khaled Hamada, and the Iraqi Kaiss al-Zubaidi set themselves apart from commercial Arab cinema by their specific ideology. Their goals, summarized by the Arab film critic Munir al-Saʿidanni, were:

- to express sincerely Arab reality and the worries of the Arab human being,
- to develop an Arab film making that derives from Arab culture and is based on it, and
- to arrange this cinema in a way that attracts audiences, enabling it to play a positive role in social life."[64]

In accordance with these demands, which consciously opposed commercial Arab, notably Egyptian, cinema, the participants of the festival coined the notion of Alternative Cinema *(al-sinima al-badila)*, which the Egyptian film critic Samir Farid, who helped organize the festival, had already used of the New Cinema Society in Egypt.[65] The pursuit of these goals transformed the Syrian film organization during the early 1970s into a collecting pool for a number of progressive non-Syrian Arab directors. Their films were characterized by their socialist orientation and an even stronger expression of nationalist and Pan-Arab ideas.

The Pan-Arab orientation of Syria and the close relation to Palestinian film makers led the Festival of Young Arab Cinema in Damascus to issue a statement regarding Palestinian cinema. Its promotion was seen as a support and a supplement to the armed struggle.[66] Thus, the idea of the Alternative Cinema also reached Lebanon. Adopted by revolutionary Palestinian film making, which was concentrating at that time in Lebanon, it exerted an indirect influence on Lebanese directors and found an expression primarily in the documentary field.[67]

The dominance ·of the Palestinian question in Damascus did not only express itself on a verbal level: Between 1969 and 1972 three out of five full-length feature films produced by the Syrian film organization dealt with Palestine.[68] Five years after the Six Day War and the subsequent occupation of the rest of Palestine by Israel, and only one year after Black September in Jordan, the Palestinian question was inevitably in the fore of any political discussion. Moreover, the specific commitment to the Palestinian cause has been used by the regime of Hafiz al-Assad, who came to power in 1971 supported by the small religious minority of Alawis, as a means of political legitimization. It was related to the notion of Arab unity that was evoked by the political leadership in order to strengthen Arab-Syrian nationalism.[69] Eventually, the preoccupation with Palestine helped to divert attention from the country's internal political conflicts.

The Palestinian question, as well as the second most important subject of Syrian realism, social injustice, were mainly derived from literary works by Syrian and other Arab writers, such as Hanna Mina, Haidar Haidar, Zakariya Tamir, Ghassan Kanafani, ᶜAli Zain al-ᶜAbidin al-Husaini, and Diya' al-ᶜAzawi.[70] These films include *The Leopard* (al-Fahd, 1972) by Nabil Maleh and *al-Yazerli* (1974) by Kaiss al-Zubaidi. They shared their orientation with realist Arab literature, which has dedicated itself to the ideals of sociopolitical commitment and responsibility *(iltizam)*.[71]

The Egyptian director Taufik Salih created one such 'committed' work with *The Duped* (al-Makhduᶜun, Syria, 1972), based on the realist novel *Men under the Sun* by the Palestinian writer Ghassan Kanafani.[72] Directed and adapted by an Egyptian, written by a Palestinian, and financed with Syrian money, *The Duped* must be considered a Pan-Arab production par excellence. Its story deals with the attempt of three Palestinian refugees to enter Kuwait from Iraq, hoping to find jobs there with which they can support their families in the refugee camps. A Palestinian truck driver agrees to smuggle them through the desert into Kuwait. The refugees hide in his empty watertank, which is heated by the burning sun, and wait for the truck to pass the check at the borders. Usually the formalities take only a few minutes, but this time the Kuwaiti guards are bored and want the truck driver to entertain them. While they delay the process, the sound of the air conditioners drown out the men's cries for help, and they die in the heat of the blazing tank.

Salih's film was one of the first to give Pan-Arab slogans a more solid base and to state the common responsibility of the Arab states for the disastrous situation of the Palestinians. Taufik Salih introduces the film with a documentary sequence depicting the refugees'

The Duped (al-Makhdu ͨ un, Syria, 1972) by Taufik Salih (*courtesy National Film Organization, Damascus*)

misery and their hopeless situation in the camps. He then illustrates
the difficulties of the protagonists, who have neither the money nor
valid papers to obtain a work permit in one of the affluent neighboring countries.

In contrast, *Kafr Kassem* (Kafr Qassim, 1974) by the Lebanese
Borhane Alaouié uses a historical event, the 1956 massacre by the
Israeli army of the inhabitants of Kafr Kassem, as an opportunity for
political analyses. Following the nationalization of the Suez Canal
and on the eve of the tripartite attack on Egypt by France, Great
Britain, and Israel, the Israeli army, as in the earlier raid on Deir
Yassin, was trying to set an example and prevent a Palestinian
uprising in Israel.[73] The film shows the army declaring a sudden and
unexpected curfew without informing the peasants working in their
fields outside the village. Later, when they return home they are shot
down by the patrols.

Alaouié's film reconstructs these murders only passingly. It focuses
on the daily life of the villagers and the internal conflicts that arise
from a variety of ideological points of views ranging from opportunism toward the Israelis to explicit Pan-Arabism. It underlines also
that, with the exception of a few collaborators and some marginalized

communists, the majority of the villagers perceive the nationalization of the Suez Canal as heralding their own liberation. Finished in 1974, seven years after the 1967 defeat, the film ends with the bloodbath of innocent civilians and demonstrates how much the Palestinians have been let down by their Arab neighbors.

Like *The Duped* and the three episodes of *Men under the Sun* (Ridjal taht al-shams; *not*, like *The Duped*, an adaptation of Kanafani's novel) by Nabil Maleh, Marwan Mu'zin, and Muhammad Shahin (1970), *Kafr Kassem* states the inefficiency of Arab politics regarding the Palestinian cause and faults the absence of a real Pan-Arab attitude. All three films make clear that claimed Arab solidarity with the Palestinians is characterized by hypocrisy and weakness.

Criticism of the Palestinians themselves is expressed in *The Knife* (al-Sikkin, 1972) by Khaled Hamada, based on Ghassan Kanafani's story *All That's Left to You* (Ma tabbaqa lakum). A young Palestinian leaves his country and escapes into the desert, abandoning his only sister to the mercy of an unscrupulous informer who has seduced her and forced her into marriage. The characters of the film are not meant to be read as individuals with a personal history, but as abstract symbols. The young man signifies the Palestinian refugee who abandons his country—personified by a helpless virgin—to the

Kafr Kassem (Kafr Qassim, Syria, 1974) by Borhane Alaouié (*courtesy National Film Organization, Damascus*)

attacker. The accusation that the Palestinians have deserted their homeland without struggling is clear.

The Duped uses a similarly allegorical and moralist narration. The three refugees represent three different generations of exile, whereas the truckdriver who lost his manhood during the war symbolizes the well established, careless emigré Palestinian. The film approaches the Palestinian question more on the rhetorical than on the analytical level. The defeat from which Palestinians suffered most seems a result of moral failure. It is not the complicated network of Arab and international political power games that is made responsible, but stupidity, egocentrism, cowardice, and the missing virility of the Arabs themselves.

Alternative Cinema uses almost without exception the conventions of the 'revolutionary' realism. Similar to the revolutionary Algerian cinema it aims not to represent real conditions but to revolutionize them. To use the words of the Syrian critic, Saᶜid Murad, the realism of Alternative Cinema derives its existence "from the human conflict that aims to change reality toward progress."[74] The negative representation of reality serves to mobilize the viewer in particular on the moral level and to incite him to change conditions.

Documents of daily life

Another realist tendency appeared in the course of the 1970s. In 1972, the Iraqi film *The Thirsty* (al-Zami'un) by Mohamed Choukri Jamil used, despite its fictional action, a style close to documentary.[75] In the same year in Tunisia, Brahim Babai shot his 16 mm film *And Tomorrow* (Wa ghadan, 1972), in which three unemployed young men try in vain to escape rural misery by migrating to the city. In Morocco too, during the 1970s and early 1980s several semi-documentaries and docu-dramas were produced, such as *The Days* by Ahmed El-Maanouni, *The Big Journey* by Mohamed Ben Abderrahmane Tazi, *A Thousand and One Hands* by Souheil Ben Baraka, and *The Barber of the Poor Neighborhood* (Halaq darb al-fuqara', 1982) by Mohamed Reggab.

In *The Days* (Alyam, alyam, 1978)[76] a young peasant's son recounts his daily problems and troubles. He is fed up with the hard, barely profitable work in the fields and hopes to find a job in Europe. Shots from his daily life, his family, and their domestic surrounding are undercut with performances in which the protagonists reenact events that happened to them. The slow pace resulting from the film's observant style offers the affected persons a chance to represent their daily life and their problems.

The Days (Alyam, Alyam, Morocco, 1978) by Ahmed El-Maanouni (*courtesy Institut du Monde Arabe, Paris*)

The Big Journey (Ibn al-sabil; Le grand voyage, 1982) by Mohamed Ben Abderrahmane Tazi and *A Thousand and One Hands* (Alf yad wa yad, 1972) by Souheil Ben Baraka are both framed by fictional action, but are, nevertheless, very much concerned to achieve restrained, documentary, and observant camera work. *The Big Journey* tells the story of a truckdriver whose load gets stolen. Too scared to face his boss, he decides to disappear. He sells the truck in order to escape illegally to Spain. However, the men who are supposed to smuggle him into Spain desert him on the open sea.

Tazi's *The Big Journey* offers an impressive panorama of the Moroccan underworld, the community of the dispossessed, thieves, smugglers, prostitutes, and have-nots. The truckdriver is driven into criminality by social conditions, as is the protagonist of *A Thousand and One Hands*. In the latter, an old wool dyer working for a carpet manufacturer suffers an industrial accident. His son wants to ask his father's former employer for a job so that he can support his mother and his brothers and sisters. As he is never allowed into the office of the carpet manufacturer, he decides to go to the entrepreneur's villa. The French wife of the industrialist cannot bear the sight of the young man's dirty feet on her precious carpets. When she hysterically throws him out he gets violent. Eventually, instead of getting a job, the dyer's son lands in prison.

In all three films, documentary realism is achieved by using amateur actors and illustrating extensively the surroundings and living conditions of the lower classes. Their pessimist view of the prevailing conditions is obvious. The truckdriver and the dyer are both incapable of standing up to social pressure. They are uprooted; neither the traditional social structures, family and village, nor their religious beliefs offer them sufficient security. Although the family of the wool dyer undertake a long and exhausting pilgrimage to a saint's monument they are not immune to the coming misfortune. Capitalist society is depicted as a ruthless machine in which only the rich and powerful are able to survive. The development of such a social determinist view seems inevitable in the shadow of an authoritarian capitalist system and appears in juxtaposition to various social problems, among others, the gender issue.

Aisha, the protagonist of Jilalli Ferhati's *Aisha* (ᶜAra'is min qasab; literally, 'sugar dolls,' Morocco, 1982) is an orphan growing up in the house of an aunt. Since early childhood, she has learned to obey and respond to orders without objection. The moment Aisha menstruates for the first time, she is married off. Soon after, Aisha's husband dies and leaves her alone with two children. In order to support her family Aisha takes up a job as a cleaner in an office. There she meets an employee and becomes involved in an affair with him. When she becomes pregnant, she is taken to court by her male relatives and deprived of her children's custody.

The film's action proceeds rather slowly. Observations of traditional practices, such as the preparation of tea, a visit to the Turkish bath, or the wedding ceremony are given much space. The protagonist herself hardly speaks, her feelings are rarely made visible, except for a few quite obvious reactions, such as her mourning for her husband or her crying at court when she is deprived of her children. Ambiguous feelings or rebellion do not occur. The documentary style of the film does not allow internal depictions of the characters. They are simply objects of observation.

The basic attitude of *Aisha* is pessimistic. The protagonist seems to be helplessly submissive to her fate. However, like the already cited semi-documentaries, the film does not use the stylistic repertoire of melodrama in order to underline its message. One reason for the absence of melodrama in the works of this period may be the lack of a local mass audience interested in Moroccan cinema. Moreover, the social criticism, the 'dirty' images and the amateur actors used in these semi- and quasi-documentaries may be considered a counter-reaction to the dominant folklorizing tendency of CCM's (Centre Cinématographique Marocain) productions, which aimed to show the country in the best possible light.[77] However, that a critical cinema should in fact develop was not guaranteed, as the representation of poverty and social injustice was officially disapproved of. *Spring Sun* by Latif Lahlou, which appeared in 1970, had to cut a scene in which the main character is told about the misery of his home village.[78] *The Days* was also censored and *A Thousand And One Hands* did not find a Moroccan distributor. By contrast, the social-determinist Moroccan films met with deep interest in the West: *Aisha,* for example, was coproduced by the German channel ZDF.

The fact that these films adopted the aesthetics and shooting techniques of the documentary might also be due to the low production costs of the genre. Furthermore, they appeared in a period of a general flourishing in the field of documentary. Documentary movements like 'direct cinema' and 'cinéma vérité' in the West had been supported in the course of the 1960s by liberal and leftist ideologies on the one hand and by the introduction of a sophisticated, professionalized 16 mm technique on the other. In the Arab countries too, critical, leftist-oriented documentary movements developed. Their representatives include the Syrian Omar Amiralay, the Egyptians Attiat El-Abnoudi, Hashim al-Nahas, Ahmad Rashid, and Khairy Beshara, the Lebanese Jean Chamoun, Randa Chahal, Jocelyne Saab, and Heiny Srour, and the Palestinians May Masri and Ghaleb Chaath.

Satirical realism

Satirical realism appeared in several Arab countries. Unlike conventional realism, which tends to confirm official leftist ideologies, satirical realism often takes a rather oppositional and subversive attitude. Sometimes it even parodies binarisms such as progress and tradition or power and dispossession. In general, the Arab satire is less concerned with a faithful reflection of surrounding and characters. With its ironic distortions it questions the realist representation and subverts its idealistic and propagandistic contents, particularly regarding social liberation, progress, and modernity.

In *Sun of the Hyenas* (Shams al-diba*c*, 1977), the Tunisian director Reda Behi describes the destruction of a fishing village by tourism. The inhabitants, whose lives are still dominated by traditional structures, are taken by surprise by a government plan to construct several holiday resorts in the area. The narration follows meticulously the process of modernization, which ruins the fishermen and their families, ultimately reducing them to beggars and souvenir merchants.

Sun of the Hyenas achieves its satirical effect by distorting and caricaturing many characters. While it tends to represent the inhabitants, their daily life, their fears, and joys realistically, the functionaries and

Sun of the Hyenas (Shams al-diba^c, Tunisia, 1977) by Reda Behi

the foreign entrepreneurs who are invading the area are disfigured by ultra wide-angle shots and worm's eye views. Thus, the film states its position clearly: It wants the political leadership to be exposed.

A similar criticism of modernity is formulated in the Moroccan film *Zeft* (Zift; literally, 'tar,' 1984) by the Moroccan Taieb Saddiki, adapted from a theater play called *Sidi Yasin on the Way* (Sidi Yasin fi-l-tariq). The film discredits the ruthlessly modernizing political leadership, and dissociates itself also from traditional social structures. The simple peasant, Bouazza, becomes the victim of a strange conspiracy. An old man in the village dies and is declared as a marabout by his business-oriented relatives. Unfortunately, the piece of land on which they plan to construct his monument belongs to Bouazza. His repeated complaints to the authorities, however, cannot prevent the construction of the saint's shrine on his field. A short while later, the peasant is confronted with an invasion of pilgrims, who eventually drive him off his land. However, Bouazza's expropriation is not completed yet. The authorities want to develop the region and start building huge highways. Finally, a tiny traffic island on which stands the shrine is all that is left of Bouazza's land. Its former owner roams as a vagabond along the asphalt roads.

Taieb Saddiki's satire is thus a double-edged sword. It counters the abuse of maraboutism and at the same time criticizes the thoughtless belief in progress. His main target is the political leadership, which uses both tradition and modernity to realize solely its own interests.

However, ambiguous depictions are not the only way to deconstruct political ideals. Using anti-heroes is another possibility, as the Algerian Mohamed Lakhdar Hamina proved by introducing Hassan Terro, the reluctant resistance fighter. The Syrian film *The Nights of the Jackal* (Layali ibn awa, 1989) by ᶜAbd al-Latif ᶜAbd al-Hamid uses a similar strategy. Its anti-hero is a charming but excessively egocentric peasant from the Golan who tyrannizes his family. He is particularly inflexible when his children want to follow their own ways. Against his father's will, the son has managed to settle in the city, but the daughter is prevented from marrying her beloved. The mother patiently tolerates her husband's moods. She does not even object when he wakes her up every night to drive away the jackals with a shrill whistle. Although their howling keeps him awake, he cannot chase them away himself. When the Six Day War breaks out the father is euphoric. He listens to the march music on the radio and waves his fists as if to threaten the enemy's airplanes. His feelings are dampened only when he receives the news of his son's death. Ultimately, his empire disintegrates with the country's military defeat. The daughter leaves with her beloved and the mother dies. Left alone, the proud patriarch is not even able to defend himself against the howling of the jackals.

ᶜAbd al-Hamid uses in his satirical comedy the same allegories prevalent in other works of Arab realism. The father represents the nation's leadership, who have overestimated their strength, fighting the superior enemy (airplanes) with empty rhetoric (radios) and inadequate means (bare fists). By oppressing the other members of society (the family) they have caused a weakness that has in turn facilitated the defeat. By means of his paternal anti-hero the director shakes patriarchal family structures and the male claim to leadership.

This satirical realism is first and foremost an attempt to deconstruct Arab realism's omnipresent socialist and nationalist discourses, which rely on conceptual and narrative binarisms, often dissolved one-sidedly, while deepening the gulf between pessimism and utopia, modernity and tradition.

History in cinema

After his father's death Wanis learns that his tribe is living on tomb robbery. He thinks it ignominious to participate in defiling tombs and starts asking questions about those who have been laid there to rest. Are they his own ancestors? And what do the signs mean that they have left on the walls of the tombs and temples? Soon Wanis discovers that the archaeologists who come from far away know how to decipher these hieroglyphs. Wanis's decision to betray to them the location of the tombs marks the painful process of becoming aware of his own history.

In *The Mummy* (1969) the Egyptian director Chadi Abdessalam illustrates the dangers that accompany the conscious acquisition of history. Historical consciousness may furnish a person with a sense of identity and community or, on the contrary, deprive him of his previous basis of life and force him to change his position. History is no status quo, no objective measure. Historical (and religious) documents are repeatedly called in and reinterpreted when present positions have to be legitimized. The same happens in the Arab countries, when debating the national, confessional, or ethnic identity, or while negotiating progress and tradition.

Thus, history may be used as a weapon in the fight for political or cultural positions.[79] The resulting historicism serves to strengthen the chipped identity, particularly when a society is subjected to rapid changes. "To the extent to which our surroundings are being destroyed, to which we lose our identity with places and groups of persons, they get reconstructed in the museum."[80] Historicism is a characteristic of modernity. It helps society to compensate for the decrease in familiarity resulting from rapid change and profound modernization in all its spheres of life.[81]

Cinema too can produce historicism or historicizing views. The realistic capabilities of the media, its analogies to reality, confer specific credibility on historical representations. Costumes, styles, and settings that are true to the original provide an ostensibly authentic representation and enable the historical film to suggest universality and to form our image of past ages.

History as a setting

In the Arab countries, it was the literature of the early twentieth century that had the job of reproducing history on the fictional level. Hence, the historical novel stood at the beginning of modern Arab literature and enabled it to take up a position in modernity.[82] Stories from the Prophet's time or about extraordinary historical Arab personalities served awakening Arab nationalism as self-assuring projections.

Nonetheless, the number of historical films produced by Arab countries has remained relatively low. One of the reasons is the high budgets required for this genre. Between 1935 and 1950 Egypt produced only seven seriously historical films. Another dozen works shot during the same period were furnished with historical touches and contained popular fairy-tales or legends, such as Antar and Abla, Ali Baba and the Forty Thieves, Abu Zayd al-Hilali, or Djuha. With a few exceptions, such as Ahmad Galal's *Shadjarat al-Durr* (1935) and Ahmed Badrakhan's *Dananir,* most films were not based on a modern literary model, nor did they demonstrate profound historical knowledge.

In Egypt, the first realizations of historical themes were essentially governed by business considerations. Producers seemed to be well aware of the legendary past's allure: "For the first time enchanting Arab palaces, beautiful historical buildings, patterned Arab garments, old Egyptian feasts, dances, and songs from *A Thousand and One Nights* will appear. For the first time an Arab company uses one hundred of the famous Arab racing horses who all made a name for themselves in racing. They perform wearing the prettiest decoration, presenting the most beautiful gaits while proving the elegance of their dance." Thus reads the announcement of Ahmad Galal's *Shadjarat al-Durr* whose production had been assumed by Assia Daghir, who also starred in the role of the legendary Egyptian Mamluk queen.[83]

According to the Egyptian film critic Kamal Ramzi the story line deviates only insignificantly from that of its literary model, a novel by Djirdji Zaydan, though it does not follow so much the historical events as the amorous adventures and intrigues of the main characters. Similar to Hollywood's grandiose spectacles, this movie aimed primarily to attract the audiences by its exceptional visual appeal.

Other historical films, such as *Dananir* (1940) by Ahmed Badrakhan and *Sallama* (1945) by Togo Mizrahi also exploit the hold that the pomp of past times exerts on audiences. Both films star Umm Kulthum as a musically talented slave; the first is set in the Abbassid period, the second in Umayyad times, both in the heyday of classical Islamic culture.

Besides its rich sets, the palaces, harems, and glittering garments, *Dananir* is full to the brim with famous and legendary figures, from the caliph Harun al-Rashid and his milk-brother and later adversary, the Barmakid prince Dja°far b. Yahia, to the poet Abu Nuwas (Hasan b. Hani al-Hakami), who is considered the father of unconventional Arab poetry.[84] The screenplay writers demonstrate their familiarity with the biography of these personalities as well as with historical detail.

As the film illustrates musical performances were a feature of the Abbassid court. Abu Nuwas, whose fame derives from his erotic and bacchanalian pieces *(khamriyat),* in which he praised the wine and his male lovers,[85] appears in the film also as fond of wine and poetry, although his homoerotic inclinations are inevitably concealed. The character of Dja°far's slave is also based on historical documentation.[86] In the film she is instructed in singing by a teacher called al-Mausili. The brothers Ibrahim and Ishaq al-Mausili were the most acclaimed singing teachers of that time.[87]

However, this is where the film's faithfulness to history ends. Dja°far seems imbued with loyalty to the caliph and honest friendship. His fall is put down to the malicious intrigue of his opponents at court. The interpretation of the vizier's struggle with the sovereign for power is neither realistic nor put into a proper historical context. The slave Dananir is stylized as a symbol of eternal self-denying love. The tragic finale, ending with the death of her beloved, reveals the narrative's real intentions: the events are forced into the sentimental corset of melodrama. Thus history forms the extraordinary frame of a quite ordinary drama.

The reckless adaptation of a historical subject to the conventions of a genre, the use of history as a mere setting, leads to an undermining and arbitrary reinterpretation of history. This can be seen in numerous quotations and allusions in *Dananir* to the cultural

Publicity poster for *Dananir* (Egypt, 1940/41) by Ahmed Badrakhan

achievements of a glorious Islamic past. Thus, the presentation of the culture of the period—its music, dance, and poetry—simply aims to glorify the reign of the Abbassid caliphs and to feed the myth of the legendary golden age of Islam, which in turn underlines the splendor of Arab-Muslim culture in general and serves as a cultural reaffirmation.

Similar 'de-historicizations' still occur today, as the spectacular French-Egyptian coproduction *Adieu Bonaparte!* (Wadaᶜa Bonaparte, 1985) by Youssef Chahine shows. Despite its reference to a major historical event—Napoleon's expedition to Egypt in 1788—the interpretation of characters and events mainly follow the personal views of the *auteur* director. Its story involves three young brothers, Bakr, Yahia, and Ali, as well as the French General Cafarelli. The thoughtful and erudite Cafarelli is filled with a partly paternal, partly homoerotic inclination to the charming Ali. Ali in turn is "passionately poetic and curious, ready for a discourse with the French, but absolutely willing to find his identity and to fight for it, a guerrilla of love, whose heroism lies in his disarming, passionate frankness."[88] He and Cafarelli use their encounter to learn as much as possible from each other.

As in an earlier work of Chahine, *Alexandria Why?* (Iskandariya, lih? 1978), set during the 1940s in Alexandria, the human relations of *Adieu Bonaparte!* develop across religious and ethnic borders. Parallel

Adieu, Bonaparte! (Wadaᶜa Bonaparte, 1985) by Youssef Chahine

battles are fought between Egyptian nationalists and the British, and Mamluks and the French. Chahine's alter ego, always acted by Muhsin Muhi al-Din, appears in both films as the charming, young hero who tears down the emotional borders between genders and nations.

The realist cinematic discourse supported by authentic costumes, props, and settings, pretends to reflect the "spirit of the epoch."[89] In reality, *Adieu Bonaparte!* hardly explains the historical context in which the Napoleonic expedition to Egypt took place. At most, it suggests that the conflict between nationalism and modern imperialism in Egypt may have started at that point. The French invasion, which initiated the further colonialization of the Near East and introduced the radical cultural changes that characterize its daily life today, serves the director primarily as an opportunity to reconcile with the aggressive West.

How idealizing Chahine's message is is made more apparent by its omissions. Cafarelli's enlightened openness cannot be considered representative: it scarcely corresponds with the European complacency of that time, which had been expressed in various orientalist writings and, indeed, had driven forward the military occupation of Egypt.[90] Furthermore, the characters' encounter with modern cannons and telescopes signifies the false idea of Napoleon's expedition as the starting point of enlightenment and modernity in Egypt.

The French, however, did not instruct the Egyptians, impress the elite intellectually, or leave their printing press when they retreated, nor did they circulate their famous *Description d'Egypte*, which was published in France in 1809 and translated into Arabic only in 1976.[91]

Arab culture and thinking are also misrepresented. Chahine's Egyptians, who encounter the great names of history, including Napoleon Bonaparte, comprise the director's usual repertoire of an urban family including the super-mother—the ultimate symbol of Egypt—the helpless father, the dying brother, in addition to numerous political fanatics, multi-cultural couples, and, most important, the young hero who is always possessed by love.[92] There seems to be no space in the director's private spectacle for historically documented Egyptian personalities, such as Ya°qub al-Sa°idi, the Coptic manager and constant companion of the French general Desaix who served as a mediator during the invasion, or the Muslim chronicler °Abd al-Rahman al-Djabarti, who tried to understand and draw conclusions from the French expedition in the specific light and philosophy of his own time and culture. Instead, the film underlines the idea of Egyptian technical backwardness on the one hand and tolerance on the other—after all, it is the friendly openness with which the majority of the Egyptian protagonists meet other races and religions, including the occupiers, which makes them culturally superior to their Western opponents.

Allegories of the contemporary

In Egyptian cinema the appropriation and interpretation of history became far more politically purposeful during the post-colonial era than it was during the 1930s and 1940s. While in 1941, the commander Saladin (Salah al-Din al-Ayubi) was only worth a poorly designed adventure film produced by the Lama brothers,[93] twenty years later, in Youssef Chahine's spectacle *Saladin* (al-Nasir Salah al-Din, literally, 'the victorious Saladin,' 1963), he had become a Pan-Arab national hero. In comparison with his opponents, the estranged and rapacious Crusaders, Chahine's Saladin appears as a symbol of pure justice and chivalry. His slogan leading the Arab allies to victory is 'unity.' This unity also includes Arab Christians, represented by the character of °Issa al-°Awam, who contributes decisively to Richard the Lionheart's defeat under the command of Saladin.

The parallel drawn between the medieval hero Saladin and Nasser (Gamal °Abd al-*Nasir*), the ultimate idol of the unifying pre-independence Pan-Arabism, is already apparent in the film's title, "*al-Nasir*

Salah al-Din." The struggle of the Arab prince (who was in fact of Kurdish origin) against the crusaders is equated with the relationship of the contemporary so-called Arab world to expansionist Europe. Saladin appears in an extraordinarily positive light. He does not fight back the invaders by military superiority alone but also by virtue of his justice and cleverness.

The screenplay, to which acknowledged Egyptian writers such as Naguib Mahfouz, ᶜAbd al-Rahman al-Sharqawi, and Yusuf al-Sibaᶜi contributed, corresponds to the Nasserist discourse dominating at that time. Even the work of the two set designers, Chadi Abdessalam and Wali al-Din Samih, providing historically authentic sets and costumes, does not reverse the impression that historical events are placed in a contemporary context and serve as allegories for present conditions.

Another film that rephrases a historical event in the light of a current political event is *al-Qadisiya*, produced in 1982 by the public Iraqi film organization and directed by the Egyptian Salah Abu Seif. The army of the Arab conquerors commanded by the pious and righteous Saᶜd Ibn Abi Waqqas is facing the well-equipped troops of the Persian king Yazdigird—and triumphs in the battle of al-Qadisiya. This battle was fought in AD 636 and lead to the fall of the Persian realm and its subsequent Islamization. However, according to the film, the destruction of the Sassanid kingdom is brought about not by its military or political weakness, but by the personal failure and egoism of its infidel despot, who is confirmed in his political errors by pagan religious practices including astrology. The Persian's arbitrariness and decadence are boundless in comparison to the tight organization, the righteousness, and fraternity of the Muslim Arabs.

The choice of subject for this costly mega-production, involving a huge number of Egyptian technicians and actors, was no accident. At the time when this historically decisive battle was cinematically reconstructed, modern Iraq was preparing for a long armed dispute with the neighboring Islamic republic of Iran.

Unity through Islam

Most historical films produced in Egypt during the 1950s and 1960s were set in the early days of Islam; works such as *Saladin* or *Wa Islamah* (1961) by Andrew Marton, representing the time of the crusades or reconstructing the reign of the legendary Mamluk queen Shadjarat al-Durr, were exceptional. However, the production of religious Muslim feature films—a dozen were shot between 1952 and 1972—stopped abruptly at the end of the Nasser era (and shifted gradually to television).

Similar to the purely 'historical' films, the religious features undertake a reinterpretation of history. In *Bilal, the Prophet's Muezzin* (Bilal, mu'adhdhin al-rasul, 1953) by Ahmad al-Tukhi, who also directed *The Victory of Islam* (Intisar al-Islam, 1952) and *Allah's Kaaba* (Bayt Allah al-haram, 1957), Bilal is born to a black slave who dies early and leaves Bilal in the hands of an unjust master. But the hour of liberation strikes: Bilal hears Muhammad's message, converts to Islam, and is bought and liberated by a fellow believer. Later, Bilal follows the Prophet in his flight from Mecca to Medina and there assumes the task of announcing the time of prayer.

The narration of the film is shaped by a linear assembly of anecdotes and closed sections of action including Bilal's early childhood, his conversion to Islam, his liberation, and several anecdotal scenes proving the righteousness of the former slave. One of these stories illustrates how Bilal once pawned his own person as a slave in order to help a poor man who asks him to release him from his debts.

Although the anecdotal character of the film suggests closeness to the original biography documented by the chroniclers Ibn Hisham, Ibn Sa^{c}d, and al-Tabari, among others, the cinematic and literary versions differ considerably. According to his biographers, Bilal was not only the Prophet's muezzin but also his adjutant who carried his sword. He accompanied him to all his battles, and, on one occasion, had the opportunity to get his revenge on his former master for the humiliations he had endured. When the latter was captured during the battle of Badr, Bilal arranged his arbitrary killing. These events, which might well have suited cinematic dramatization, are completely concealed. Instead, the film emphasizes the image of a peaceful martyr-like Bilal. As in some Western films on early Christianity, the believer is denied a contradictory or aggressive nature and is transfigured into a righteous saint.

The film does not aim to give a historically correct interpretation, but wants to give moral instruction, as becomes clear at the end when a hadith[94] of the Prophet is quoted, summarizing the film's message: "Paradise to him who obeys me, even if he is an Ethiopian slave; Hell to him who disobeys me, even if he is an aristocrat of the tribe of Quraysh."[95] Produced just one year after the end of colonial dependency and still before the nationalization of the Suez Canal and the complete withdrawal of the British troops, the film might be read as an apology of the colonized Muslim defending his conviction as ethically and morally superior. Ironically, its clear anti-colonial appeal stating the equality of all races is eventually subjected to the ethnocentric norms of Egyptian film industry. The main character is not

Amina Rizq (center) as a Muslim believer in *The Dawn of Islam* (Fadjr al-Islam, Egypt, 1971) by Salah Abu Seif

performed by a black person but by film star Yahia Shahin, whose Arab features are meagerly blackened.

Bilal, the Prophet's Muezzin is one of the first films to develop the stereotypes of the early Muslims. They are hardly depicted as individuals but entirely transfigured into unworldly saints and furnished with a martyr-like aura similar to the image of the tortured Jesus Christ. Films such as *The Dawn of Islam* (Fadjr al-Islam, 1971) by Salah Abu Seif and *Shayma', the Prophet's Sister* (al-Shayma' ukht al-rasul, 1972) by Husam al-Din Mustafa contribute to shaping the discourse of the virtuous *(salih)*, selfless, and self-sacrificing Muslim. This characterization is not only underlined by the acting but also by the costumes. In contrast to the vicious pagans, early Muslims generally appear in white gowns.

In these films the decisive dramatic turning point occurs with the conversion of the protagonists, who is finally lead to his proper destiny. At this point the characters experience a complete change—they switch their signs, so to speak. This often stereotypical process contributes to the action's affirmative character, emphasizing that confessing Allah's oneness[96] is the key to Paradise, not only in the hereafter, but also in this life.

In Niyazi Mustafa's film *Rabᶜa al-ᶜAdawiya* (1963), the heroine experiences a similar turning point. She is a nominal Muslim at the beginning of the story, but her thirst for adventure and her work as a dancer and singer make her needy of true conversion. After repenting, she becomes a holy figure.

The story line of the film is based on the biography of Rabᶜa al-ᶜAdawiya, a freed slave from the ᶜAdi tribe, who originally came from Basra and died most probably at the end of the second Islamic century in Jerusalem. Rabᶜa is considered as one of the first Sufis, an unworldly personality who preached self-sacrifice and underlined her conviction by withdrawing into the desert where she practiced chaste asceticism. Several mystic sayings concerning 'pure love' of God are ascribed to her.[97] Some of these utterances are quoted in the film. The historically documented revering of Rabᶜa as a saint is underlined in the film by transfiguring and idealizing her personality. However, the film makes no differentiation between the traditions of popular Islam and the orthodox doctrine that might have led to a dissociation from its main character, nor a proper introduction to the sociopolitical context of Sufi thinking. Instead, the dichotomy of good and evil, pleasure and asceticism, this and the other life, structures the narration. The adventurous young singer is simply transformed into a transcendent, virtuous believer. Islamic history and the interpretation of its legendary figures is reduced to a simple, single, and sole possible moral discourse.

In spite of the secular orientation of the Nasserist regime and the ideal of national unity *(al-wahda al-wataniya)* between Copts and Muslims that has been constantly evoked since the common nationalist rebellion in 1919, it is evident that Islam has increasingly became an essential factor in Egyptian national identification and unification. A comparable juxtaposition of nationalism and latent confessionalism can be found in some Algerian films dealing with the war of liberation.

The Opium and the Baton (al-Afyun wa-l-ᶜasa, 1969) by Ahmed Rachedi, for example, presents religion as the sole, though essential, difference between Algerians and French.[98] Ali, a resistance fighter, is offered a piece of meat by a French soldier. In spite of his hunger he refuses, explaining that the consumption of pork is considered a sin in Islam. All the Frenchman's assurances that it is beef fail to convince Ali. In the same film, an old peasant rallies a group of villagers to unify as "one man" against the infidels *(kuffar)*. In the following scene the imam of the same village gathers the men for prayer in the mosque while they wait for a French attack to come.

In *Chronicle of the Years of Embers* (Waqa'iᶜ sanawat al-djamr, 1974) by Mohamed Lakhdar Hamina, the imam again plays a mobilizing role. Only with his assistance can the intellectual Larbi induce workers and peasants to a joint act against the occupying power. It is the Muslim cleric who administers the access to history: he is the one who after his return from abroad tells Ahmad the tragic story of his home village pestered by drought, colons, and the French army.

The mobilizing effect of Islamic slogans is not a projection of the present on to the past, but a historical fact. The members of the Algerian FLN called during the war of liberation for Holy War, the *djihad* against the infidel *(kuffar)* colons.[99] The revival of these notions in state sponsored films shows that the juxtaposition of superficially secular-oriented, revolutionary nationalism, and the "cultural rehabilitation" of Islam *(asala)*, as Maherzi calls it,[100] continued after independence.

Mythological history

In *The Opium and the Baton* (al-Afyun wa-l-ᶜasa) by Ahmed Rachedi, members of the FLN urge the doctor, Bashir, to join the *Mudjahidun*. He leaves Algiers and travels to his home, a village in the mountains of Kabylia. From there he is led to the hiding places of the resistance fighters. His brother Ali and his brother-in-law have joined them already. These two are the real main characters of the film. During a guerrilla operation, both of them are captured. Ali survives with the help of a French soldier, but the army destroys his paternal home and blows up the olive plantations of the village. The partisans success-fully prepare to retaliate, whereupon the French army steps up its violence against civilians. Before driving the villagers out, the soldiers shoot Ali in front of his family.

Long chases are used in *The Opium and the Baton* to create suspense. Sudden turning points, such as the decision of the French soldier guarding Ali to join the partisans, help to resolve dangerous situations. The mises en scène of the military confrontations are extremely vivid, entailing an immense output of ammunition. Yet, the most effective means for fighting are not weapons but the courage and cunningness of the Algerian resistance fighters. Judging from the number of Frenchmen killed in these scenes, one might have expected the Algerians to have won the war in a few months.

Ali and his brother-in-law are prototypes of the intrepid partisan. They never seem to be tired or scared. The urban academic Bashir is cast in a different mold. Walking through the mountains he gets sore feet. After his arrival in the guerrilla camp he meets his brother, who explains the situation: "There is no rest for us, the word has lost its

The Opium and the Baton (al-Afyun wa-l-ᶜasa, Algeria, 1969) by Ahmed Rachedi
(*courtesy Institut du Monde Arabe, Paris*)

meaning. You will get used to it in a few days and you will not want
to talk about it any more."

The representation of the resistance fighters has no psychological
depth, but follows fixed stereotypes that are repeated in other
Algerian films too. "We are not dealing with human beings but with
admirable giants, with gods who have descended Mount Olympus.
They are lacking nothing, neither strength, agility, intelligence, nor,
last but not least, beauty."[101] The simultaneous, detailed, and largely
accurate depiction of the environment, or in other words, realist
conventions on the technical and formal level, help to 'naturalize'
these supernatural heroes and conceal the misrepresentation of
history that is achieved by them.

The Algerian *Mudjahid* who emerges from colonialization as a hero
is supposed to become the model of the post-colonial Algerian. In the
first place, however, he must be considered as the projection of a
shattered national identity. His impersonal and generalized characterization suggests the existence of a closed nation without any
linguistic, ethnic, or social deviances, which can face the infidel
invader as "one man." Consequently, no reference whatsoever, visual
or linguistic, is made in *The Opium and the Baton* to the Kabyle

(Berber) origins of the protagonists or to the cultural specificity of the region where the story takes place. The generality of the heroes helps them to embody Algerian national unity and conceals real existing differences.

In Algerian cinema, peasants were subjected to a similar monumentalization. In *Chronicle of the Years of Embers* by Mohamed Lakhdar Hamina a peasant family represents the Algerian people as a whole experiencing the three historical phases of colonialism, described in the film as the years of ashes *(sanawat al-ramad)*, the years of the chariot *(al-ᶜaraba)*, and the years of embers *(al-djamr)*. Threatened by the drought, Ahmad and his family leave their village and move to a county town where he finds work in a quarry. The working conditions are humiliating and inhumane. The incipient economic crisis adds to the family's ordeals. Soon, a contagious disease spreads among the undernourished natives. The authorities evacuate the French, while the Algerian inhabitants are kept in quarantine. Ahmad's whole family falls victim to the disease. He returns alone to his home village, but conditions have worsened there too. The peasants are at the mercy of the colons and the native landowner. Ahmad objects but is drafted to the army and sent to Europe to fight in World War II. After the end of the war, he returns to his country and assists in setting up the resistance against French occupation.

Even Ahmad's physiognomy corresponds to his scarcely individual character. His internal stirrings are only reactions to external events. He has no negative attributes. The majestic cinemascope close-ups of his face, shot from a fish eye's perspective, undercut with the cracked arid soil on which he gazes during the opening scenes of the film, invoke his archaic closeness to the earth. This relationship is emphasized and placed into a mythological context in the subsequent images of a rite conjuring up the rain. Man and earth are one: as the director remarked, "The peasant's rootedness in his land is well-known. My father used to say, you love your land first and then your family."[102]

The epic narration of the film and Ahmad's timeless, earthbound character provide the hero with the air of a legendary figure. The different periods of recent Algerian history from the 1930s until national independence leave no visible marks on him. He is the hero of a myth, as it has been defined by Roland Barthes: "A trick is going on in which the real has been turned over, emptied of history and filled with nature. . . . By changing from history into nature the myth achieves an elimination. It abolishes the complexity of human actions. . . . It organizes a world without contradictions."[103]

A decisive factor in the heroes' mythical monumentalization in *The Opium and the Baton* or in *Chronicle of the Years of Embers* is their virility. Women play only a marginal role in the films dealing with the war of liberation. As Maherzi states, except in *Wind from the Aurès* and *Noua*, no main characters were women in the twenty-four films produced until 1979 that dealt with the war of liberation.[104] The few women who appeared represented either mothers and wives or abused young girls. The female resistance fighters, the *Mudjahidat*, who played a considerable role in reality, hardly figure in these films.

In post-colonial Arab cinema, the variations on the 'mythical hero' are numerous, ranging from Youssef Chahine's peasant in *The Earth* (1968) to the worker in *Sejnane* (1978) by the Tunisian Abdellatif Ben Ammar. The immortality of these heroes conflicts massively with the conventional realist depiction of the films in which they appear, which usually spares no detail of the huts of the poor.

Some Algerian cinematographers have started to counter these myths. *The Uprooted* (Bani Handal, 1976) by Lamine Merbah is one of the few films that do not compensate for the humiliations of colonialism and the ordeals of the struggle for liberation with perfect heroes. The story, which is based on a sociological study, is set at the end of the nineteenth century and depicts the gradual dispossession of a tribe by the colonial administration. Because its members cannot offer any official papers for the land they have cultivated for generations, the authorities are able to confiscate it easily. In cooperation with Algerian notables and by using well-directed pressure on the remaining small farmers, the Pieds Noirs take the land in their place and subsequently acquire huge estates. The native population is pushed into dependent labor or, worse, into homelessness. Those who do not want to bow are quickly dismissed as outlaws. The film ends with a homeless 'beggar' opening fire on a Pieds Noirs party.

Other works achieved a demythologization by using comic or satirical means. Mohamed Lakhdar Hamina's comedy *Hassan Terro* (1967) was the first Algerian feature film to profane the myth of the partisan. The bourgeois Hassan, played by the popular comedian Rouiched, who also participated in writing the screenplay, works for the French radio program and lives in an elegant suburb of Algiers. He is a coward and prefers to have nothing to do with either the French soldiers or with the resistance. But when activists of the FLN force him to hide a wanted resistance fighter in his home, the anxious opportunist Hassan becomes a reluctant hero.

The director Mahmoud Zemmouri also deconstructs the image of the heroic Algerian resistance in his coproduced satire *The Mad Years of Twist* (Les folles années de twist, 1986), illustrating the life of a

Rouiched in *Hassan Terro* (Algeria, 1967) by Mohamed Lakhdar Hamina

The Mad Years of Twist (Les folles années de twist, Algeria, 1986) by Mahmoud Zemmouri

small Algerian town on the eve of independence in 1963. The two young protagonists are real anti-heroes who are interested, first and foremost, in having fun. They don't think much of work or of armed resistance. They have a lot of respect for the French and the colons, but this does not prevent them from plundering their orange plantations. Their anxiety about French patrols is overcome by their desire for money. One day they stroll through the crowded market place. As soon as a patrol approaches and the frightened crowd quickly disperses, the two young men empty the merchants' cash boxes. The war of liberation has its human side too.

A far more painful deconstruction is offered by Okacha Touita's *The Sacrificed* (al-Qarabin; Les sacrifiés, 1982), which was also coproduced with France. It is one of the few works that bluntly uncovers the internal power struggles of the FLN and does not shrink from depicting the psychological burdens that have caused some underground fighters to break down.

Counter-histories

How does a child see it when a coarse adult insults another, accusing him of being a traitor, and knocks him to the ground? What does a little boy feel when he sees his mother humiliated by her father and

Paternal violence in *Dreams of the City* (Ahlam al-madina, Syria, 1984) by Mohamed Malas

called a slut? Little Dib, the main character of *Dreams of the City* (Ahlam al-madina, Syria, 1984) by Mohamed Malas, has moved to the city with his mother after having lost his father. There, he is obliged to work in a laundry, and is introduced to the world of adults, observing how they form alliances, quarrel about politics as well as private issues, how they love, beat, and even kill each other.

Dib's eyes are everywhere, but they are still innocent. He does not side with anybody. His impartial perspective rids the narration of imposed political rhetorics. On his way to work Dib witnesses how a supporter of the opposition nationalist leader Quwatli beats a regime collaborator. The boy is scared and subsequently gives the man a wide berth. But the man is not as vicious as he seems at first sight; he realizes that he has scared Dib and gently tries to win his liking. The people Dib comes to know are all like this man, be they Nasserists, nationalists, travelers, or informers—they are neither heroes nor complete wrongdoers. Their political point of view is as contradictory as they are. These attributes help to create a second narrative level, eclipsing the representation of the conflicts that dominated the different political camps in Syria during the 1950s. They make it possible to qualify the different ideological positions and avoid a one-sided representation. The subjective perspective of the child, which defines the course of the film, is essential in creating intellectual distance.

Awareness of history is doubtless a matter of perspective, a fact that is emphasized in Assia Djebar's historical experimental film, *Zerda and the Songs of Oblivion* (La zerda et les chants de l'oubli, 1982).[105] In cooperation with Malek Alloula, the Algerian writer viewed all the available archival material shot in the Maghreb between 1912 and 1942. For her film she used mainly documentary left-overs shot by French cameramen.[106] She arranged them into five 'songs,' the songs of rebellion, of refusal to compromise, of isolation, of emigration, and of the dead, thus representing the historical periods of French colonialism in the Maghreb. The images of feasts, official visits, and important historical events help to expose the colonial perspective. Juxtapositions and contrasting images underline the contemptuous gaze with which the colonial masters regarded the indigenous population.

"In spite of their images and starting out from what lay outside of the range of their sight, we tried to emphasize other images, scraps of a despised ordinariness. First of all, anonymous voices woke up behind the veil of that reality, revived or reinvented, the soul of the united Maghreb and of our past."[107] Thus put in a new context, the gesture of a French officer being welcomed by young, traditionally dressed, Algerian girls seems unbearable. When the man tries to kiss the girls they visibly shrink back, but he insists with an additional, intrusive touch. Assia Djebar's editing sets store by the girls' silent resistance, and thus makes room for their suppressed protest. Historiography in *Zerda* means rewriting history, to re-interpret and counter a dominant historical discourse.

There are few attempts in Arab cinema to write counter-history or to shoot films which, in Marc Ferro's words, are not "in accord with common—dominant or minoritarian—currents of thinking," but permit "conversely an independent and new view of society."[108] The rare attempts are mostly confined to the documentary or experimental field.

The Lebanese film maker Heiny Srour tries to reconstruct regional female history in her semi-documentary *Layla and the Wolves* (Layla wa-l-dhi'ab, 1984). Using a variety of archival material, reconstructed (enacted) historical events, and a subjective commentary that is loosely embedded in a fictional framing story, the director manages to uncover the participation of Palestinian women in the struggle for independence. She shows women who smuggle weapons, stall soldiers with stones and boiling water, and stand up fearlessly to the use of force. Thus, Heiny Srour refutes the image of the helpless female victim and its equation with the robbed and violated homeland that has been so popular in the works of many male Arab directors.

The films of the Palestinian director Michel Khleifi, particularly his documentary *Fertile Memory* (al-Dhakira al-khisba, 1980), similarly try to undermine the common Arab discourses on the Palestinian question. In *Fertile Memory*, Khleifi portrays two Palestinian women of very different backgrounds: the now acknowledged feminist writer Sahar Khalifa from Nablus in the occupied territories, and his own aunt who lives in Galilee, Israel. Sahar represents the type of young, emancipated woman. At the age of thirty she filed a petition for divorce and started studying. In 1980, when the film was shot, she was working as a writer and teacher and living alone with her daughter. In contrast, Khleifi's widowed aunt has remained faithful to traditional ideas. She thought it improper to remarry after the death of her husband. She has, however, been very independent, has brought up her children alone and supported them by working, first as a housekeeper and then as a seamstress. She, too, stands up for a political point of view. Despite her children's insistence, the widow refuses to give up her legal claim and accept compensation for a piece of land that has been confiscated by the Israelis.

Fertile Memory uncovers the traces of a double occupation in the life of its protagonists. The women not only suffer from the Israeli domination but also from their men's claims of ownership and the restrictions imposed on them by patriarchal society as a whole. Hence, the Palestinian male occupies in the film the position of culprit and victim at once. This is a view that Sahar Khalifa expresses in her literary and feminist work. Her position opens the notion of Palestinian resistance to a concept comprising the entire society and counters the image of the passive, abused, female Palestinian.

These various attempts to question the historicism of post-colonial, nationalist-oriented film making strive to challenge cherished ideological positions—the myths of virility, or the undivided nation—and to replace dominant historical discourses by images of oppressed counter-histories, including those of women. However, they do not always question the dubious concept of historical authenticity that automatically sneaks in with the realist mode of representation. Only exceptionally do films leave behind historicization. Chadi Abdessalam's *The Mummy*, for example, and Assia Djebar's *Zerda and the Songs of Oblivion* are rare films that problematize the awareness of history as such.

Nevertheless, these films remain completely marginal to the historicizing mainstream, which tends to reflect more generally accepted views. It is no accident that historicism developed first in commercial cinema. Its allusion to a glamorous past, the use of political allegories to create modern nationalist myths with a clearly apologetic and anti-colonialist character, involve it actively in the construction of modern national identities and entities. It is no wonder that apologetic and unitarian historicism persists in mainstream cinema and, more decisively, in the far more widely distributed Egyptian television productions, such as the recent spectacle *Nasser 56* (1995) by Muhammad Fadil. In so doing, it shapes the views and perceptions of coming generations.

Cinéma d'auteur

The notion of *cinéma d'auteur* has been used in various ways. As a genre it partly merges with the notion of 'art film,' which became associated in the early 1960s with a group of European film makers in films such as *L'avventura*, *Hiroshima mon amour*, and *La Dolce Vita*. Micelangelo Antonioni, Alain Resnais, Frederico Fellini, and Ingmar Bergmann, "these four—though perhaps Resnais less then the others—served to define the 'conventions' of the developing 'art-movies' genre: deliberately and obviously intellectual (there is nothing more deliberate than the final scene of *La Dolce Vita*), with extremely visible individual stylistic characteristics."[109]

However, it is hard to assign the art film and more specifically *cinéma d'auteur* to a specific genre.[110] While a genre film corresponds to an industrial norm and is rather dissociated from the personality of its director, the most important concern of art film is using the media for the author's personal vision.[111] The camera is transformed into a literary means of expression, a *caméra-stylo*,[112] relying on the concept that "The eye of the camera only starts seeing when a literary consciousness is behind it."[113]

The notion of the film author or *auteur*, which appeared in the 1950s in François Truffaut's contributions to the magazine *Cahiers du cinéma*, and elsewhere, was originally not confined to the art film but served to describe the style or 'personal handwriting' *(écriture)* of extraordinary directors such as Jean Renoir or Marcel Carné.[114] The notion of the *auteur* was used about mainstream Hollywood directors such as John Ford and Howard Hawks. Their specific form of commercial cinema "knew its audience and its expectations but often provided something extra. This extra is the concern of the *auteur* theory."[115]

The "something extra" of a film may concentrate in the person of the *auteur* and manifest itself in certain formal and thematic characteristics. A structural procedure, according to which the work of the individual has to be searched for constant parameters, may be useful in defining an *auteur* film.

However, it might be more helpful to undertake such an analysis not only in respect to the personality of the author. The particular has inevitably to be measured against the regular and general, the norm, and defined in comparison to it. The work of a director cannot exist completely independently of the social and economic framework, even if he or she has total control of the artistic representation and the financial means. "The logical basis of the *auteur* theory lies in the fact that film can never, even under the best conditions, be completely personal. The purity of personal expression is a myth of textbooks."[116]

The economic situation of a film maker is certainly one part of the framework that shapes his style. This factor played an important role in German *Autorenfilm*, for example. The *Autorenfilm* appeared first in West Germany when the signatories of the 1962 Oberhausen manifesto renounced "Papas Kino" (Daddy's cinema) and tried to pave the way for a more unconventional film language. They linked the idea of wholly independent film making with the attempt to create alternative production modes. Public funding was meant to secure the independence of the *Autorenfilm* from producers and subsequently from the commercial structure of the film industry. The *Autorenfilm* was thus conceived as the opposite of the 'producer film' *(Produzentenfilm)*, which is governed by commercial considerations and offers a director fewer opportunities to develop a personal 'writing.' Beside the alternative financing, a quasi pre-industrial production mode with a low degree of labor division was introduced in order to allow the director to control all aspects of the production process.[117]

In practice, the realization of a genuine *auteur* film comes up against numerous obstacles. While producing a full-length feature film the 'artisanal' production mode can be applied only partially at best. Only an amateur, in the spirit of Maya Deren, can control the process of production completely. However, a film that wants to reach a certain technical standard has in general to rely on industrial labor division. Thus, individualism in cinema is possible only to a certain extent. The individual or particular of a work is not absolute, but is rather the product of an antagonism between film maker and the surrounding conditions. It is the result of a struggle for the greatest possible independence from social frameworks on which one is in fact permanently, and inevitably, dependent.

Since the 1970s, Western TV channels and cultural institutions have developed an increasing interest in promoting productions from the so-called Third World. In particular, France has invested in its former francophone North African colonies and created a relative economic dependency of native cinema on French coproduction, quite similar to that of West African cinema.[118] Due to its individualism and intellectuality, *cinéma d'auteur* is much more suitable than regional popular cinema for this mediating role.

New Arab Cinema and the *cinéma d'auteur*

Since the late 1970s new cinema currents have made their appearance in the different Arab countries. The notion of 'les nouveaux cinémas arabes' (New Arab Cinemas) was circulated in France, among others, by the film critic Claude Michel Cluny and the publications of CinémAction, edited by Guy Henebelle.[119] In French, the use of the plural indicates the variety of different currents in cinema, ranging from New Egyptian Realism *(al-waqiʿiya al-djadida)*[120] to experimental art cinema. In Arabic, the notion of New Arab Cinema is used in the singular and hence appears more diffuse in terms of regional, conceptual, and stylistic specifications. In reality, it comprises numerous directions, including *sinima djidid* (New

Cinema) in Algeria,[121] Young Cinema *(sinima al-shabab)* in Egypt,[122] and Alternative Cinema *(al-sinima al-badila)* in Syria.[123] These classifications rarely differentiate between genres. They refer to realist works as well as to *auteur* films, as they are often undertaken according to subjects and messages, i.e., the sociopolitical commitment *(iltizam)* of a work, rather than to formal criteria.

However, the essentially new in Arab *cinéma d'auteur* is, unlike other forms of committed cinema such as realism, the radical striving for personal expression, be it on the aesthetic and formal level, or with regard to content. Also innovative is its dissociation from global political messages and ostensibly objective analyses. The following words of the Syrian director Mohamed Malas, author of the semi-autobiographical film *Dreams of the City* (1986), may clarify this tendency:

> As we mostly work out our subjects and screenplays ourselves, they are not simply adaptations of projects rather than reflections of inner ideas and anxieties. . . . To me cinema represents a personal means of expression and not a profession that is supposed to secure me material or moral profit, . . . particularly because I realize only films that express our inner disquiet and concern. They are related to me as a human being and individual, but also as a product of a whole generation, of a specific epoch, of a society, and a country. Hence, all my films are related, starting with their titles—*Dream of a Little Town, Memory, Dreams of the City, The Dream, Notes of a City*[124]—and ending with their contents.[125]

As elsewhere, Arab *cinéma d'auteur* strives for an independent economic basis. Its financial sources range from state owned production companies and public funding to foreign coproducers. Film funds that are administrated by film makers themselves, as in Germany for example, do not exist.

In Syria, the emergence of a *cinéma d'auteur* would have been unthinkable without the support of the public National Film Organization. As in Algeria, the degree of freedom a film maker is able to force out of bureaucracy and its censorship depends on his or her readiness to struggle and take risks.

At the end of the 1960s the members of the New Cinema Society *(Djamaʿat al-Sinima al-Djadida)* in Egypt tried to minimize the disadvantages of state production by themselves contributing to the financing.[126] However, the group realized only two films. Further plans were thwarted by the reprivatization of the public production company. Public initiative in Egypt had in any case offered no alternative to commercial production modes. Egyptian directors such as Taufik Salih or Chadi Abdessalam, who were turned down by the private sector, also had great difficulties realizing their plans in the public sector.

Given this situation, Youssef Chahine tried to create a private production base for himself. Since the production of his film *The Sparrow* (1971), the director has managed, together with other members of his family, to establish a production company, Misr al-ᶜAlamiya (Misr International). The company survives by foreign, mainly Western, financial support. Coproductions first with the former ONCIC in Algeria for *The Return of the Prodigal Son* (1976) and *The Sparrow*, and later with the French ministry of culture and French television, allowed Chahine to complete his more expensive projects, such as *Adieu Bonaparte!* (1985), *Alexandria Now and Forever* (Iskandariya, kaman wa kaman, 1990), and *The Emigrant* (al-Muhagir, 1994).[127]

Tunisian and Moroccan *cinéma d'auteur* is in the same situation. Although generally it can rely on public funds, it could hardly survive without Western coproductions. This situation, however, endangers its cultural legitimacy and at the same time its economic existence.

The defeat

The essential innovations of Arab *cinéma d'auteur* are its choice of subjects and its dissociation from conventional narrative structures. Some of the early films that fit into this category are the Tunisian *Khalifa the Bald* (1969) by Hamouda Ben Halima, and the Moroccan *Wechma* (1970) by Hamid Benani. The latter is characterized by a constant merge and interaction of past and present, a feature that also characterizes the Syrian works, *The Knife* (al-Sikkin, 1972) by Khaled Hamada and *al-Yazerli* (1974) by Kaiss al-Zubaidi. In *al-Yazerli*, which was adapted from the novel *On the Sacks* (Fauq al-akyas) by Hanna Mina, flashbacks, dreams, and visions of the adolescent protagonist break the action's linearity. The framing narrative as such contains social critique but attains, through the intertwined fantasies, an air of expressionism. Thus, the basic realist discourse on a materially and sexually deprived youth, confronted with oppressive working conditions, is relativized and elevated to a more fictional level.

According to the Tunisian director and scriptwriter, Nouri Bouzid, one reason for the changes that occurred in parts of Arab cinema and contributed to the emergence of the so-called New Arab Cinema was the 1967 debacle. He calls the film making that has appeared since then "sinima al-waᶜy bi-l-hazima," the cinema that is conscious of the defeat.[128] The Six Day War left deep traces in the intellectual life of the Arab world and had repercussions on film making as well.

While during the late 1960s and early 1970s in Algeria, and less so in Tunisia, film makers were assimilating the war of liberation and new social conditions, and creating a new self image, the 1967 debacle was echoed directly in Egyptian and Syrian cinema.

The most immediate reaction to it, which also had a touch of youth rebellion about it, was the foundation of the New Cinema Society in Egypt. Its members consisted of scriptwriters, directors and film critics.[129] The Palestinian Ghaleb Chaath was one of its founders, although, being a foreigner, his name could not appear on the members' list. Chaath, whose family had sought refuge in Egypt, studied cinema in Vienna and returned to Cairo after the 1967 war, introducing his colleagues to the ideas of the Oberhausen manifesto.[130] The new society, which was eventually founded in 1969, aimed to produce politically committed films that differed from the prevailing Egyptian mainstream cinema. The two full-length feature films directed by its members are *Song on the Passage* (Ughniya ᶜala al-mammar, 1972) by Ali Abd El-Khalek and *Shadows on the Other Side* (Zilal ᶜala al-djanib al-akhar, 1973) by Ghaleb Chaath. Both films are based on literary works and announce on the formal level a certain 'polyphony' that disrupts the omniscient, realist discourse, and creates a variety of subjective voices and perspectives.

Song on the Passage is a clumsy debut film but, like *Shadows on the Other Side*, contains a narrative structure that was uncommon in Egyptian cinema of that time. During the Six Day War a group of soldiers has entrenched itself in a mountain passage. Later, when they discover that their troop has already retreated they have to decide whether they want to keep their position or flee. The soldiers start talking about themselves and their lives before the war. Their accounts are partly contradicted and even exposed by the screen images, which sometimes portray a completely different events. The opposing political convictions of the protagonists clash, while individual self indulgence and egocentrism are denounced and held responsible for the debacle.

In the second, artistically far more sophisticated production linked to the society, *Shadows on the Other Side*, the perspective of the supposedly objective narrator is completely eliminated and the story is told several times anew from different angles. These competing narrative versions are linked to the five main characters. Rose is a fragile young girl who suffers emotional deprivation because of her foster mother's coldness. She falls in love with Mahmud, an art student, who invites her from time to time to his houseboat where he lives with three fellow students. Rose becomes pregnant, but Mahmud drops her. Out of sympathy for Rose, Mahmud's friends start criticizing his behavior. Their statements, however, derive from

Nagla' Fathi as Rose in *Shadows on the Other Side* (Zilal ʿala al-djanib al-akhar, 1971) by Ghaleb Chaath

different motives, from envy, idealism, and morals. Hence, each young man develops his own version of the story. Their debates all point to one theme, social responsibility. Finally, it is ʿUmar, the Palestinian, who responds most decisively to his private and political situation. After a visit to the occupied territories he changes the subjects of his exams from refugees *(ladji'un)* to resistance fighters *(fida'iyyun)* and decides to settle in Jerusalem (Ghaleb Chaath himself followed the example of his protagonist and moved in 1974 to Beirut, where he directed documentaries for the Palestinian organization Samed). The unconventional narrative Chaath chose for his film enabled him to reflect a controversial debate and, simultaneously, to discuss the reasons for the defeat on several levels.

The Sparrow (al-ʿUsfur, 1971), directed by Youssef Chahine in 1971, again showed signs of disintegrating the realist narrative discourse and indicated the director's new formal orientation, his shift from mainstream and realist cinema toward the *auteur* film. Ra'uf, a young police officer, is stationed in a small village in Upper Egypt. The inhabitants suffer from the harassment of Abu Khidr, who owns a closed down factory nearby and seems to be involved in suspicious transactions. Ra'uf's stepfather, a high-ranking police officer, is expected in the village to end the dealings. Additionally, the journalist Yusuf arrives, but his investigations are not welcomed. He is put in custody while Abu Khidr gets killed by the non-local police, preventing Yusuf from learning more about him. Ra'uf and Yusuf meet again in Cairo at the home of their common friend Bahiya. Her house hosts all kind of discontented people. Yusuf, whose work is constantly obstructed by state security, is still determined to throw light on the case of Abu Khidr and asks Bahiya's friends for assistance. Gradually, the scale of Abu Khidr's involvement becomes clear: weapons and machinery mysteriously disappear from public factories and reappear later as private property. Even high officials seem to contribute to the transactions. At the height of the investigations the news of the Six Day War and the subsequent defeat bursts in. As President Nasser declares his resignation and the demonstrating masses fill the city, trucks loaded with stolen goods sneak away through dark side streets.

Chahine's film was shot in 1971 but was only released two years later, after Egypt's October 1973 (Yom Kippur) war against Israel. Its aggressive attitude did not please the political leadership at the time. The film, however, was rather unconventional: its basic dramatic narrative, the crime and its investigations, is disintegrated by the imposed epic structure. Various parallel actions merge at points to form dramatic situations, such as Ra'uf's trip back to Cairo, the death of his brother in a trench, or Nasser's resignation. Flashbacks and associations interrupt the different lines of action. The 'objective' film surface seems scattered, its reflection distorted. Reality after the defeat seems to have more than one face.

Autobiographic cinema

An essential innovation brought about by Arab *cinéma d'auteur* is the introduction of the autobiographic film.[131] Youssef Chahine's *Alexandria Why?* (Iskandariya lih?) completed in 1978 is one of the first quasi-autobiographic films shot in an Arab country. With a script written by Youssef Chahine in cooperation with Muhsin Zayid, the film is the first of a trilogy made up by *An Egyptian Fairy Tale* (1982) and *Alexandria Now And Forever* (1990).

Yahia, the main character of *Alexandria Why?*, is about to graduate from the prestigious Victoria College in Alexandria, but is much more interested in Hollywood films starring Ginger Rogers and Fred Astaire. He dreams of becoming an actor. But Egypt is living through a difficult time. It is 1942, at the height of World War II. German troops are approaching Alexandria. Speculation and the black market

Alexandria Why? (Iskandariya lih? Egypt, 1978) by Youssef Chahine

flourish. Yahia's family is in an economic crisis. The father, an idealistic lawyer, prefers to go fishing than to deal with unjust jurisdiction,
while the mother is desperately trying to make ends meet by selling
the piano and other pieces of furniture. Yahia's prosperous fellow
students are already planning their studies abroad, while he himself is
forced to start a boring banking training. When, against all expectations, he is granted a scholarship to the United States, the family
collects its last savings in order to enable him to travel.

However, Yahia's story is not the only one told in *Alexandria Why?*
The framing autobiographic narrative is intertwined with numerous
little secondary stories populated by an enormous number of characters. There is, for example, the father of a fellow student who has
become rich by speculating and now holds grandiose parties to
impress the influential heads of the country. Elsewhere, a young
patriotic aristocrat indulges a strange vice: he buys kidnapped British
soldiers and shoots them. Other side-stories present a group of young
nationalists who are planning the assassination of Churchill, and a
love relation between a Muslim leftist and a Jewish comrade.
Together they form a subjective portrait of cosmopolitan pre-
Nasserist Alexandria.

The center of gravity that links all these actions and characters is
Yahia, the director's alter ego. Chahine himself, whose family stems

originally from Lebanon, was born in 1926 and grew up in Alexandria. He lived in the solid middle-class neighborhood of Ibrahimiya and was educated at the elite schools Saint Mark's and Victoria College. In 1946 Chahine traveled to the United States in order to study acting at the Pasadena Playhouse, and there switched to directing.[132]

In 1982, Youssef Chahine completed his second semi-autobiographic film, *An Egyptian Fairy Tale*, for which he wrote the screenplay on his own. In this film Chahine depicts his career as a director. As usual, he also addresses political issues, displaying his admiration for Nasser while at the same time mourning Europe's lack of interest in the so-called Third World. The film shows his own renunciation of the Western dream—how, as an Arab film maker, he loses hope of being recognized at Cannes or elsewhere in the festivals of the 'First World.'

The explicit political statements Chahine made in his first two autobiographical films fit partly into the anti-colonial discourse prevalent during this period—even if they contradict his personal experiences on the production level. After the release of *An Egyptian Fairy Tale* he succeeded in collecting the necessary funds from French institutions to produce his grand spectacle *Adieu Bonaparte!* (1985), starring the French stars Michel Piccoli and Patrice Chéreau.

Chahine's sometimes simplified political messages are partly disguised in allegorical narratives, for example in scenes depicting Alexander's invasion of Egypt in his most recent self portrayal, *Alexandria Now and Forever*, and the side-story of a group of young nationalists in *Alexandria Why?* The nationalists are planning to assassinate Churchill while entertaining contacts with the Muslim Brotherhood. With this story the director alludes to the emergence of the nationalist movement—the Free Officers—and their cooperation with Muslim fundamentalists on the eve of independence, and sets it against the background of his own personal experiences.

It is worth noting that these political insertions oppose the main story line, that is, the autobiography on the narrative level. Whereas the latter takes a largely subjective narrative perspective and is restricted to the main character, the allegorical side-stories are narrated in a quasi-objective and omniscient way and are based on the absence of the protagonist. It is possible that Chahine's attachment to political allegories and the fact that he does not refrain completely from the omniscient type of narration are part of the legacy of the *iltizam* he had devoted himself to during his earlier, realist phase:

No doubt, June 5 [the Six Day War] has contributed strongly to my awareness of the artist's responsibility toward society. Yet, to be honest, already after the revolution in 1952 I became aware of that responsibility—though in an abstract and diffuse way—when I found myself given a choice between participating in the events of reality that surround me or being content to observe them. This was maybe expressed in *Mortal Revenge*. After June 5 I started changing: first I moved from bourgeois entertaining cinema by addressing certain topics within that cinema and started then to make films that correspond to society's needs. You have to produce films that are indispensable.[133]

The adherence to *iltizam* or social commitment can also be found in *Summer Thefts* (Sariqat sayfiya, 1988) by Yousry Nasrallah, one of Chahine's former assistants. An essential difference, however, is expressed in the fact that the director largely abstains from political allegories. From the perspective of a little boy, he depicts the social and private tensions that arise in an upper-middle class family during a summer vacation spent on their estate. After the Nasserist agrarian revolution, the affluent family fears the nationalization of its properties. At the same time, their standing among the peasants is threatened by the increasing influence of state functionaries. The boy himself has an ambiguous relationship to the peasants. When he steals something from his aunt and his best friend, a peasant boy, is suspected, he does not exonerate him. An older cousin is more conscious about the needs of the moment. She hijacks all the radios available in the house, in order to give the peasants an opportunity to listen to Nasser's agitating speeches concerning the agrarian revolution.

Nasrallah's *Summer Thefts* is one of the first Egyptian films not to schematize the higher bourgeoisie. The author sympathizes with both sides. He describes the difficulties of the parents' broken marriage, depicts the extravagance and egocentrism of their bourgeois relatives, and contrasts it with the solidarity and spontaneous warmth of the servants. Nasrallah's narrative touches on the situation of peasants facing up to the new system and their problems in developing adequate consciousness. Nasrallah also shows, by means of the cousin's subversive action and the decision of an elegant aunt to marry a Nasserist functionary, how much class consciousness can change. Indeed, the hero is ready to learn his lesson. He comes back as a grownup searching for the friend who had been wrongly accused of theft.

The summer depicted is not any summer but the summer when the little boy's parents decide to separate, as did the director's own parents. The allusions to political conditions overlie the images of this painful personal memory almost as a superstructure. Nasrallah does not, however, transform them into a uniform ideological statement. Via the various sympathetic characters who belong to the privileged (dominating) as well as underprivileged (oppressed) classes, sufficiently diverse opinions and interests are expressed to achieve a suitable polyphony.

Social commitment along with autobiographic tendencies has also manifested itself in the work of other Arab directors, such as Néjia Ben Mabrouk, Nouri Bouzid, and Mohamed Malas, while toppling the explicit political discourses almost completely.

In *Man of Ashes* (Rih al-sadd;[134] *L'homme des cendres*, 1986) the Tunisian scriptwriter and director Nouri Bouzid depicts the difficulties in adapting to their surroundings of two young carpenters, Hashimi and Farfat, who have been sexually abused during their childhood by their master craftsman. Farfat is defamed by neighbors as being homosexual, which makes his father throw him out of their home. Hashimi is in trouble too. His family is preparing for his wedding, but he takes no real interest in the event. He upsets his parents by avoiding his paternal home and the guests. His mother believes in black magic, which she tries to counter by calling a woman magician. Her husband, however, undertakes more rigorous actions: he beats his son with a belt. But none of this helps Hashimi

Man of Ashes (Rih al-sadd; *L'homme des cendres*, Tunisia, 1986) by Nouri Bouzid (*courtesy Institut du Monde Arabe, Paris*)

solve his problem. His insecurity has a long past, depicted by inter-cutting visual flashbacks related to the claustrophobic memories of the master's sexual assaults.

Hashimi drifts around. Accompanied by Farfat and some other friends he visits a brothel. When the young men mockingly allude to Farfat's dubious masculinity, he is seized by rage. He storms out and through the streets looking for his master, and when he finds him, stabs him with a knife.

Nouri Bouzid's film illustrates different types of violence to which children and adolescents are subjected as a result of the dominating patriarchal family structures. Despite the social implications of his subject the director does not work in any political allegories. He sticks close to the daily life of his protagonist and his personal impressions and memories. It is not Hashimi's conflict with his environment that structures the narrative, but various almost impressionistic scenes, including an excursion to the beach, a visit to an old Jewish music teacher, walks through the town, the visit to the brothel, and some flashbacks. They create the film's basic, epic character.

Man of Ashes does not include events that are strictly autobio-graphic—Nouri Bouzid was not abused as a child.[135] It is, however, closely connected to the director's personal experience:

> Both *Man of Ashes* and *Golden Horseshoes*, are, indeed, very much related to my life in Tunisia. The two films, particularly the last one, were a sort of catharsis, a sort of exorcism to me. I wanted to liberate myself from everything that had preoccupied me immensely during the last years, that made me unhappy in my country. In my films I wanted to approach what my generation has experienced. I wanted to address with my films what makes up our present situation of crisis, the bankruptcy of our society. Thus, my first film addresses childhood, not exactly mine but rather my generation's, how we were 'broken' from the beginning, how we suffered from adult violence.
>
> The second film, *Golden Horseshoes*, is closer to my biography. I felt somehow compelled to tell what happens to a critical generation in an Islamic country. It was a opportunity to share my anxieties with the audience. This already explains why the film has a hard time getting screened in public. After that film I felt liberated to deal again with other topics. My next film will not be so strictly autobiographic: my view is directed now toward the society which surrounds me.[136]

In fact, the story of *Golden Horseshoes* is much more closely linked to the film maker's life. Nouri Bouzid spent five years in Tunisian prisons because of his political conviction and, like his protagonist, was humiliated and tortured.[137]

Odysseys

The individual that is brought to the foreground by autobiographic cinema is sent in a few films on a frightening odyssey. In the Tunisian film, *Crossing Over* (ᶜUbur; Traversées, 1982) by Mahmoud Ben Mahmoud, an Arab intellectual travels by boat from Belgium to Great Britain. Although he has a valid visa he is denied entrance at the border. The frontier police suspect him of terrorism and subject him to a degrading body check. Finally, together with an East European, he is send back to the ferry. The boat travels back but neither man has a visa for Belgium, and both are prevented from leaving the boat. Without any alternative, they try to come to arrangements with the crew. While the East European gets casual work on the ferry, the Arab escapes into the higher spheres of poetry and love.

The Arab protagonist of *Crossing Over* is characterized by pride and unapproachability, which sets him apart from his East European fellow sufferer. Considering his desperate situation his attitude seems inadequate and inappropriate. Having his eyes made up with kohl, he cites Arab poetry to the European lover he has found on board. His reference to his great culture, however, cannot affect his real problem. He cannot return to his own country—which evidently cannot cope with a secular, liberal intellectual of his kind—but is not permitted to enter the so-called liberal world either. Accordingly, the Arab intellectual is in limbo, caught between irreconcilable contradictions—past and present, East and West, reality and ideal. His future has no perspective.

According to Ben Mahmoud, the story is based on a personal experience during his studies in Belgium. On a trip to Great Britain he was held at the border. He, in fact, was able to return to Belgium, but a Yugoslav traveler on the same boat did not have an entry visa for either country.[138]

The protagonist of *Wanderers in the Desert* (1984) by the Tunisian Nacer Khemir suffers a similar fate. A young man (the role is acted by the director himself) travels to a remote town, deep in the desert, in order to start a job as a teacher there. When he arrives, he finds himself in an ancient town whose clay towers are untouched by modernity, but whose formerly flourishing gardens have sunk into dust. Soon, he discovers that it is inhabited only by women, children, and old men. All the young men have mysteriously disappeared, but are occasionally seen, far away, as a group of ghostly shadows crossing the horizon. The teacher's attempts to find out about their fate are unsuccessful, not least because those left behind have lost any sense of reality. Most of the town's inhabitants spend their time searching for treasure. Only one boy has a different dream: he wants to sail to the 'legendary' Cordoba on a ship that has been mysteriously abandoned in the sand dunes. Eventually, he too disappears in the desert, followed by the young teacher.

The film shifts constantly between fantastic and realistic events, so that the borders between the (supposedly) objective and the subjective perception blur. Although Nacer Khemir used the clay brick architecture in the south of Tunisia for his shooting, the town and its inhabitants do not resemble any real place. The costumes and behavior of the people belong to another world, while the visual arrangements, colors, and motifs follow Islamic miniature painting and in part create an aesthetic idealization. The fairy tale-like images are neither related to the present nor to the specific historical period that can be recognized from the details of the costume and the setting. Thus, cultural history is reduced to a diffuse, remote, though highly aesthetic, formula.

The integration of his cultural heritage in daily life seems impossible to the protagonist, as it does also to the film maker: "In the morning, when I walk through the streets at home and see that, again, they have destroyed a beautiful door or cut down a tree, I get into trouble. . . . I cultivate my absence from home by advancing further into a geography of the imaginary."[139] As a result, Nacer Khemir lives in Paris and not in Tunisia. The director establishes the connection to the mythical town depicted in the film, which embodies classical Arab culture and its civilizing achievements within as well as outside the film, by leaving on a binary, real and imaginary, journey. In the film, eventually and unexpectedly, the journey becomes an odyssey during which the individual is entirely lost.

In the Egyptian film *The Search for Sayyid Marzuq* (al-Bahth ʿan Sayyid Marzuq, 1991) by Daoud Abd El-Sayyed, it is not the unresolved relationship to his own culture that leads the protagonist astray but the confrontation with the dominating social system. One day, Yusuf, a simple employee, wakes up late and rushes to his work, only to discover he has made a mistake—it is a holiday. For twenty years, he has hardly been out, and now he enjoys spending the day drifting. On his walk he meets some odd people, including an organ-grinder who plays early in the morning on an empty square in front of closed doors and windows. In the middle of a party, frogmen appear, who are retrieving the body of a drowned person from the Nile. This is when Yusuf meets Sayyid Marzuq, a rich businessman, who invites him out so that he can tell him his story. In the evening, Marzuq asks Yusuf to look after his expensive car for a moment. A short while later, a police officer accuses Yusuf of stealing it. Yusuf flees through the city, with the police in hot pursuit. They do not stop chasing him even when the error has been cleared up and the car has been returned to his owner. More than once, Marzuq appears, followed by a group of musicians, and invites the exhausted Yusuf to a ride on his boat or gives him a precious birthday present, then leaves him again to his pursuers.

The kafkaesque chase seems absurd and has no logical explanation. The events and people's behavior are arbitrary and unpredictable. The simple citizen who has not left his house, except to go to work, for twenty years (i.e., since Nasser's death in 1971) finds himself in a world that is controlled by an omnipresent and unreasonable police apparatus.[140]

The absurdity of events is reflected in the narrative structure of the film. As if in a dream, normal spatial and temporal rules are distorted and neutralized. The representation of Marzuq and most other characters who surprisingly appear and repeatedly disappear during that endless night and whose intentions and identities remain unclear is not governed by logic or causality, thus reflecting an obviously incomprehensible reality.

Rebellion of sons

The 1967 defeat led not only to a changed perception of the individual and his position in society, but in some films also challenged the prevailing myth of virility. In the 1970s, several *auteur* films began questioning the traditional view of manhood and its negative sociopolitical effects. The ideological background to this has already been discussed in connection with *The Duped* (1972) by Taufik Salih. It is embodied in the allegorical character of the Palestinian truck driver who smuggles his compatriots into Kuwait for money. He does not care about the fate of his people; his only satisfaction is his personal enrichment. His attitude stems from a war wound that took away his manhood and consequently his sympathy and positive emotions.

The film clearly equates virility with honor, with national pride, and the readiness to make sacrifices. This association means inevitably that women lack these characteristics. Indeed in *The Duped* they are merely helpless and passive secondary figures. Some *auteur* films questioned this binary gender representation.

The Syrian scriptwriter and director Samir Zikra shows in *The Half-Meter Incident* (Hadithat al-nisf mitr, 1981) that male machismo constitutes a basic element in the psychological make-up of the petit

The Half-Meter Incident (Hadithat al-nisf mitr, Syria, 1981) by Samir Zikra
(*courtesy National Film Organization, Damascus*)

bourgeoisie, and that the 1967 defeat reinforced rather than weakened it. The main character of *The Half-Meter Incident* is an apolitical and sexually frustrated white collar worker who supports his mother and his little brothers and sisters. This prevents him from having an own family. As a result, women and sex occupy a large part of his thinking, until he meets a young student who is willing to start up a relationship with him. Gradually the shy young man mutates into a self-aware gigolo. When his girlfriend becomes pregnant, he abandons her. Meanwhile, he has been able to attract the attention of his superiors by his opportunism and cooperativeness, and they put him in charge of organizing a civil defense. However, the Six Day War ends as quickly as it starts. Its disastrous outcome has no negative effect on the protagonist. On the contrary, he has obtained a promotion because of his useless commitment.

Apparently Samir Zikra attributes no cathartic effects to the defeat, but believes instead that it further reinforced the dominant conditions in his country. Consequently, the increased repression due to political insecurity and the close attachment of the petty bourgeoisie to the system contributes to the reinforcement of patriarchal norms. Zikra's analysis clarifies the conditions that create a moral double standard regarding women.

The Palestinian director Michel Khleifi also criticizes the ethics of

Wedding in Galilee (ᶜUrs al-Djalil, Palestine, 1989) by Michel Khleifi

patriarchal Arab society, in particular the concept of male honor *(sharaf)*. In Khleifi's feature film *The Wedding in Galilee* (ᶜUrs al-Djalil, 1989), a Palestinian *mukhtar*, the head of a village, wants to celebrate his son's wedding. Because of the curfew he has to ask the Israeli administration for permission. They agree, on the condition that the military governor and his entourage may participate in the celebration. The *mukhtar* has no choice but to accept. The wedding is organized according to traditional customs, but once he is left alone with his bride the son finds it impossible to consummate the marriage, and the guests are made to wait for the required tissue with the sign of the defloration. The groom is seized by helpless rage against his father, and in order to relieve him the bride deflowers herself. But it is too late: the guests have already left, chased away by Israeli patrols.

In spite of the state of emergency imposed by the Israeli authorities, internal and traditional power relations remain intact. The head of the village who yields to the Israelis is nevertheless an authority whom even his opponents in the village, who prefer unconcealed resistance, still accept. Even his son cannot escape his control. He vents his anger only passively and self-destructively, resulting in his impotence. The latter is the more fatal, as the groom's virility is bound up with his father's reputation. This notion of manhood can only be proven by means of penetration and defloration.

In the context of the occupation, the political oppression, and the deprivation of Palestinian society, Michel Khleifi tries to show how meaningless such a notion of virility is. He argues for an admission of weakness instead of a shallow demonstration of power:

> Here, a rehabilitation of the Arab individual with his contradictions and weakness takes place. It is only weakness that allows him to mature and to face problems in a balanced manner. I wanted to put aside slogans in order to allow the mental condition of Arab society to come to light. Only liberated individuals can fight oppression, which means weak individuals who are presented in their weakness and inability. What I wanted to express with this film is summarized in that fragile child in the first shot who is running while he hears the noise of shots. Certainly it is an image of weakness but it also testifies a terrible force.[141]

The representation of force and weakness in *The Wedding of Galilee* focuses on two antagonisms: male and female, steadfastness and compliance. They shape the film's movement by a constant up and down. An Israeli female soldier faints, overwhelmed by the heat, the sumptuous meal, and the smells. The Palestinian women carry her into the house, take off her gray uniform, and wrap her in a colorful, embroidered Palestinian gown. When she wakes up she finds herself surrounded by the subdued light of the house, gentle voices, and soft fabrics. The aggressive male power that she has symbolized hitherto is absorbed by the 'female' interior of the Arab house. "The architectural thinking of the film is really part of Palestinian society: the logic of violence on the male side and the logic that spoils this violence on the female side. The whole writing *(écriture)* is carefully arranged around this quasi-architectural opposition between a violent and an 'escaping' material."[142] When an Israeli soldier tries to get into the house to search for his female colleague, he finds himself encircled by women and prevented from entering. His vigor is cushioned by their soft, but determined movement and subsequently challenged by their seductive mockery. Michel Khleifi's binary notion of gender certainly draws from traditional ideas, but invalidates them by changing and twisting their signs, or precisely, by linking putative female weakness with power and male power with weakness.

In works by Arab *auteur* directors, the rebellion of sons against the dominant patriarchy frequently ends in self-destruction. Already in the Moroccan film *Wechma*, shot in 1970, the father's severity leads to his son's destruction. More recent films, such as Nouri Bouzid's *Man of Ashes*, take up similar themes. Hashimi's relationship with his father is marked by violence and hostility. His relationship with his 'substitute' father, his master ᶜAmmar, is also overshadowed by the trauma of aggression (embodied by sexual abuse). The only positive paternal character is an old Jew who is excluded from the patriarchal power structure by his physical frailness and his social marginality.[143] Thus, Hashimi in his turn can react only in despair and violence. He rejects the proposed marriage, in other words his family's requirements, while his alter ego Farfat attacks the master with a knife and escapes.

The political activist Yusuf in *Golden Horseshoes* destroys himself too. He fails to find a place in the political system and loses contact with his grown-up children. They in turn despise their father, who cares more about politics than their well-being. Yusuf's attempts to initiate changes are in vain. His ultimate solution is suicide.

In his analysis of the Bourguiba period in Tunisia Aziz Krichen states that Bouzid's generation suffered a whole succession of destroyed father-son relations. "The drama determining Nouri Bouzid's work and giving it at the same time its strength and homogeneity is the drama of affiliation from which there is no return and that is expressed in the loss of a sense of identity and belonging. It turns those who suffer from it into isolated individuals who are unable to recognize others, to commit themselves and to act, like the scattered parts of a broken transmission chain."[144]

Essentially, Krichen considers the failed affiliation and the resulting identity crises the legacy of colonial oppression and humiliation—of which the 1967 defeat is a part—which have bequeathed self-hatred and national pride to the colonized as the two sides of one coin.[145] This legacy is still effective and continues decisively to shape post-colonial society.

Feminization of Arab cinema

The position of women in the Arab countries is one of the most contentious issues separating progressive and fundamentalist tendencies. Various works of the revolutionary Algerian Cinema and Egyptian realism have objected to discrimination against women. They criticize the arranged marriage *(The Open Door, A Wife for My Son)*, the disadvantaging and molesting of women at work (Salah Abu Seif's *I Am Free*, Ana hurra, Egypt, 1958; Sid Ali Mazif's *Layla and Her Sisters,* Layla wa akhawatiha, Algeria, 1977), or family oppression *(Sahara Blues, South Wind, Aziza* by Abdellatif Benamar, Tunisia, 1980). Many male directors, however, expressed in their films the need for female emancipation but often simply as a means to achieve national goals, such as technical and cultural progress, or political independence. Examples include the Algerian film *The South Wind* (1976), or *The Open Door* (al-Bab al-maftuh, 1963) by the

Layla and Her Sisters (Layla wa akhawatiha, Algeria, 1977) by Sid Ali Mazif
(*ONCIC (former)/Ministry of Culture, Algiers*)

Egyptian Henri Barakat. In many other cases, women remain helpless victims, as in the Moroccan melodramas *Badis* (1989) by Mohamed Ben Abderrahmane Tazi and the realist *Aisha* (1981) by Jilalli Ferhati. Only in the late 1970s did the *cinéma d'auteur* start presenting a differentiated and deconstructive image of women.

In contrast to his first film, *Aisha*, Jilalli Ferhati's more recent *The Beach of the Lost Children* (Shati' al-atfal al-da'i^cin, Morocco, 1991), for which he wrote the screenplay himself, gives a contradictive image of women's life in so-called traditional society. Mina is a rebellious girl who lives with her father, grandmother, and young stepmother in a remote fishing village. She likes to roam about the beach with the neighbors' children, instead of spending the day at home with her stepmother. Then Mina has an affair with a taxi driver. When she asks him to marry her, he refuses. Outraged, but unintentionally, the girl kills her lover. She hides his body in the huge salt piles at the beach. A short while later, Mina discovers she is pregnant. When her father finds out, he locks her up. He tells the people in the village that Mina has gone to visit relatives, and persuades his wife to pretend that she is pregnant. However, when Mina delivers her child she does not want to leave it in her stepmother's custody. She takes her child and escapes, with the villagers looking on. The film leaves it open as to whether she will succeed and how the village will react.

Ferhati avoids clichés. His characterizations attach importance to a profound psychological description. He carefully depicts the ambiguous relation between Mina and her infertile stepmother, who is almost the same age as her. Importantly, her father is not represented as a violent, omnipotent patriarch who would prefer his daughter dead after she has besmirched his honor. Instead, he is torn between compassion for his daughter and the necessity of maintaining his social reputation. In Ferhati's film, men and women alike come into conflict with society and try actively to resolve that conflict.

Female *auteurs*

Women are underrepresented in Arab cinema in every respect. Female problems and circumstances of life remain marginalized in general. The phenomenon of women producing and realizing films is relatively recent in Arab film history, if we disregard the female pioneers of Egyptian cinema, such as ᶜAziza Amir, Fatima Rushdi, and Bahiga Hafiz in the 1920s and 1930s.[146] Today a considerable number of women write screenplays, direct for television, or realize documentaries, for example the documentarists Attiat El-Abnoudi, Nabiha Lotfi, and Firyal Kamil in Egypt, and Selma Beccar in Tunisia. The Palestinians May Masri and Mouna Hattoum work in the fields of documentary and experimental cinema respectively.

In feature film production, however, women are still particularly underrepresented. In Syria, not a single woman has had the opportunity to direct a long feature film. In Iraq, only one woman feature film director is known, Khayriya ᶜAbbas, who directed a film called *6/6* in 1987. Morocco has two female directors, Farida Ben Lyazid and Farida Burqiya. In Algeria, the writer Assia Djebar directed two semi-documentaries for television. The first conventional fiction film, *Female Demon,* shot by an Algerian woman, Hafsa Zinat-Koudil, was completed in 1993. In Lebanon the best known female documentary film makers, Jocelyne Saab, Randa Chahal, and Heiny Srour, have to date directed either one or two full-length fiction films each. They all live in Europe and finance their projects either themselves or with the support of Western producers. The same applies to the Tunisian director Néjia Ben Mabrouk. Moufida Tlatli and Selma Beccar, who live in Tunisia, also have to rely on coproductions. Each of them has directed one full-lengh feature film. In Egypt only a few woman directors have entered the film industry in recent years, including

Inas al-Dighidi, Nadia Hamza, and Asma' al-Bakri. Their work scarcely differs from the products of their male colleagues. One of the various reasons why few women join the film industry is certainly moral. Film, showbusiness, and particularly acting are associated with moral laxity.

Some Arab woman directors, including Assia Djebar, Farida Ben Lyazid, and Néjia Ben Mabrouk, have accessed cinema through writing. Néjia Ben Mabrouk, the director of *Sama* (The Trace), explains this phenomenon by referring to the inadequate educational situation in her homeland and the absence of native female examples:

> At that time I didn't want to make my own films—maybe because I was missing examples of women film makers. All directors were men, so it seemed more natural to me as a young woman to tell stories through writing. I wanted to write novels. At that time, in the late 1960s, no film school, no acting school existed, nothing that could have allowed a young woman to make films. Even television was not functioning yet.[147]

Ben Mabrouk studied cinema in Brussels at the INSAS (Institut National Supérieur des Arts et du Spectacle). Her first full-length feature film, *Sama,* contains elements of her own biography. It describes the struggle of a young woman to obtain an adequate education and the right to determine her own life. The narrative of *Sama* constantly shifts between past and present, between the protagonist's childhood and her vain efforts to graduate from high school. The imagery is divided into the hostile public space—the streets, with their male harassment and the school with its unrelenting male French teachers—and an intimate space—her parents' house, her accommodation in town, and her girlfriend's apartment.

The interior of the house is defined by Mabrouk as the female domain, which men rarely enter, the realm of the embracing, protective, but also devouring mother. This juxtaposition is made already at the beginning of the film in a dream of the protagonist. The hands of the mother appear in a dim room wrapping a tiny stone in paper, hiding it eventually in a small round tin before shutting it away in a drawer. Then they sew the key of the drawer into a small cushion, while the protagonist's voice desperately asks for her little tin.

None of Néjia Ben Mabrouk's male colleagues has succeeded in presenting a similarly claustrophobic description of a female environment. As the protagonist is able to liberate herself neither by adopting the maternal role nor by finishing her education, she chooses emigration as an escape. This seems also to have been the only way out for the film maker herself, who lives today in Belgium.

The adolescent hero of Jocelyne Saab's *The Razor's Edge* (Ghazal al-banat, literally, 'girls' flirtation'; Adolescence sucrée d'amour, Lebanon, 1985)[148] discovers a different freedom, which is war. Her parents are occupied with taking care of daily supplies and unable to provide proper attention or education for their children. The girl roams through the destroyed city, explores ruins and abandoned houses, and makes strange and sometimes dangerous acquaintances, including a disillusioned painter and a cynical sniper. Together with a girlfriend she spends her time in a bombed stadium acting out love scenes from Egyptian movies. Neither her parents nor her grown-up friends can act as an example for the girl, and she has no regard for what they think. The destructive war has created a vacuum in which, at the most, the imagery of the Egyptian dream-factory provides a continuity. However, the question of whether the war was able to create new, permanent, liberal structures is not answered by the film.

Some films by female authors set out consciously to invalidate certain predominating discourses on women's liberation, be they national or Western. One such film is the Tunisian feature film *Silence of the Palaces* (1994), directed by Moufida Tlatli. The story is set in the early 1950s, on the eve of Tunisia's national independence, in the palace of some Tunisian beys, where several female servants are kept almost in slavery and have to do their masters' will in any respect.

The film centers around an adolescent girl who witnesses the sexual abuse of her mother by the beys. In spite of the women's seclusion, the palace is not a closed entity. The camera never leaves it, but the outside interferes constantly in the events that take place inside, especially politically. One of these intrusions is brought about

Silence of the Palaces (Samt al-qusur, Tunisia, 1994) by Moufida Tlatli

by a young nationalist teacher who is hunted by the police for his activities and is hidden in the house by the servants. He makes the heroine fall in love with him, and eventually releases her from the golden cage in which she was brought up. However, when they leave the palace together, he does not marry her because of her social and moral status, but puts pressure on her instead to abort their child.In this way, Moufida Tlatli disconnects national liberation from women's liberation, showing that the one does not necessarily result in the other. This conviction has also been expressed—though not in so sophisticated and formal a way—by male directors, such as the Algerian Rashid bin Hadj, who directed the feature film *Touchia* (1993). His heroine is raped by compatriots the same day national independence is declared.

Another rare view on the gender issue is that of the Moroccan scriptwriter and director, Farida Ben Lyazid, who reflects on Western-oriented ideas of women's liberation. For her, female self-realization is not achieved by submitting to a national project, nor by destroying traditional structures, nor by escaping abroad. Instead, in her directing debut, *A Door to the Sky* (Bab al-sama' maftuh; Une porte sur le ciel, 1989), she searches Islamic culture for ways to emancipate women.

Nadia, whose father is dying, returns from Paris to Fez. She and her siblings have grown up in two cultures, the children of a Moroccan father and a French mother. Each of them has chosen a different type of affiliation. Driss, the brother, wants to be entirely French. After his father's death he decides to sell the paternal home, a huge traditional house in the old city, as soon as possible, and to return to France. In contrast, Nadia's sister Layla is married to an affluent Moroccan and has adapted to the convenient but dull life of the native bourgeoisie. Nadia herself says, "J'ai rien choisi, je veux tout" (I have chosen nothing. I want everything.) She thinks of going back to France but does not want to give up her father's house. During her father's funeral she meets a *muqaddima* who recites the Quran at the women's mourning ceremony. The wisdom of the old woman touches Nadia so much that she gets involved with her in a debate on doubts and belief. The *muqaddima* advises her to read the texts of the old Sufi scholars and mystics, such as al-Halladj and al-Ghazali. Supported by her religious adviser, Nadia decides to transform the house into a *zawiya*—in the Maghreb usually the settlement of a Sufi brotherhood, in this case a religious institution offering lodging and teaching for women in need. At the same time Nadia ends her relationship with her French lover and withdraws from the world into her *zawiya*. The house becomes a place of refuge and contemplation where religious feasts are held. During a *hadra*, a ceremony including religious dances and recitations cumulating in trance, Nadia is blessed with visions and discovers that she has healing powers *(baraka)*.

The director dedicated her film to Fatima al-Fihriya, who founded the first university in Fez in the tenth century, thus clarifying her subliminal political message. On the one hand, *A Door to the Sky* wants to support native feminists by reminding them that women held important social positions in classical Islamic times. On the other hand, the author takes a position on Western feminism by illustrating that such 'progressive' institutions as shelters for battered women have a long tradition in Islamic culture and that female self-realization can take place in a traditional framework. In keeping with this, Farida Ben Lyazid leaves the shelter in her film in its traditional surroundings and embeds it in a religious foundation or *zawiya*.

The film does not, however, suggest a return to orthodox Islam but rather a reevaluation of the knowledge and rites of Sufi mysticism that form part of popular belief in the Maghreb. Farida Ben Lyazid aims to strengthen the notion of a tolerant Islam combining belief and social commitment, but consciously places both in an entirely regional context. Hence, she makes the *muqaddima* tell the women that while Islam is unchangeable, its interpretations are open to change. She explains the hostility of some women to the admission of a francophone former convict by reference to their limited knowledge and tries to persuade them to show more sympathy.

Despite the profound change the heroine undergoes during the film, Nadia does not resolve her original dilemma. She solves the problem of her national affiliation by taking a one-sided decision. She reconciles only with her Moroccan heritage, but cuts her relation to France abruptly and thoroughly, leaving again a wide fissure between tradition and modernity as absolute contradictions, at least on the material level. Hence, her search for identity concentrates on metaphysics. Accordingly, her eventual marriage to a young man she has cured is not realistically described. The two of them do not lead the daily life of a married couple, but start a journey through the mountains, visiting holy places. Their transfigured embrace seem to unify them with each other and with nature. These scenes may be read as symbols of a spiritual journey and draw from the traditional Sufi ideas of love and the believer's devotion to the creator. Through this symbolism the film transfers the conflict of this life to a metaphysical level. The problem of identity is solved by immersion in a spiritual sphere that in its core is common to all cultures.

4

FROM THE NATIONAL TO THE TRANSNATIONAL?

The struggle for national cinemas

Since the advent of cinema and on several occasions, through the events of decolonization, revolutions, and civil wars, many Arab countries have been caught in a bitter struggle to develop or keep up their national film production and ensure their distribution. .This applies especially to the period from 2005 to 2015. The reanimation of the Lebanese media and film industry, the strengthening of the Moroccan film industry, and the rise of media hubs in the Persian Gulf, most notably in the UAE, are integral to this development. In particular the Emirates and Qatar have worked hard during recent years to encourage film and media production in their countries, by encouraging Arab and international film culture through festivals, investment, and funding opportunities. Also some presumably national cinemas, most notably the Lebanese and the Moroccan, have managed to enhance the economic basis of their productions and cross over into the regional and international markets with a handful of exceptional films without necessarily increasing their local market share. At the same time, the Egyptian industry is struggling for survival on the level of production even though it has still kept its traditional assets in most of its former markets. And of course the

continual shifts of national borders due to the ongoing international and regional power struggles, as well as the effect of
transnational social and political movements and forces linked to
it, such as the Muslim Brothers and the Islamic State (IS), and the
resulting displacement and ethnic cleansing, are affecting so-
called national production in the region and its relation to the
outside world.

Of course the very meaning of 'national' cinema has to be discussed, in any case, because common definitions of national
cinema seem at odds with the actual situation in many countries. In
some festival catalogues the national affiliation of a film often follows the nationality of the director. Others add the nationality of
coproducers and funding institutions. However, does that suffice
for a film to become part of a national cinema? In his analysis of
British national cinema, Andrew Higson, for example, mentions
three defining aspects: First, the existence of working infrastruc-
tures in the field of production, distribution, and exhibition within
one's national borders; second, market shares, or the extent to
which audiences perceive and interact with national production;
and third, the question of cultural specificity or identity, a process
that might give preference to certain films at the expense of others,
for instance, committed or art cinema as opposed to supposedly
trivial or alienated popular cinema.[1]

Applying the first and second aspects to the situation of Arab
countries would exclude most of them from being able to claim
having a national cinema. This holds true even more in view of the
fact that so many of them have to rely on the system of coproduction and foreign funding to ensure the making and shooting of films
within their borders. Of course the third aspect plays well into the
discussion of what is allowed to represent the nation and what isn't
and for what reason. It also fits into theories that underline either
the construction of narration through the nation or vice versa—that
the nation may be imagined by narration and its audio-visual extension, the fiction film. Naturally it is preferable not to perceive these

theories as opposed but rather complementary, in order to be able to understand the dialectic and transitory relation between nation and narration. It goes without saying that the actual gap between the nation-state and the nation, namely between the largely arbitrary geographic boundaries and the degree of linguistic, ethnic, and religious diversity, reflects on that dialectic.

Another important defining aspect of national cinema is the power relations that govern the international market and have produced different forms of national cinemas, if we follow the model proposed by Stephen Crofts, who speaks of seven different variations of 'national cinema.' In his view, most of them had to operate according to an agenda set by Hollywood that parallels to a certain degree the unequal global economic and cultural exchange. Some of Crofts' variations overlap; this is why I prefer to mention only the most crucial. First, there are specialized cinemas that differ from Hollywood and cater to a distinct market sector, like European art film. Second, there are cinemas that may or may not critique Hollywood, without competing with it, such as Bollywood, for example. They may even ignore Hollywood entirely. Third, there are European and Third World entertainment cinemas which compete with Hollywood and have difficulties in defending their national markets. Anglophone cinemas that try to beat Hollywood at their own game, such as the British and the Australian, are the most successful type of this model. Fourth, there are state-controlled and fully or partly subsidized industries, like former Soviet cinema. Fifth are the regional or national cinemas that keep their distance from the nation-states that surround them, such as Catalan or French-Canadian.[2]

At first sight, the Egyptian film industry certainly fits into the variation of struggling entertainment cinemas, while Moroccan cinema shifts between subsidized, art, and entertainment cinema. Others, such as the Tunisian and the Lebanese, manage only occasionally to arrive at the stage of entertainment and are stuck largely in the first variation, that is, art cinema. However, unlike the most successful type of European art cinema, namely the French, they have almost no audience at home. Yet still the question needs to be posed whether the current regional and transnational economic and cultural exchange is as unbalanced as Crofts' model would suggest. Is it indeed governed by one-sided power relations that produce a hegemonic center, such as Hollywood and its regional competitors, like the Egyptian film industry? Or would another model be more appropriate to describe the situation? But then how to assess recent developments in the field such as the emergence of new national cinemas in the Gulf region, and those with negligible national market shares but an increasing influence on the film economy of other Arab countries, first and foremost Egypt?

A changing mediascape

On the historical level it is evident that the development of Arab cinema was marked by an imbalance in its regional cultural and economic exchanges, preferring a largely one-way flow from the center of production to the periphery of consumption. To be more precise, as we have seen in the first part of the book, the Egyptian film industry and its mainstream production has dominated Arab film culture for many years, and was later, in the era of decolonization, denounced for that reason as a dream factory and blamed for its presumed escapism.[3] It was increasingly challenged by the advent of other Arab national cinemas in North Africa and the Fertile Crescent. In particular, filmmakers who perceived themselves as the representatives of New Arab Cinemas—or what I have chosen to describe as *cinéma d'auteur*—considered that popular Egyptian cinema was being produced and distributed at the expense of other national productions and were thus eager to denounce it and to work on curbing its popularity with local audiences. This applied also to post-independence film critique in Egypt itself, which dismissed the cinema that preceded the 1952 coup and revolution as royalist and backward.[4]

On the political level Egypt's special position mirrored its immense historical, human, and cultural potential as well as its unique geo-strategic position and the leading role that it played particularly in the first years of decolonization under the rule of Nasser, a status it started to lose gradually after the 1967 defeat and the Camp David Accords in 1978. These two events isolated the country regionally to a certain extent and coincided with the rise of other national Arab cinemas. Viewing Ferid Boughedir's 1982 Tunisian documentary *Caméra Arabe*, the polarization between mainstream or popular cinema and what he calls New Arab Cinemas becomes very apparent. In this context he lists the names of committed directors, such as Youssef Chahine, Taufik (Taufiq) Salih, Ridha Behi, and Borhane Alaouié, among others, and their respective works that appeared in the first post-colonial era and deviated from the formulae of commercial Egyptian genre cinema, its melodrama and musicals. In a way his argument is reminiscent of Solonas' and Getino's classification of first, second, and third cinema. According to the logic of this model, the Egyptian film industry would be considered a second cinema representative, that is, a Third World dream factory that caters to a Third World people copying the alienating and deceptive representational methods of First World industry, to the disadvantage of its people.

As Stephen Crofts emphasized, "Hollywood has successfully exported and naturalized its construction of the cinema as fictional entertainment."[5] He quotes Thomas Elsaesser that "Hollywood can hardly be conceived as totally other, since so much of any nation's film culture is implicitly 'Hollywood.'"[6] In contrast, "in Western discussions, Hollywood is hardly ever spoken of as a national cinema."[7] This naturalization has made Hollywood cinema into the international norm, *the* cinema per se, while other national cinemas are likely to be perceived as exceptional, despite the paradoxical fact that on the level of representation Hollywood sticks primarily to elements of its national culture, be they emotions, locations, language, narration, or tropes.

At this point the question arises whether Second Cinemas like the Egyptian have achieved a similar naturalization on the regional level. In fact, Egyptian cinema has long remained equivalent to Arab cinema in general, particularly during the colonial era. This also explains why its dominance had to be challenged in the period of decolonization, in which other Arab countries had been busy constructing and cementing their respective national identities. Egyptian films have been circulating in all the other Arab countries since the 1930s in varying degrees, either on the silver screen or in video sales, reaching at times an exceptional 45 percent of local market share, as in Saudi Arabia, for example.[8] On the other hand, the Egyptian market has been closed to films from other Arab countries with some very rare exceptions, such as Syrian films by Doureid Laham in the 1990s or some Lebanese films, most recently Nadine Labaki's *Where Do We Go Now?* (Wa halla l-wayn, 2011), thus creating an imbalance in terms of cultural and economic exchange.

Yet this is only one side of the picture. So-called cultural hegemonies tend also to be challenged or subverted by subjecting their cultural expression to subversive mimicry and to carnivalist (in the Bakhtinian sense)[9] or even 'cannibalist' recycling.[10] They may also make concessions to their foreign recipients. Since the 1940s, Egypt's productions have integrated Lebanese singers, actors, and characters, and included songs and dances from other regions, while distribution was partly dominated by Jordanian and Lebanese enterprises. True, in the 1950s and 1960s Egyptian genre cinema served as a role model, and still does for emerging mainstream-oriented film industries in the region. However, in the 1980s audio-visual products from Egypt were used regardless of their quality as an advertisement medium for commodities relevant to the Gulf States, while distribution became increasingly dominated by Kuwait. This caused Egyptian cinema to be hijacked and adapted to the needs of neighboring countries with stronger economies, despite its clearly Egyptian character in terms of dialect, topics, and stars. At home, this has led to Egyptian films becoming a sort of Trojan horse for the so-called 'new morality' and religiosity, strongly inspired by the Saudi Arabian fundamentalist Wahhabism that has spread in Egyptian society since the 1970s. It culminated in the development of a so-called 'clean cinema,' or *sinima nazifa*, since around 2005, a cinema that exerts self-control with regard to the moral image and permissiveness of its leading stars, of both sexes, as well as to female clothing. At the same time formal elements of Egyptian mainstream have been recycled, ridiculed, or embellished by nostalgia in Arab arthouse cinema, such as Ferid Boughedir's *Halfaouine* or Jocelyne Saab's *The Razor's Edge*, among others.

Hence, it seems more useful to move away from the rather polarizing concept of center and periphery to a more complex model proposed by Arjun Appadurai, namely, the notion of scapes and flows. In his view, global exchange presents five different "landscapes" defined by constantly shifting, distinct, and not necessarily interdependent flows: finanscapes, technoscapes, ethnoscapes, ideoscapes, and mediascapes. This view allows us to map the traveling of people, inventions, money, ideas, and media that form our imagined world.[11] With regard to cinema, this concept qualifies Crofts' model considerably, in that it refuses to deal with cinema as a separate phenomenon, but perceives it instead in the framework of an interrelated process that implies national and international creation and dissemination of information and ideas at once. It permits film production, distribution, and exhibition to be viewed in their processuality, that is, as a form of transnational interaction. This interaction has been enhanced and fostered by technical developments, namely the advent of new media or, in other words, the digital turn that has affected production and distribution on the level of practices and economy, but also in terms of regional and international exchange which even Egypt's cinema has started to be affected by.

Egypt's film industry: A battle for survival

Egyptian cinema continues to play a certain role as a fiction-film supplier for the region, as well as in producing entertainment programs and dramatic serials *(musalsalat)* for transnational Arab television channels. (Until the outbreak of the civil war, Syria was its strongest competitor in the field of Arabic-speaking serials.) In contrast to the Moroccan situation, the Egyptian film industry works below capacity, but ranks high with regards to stable distribution and, recently, its remarkable growth in the number and technical standard of movie theaters. Since the 1990s the number of cinemas in the country has risen to 544,[12] some of which are furnished with digital and 3D screening facilities. In 2010, there were twenty-eight digital screens, so that the country ranks thirteenth worldwide in terms of introducing the new digital technology.[13]

Egypt's authorities offer little in terms of long-term and sustainable development policies, including funding. The film economy is run almost entirely on a private basis and has to rely on the recuperation of production costs through distribution. This means that the industry does not enjoy complete independence or self-sufficiency: as production has been export-oriented since 1933, it has always been at the whims of non-Egyptian distributors. Egyptian films exports have ranked highest at the box office in Qatar and Bahrain. Since the 1990s approximately 25 percent of its exports went to Gulf countries, and around 7 to 10 percent to Lebanon, Syria, and Jordan.[14] For decades this business has been monopolized by Lebanese, Jordanian, and more recently Gulf distributors. Today, companies from the Gulf have gained considerable influence as coproducers or main financiers and are suspected of exercising pre-censorship on Egyptian films.[15] The largest of these companies is the Rotana Group, whose biggest shareholder is the Saudi prince al-Walid ibn Talal. The Rotana Cinema channel is said to have purchased the negatives of hundreds of old Egyptian movies from ERTU (the Egyptian Radio and Television Union), which now lacks the means of acquiring the rights to air more recent Egyptian films.[16]

Egyptian production numbers have varied considerably in the last two decades, often affected by political or social unrest in the region. For example, production crashed suddenly from an outstanding peak of seventy fiction films in 1992 to sixteen in 1997—the lowest output since the 1930s—during the time of the 1990 Gulf War and the introduction of transnational Arab television channels. Since the turn of the millennium, Egypt's film industry has been able to stabilize and slightly increase its annual output, to twenty-four films in 2004 and thirty-nine in 2006. According to some analysts, the recovery was primarily due to the industry's adoption of improved technologies in the realms of sound, film laboratories, and computer graphics,[17] in addition to the more recent willingness of private transnational Arab satellite channels, such as ART and Rotana, to invest in the production of movies.

Similarly, between 2009 and 2011, the year of the outbreak of the rebellion which hit the industry strongly in the first year and brought almost everything to a halt for security reasons, the number of film releases ranged between twenty-two and thirty-three. Yet the situation began to reverse itself almost immediately, and the Ministry of Culture counted a total of sixty-two productions for the years 2012 and 2013.[18] At the same time, and unlike all other Arab countries, Egypt has kept the number of foreign releases low, thanks to restrictive legal measures. In 2011, for example, the Egyptian local market share was 83 percent, while the remaining 17 percent was held by American productions.[19]

Technical standards have improved since the introduction of digital technology for shooting and projection. Moreover, producers are increasingly making use of post-production services abroad. Budgets, as well as production costs in general, have been on the rise since the deterioration of the economic situation in Egypt, particularly after 2011. A typical budget is currently between seven and eight million Egyptian pounds, or slightly more than US$1 million.[20] Even harmless comedies, like Sandra Nash'at's *Thieves in KG2* (Haramiya fi KG 2, 2001) and *Molasses* (ᶜAssal aswad, 2010) by Khaled Marei (Khalid Marᶜi), show evidence of expensive effects, props, and locations. Monopolies also play a role within the industry. Between 2002 and 2011 only nine companies produced the majority of a total of 378 films.[21]

One exception was represented by Good News, a daughter company of the Gulf-based Good News Media Group that operates in eight different MENA countries and owns several theaters in them. Since 2011 it has abandoned film production. In the time before the uprising it produced a limited number of high-profile productions and its budgets exceeded at times the 30-million-Egyptian-pounds mark.[22] This made production standards rise considerably and achieve international visibility for Good News productions like *The Yacoubian Building* (ᶜImarat Yaᶜqubiyan, 2006) by Marwan Hamid, an adaptation of Alaa al-Aswany's international bestseller. Another expensive Good News production was *Ibrahim Labyad* (2009), an action film by the same young director Hamid. It capitalizes on complicated chases, fights, special effects, and very particular sets. Even though Good News gave up on production, Hamid directed more recently another technically ambitious film, *The Blue Elephant* (al-Fil al-azraq, 2014), a horror movie that successfully applies genre-specific effects.

Simultaneously, Egypt witnessed the emergence of the so-called shopping-mall film, specifically designed to reflect the interests and lifestyle of middle-class youth. The most successful of these were *Sleepless Nights* (Sahhar al-layali, 2003) by Hani Khalifa and *Leisure Time* (Awqat al-faragh, 2006) by Muhammad Mustafa. This category received its name from the specific movie theaters through which it attracts its privileged audiences. Situated in newly constructed shopping malls in the extended suburbs of Egypt's metropolises, these theaters are equipped according to the latest technical standards, profiting from and contributing to the comforts these specific, modern urban sites have to offer the Egyptian middle class.

In general, since the 1990s the Egyptian film industry has begun to rely less on melodrama and more on action films as well as on 'new comedy,' which started sweeping movie theaters and introducing a new generation of comedians, most notably Ahmad Helmy (Hilmi),

Muhammad Saʿd, Muhammad Hinidi, and Hani Ramzi. Some of the outstanding box-office hits achieved by these stars' film cycles, including *Hamam in Amsterdam* (Hamam fi Amsterdam, 1999) and *al-Limbi* (2002), made profits ten times higher than expenses, but they did not remedy the general crisis as expressed in weakened production rates for the simple reason that producers did not sufficiently reinvest their profits into the industry.[23]

From regionalism to international art house

The new millennium brought a diversification in genres and stylistic approaches even though moralist conservatism persisted. Khaled Youssef directed a (moderate) horror-thriller in 2006 called *Ouija*, for example. Sherif Arafa, who undertook the sequel *The Island* (al-Jazira, 2007 and 2014) and the espionage film *Cousins* (Wilad al-ʿamm, 2009), among others, Sandra Nash'at with *The Hostage* (al-Rahina, 2007), and Marwan Hamid tried to catch up with international standards in their action movies by importing South African expertise for action scenes and special effects. On the other hand, the preference for shooting abroad, for example Nash'at's comedy *Thugs in Thailand* (Haramiya fi Thailand, 2003), a trend that started earlier with *Hamam in Amsterdam* (1999) by Saʿid Hamid, died out gradually.

  At the box office, comedy and musical farce have remained highly successful, for instance *al-Limbi* by Wa'il Ihsan starring comedian Muhammad Saʿd. It was strongly attacked for its supposed triviality in presenting a constantly drugged, infantile, lower-class male character. *Omar and Salma* (ʿUmar wa Salma, 2007) by Akram Farid, a soap-opera-like comedy about a quarrelsome young bourgeois couple, was so popular that two sequels followed. The new-generation comedian Ahmad Helmy, who was well received in *Snakes and Ladders* (Sulum wa thuʿban, 2001) among other films, rose to the top with *Keda Reda* (Kidda Ridha; literally, 'Ridha like that,' 2007) and later *X-Large* (2011).

The new comedy, as well as action films in the style of Sherif Arafa, however, are impregnated with conservatism, particularly with regard to gender relation and sexuality; it has been dubbed "clean cinema" or *al-sinima al-nazifa*. Certain stars, such as Mona Zaki, Ahmad Helmy, Ahmad al-Saqqa, Muhammad Sa^{c}d, and Muhammad Hinidi, have become the backbone of this type of cinema that decidedly refrains from showing any signs of eroticism, even kisses between men and women or sexy outfits. Their attitude is based on the consciousness that audiences create an imagined persona of popular stars, merging their fictive and real characters.

Consequently, performers who want to appear morally respectable try to avoid playing loose characters or getting involved in stories that do not have a clear moral orientation. This has made it very hard for directors like Daoud Abd El-Sayed, for instance, who consciously addresses political and moral taboos, to get his films produced. El-Sayed's *Messages from the Sea* (Rasa'il al-bahr, 2010) thus remained in the pipeline for many years. Since none of the above-mentioned stars was ready to accept the lead role, it was nearly impossible to raise the necessary funding. After years of struggle the film was eventually realized with lesser-known actors and the help of ministerial support offered through public post-production services.

The New Realist wave died out in the late 1990s in spite of veteran Mohamed Khan's constant attempts to revive it with, among others, *Factory Girl* (Fatat al-masna^c, 2014), one of his latest independently produced films. Realist motivation and related stylistic approaches have persisted to a certain extent in the work of other directors as well, including even Khaled Youssef (Khalid Yusuf), the co-director of Youssef Chahine's *Chaos* (Hiya fawda, 2007), who tends to use exploitative strategies for his films. His *Until Further Notice* (Hina maysara, 2008), for instance, is situated in an informal neighborhood or slum. The selling point is certainly the promiscuity of its characters. At the same time the film displays the immense degree of social injustice and human rights violations that prevail in the Egyptian environment. The finale, with the bombed and burning slum, destroyed as a result of the conflict between Islamists and the police, has an almost prophetic quality, predicting the unrest that has followed the 2011 uprising involving the Egyptian army and the Muslim Brothers.

The persistent 'realist' motivation of some filmmakers implied the presentation of daring topics, which in turn often touch upon gender relations. *Girls' Secrets* (Asrar al-banat, 2001) by Magdy Ahmad Ali, for example, deals with female genital mutilation and teenage pregnancy; Yousry Nasrallah's *Sheherazade, Tell Me a Story* (Ihky ya Shahrazad, 2009) with domestic violence; *1:0* (2009) by Kamla Abu Zekry with the personal status of Coptic women; *678* (2010) by Mohamed Diab with sexual harassment; and *Asmaa* (Asma', 2011) by ᶜAmr Salama with the moral stigmatiza-tion of AIDS/HIV-positive patients. Oussama (Usama) Fawzi's *In Natural Colors* (Bi-l-alwan al-tabiᶜiya, 2010) tries to address the dichotomy between modern art and lifestyle, artistic and sexual lib-erty, and religious conservatism, although in a quite polarizing way that caused a stir.[24] Ahmad Abdalla's unconventional *Décor* (2014), shot in black and white, about a schizophrenic woman struggling to liberate herself from her relationship to two different men, pays homage to the psychological thriller *The Last Night* (al-Layla al-akhira, 1963) by Kamal El-Cheikh.

ᶜAmr Salama's *Excuse My French* (La mu'akhza, 2014) is a social comedy with a unique, music-clip-inspired *mise en scène*, about the discrimination against Copts in Egypt. It features a boy from a Christian middle-class family who are in a financial crisis and have to transfer him from a fancy English-language school to a public school, where the greatest offense you can commit is to be diligent, bring your mother to complain—or be Christian. The boy's struggle to find his place without denying his religious affili-ation gets him into a lot of tricky situations that reveal a great deal about the hypocritical attitude of Egyptian society toward the issue of religious tolerance.

Muhammad Amin, in contrast, presented two politically critical and sexually quite uninhibited—not on the graphic but on the verbal and symbolical level—satires, *The Night When Baghdad Fell* (Laylat suqut Baghdad, 2005) and *Black February* (Fibrayir al-aswad, 2013). He prefers a TV and farce-like style. The bitter social satire *Ant Scream* (Sarkhat namla, 2011) by Samih ᶜAbd al-ᶜAziz is more realistic in its *mise en scène*. It was conceived before the revolution but added some revolution-related scenes during its realization.

The outbreak of the January 25 Revolution and the subsequent political unrest have been portrayed as well, from right on the spot in *18 Days* (18 Yaum, 2011), an episode film by ten directors including Nasrallah, Abu Zekry, Hamid, and Arafa. *After the Battle* (Baᶜd al-mawqiᶜa, 2012) by Yousry Nasrallah and *Winter of Discontent* (al-Shita illi fat, 2012) by Ibrahim El-Batout (al-Batut) are political films that discuss some of the social and personal implications of the revolution. El-Batout and Ahmed Abdalla represented first and foremost the independent and alternative film scene that had started to develop in the mid-2000s, that is, before 2011. This wave was followed by others and crystallized in a number of independent, sometimes collectively produced, art house films of varied quality.

Another novelty is the increase in full-length documentaries, some of which made it to movie theaters, like Amir Ramses' *The Jews of Egypt* (ᶜAn yahud Misr, 2013). The new wave of quality documentaries starting with Tahani Rashid's *These Girls* (al-Banat dul, 2006), and most notably post-revolution films such as *Waves* (Mudj, 2014) by Ahmed Nour (Ahmad Nur), have also benefited from the new funding policy of the Gulf states. This also applies to independent fiction films with a unique cinematic approach, like Hala Lotfi's (Lutfi) *Coming Forth by Day* (al-Khurudj ila al-nahar, 2012), or works that rely on good character studies, such as Ayten Amin's charming and autobiographically inspired portrait of an aging, capricious man in *Villa 69* (2014).

On the ideological and moral level, the uprising in 2011 has shaken up and polarized everyone involved, and of course it has also served as a catalyst for already existing innovative approaches. Numerous film professionals took part in the various sit-ins in Tahrir Square, including the directors Daoud Abd El-Sayed and Yousri Nasrallah, and the performers Khaled Abu El-Nagga (Khalid Abu'l-Nagga), Amr Waked (ᶜAmr Wakid), and Basma, although not the representatives of 'clean cinema' and the very top stars. The aging Egyptian "King of Comedy" ᶜAdil Imam, for example, whose films since the end of the 1970s were inevitably box-office hits, strongly supported Mubarak in a television interview during the uprising. With Mubarak's resignation on 11 February, Imam lost so much of his popularity that a Vodafone advertising campaign launched a short time earlier with him at the helm had to be cancelled. In spring 2012, however, when the Muslim Brotherhood started to gain ground politically, this very same Imam was charged and convicted because he supposedly defamed Islam in a work created decades ago, which assured him the solidarity of his fellow actors, artists, and parts of the public. Some of them were very outspoken supporters of the revolution, like Khaled Youssef, but backed the military coup in June 2013. Others, most notably Abu El-Nagga, the lead player in films by Mohamed Khan and Daoud Abd El-Sayed, did not budge in his demands for free speech and thus became the object of a smear campaign in 2014 with regard to his sexual orientation.

Abu El-Nagga has also served as a bridge between mainstream and so-called independent cinema, which started gaining ground in the mid-2000s. Some of its representatives were even able to succeed in the international arthouse festival circuit and have subsequently pushed into the Egyptian market. Considering the circumstances of the Egyptian film industry, traditionally dominated by its star system and monopolized by a few powerful transnational distributors, films without a popular actor—or, in some exceptional cases, an actress—attached to them normally stand almost no chance of being made or distributed. Nevertheless, a few directors, such as Ibrahim El-Batout and Ahmad Abdalla, sought to move into new terrain with narrative styles and production methods that were relatively independent from the industry. Others followed.

The first work that needs to be mentioned in this context is *Ain Shams* (2009) by El-Batout, about a small girl from Cairo's impoverished neighborhood of Ain Shams, who is suffering from cancer. All her life she has wanted to see Cairo's inner city, but her father, a humble taxi driver, has his hands full: apart from his own taxi, he has to chauffeur a rich industrialist and, in addition, grapple with the latter's family problems. *Ain Shams* is distinguished by its minimal budget and absence of stars, its open and almost fragmentary narrative structure with multiple parallel stories, and an obvious improvisational spirit that derives from the fact that the play and stories originated in a theater workshop whose members included both professional actors and amateurs.

Purely in terms of production technicalities, El-Batout set a precedent with this film when, circumventing the usual laws and protesting state censorship, he produced his movie without a film permit. However, before its commercial screening, he had to reach a compromise with the authorities and obtain a formal release. The controversy pertained not to the film's content per se but rather to the fact that he challenged standard procedures. Yet the kaleidoscopic, fragmentary narrative style of this film has to be understood in the framework of a trend. Tending toward a collective orientation, other films emulated this narrative form after the revolt as well, such as Maggie Morgan's *Asham: A Man Called Hope* (cAsham, 2012), which features actors improvising various episodes linked by only one thing, namely an encounter with a cheerful casual worker called cAsham (literally, 'hope, expectation'). The author's attempt to use improvisation to escape a strict dramatic narrative generates a shift from the large, meaningful narration to the small detail, while the concentration on individual episodes creates a kaleidoscopic perspective.

A clear exception to this narrative approach, but still the result of collective spirit, is Hala Lotfi's *Coming Forth by Day* (2012). Its success on the European art house and film festival circuit, despite its low budget, has underlined the viability of new collective-oriented production concepts. It was produced by al-Hasala ('the money box'), a group of film professionals who have also been involved in the production of documentaries, such as *Mother of the Unborn* (Umm ghayib, 2014) by Nadine Salib. *Coming Forth by Day* had already been in progress years before the revolt, but could only be completed in 2012. With a strongly observative camera and great care for tiny details, the filmmaker follows a young woman for a day and a night while, between the healthcare needs of her father, bedridden and near death, and the moods of her exhausted mother, she tries to inject a little joy and dignity into her own daily routines.

As its title suggests, the film builds on the ancient Egyptian idea of the soul's journey after death, and thus is also intended as a meditative confrontation with the experience of parting and passing away. Close to what André Bazin describes as realist cinema, this film uses primarily long shot and long take as stylistic devices, thus embedding the characters in their social environment. Hereby it has become one of the most radical Egyptian art house films. Unsurprisingly, it received funding from the Doha Film Institute and Abu Dhabi's Sanad, toured many international film festivals, and eventually found a non-commercial German distributor. An important factor that has facilitated this type of independent production and their diversification is certainly the use of the new, much more affordable digital technology that spread with the so-called digital turn.

Ahmad Abdalla's work is likewise pivotal, starting with *Heliopolis* (2009), a conglomeration of almost unrelated strings of actions united only by their spatial location, the deteriorating, upscale, architecturally unique neighborhood of Heliopolis. *Microphone* (2010), by the same director, is a kaleidoscopic music film that deals with the exclusion of the Alexandria alternative art scene—including rappers, filmmakers, and graffiti artists—from the state's Art Center in favor of more assimilated artists. At the same time it examines the individuals' private lives. It owes its charm and spontaneity to the fact that its protagonists, the musicians and artists, developed their stories and characters themselves; thus the result should be viewed as a collective effort. This combination is what lends the film its polyphony. As a heavy lifter for the box office, the famous actor Khaled Abu El-Nagga joined the team in a secondary role. He also contributed to the film's budget.

The precursors of kaleidoscopic storytelling in Egypt were female and male 'buddy' stories, usually revolving around three friends, often from different social backgrounds or representing different problems and solutions to controversial issues, generally sexuality and gender relations. Examples are *Cheap Flesh* (Lahm rakhis, 1995) by Inas al-Dighidi, *My Life My Passion* (Ya dunya ya gharami, 1996) by Magdy Ahmad Ali, and *Cultural Film* (Film thaqafi, 2000) by Muhammad Amin. The recent films, however, have taken the narrative structure further, using parallel stories that are only loosely related, or start out completely unrelated and reveal a superficial connection between the characters at a very late stage, as in *Aquarium* by Kamla Abu Zekry (Djunaynat al-asmak, 2008) by Yousry Nasrallah or *1:0 (2009)*.

The film *1:0* breaks up the classical, morally polarizing plot of the embattled individual or group into an observing quasi-documentary fiction. It presents a conglomeration of various characters from completely different origins, including a Christian woman who is unable to marry her beloved because she cannot receive a divorce from the Coptic Church and two impoverished young sisters. One of these sisters works as an advertisement and party girl for the sake of money, and the other, who is too religious to follow her sister's career, works as a visiting nurse in the homes of affluent people and meets with her admirer on the streets, as they have no other place to go. Their different personal dramas are primarily united by the same spatial and temporal framework, namely the city of Cairo on the day of the Africa Cup of Nations final in 2008. While Egypt meets Cameroon in the last decisive soccer game, the film's main characters end up in custody at the same police station. With Egypt's sporting victory at the end of the film, only one string of dramatic entanglement is resolved. The police officer in charge is so happy with the outcome of the game that he releases everybody. This, however, discloses the ambiguity of the national success and its resolution into a kind of bittersweet open ending, for, in fact, the general condition of the heroes and heroines does not change. Even though they join the flow of happy, celebrating people on the streets, they personally remain defeated by the system's arbitrary rule. Yet they are all linked through the same pulse and pace that dominates the space. In the same vein the new independent films, as we saw above, use places, such as Alexandria or the Cairo neighborhoods of Heliopolis and Ain Shams, as the main connection between characters and action.

Most importantly, in all these films we find recurrent, almost ritualistic encounters of the characters with arbitrary state abuse and violent policing. These encounters take a variety of forms: the young couple in *1:0* gets arrested because they are forced, like many poor young couples in Egypt, to have their rendezvous on the street; the young man in *Microphone* who sells music cassettes on the streets of Alexandria is beaten up by a number of policemen. These encounters are not just dictated by the narratives nor do they serve simple allegorical purposes. They lie at the heart of any possible transgression as they mark the borderline that has to be crossed into a more liberated and collectively organized existence.

In *Microphone*, this 'breaching' into freedom marks the end of the film. The characters rally at the seaside after they have been driven out from the courtyard of the cultural center, and they challenge the authorities by finally performing the concert they have been preparing. Thus the recurrent depictions of state abuse offer the necessary cathartic moments for activating the transgressive force of the narrative. The more the characters are threatened by these encounters with the representatives of the system, the more significant becomes their temporary or complete escape from this grip, which is felt as an act of resistance.

Digital turn and collective spirit in the wake of the Arab rebellion

Not only in Egypt but in almost all Arab countries, including Saudi Arabia, the introduction of digital technology around the turn of the millennium, long before the uprisings, supported by online editing devices compatible with ordinary PCs, engendered a new generation of independent, avantgardist, 'secessionist,' or simply critical currents. Haifaa al-Mansur's documentary, *Women without Shadows* (Nisa' bila zill, 2005), on women's rights and position in Saudi Arabia, is one example. Acting as her own camerawoman, Mansur toured the country seeking to determine the status of women today in her homeland. In Kuwait, the full-length *Cool Youth* (Shabab cool, 2004) by television director Muhammad Dahham al-Shammari was shot in digital and then transferred to 35mm for screenings in commercial theaters. The same applies to *Midnight* (Muntasaf al-layl, 2004) by ᶜAbd Allah al-Salman. In Bahrain, Bassam al-Thawadi (al-Dhawadi), director of the country's first full-length feature film, had already chosen the same medium by 2003 for his second film, *The Visitor* (al-Za'ir). Also, more than one film director from 'elder' film countries, like Egypt and Syria, has turned to digital video for fiction film shooting as a means either to save production costs or to create new aesthetics and genuine film style. One example is Yousry Nasrallah, director of *The City* (al-Madina, 1999), who wanted to give his actors more space for improvisation. An additional reason for the increasing use of digital video is film economy. Mohamed Khan's self-produced *Klephty* (2004) offered the director an opportunity to return to his earlier observative, socially committed realism, while Muhammad Malas, encouraged by foreign funding, took for the first time the opportunity to realize a feature, *Passion* (Bab al-maqam, 2005), without the support of the Syrian National Film Organization. The Moroccan filmmakers Nabil Ayouch, Abdelkader Lagtaa (ᶜAbd al-Qadir Laqtaᶜ), and Mohamed Ben Abderrahmane Tazi turned to the digital format in 2003.[25] Meanwhile, of course, the use of digital cameras has increasingly replaced 35mm and 16mm in the production (and in projection) of all formats, even high-budget fiction films.

Filmmakers and video artists interested in formal experiments have also emerged along with the digital turn. Without a doubt, Lebanon must be considered the vanguard in this respect. With the end of the war and the gradual return and/or coming of age of a younger generation of filmmakers and artists, a vibrant independent and innovative art and video film movement developed.[26] One of its major achievements was the creation of the Arab Image Foundation (Mu'assasat al-hifaz ᶜala al-turath al-ᶜarabi al-musawwar) by Fouad Elkoury (Fu'ad al-Kuri), Samer Mohdad (Samir Muhdad), and Akram Zaatari (Zaᶜtari). Zaatari, who studied photography, developed a deep interest in film. He directed more than thirty videos on daring topics, such as homosexuality in *Crazy about You* (Madjnunak, 1997) and *The Red Chewing Gum* (al-ᶜAlka al-hamra', 2000). He also investigated the process of image and visual discourse formation, as in his homage to the Armenian-Egyptian photographer Van Leo in *Her and Him* (Hiyya wa huwwa, 1997).

It is Mohamed Soueid, however, who may be considered the real godfather of postwar Lebanese independent and experimental documentary. He began his career with his first video in 1990 and later directed *Cinema al-Fouad* (Sinima al-fu'ad, 1994), which was at the time the most unconventional portrait of a Lebanese transvestite. He also opened unprecedented production venues for himself and others with Future TV. Soueid's most accomplished documentary, *Nightfall* (ᶜIndama ya'ti al-masa', 2000), part of a trilogy on the civil war, focused on a Lebanese student squad of the Palestinian Fatah movement, to which the director himself belonged. As a one-man crew, Soueid succeeded in capturing the painful but also trivial disillusionment of this group, whose members seem to have sought refuge, if not in death and the arts, then in alcohol.

Soueid's ideas and presence encouraged the creation of another backbone of Lebanese alternative film art, namely the association Beirut DC (Development Cinema), founded in 1999 and run by Hania Mroue (Muruwwah) and Eliane Raheb (Rahib). The association's major goals are training, networking, documentation, and the promotion of independent film in Lebanon through coproduction and screenings. One of its most effective cultural initiatives is the biannual Ayam Bayrut al-sinim'iya, the Beirut Film Festival, as well as a touring Arab Film Week. Beirut DC has contributed to creating a cultural atmosphere in which a more innovative film culture could grow, even if this does not translate into a massive re-education of Lebanese audiences, who still flock to the latest American releases.

Since 2003, Mohamed Soueid has also promoted, against all odds, the production and airing of Arab documentaries, old and new, on MBC's transnational Arab news channel, al-ᶜArabiya. Al-ᶜArabiya's and al-Jazeera's initial readiness to encourage Arab documentary filmmaking (though only on politically spectacular topics) boosted production and helped for a while to develop a critical, if not always inventive, documentary film movement. Among the movement's most fruitful results were the documentary series produced by Assad Taha in 2004–2005, *Prison Literature* (Adab al-sudjun) and *Once Upon a Time* (Yuhka anna), which relate, among other things, the painful memories of political prisoners in the Arab world from Morocco to Syria.[27]

The supportive attitude of O3 productions, an MBC subsidiary for documentary production and post-production services toward creative documentary did not last for long and rolled back to standardized TV production. However, the increase in so-called creative documentary suitable for theatrical release has been facilitated by different regional (temporary) training programs, such as

Doc Med run by Beirut DC, the German Documentary Campus, the Beirut Screen Institute, and the Arab Fund for Arts and Cultures, as well as the various Gulf-based film funds. In particular, Gulf film festivals and the attached platforms, most notably the Dubai Film Connection with its coproduction market, became a catalyst for this format. It promoted coproduction but also allowed an exchange of ideas, experience, and professionals between different Arab countries. One of the problems of this system, however, is that films remain locked in the festival circuit. Only very few are able to cross over into the commercial distribution and exhibition system, either movie theaters or television, to be exposed to a larger audience.

Despite the hegemony of the film industry on the national level, Egypt too can claim to have brought to light a body of experimental films presented by multimedia artists—among others, Wael Shawky (Wa'il Shauqi), Hassan Khan, Shady el-Noshokaty (al-Nushuqati), Maha Mamoun (Ma'mun), and Hala El-Koussy (al-Kusy). Other less formally oriented filmmakers have displayed boldness in their short videos, for example in their depiction of sexuality and gender relations. Ahmad Khalid's *The Fifth Pound* (al-Junayh al-khamis, 2005) is about a couple trying to find some intimacy on public transportation, and Hadil Nazmi's *Elevator* (Ascenseur, 2005) features a young girl who, while stuck alone in an elevator, gives in to a mobile phone flirtation, taking off her veil. The film caused a stir when an Islamic web site and a weekly magazine falsely claimed that it was made by Christians for the purpose of attacking Muslim veiling. More recent examples of daring shorts are *Senses* (Hawas, 2010) by Mohamed Ramadan or Omar (ʿUmar) Khalid's *Payback* (al-Hisab, 2012), produced by the film cooperative Semat.

New media have doubtless changed the traditional understanding of commercial spectatorship, with all the platforms that offer films for free, like YouTube and Vimeo. These venues have also become crucial for political activism, a fact that became even more evident during the Arab uprising. Indeed, one of the most striking phenomena in the field of independent film that foreboded and accompanied the massive protests which started in 2010/2011 is the creation of film cooperatives or collectives. The previously mentioned Semat, institutionalized and directed by Hala Galal, has been producing short films and training programs since 2001, as well as alternative distribution programs. Al-Hasala (literally, 'The Money Box') was created in 2010 to facilitate the production of Hala Lotfi's (Lutfi) *Coming Forth by Day* (al-Khuruj ila al-nahar, 2012). The full-length docu-drama by Tamir El-Said (Tamir al-Sacid), *The Last Days of the City* (Akhir ayam al-madina), which went into production in 2008 and was eventually released at the Berlinale in 2016, facilitated the creation of two initiatives: first, the (no-longer operative) collective Mosireen founded in cooperation with actor Khalid Abdalla (*The Kite Runner*, 2007), and second, the alternative film center Cimatheque, which is equipped with a screening hall, lab, archive, and library, and offers all kinds of training opportunities.

The members of Mosireen dedicated themselves to people's journalism and created an archive of footage shot during the Egyptian uprising and the events that followed. Some have meanwhile succeeded in shooting feature-length documentaries, like Philip Rizk (Rizq), Yasmina Metwally (Mitwally), and Salma al-Tarzi. *Out in the Streets* (Barra fi-l-sharic, 2015) by Rizk and Metwally, for instance, documents a theater workshop with unemployed workers who reenact their individual experiences in the dismantled factory they have been working in. In Alexandria two production cooperatives were created on the eve of the revolt, Figleaf Studios and Rufy's. The latter produced an original short film compilation under the title *Mice Room* (Udat al-firan, 2010), which used props and equipment provided by the production of Ibrahim El-Batout's *The Magician* (al-Hawi, 2010).

Decentralization and collectivism have played a role for artistic activities during and after the uprising in Tunisia as well. First of all there was an attempt to extend the principle of collectively run institutions to formerly-dominated realms. Cineasts urged the creation of a self-governing national film center to control film ratings and support films. Despite substantial preparatory work on its statutes, to this day the center is still not really independent from state administration. In November 2012, Tunisian producers and filmmakers complained that the appointment of the center's conservative director was made over their heads.[28]

Notwithstanding, other small cooperatives emerged, such as the ATAC (Association tunisienne d'action pour le cinéma)—which chiefly organizes workshops and traveling performances in the provinces—as well as the film group Exit. Along with Ismaël (Isma^cil), the group includes Youssef Chebi (Yusuf Shabbi) and Ala Eddine Slim ('Ala' al-Din Salim). Stylistically, their joint film *Babylon* (Babil, 2012) can be categorized as 'direct cinema,' particularly since the filmmakers document the construction and later dismantling of a Tunisian refugee camp near the Libyan border without commentary and through long, observational shots. In the process, they depict the major and minor adversities and pleasures of the refugees, as well as those of their supervisors, from countries throughout the world from Bangladesh to West Africa, situating them in relation to the harsh natural environment of the surrounding desert. The film deliberately avoids rendering the camp's prevailing linguistic chaos accessible through subtitles so that the viewer, too, remains helplessly exposed to the camp's Babylon effect.

In Jordan, Hazim Bitar created the Amman Filmmakers Cooperative (Ta^cawuniyat ^cAmman li-l-aflam) as early as 2002. It has run training programs and has sponsored the production of several shorts. In Ramallah, Mohanad Yaqubi (Muhannad Ya^cqubi) co-founded Idioms Films. In Saudi Arabia the short-lived Talashi collective made headlines with a number of shorts in 2009. An initiative which was born under much more difficult and extreme conditions is the Syrian Abounaddara (The Man with the Glasses) collective. It was founded in 2010 by self-trained filmmakers and started to produce anonymous shorts during the uprising in Syria, representing different camps and focusing primarily on human commonalities.

The works are accessible through their website.[29] The option to release films on the uprising online, thus circumventing official and traditional media, has also been chosen by individual 'citizen journalists,' such as Nadir Bouhmouch (Buhmush), who created the documentary *My Makhzen and Me* (Ana wa makhzany, 2012). It is a personal account of a Moroccan student who returns from the United States to document the political activism that had started spreading in his homeland, and discusses his and others' relation to the political system as embodied by al-makhzan (i.e. the king).

New media, however, have not only propelled liberal and revolutionary content but have also become a playground for extremists. The professionally staged videos by the Islamic State showing the assassination of hostages, such as the beheading of twenty-one Copts in Libya on 12 February 2015, bear sad witness to this fact. Palestinian Hamas has also produced videos that circulate on the internet. In October 2012, *The Dispersion of Illusion* (al-Wahm al-mutabaddad), a documentary produced by Hamas and its armed wing, the cIzz al-Din al-Qassam Brigades, which documented and restaged the abduction of the Israeli soldier Gilad Shalit and the preparations preceding the act, started circulating online. The purpose of the film was expected to reinforce the 'cultural' Palestinian identity and the spirit of sacrifice.[30]

Neither the collective spirit nor the space and opportunities offered by new media can hide the fact of financial dependency and transnational embedding. Most cases, even the above-mentioned initiatives which support liberal ideas and an innovative, individualistic approach to the arts, have been sustained by donors from outside their national borders. These supporters may be Arab, such as the Gulf-based funds; cultural development funds, like the Arab Fund for Arts and Culture and al-Mawred al-Thaqafi; or European, such as the Euromed Audiovisual program or cultural institutes like the British Council or the German Goethe Institut. This inter-dependency has meanwhile also seized committed Egyptian cinema.

The coproduction system between the national and the transnational

As described in the first part of this book, European funding has contributed to the creation of a considerable number of Arab art films since the 1980s and has certainly also added to the region's cinematic diversity and boldness. Some of these films would never have appeared if they had not been coproduced by European entities or set in Europe. *Salvation Army*, by the Moroccan director Abdallah Taia, is one of the first Arab films to focus solely and explicitly on the biography of a male homosexual. It was shot partly in Morocco and coproduced by Nabil Ayouch's Ali'N Production. This contrasts with Algerian Amor Hakkar's story of a bisexual love triangle, *A Few Days of Respite* (Quelques jours de répit, 2011), which is set entirely in France. The extremely daring *The Warmest Color is Blue* (Le bleu est une couleur chaude, 2013), also set in France and by the Tunisian Abdellatif Kechiche (ᶜAbd al-Latif Kashish), includes several graphic scenes of lesbian sexuality.

That these films are all French-produced is no accident. France is still the largest market for Arab art house films. In the years between 2006 and 2011, for instance, more than one-third (37 percent) of all Lebanese coproductions were undertaken with France. Germany has also been crucial for film financing in the region, with Qatar and the UAE at a much lower level. While it is true that 20 percent of all Lebanese productions received money from the UAE, the great majority of French coproduced films were fiction films, while money from the Gulf went primarily into documentaries.[31] In other words, despite the great hype that was created around the resources offered by the Gulf region, its actual input into Arab fiction films was less substantial than might have been expected.

Doubtless the creation of all the various Gulf film festivals, which will be described in more detail later, had a positive effect on the Arab festival circuit in general and has propelled the production of documentaries and art house films. However, their overall impact on Arab film industries and infrastructure has to be qualified. First, these institutions are competitive with regard to other regional funds. For that reason they apply exclusive funding policies, which prevent the accumulation of funding resources for each project.

Second, the sums offered are small in comparison to overall film budgets, often not exceeding US $25,000 to $50,000. Thus their general economic impact has to be considered promotional rather than substantial, particularly for fiction films. Third, the respective selection committees include a high proportion of Western consultants, whose choices generally comply with standards of the international festival and art house circuit. Popular mainstream as well as TV formats, for both fiction and documentary, are not admitted. This dichotomy is also reflected in distribution and exhibition.

Moreover, the persistence or stabilization of regional mainstream output, such as in Egypt or Morocco, that may compete commercially for local audiences does not necessarily indicate a strong competitive industry. The same applies to the occasional success of Arab films in international festivals and their release in one or more Western countries. This is also related to the general structure of international distribution circuits. There is, first of all, the commercial-industrial film market, profit oriented and entirely box office-dependent. Then there are the various so-called low- or non-profit circuits, ranging from indies (independent production) and related art house, to film festival distribution, to merely grass-roots and educational uses.

Not every Arab country has the same access to these different circuits, which generally correlates to the type of filmmaking that is possible in each of them. Until recently, Egyptian cinema has had a weak presence in the general art house circuit, unlike Morocco, Algeria, Tunisia, Syria, Palestine, and Lebanon, but it is still the only Arab country that has market shares in other Arab countries. Lebanon has broken that rule recently with films directed by Nadine Labaki, but it is still far from challenging Egypt's position. Egypt, in turn, has been unable to reduce the role of American productions at the Arab box office.

While Arab films in general, either mainstream or art house, almost never make it into the competitions of any of the A-festivals in Berlin, Cannes, Venice, or Locarno, they show a stronger presence in sections for innovative cinema, such as the Forum in Berlin, the Quinzaine des réalisateurs in Cannes or Orizzonti, in Venice. At the same time, it must be stated that films from the region have been almost absent from international sales, except for France. In fact, the market share of non-European and non-American films is minimal and confined to the likewise highly competitive art house circuit due to the fact that the European film market itself is dominated by US productions. In general, if at all, it is far more likely for a European coproduced Arab film to be distributed abroad than a nationally produced one. Paradoxically, these coproductions stand almost no chance of being exhibited in the countries of their directors, either because of the Egyptian or American mainstream monopolization or because of the high screening fees of their foreign distributors.[32]

It also remains difficult to distribute anything from the Arab and Muslim world in Europe that offers alternative or simply unspectacular stories that go beyond the dominant discourses on the region.[33] Looking at the films that received the most interest and widespread art house circulation since the 1990s, four major subjects can be singled out: gender inequality, violent Islam, the Palestinian question, and, to a certain extent, political and social underdevelopment and more recently the Arab rebellion. While Palestinian cinema since the Oslo Accords has been welcomed because of the pivotal position of the Palestinian national cause in European politics, Tunisia's capitalization on gender, as we will see later, could draw upon a more historically rooted interest. Since colonial times, the presumed Muslim oppression of women has formed one of the backbones of Orientalist discourse, even offering a pretext for interference in the region.[34] The predominance of the trope of unequal gender relations—the either absent or cruel father and dominated mothers, daughters, and sons—must thus be considered in part the product of European expectations and preconceptions. Consequently, some of the coproductions that succeeded in finding their way to Europe, disregarding complex realities on the ground, have tended to emphasize (presumable) cultural differences between North and South.

At this point it seems necessary to investigate the historical development of European art house itself. It reflects Europe's own post-Second World War battle against American screen supremacy and for that reason has collapsed its national cinema into the kind of art cinema that flourished in the 1960s and 1970s. As Crofts points out: "This model aims to differentiate itself textually from Hollywood, to assert implicitly or explicitly an indigenous product."[35] The discourses which support this model tend to be bourgeois nationalist and elitist in orientation.[36] Moreover, the arguments about quality make this type resort frequently to literary sources and try to consolidate them as a national tradition.[37] Hence, the devaluation of mainstream or popular forms of cinema is intrinsic to European art film and the cultural funding policies that helped generate it. Understandably enough, Arab anti-colonial Third-Worldist cinema that developed during decolonization and took a stand against the Hollywood model and its Egyptian representative could easily be accommodated to that national and elitist model, declaring it more indigenous and therefore more authentic.

This logic, however, does not acknowledge the attachment of Arab spectators to their popular cinema, which may create a sense of identification, national pride, and belonging and, even more importantly, caters to their emotions. In fact, popular genre cinema relies essentially on the idea of transgression, as Rick Altman puts it in his analysis of generic developments and the functionality of American film industry output: "For ninety minutes, Hollywood offers generic pleasure as an alternative from cultural norms" and "authorized opportunities for countercultural activity."[38] Thus, generic pleasure is thought to be rooted in the transgression of cultural values, an augmenting transgression, as it moves from breaches of etiquette to adultery, from brawls to murder, from slight creepiness to bloody carnage, but also toward utopia in its temporary reconciliation of social difference, for example. In connecting to the popular, some Arab filmmakers, like Nadine Labaki or Nabil Ayouch, have rediscovered the necessity of transgressive utopia so much neglected by the ostensible 'realism' of committed cinema, by constantly revived harsh social conditions, or by alienating, innovative film styles. No wonder the American film scholar Bill Nichols has equated cinematic fiction with "documentaries of wish-fulfillment" that "give tangible expression to our wishes and dreams, our nightmares and dreads. They give a sense of what we wish, or fear, reality itself might be or become."[39] It is for precisely that reason that popular cinema is also capable of expressing and representing collective national concerns.

Futhermore, the transgressiveness of the popular exceeds the mere reproduction or utterance of dreams and desires relevant to the spectator. Despite its constant production of sexual, social, and racial difference, popular cinema has been less concerned with cultural polarization on the formal level. It lives through recycling, juxtaposing, mixing, and even cannibalizing standardized film forms,[40] amalgamating them into an oscillating 'international' hodge-podge,[41] and trivializing already 'trivial' genres even more. No wonder it is considered unacceptable, if not repulsive, in international art film circuits. True, its violation of standards and artistic order also applies to Western trivial art, but in the context of international film commodity circulation, it has been tied, as pointed out earlier, into the post-colonial East–West divide and power constellation, becoming a site of negotiation between elitism and popularity, between dominant discourses and subversive ideas.[42]

This is also why I would argue that Arab popular film is at times more capable of representing the mixed, impure, contradictory, fragmented, and globalized realities of the Middle East and North Africa for its audiences. This is why it is put into practice excessively and more or less consciously by producers and directors in the Egyptian film industry, and meanwhile also in the Moroccan industry, becoming abundant and spontaneous in cases dominated by generic cycles and star personae and conscious in the cases of innumerable works by committed directors. The most recent examples are: Youssef Chahine's French coproduction, *Alexandria . . . New York* (2004) and Daoud Abd El-Sayed's Egyptian-produced *Land of Fear* (Ard al-khawf, 2000), which is much more sophisticated in approach and style and is a multi-layered secret-agent story open to a variety of existential and political readings. Stretching over more than two decades, from Nasser to Mubarak, it follows the career of a dedicated officer as he becomes ensnared in the world of large-scale drug dealing. He is originally put in charge of infiltrating criminal circles, and succeeds very quickly, but his real identity is obliterated over the years as a result of consecutive changes in the constellation of political power. He is ultimately

Land of Fear (Ard al-khawf, 2000) by Daoud Abd El-Sayyed
(courtesy Daoud Abd El-Sayed, Cairo)

doomed to a life of criminality with no prospect of return. The biblical fallen-angel motif is clear, but the film also expresses a more general sense of loss and ephemerality linked to the country's recent social and political changes.

Another example is *Ali Zoua, Prince of the Streets* (ᶜAli Zawwa, 2000), which was realized in cooperation with Casablanca street kids and represented an imaginative and not at all melodramatic Moroccan version of the Indian film *Salaam Bombay* (1988). *Ali Zoua* is narrated from the children's perspective and dwells on the gap between reality and dreams, on the protagonists' desires and multiple deceptions of themselves and others. The positive reception of this film in Morocco proves the ability of director Nabil Ayouch (ᶜAyush), born to a French mother and a Moroccan father, to mix a European art film orientation with popular elements in order to attract audiences. His first work, *Mektoub* (Maktub, 1997), already capitalized on thriller film elements.

The importance of contemporary popular culture also has been grasped by art house oriented directors or *auteurs* such as Philippe Aractingi, Nadia al-Fani, and Elia Suleiman, to name only a few. In their films, they question the paradigms of highbrow art, purity of form, and stylistic consistency, with a conscious inclusion of 'trivial' elements of global culture that reflects the porosity of culture instead of pretending the existence of stable borders.

Suleiman's virtual Palestinian resistance fighter (or ninja) is but one example of this porosity. The same applies to Aractingi's use in *Bosta* of the Lebanese *dabka*, a form of traditional and folkloric dance, also used in innumerable Egyptian and Lebanese popular films of the 1940s and 1950s. In Aractingi's film, the *dabka* does not serve as a spectacle, but rather is portrayed as the very site of identity struggle. Following a newly formed dance group on its tour, the film works out their attempts to reinterpret the rhythms and representational habits of the conventional dance, mixing them with modern, more disruptive elements (such as techno) while insisting on winning the conservative audience. This is not an easy task to fulfill, of course, as the protagonists simultaneously have to come to terms with the legacy of war and their personal biographies.

Of course, recourses to popular culture do not always serve the purpose of pleasing local audiences. At times they are tied instead into an avant-gardist cinematic approach. A move in this direction is represented by Ghassan Salhab's postwar Dracula tale of a doctor turned vampire, *The Last Man* (Atlal, literally, 'ruins,' 2006), Nadia al-Fani's *Bedwin Hacker* (2002), and Nabil Ayouch's *One Minute of Sun Less*, as they borrow narrative structures from popular film forms, most notably detective films and thrillers, while destabilizing the borders of the real, of national self-perceptions, and of sexual difference. In breaking away from the usual dualism of Tunisian feminist 'women's cinema,' *Bedwin Hacker*, for instance, displays an entirely postmodern vision, featuring the quest for a mysterious Tunisian hacker who is able to disturb Western television transmissions and who turns out to be a bisexual woman living in the southern part of the country.

Unquestionably, some Arab filmmakers attempt to rediscover popular culture to address local audiences and cross their national borders into neighboring countries with it. This plus the occurrence of the digital turn, the advent of new media, and the festival circuit have strongly increased inter-Arab and transnational cooperation and exchange. In that sense, and to different degrees, Arab cinemas may be considered as much national as they are transnational.

For that reason it must be emphasized that the borders of all these national cinemas are strongly permeable and governed by multiple and imbalanced flows of money, know-how, professionals, ideas, and images. Even Egypt, as we have seen, is not in complete control of its own production but is dependent on its customers in the neighboring countries, particularly in the Arab peninsula. The Gulf countries in turn have the money to encourage and improve Egyptian mainstream production and to promote art house films, primarily documentaries, from the rest of the region, but are still unable to sustain their own national cinemas and provide a market for themselves, as we will see in the following chapter.

5

TWENTY-FIRST CENTURY ARAB CINEMAS BY COUNTRY

This chapter first sketches out the strong divergence between the cinemas of different Arab countries (except Egypt, discussed in chapter 4) on the level of production, distribution, and exhibition, and then maps different forms of exchange and interdependency between them. As discussed earlier, cinematic development in the various Arab states has taken completely different roads. Some are still marginal and underdeveloped, economically as well as professionally, like Yemen, Oman, Sudan, Mauritania, and Libya, while others are striving hard to keep their status quo, for instance, Egypt, Algeria, Tunisia, and Lebanon, or to become international players, such as the UAE or Morocco.

At the same time it has to be underlined that I chose to discuss most of the films in the context of their directors' national affiliation. Yet it should also become evident throughout the following and preceding discussion that there are multiple ways in which films connect or disconnect from the nation. While for some cineastes the Egyptian 'industrial' mode of production equals national cinema and most of its products can indeed be defined as 'national' because they are locally financed, others prefer to consider art films as the real representatives of national cinema because of their highbrow cultural value, which has been additionally underlined by their acceptance on the international art house and festival circuit. On the other hand, it cannot be denied that the cultural mode in which state-supported films have often been situated[1] has at times been instrumental in cementing the legitimacy of the national leadership, as in Tunisia before the Rebellion, or to underline the myth of the nation-state, as in Algeria. Palestinian cinema, in contrast, deprived of such a state, has worked as hard to imagine that nation as to deconstruct some of its premises. Along with other so-called national cinemas, such as the Lebanese, the Syrian, and the Iraqi, however, it has hardly surpassed the range of a regionally marginalized intellectual and elitist cultural activity that stands for diversity and tolerance but is unlikely to challenge sectarian and secessionist realities on the ground.

On the margins: Sudan, Libya, and Mauretania

In Sudan, government-backed efforts have resulted in the production of a number of documentaries, such as those by Gadalla Gubara (Djad Allah Djubara), who started with educational films and reports back in the 1950s. Meanwhile, fiction film production remained exceptional. One of the few examples is the 16mm black and white film *Hopes and Dreams* (Amal wa Ahlam, 1970) by Ibrahim Mallassy, which was followed in the 1980s and early 1990s by four more feature films. These efforts, as well as attempts to promote film culture, for example through the Sudan Film Club, came to a long halt following the Islamic military coup in 1989.[2] The cruelty of the new order found its expression in an experimental short, *Insan* (literally, 'human being,' 1994) by Ibrahim Shaddad, which has much to contribute to a discussion on subjectivity and disrupted nationhood.[3]

In Libya the situation has to be considered the same, if not worse, even after the ending of the long-lasting cultural isolation and the economic embargo that resulted from the outbreak of the Arab rebellion. The politically unstable situation after the ousting of the Gaddafi dictatorship, with the country still in a state of civil war, has not helped to improve the situation. Nevertheless, the Libyan researcher Amal al-ᶜUbaydi unearthed some crucial information that complements the film history in her homeland. One of her most interesting insights is that significant efforts have been made, starting in 1947, in the field of documentary film, which was, however, soon to be monopolized by state entities. She notes that the film activist and director Muhammad al-Farjani had already made a purely Libyan full-length feature film, *The Splinter* (al-Shazaya), by 1983, along with the more widely acknowledged productions by foreign directors like the Syrian al-Akkad, the Palestinian Qassim Hawal, and the Moroccan Abdalla Mesbahi (ᶜAbd Allah al-Misbahi).[4]

However, cultural and political isolation, along with unsystematic state intervention, have been the main reasons preventing any continuous production. In addition, private enterprises have been rare and movie theaters almost nonexistent. According to a report by the Euromed Audiovisual program, there was one cinema operating before the uprising, which has been closed now for security reasons.[5] The only possibility to go to a 'cinema' has been a film club that shows films on DVD twice a week. Public television does not commission any kind of works from the independent sector. There are no production or distribution companies in the country. Production is confined to young amateurs or diaspora filmmakers, including young talents such as British-Libyan Naziha Arebi and Egyptian-Libyan Abdullah al-Ghaly, who self-produce their shorts or documentaries without any financial support from the Ministry of Culture.

While Libya has not succeeded so far in producing any significant feature film, Mauretania has seen exceptional, high-profile productions, most notably *Heremakono: Waiting for Happiness* (Fi intizar al-saᶜada, 2002) and *Timbuktu* (2014) by Abderrahmane Sissako (ᶜAbd al-Rahman Sisaku) which was shown at the Cannes Film Festival in 2014 and deals with the rule of the Islamist militia in Mali. Sissako, who also has family ties in Mali, produced this film in Mauretania because of the tense security situation in Mali. Generally, his work has always displayed strong pan- or trans-African interest. Since it is a product of his individual efforts, it cannot be fully related to any growth of the film industry in Mauretania. However, in 2002 the director helped to create an association in his homeland, Dar al-Sinima'iyin (The House of the Cineasts/La maison des cinéastes), which is backed by the Ministry of Culture and runs a festival. With some foreign support, it has also offered training and financing opportunities for filmmakers. Several documentaries and shorts were produced with the help of the association. One of the trainees of the association, Salem Dendou (Salim Dandu), who also appeared in *Timbuktu*, is currently in post-production of his first full-length fiction film. The production was even able to attract private Mauritanian financers.

Jordan

Since 1958, the 'newcomer' country Jordan has seen occasional attempts to direct films of all formats, often on topics related to the Palestinian question, but these efforts went largely unrecognized.[6] Private investors during that period oriented themselves toward the Egyptian, Lebanese, and Turkish film industries instead.[7] Initially, public involvement started in 1964 with the Department of Film and Photography attached to the Ministry of Culture and resulted largely in the production of shorts. The main novelty in this regard was the creation of the Royal Film Commission (RFC) in 2003, which is a financially and administratively autonomous governmental organization directed by a board of commissioners and chaired by the king's brother, Prince Ali b. al-Husain.

Today the scale of production is still very limited and largely based on either indirect public funding or the system of coproduction. Nonetheless, there are serious attempts on the part of film professionals to create sustainable production conditions and to push for more public support, even though the latter has been cut back after an initial involvement in the field. As in Doha and Dubai, the RFC has recently suffered from unexplained budget cuts, although at first it boosted the cinematic activities in the kingdom considerably. Since 2011, the RFC has also started the Jordanian Film Fund in support of local producers and filmmakers. Training programs and screenings at the RFC Film House have helped young filmmakers from Jordan to enter the field. In addition, it has had an impact on the development of film in the region by offering trans-Arab training programs. The commission's two main regional programs—the Rawi Screen Writers Lab, run in collaboration with Sundance, and the Med Film Factory, funded by Euromed Audiovisual for a time span of three years—have thus contributed to improving storytelling skills and the professionalism of producers, for Jordanians and non-Jordanians. The founding of the Red Sea Institute of Cinematic Arts in 2008, a semi-private film school in Aqaba, has contributed to the dissemination of expertise as well. A joint venture between the California University Film School and the Royal Film Commission, the school was suspended in 2013 for undeclared reasons. It is suspected that they are related to the same budget cuts that curbed the activities of the commission, and that they probably involve the royal family.

Notwithstanding, Jordan has seen the production of a number of feature-length documentaries and fictions, an average of one film per year between 2006 and 2009. Some of them enjoyed considerable success in the festival circuit. This applies even to the productions of the first year, 2006: the documentary *Recycle* (I‘adat khalq, 2006) by Mahmoud al-Massad, the portrait of a failed fundamentalist, and the fiction film *Captain Abu Raed* (Captain Abu Ra'id, 2006) by Amin Matalqa. The latter depicts an aging airport janitor who lives in humble circumstances. One day he is mistaken for a captain by some neighborhood kids. He eventually develops into their fatherly friend, advisor, and protector.

Since 2010, the Jordanian output has ranged from two to five films a year.[8] Finding a screening opportunity at home is not an easy task, though. Jordan is relatively advanced in terms of well-equipped screens and the number of multiplex cinemas, yet the market share for locally-made films is negligible. In 2012 a total of 186 films were released, but only fourteen were in Arabic. Among them was the humorous romance *When Mona Lisa Smiled* (Lamma dhahikat al-Monalisa) by Fadi Haddad as the sole Jordanian production. Interestingly however, even though the number of American films has been overwhelming, the highest ranking in terms of admissions was the Egyptian farce on a young married couple *Omar and Salma 3* (2012) by Muhammad Samy. It occupied three screens for thirty consecutive weeks. *When Mona Lisa Smiled* stayed on one screen for eight consecutive weeks.[9]

In fact, several films were trying to lean toward the mainstream, to present accessible but socially critical topics using love stories for their basic plots, like *Line of Sight* (ᶜAla madd al-bassar, 2011) by Aseel Mansour (Asil Mansur) or *Seven Hours Difference* (Farq sabᶜ saᶜat, 2010) by Deema Amr (Dima ᶜAmr). The latter film also addressed the issue of cultural difference and Westernization. By means of comic entanglements it depicts the problem of a young Jordanian woman trying to find the courage to introduce her American boyfriend as a future groom to her conservative family.

In contrast, *The Last Friday* (al-Jumᶜa al-akhira, 2011) by Yahya al-Abdullah, which was produced in the framework of the RFC training program, as well as the much praised historical spectacle *Theeb* (*Dhib*, colloquial for 'wolf,' 2014) by Naji Abu Nowar (Nuwar), have much more the air of typical international art house movies. They rely on thorough character studies, strong visuality, and low-paced action. Both films toured international festivals and received important awards. Exceptional in terms of popularity was the humorous *Amreeka* (Amrika, literally 'America,' 2009), an American Arab-immigrant drama by Cherien Dabis (Shirin Daᶜbis), who grew up in the United States with a Palestinian father and a Jordanian mother. In distribution circuits her film was considered Palestinian rather than Jordanian. However, Dabis was one of the first Jordanian Rawi

Theeb (Dhib, 2014) by Naji Abu Nowar (courtesy Naji Abu Nowar)

alumni and her film was well received in festivals as well as in the
United States, where it was also distributed. Apart from that,
Jordanian filmmakers have recently underwritten a number of distinguished creative documentaries, such as al-Massad's *Recycle*
and his subsequent *This Is My Picture When I Was Dead* (Hazihy
surati wa ana mayyit, 2010), Sandra Madi's *Perforated Memory*
(Zakira mathquba, 2008), Aseel Mansour's *Uncle Nashaat*
(ᶜAmmu Nash'at, 2011), Mais Darwaza's poetic essay film *My
Love Awaits Me by the Sea* (Habibi biyistanani ᶜand al-bahr, 2013),
and Yahya al-Abdullah's *The Council* (al-Madjlis, 2014). All of
these works except for *Recycle* deal with topics related to Palestine
and Palestinians, which is no wonder, given the strong presence of
Palestinians in Jordanian society.

The emergence of new players: The Gulf states

The cinematic development in the Arabian Peninsula shows a great
disparity, ranging from endeavors to create a local film culture and
build up a sustainable infrastructure to the other extreme of almost
complete neglect and marginality. The latter applies primarily to
Oman and the economically and politically marginal Yemen.
Yemen's first full-length feature film productions were *A New Day in*

Old Sana'a (Yaum djadid fi Sanᶜa' al-qadima, 2005), a Yemeni–British coproduction by Bader Ben Hirsi, and *I Am Nojoom, Age 10 and Divorced* (Ana Nujum bint al-ᶜashara wa mutallaqa, 2014) by Khadija al-Salami. Oman has produced *al-Boom* (al-Bum, 2006) by Khalid al-Zadjali, a kind of modern fairy tale dominated by television film aesthetics. As in Mauretania, cinema in these two nations rests on the shoulders of individuals who are predominantly based abroad.

On the other hand, since the turn of the millennium a rising number of Gulf countries have become involved in full-length feature film production. Due to a lack of artistic quality and narrative originality, the very first works from these countries did not attract any international attention. This has changed drastically with films by the Emirati ᶜAli F. Mostafa (Mustafa) and the Saudi Arabian Haifaa al-Mansour (Haifa' al-Mansur). Because of increased governmental commitment the Gulf States, primarily the UAE and Saudi Arabia, followed by Bahrain and Qatar, have seen a considerable change during the last decade, hosting increasingly diverse cinematic activities in addition to laying the foundations for a more sustainable cinematic infrastructure. The UAE and Qatar in particular have made headway in that respect, even though their progress has been hampered recently by the quite arbitrary character of official intervention, which often depends on the rulers of the countries or individuals related to them. An additional obstacle has been the dubious cooperation and involvement with Western institutions and professionals, which has led to immense spending as well as to conflicts about questions of adequate cultural representation.

Taking Qatar as an example: The Doha Tribeca Film Festival, founded in 2009 and run by the Doha Film Institute under the auspices of Sheikha Mayassa Bint Hamad al-Thani, a member of the royal family, was stalled after four sessions. It was at first run in cooperation with the American Tribeca Enterprises and headed by the Australian media and film executive and former al-Jazeera presenter Amanda Palmer. Palmer resigned in 2012 to be replaced by a local CEO. In order to be able to attract international and Arab producers and filmmakers to its film market, the Institute, like other Gulf funding institutions, offers financial support to all stages of production. In 2013 the festival and film funds were restructured, and a substantial part of the staff was laid off.[10] The festival has been redesigned to focus on first- and second-time film directors, yet its 2014 session was postponed to 2015. At the same time the Institute reportedly made a hundred-million-dollar deal with a US company to produce films in various formats.[11]

The restructuring of the film festival occurred after the resignation of Palmer and the $55 million flop *Black Gold* (2011) by Jean-Jacques Annaud. The historical spectacle starring a number of international stars, first and foremost Antonio Banderas, was copro-duced with the Tunisian TV mogul Tarek Ben Ammar and recouped only one-sixth of its expenses. It also displayed a strongly Orientalist orientation. Discussing the experience, Arab critics deplored the huge discrepancy between the enormous budget of this single, supposedly prestigious, international multi-million-dollar production and the small amounts spent in support of nascent Qatari film culture, as well as for other Arab films which received funds from the Doha Film Institute that never exceeded a few thousand dollars.[12]

A similar case was reported from Abu Dhabi. Image Nation, a government-backed film company, produced the first Emirati horror film, *Djinn*, in 2012. It was directed by the American Tobe Hooper, the director of the infamous *Chainsaw Massacre* (1974). The film—not be confused with an American movie called *Jinn* (2014) by Ajmal Zaheer Ahmad—is said to have been shelved because of its representation of the UAE. A member of the royal family considered the film "subversive." This caused *The Guardian* newspaper to lament: "The old suspicion surrounding the Emirati industry had risen again: that it was too tightly supervised from above (usually through the National Media Council censorship body) to blossom freely."[13]

In the same year, 2012, Abu Dhabi Film Festival director Peter
Scarlet, along with other Westerners in high-profile positions, such
as the head of the film commission and the head of the Media Zone
partner company twofour54, were replaced by Emiratis. These
changes led to a short-term freezing of financial support offered by
Sanad, the film fund attached to the Abu Dhabi Film Festival. The
latter had been operational since 2007 but was called off in 2015.
Still operative is the internationally oriented Dubai International
Film Festival, founded in 2004, which also has a film fund
attached, Enjaaz. The regional Gulf Film Festival was created in
2008. In 2014, a decade after its creation, the Dubai Festival suffered severe and arbitrary budget cuts for unclear and most
probably personal reasons related to the ruling family. It resulted
in the temporary closing of the most successful Gulf film coproduction market so far, the Dubai Film Connection, among others.
In general the major Gulf festivals have been acting in a strongly
competitive and exclusive manner with regard to resources, projects, films, and Western expertise.

There is no way, however, to deny the general boosting effect
these activities and investments have had on the regional film culture and economy. Image Nation has so far coproduced more than
a dozen films, some of them very successful. They include international mainstream, such as the Bollywood film *My Name is
Khan* (2010) by Karan Johar (Djuhar), as well as successful Arab
art house films, for example the Jordanian-American production
Amreeka (2009) by Cherien Dabis. The UAE has also offered
opportunities for smaller enterprises, such as Nayla al-Khaja's D-
Seven Motion Pictures, which has specialized in film branding and
promotion. Al-Khaja has also made a name for herself as one of
the first talented women filmmakers, with a number of short fiction films addressing gender issues, such as *Malal* (literally,
'boredom,' 2010) and *Once* (Marra, 2013), as well as child abuse
in *Arabana* (2006). She also established The Scene Club for featuring independent films.

The first UAE full-length film, *Dream* (Hulm) by Hani al-Shibani, was directed in 2005 and the first to gain international recognition as a result of being promoted by the Dubai Film Festival was *City of Life* (Dar al-haya, 2009) by Ali F. Mostafa. The fast-paced and high-standard technical production with an international cast reflects on the cultural mishmash in the Emirates, presenting a number of parallel and increasingly intertwining stories of different UAE residents with their specific problems, including a European stewardess, an Indian driver, and a spoiled young Emirati. Multiculturalism and the crossing of national borders play a decisive role as well in Mostafa's subsequent film, *A to B* (Min alif ila ba', 2013), a road movie that follows three Arab childhood friends from different national backgrounds on a journey from Abu Dhabi to Beirut.

Gender relations and generational conflicts frequently serve as main topics in Emirati film and in Gulf cinema in general; one example is the strong portraits of women by the female poet Nujoom al-Ghanem (Nudjum al-Ghanim). Nawaf al-Janahi's second feature film, *Sea Shadow* (Zill al-bahr, 2011), is a coming-of-age story with slightly stereotypical protagonists, but it stands out by its unpretentious and sensitive *mise en scène*. Its action focuses on an errand boy who is torn between two attractive girls, one of whom comes from a family on the verge of collapse. Neglected by her strict and cold father, she falls prey to the sexual harassment of his Indian hairdresser. In contrast, al-Janahi's first film, *The Circle* (al-Da'ira, 2009), a UAE–Kuwaiti coproduction realized with TV money (MBC-Group), departs a bit from the prevalent thematic orientation, as it features the existential crisis of a poet and journalist who reconsiders his life the moment he discovers that he has a mortal disease.

Identity crisis due to neocolonialism has been addressed in Bahraini cinema by its godfather, Bassam al-Thawadi. In 2006 he directed *A Bahraini Tale* (Hikaya bahrainiya), the story of a middle-class family against the backdrop of the Six Day War in 1967 which resulted in Egypt's defeat and the decline of Nasserism and social-ist thought in the Arab world. Despite its political subtext the film has a quite cinematographic appearance. Other Bahraini films, even those in which Thawadi has served as executive producer such as *Four Girls* (Arbaᶜ banat, 2008) by Husain al-Hulaibi, rely strongly on TV-style acting and *mise en scène* reminiscent of Egyptian entrepreneur or *muqawalat* films of the 1980s. *Four Girls* provides a funny take on gender inequality. In telling the story of four women who make the unconventional decision to open a car wash, it depicts the challenges Bahraini women encounter when they plan to enter the male-dominated realm of labor. Following the typical modernist argumentation, the film presents a Muslim fundamental-ist as the main opponent of the women and their business project. Al-Hulaibi follows the same standardized and stereotypical repre-sentation in his film *Longing* (Hanin, 2010), which depicts the rise of a polarizing sectarianism in a mixed Sunni–Shiite family during the period from 1982 until the millennium.

Along with these more old-fashioned takes on cinema there is also a remarkable interest in certain mainstream genres, first and foremost horror film and science fiction, although this interest has been expressed largely in parodies. The English-language *Silveraven* (2012) and *Dead Sands* (2013), both by the Bahrain-based Pakistani Zeeshan Jawed Shah, represent comedies that contradict the genre rules by their slow-paced action and long takes. A similar interest in the horror film genre can be sensed among young directors in Kuwait. *Ghost Pain* (no Arabic title, 2010), a short amateur film by Ahmad Haji Ali, likewise mocks the genre: the ghost in the film turns out to be the protagonist's dis-guised friend.

In general, Kuwaiti cinema, similar to Bahraini cinema, has pro-duced a very limited number of TV-style fiction films, such as *The Lost Years* (Sanawat al-dayaᶜ, 2008) and *Whispers of Sin* (Hamasat al-khati'a, 2010), both by Abd al-Rahman al-Khalifi. Both films tell moralistic tales about young people who lose their way because of familial neglect and paternalism. In contrast, the road movie *Tora Bora* (2011), by Walid al-Awadi, focuses on Abu Tariq and Umm Tariq, who set off on a journey to search for their youngest son Ahmed who, after being brainwashed by extremists, has decided to leave Kuwait for Afghanistan. This film displays a much stronger visuality even though it sticks to the usual melodramatic tone of Kuwaiti and Bahraini films, which in turn are strongly reminiscent of Egyptian cinema in the 1970s and 1980s.

Little progress has been made in either Kuwait or Bahrain in terms of creating an infrastructure for production similar to the one in the UAE, yet there have been attempts to reach out to the region through coproduction. Desert Door Productions, for example, a Kuwaiti production company with a representative office in UAE, produces Walid al-Awadi's films and coproduced the Palestinian feature film *Pomegranates and Myrrh* (al-Murr wa-l-Rumman, 2009) by Najwa al-Najjar. Talal al-Muhanna, an independent Kuwait-based producer, is making a name for himself in the field of regional art house production, and has meanwhile undertaken coproductions in the field of Arab documentary, most notably *Fidaï* (Fidaᶜi, 2012) by Damien Ounouri (Anwari), a French–Algerian–Chinese production.

The most remarkable change in terms of film culture has occurred in Saudi Arabia since 2006, where a small but quite diverse number of feature-length films has appeared, directed by both Saudi men and women. This has taken place despite the fact that, unlike in other Gulf countries, film culture has been highly contested and any attempts to organize public screenings have been eyed with suspicion.

Ironically, movie theaters were not officially banned in Saudi Arabia until 2009. In the 1970s and 1980s, it seems, some improvised theaters existed, but they fell into disuse after the rise of religious conservatism. In 2008 the then minister of information and culture made a request to the Shura Council to open a cinema hall, but to no avail. Instead, one year later a private petition to ban movie-theater construction was approved by the minister of interior. It has to be suspected that these strict measures are primarily due to the pressure exerted by clergymen with close ties to the king. Moreover, they are not really in accordance with public opinion. According to a MEMRI study, a "recent poll found that 90% of Saudis agree to the opening of movie halls in Saudi cities, as long as they screen films that are 'realistic' and whose content does not contravene the values and customs of Islam."[14]

Indeed, since mid-2000 Saudi cultural activity has made inroads into the field of cinema. The Rotana Group, which belongs to the king's nephew al-Walid ibn Talal, organized Saudi Arabia's first film festival. It took place in July 2006, in Jeddah, under the title "The Jeddah Visual Shows Festival." It included sixteen movies, eight of them from Saudi Arabia (according to MEMRI). However, the most widely acknowledged Saudi productions of that year, the two full-length feature films *Shadow of Silence* (Zilal al-samt, 2006) by ᶜAbd Allah al-Muhaisin and *Keif el-Hal* (Kayf al-hal, literally: How's It Going?, 2006) by Izidore Mussalam, were entirely shot abroad.[15] *Shadow of Silence* has been described as "a film which reflects the long experience of its director, who in 1975 founded the Transworld Company, the first commercial cinema and TV production company in Saudi Arabia and a producer of numerous films and TV programmes."[16] It tells the story of a wife who is in search of her husband, a liberal leftist intellectual. He has been abducted and sent to a government reprogramming center in the desert. *Keif el-Hal* was directed by Izidore Mussalam, a Palestinian-Canadian director, and commissioned by Ayman Halawani, a producer at the Rotana Group. It was conceived as a mainstream comedy on intergenerational conflicts and love marriage as opposed to arranged marriage. Its main character is Sahar, a young woman whose fundamentalist brother Khalil conspires to give her away for an early marriage. Yet she prefers to become a journalist and write about the film and theater director Mansour, for whom she falls.

Despite Rotana's endeavors the fourth edition of the Jeddah festival was called off in 2009 because of the already mentioned ban
on movie theaters, but was resumed the following year. In the very
same time span, however, a first public screening was held showing the Saudi film *Menahi* (Manahi, 2009), another Rotana
production. According to *The World Post*, the film was shown to a
mixed audience in the "more open western seaport city Jeddah" as
well as in Taif. A Rotana spokesman stated that a total of 25,000
viewers watched the movie, including 9,000 women.[17]

Under different circumstances *Menahi* could have certainly
attracted more audiences, as it has all the elements of a popular mainstream film following the Egyptian school. Starring popular Saudi
TV comedian Fayiz al-Malki, the film presents several musical numbers and draws otherwise on Arab farce traditions relying on stylized
acting and the use of different Arabic dialects as a source of comedy.
The story is as timely as it is standardized, focusing on a naïve Saudi
Arabian Bedouin who gets hijacked because of a political conspiracy
and ends up as a billionaire in Dubai, against all odds and despite the
constant interference of his rich and influential opponent, Abu Nasir.

Cinematic activities and aspirations in Saudi Arabia have not
been confined to high society, but have also spread among younger
and less privileged circles. Media collectives and promising young
women filmmakers have appeared and directed well-received short
films. For example Shahad Ameen (Amin) has directed two shorts
so far on gender inequality, *Layla's Window* (Nafizat Layla, 2011)
and the visually stunning, highly allegorical *Eye and Mermaid*
(Huriya wa ᶜayn, 2013). ᶜAhd Kamel (Kamil) directed *Sanctity*
(Hurmat, 2012), tackling the social pressure that is exerted on a
widowed single mother. She also appeared as a lead player in
Haifaa al-Mansour's *The Girl Wadjda* (Wadjda, 2013), which was
shot entirely in Saudi Arabia and distributed worldwide. This film,
too, deals with the difficulties women face due to religious conservatism at home, depicting the struggle of a little girl to be able to
buy and ride a bicycle like the boys in her neighborhood.

The Girl Wadjda (Wadjda, 2013) by Haifaa al-Mansour
(courtesy Razor Film Produktion GmbH/photographed by Tobias Kownatzki)

Daring topics, first and foremost the sexual abuse of a minor boy in *Sunrise/Sunset* (Shuruq wa ghurub, 2009) by Muhammad al-Zahiri (2009), were presented by the collective Talashi Films. As of 2009, Talashi was composed of ten members and had produced seven shorts, including *Shadows* (Zilal, 2009) by Mohamed Alhamoud.[18] The films of the group, which has since disintegrated, not only experimented with film form but were also eager to touch on taboos, such as gender relations, the status of women, or merely behavior, dress code, and language. In spite of the current conservatism of the political leadership, after the first suppressed wave of protests in 2011 and the war that Saudi Arabia is conducting in Yemen, it is expected that this form of cultural resistance will reappear.

Iraq: A failed national cinema?

In contrast to the Gulf States, filmmaking in Iraq has been a great challenge in recent years. Today, national sovereignty is practically lost and the country is on the verge of complete fragmentation, with huge territories in the north either under control of the Kurds or the Sunni Islamic State militias and the south practically dominated by Iran. The country's public institutions are still struggling to rise from the rubble of boycott, invasion, and terrorist attacks. In fact, Iraqi cinema has never really had an easy time. Only in pre-Saddam times was the country able to produce a few love stories and musicals à la Hollywood-on-the-Nile. Some of them were even successful at the national box office, such as *Alia and Issam* (Aliya wa ᶜIsam, 1947) by Frenchman André Shatan, inspired by Romeo and Juliet and set in a Bedouin environment, and *Fitna and Hassan* (Fitna wa Hasan, 1955), also a tragic love story directed by Haidar al-ᶜUmar. This film enjoyed a particular popularity because of its supposedly genuine Iraqi character.[19] Iraq's more socially committed, realist-oriented tradition also attracted attention, starting with *Who's Responsible?* (Man al-mas'ul?, 1957) by ᶜAbd al-Jabbar Wali Taufiq, *Saᶜid Effendi* (1957) by Kamiran Husni, *The Thirsty* by Mohamed Choukri Jamil, and *The Night Watch* (al-Haris, 1967) by Khalil Shauqi.

This is about the time when the first state interference in cinema took place, with the Ministry of Information beginning to monopolize film imports after 1972.[20] After Saddam's complete takeover of power in 1979, the state eventually dominated most film activities. Cinema was increasingly used for means of propaganda, with a number of features in the early 1980s praising the dictator.[21] Political films like *Mutawiᶜ and Bahiya* (1982) criticized Egyptian president Sadat's peace initiative with Israel, and mega productions, most notably *al-Qadisiya* (1981) and *The Great Question* (al-Mas'ala al-kubra, 1983), starring British actor Oliver Reed, conjured up national liberation and unity while mobilizing against neighboring Iran. Given the ongoing military conflict, war films in the 1980s were complemented by light comedies in an attempt to cheer up the public. Some of these enjoyed considerable popularity, particularly Sahib Hadad with his *Building 13* (ᶜImara 13, 1989). Films by Khairiya al-Mansur, the only Iraqi woman fiction filmmaker of the time, such as *6/6* (Sitta ᶜala sitta, 1988)[22] and *100 Percent* (Mi'a bi-l-mi'a, 1992), belong to this comedic category.

The last big production of the period, again a national epic, was Mohamed Choukri Jamil's *King Ghazi* (al-Malik Ghazi), released in 1993 before the effects of the embargo started to take root. At the start of the 1990s, the Ministry of Information called on business-men to invest in founding film companies, while the absence of film stock led some directors to shift to using television cameras, mak-ing what came to be known as 'screen films' *(aflam al-skrin)*, in an attempt to meet the demand.[23]

One of the supposedly last Iraqi films made before the fall of the regime and the allied incursion (as reported by American online sources) was *Hafr al-Batn* (2001) by Abdul Salman al-Adhami, a film that is said to show how Iraqi soldiers were mercilessly tar-geted by American troops.[24]

The American invasion of Iraq, contrary to expectations, did not facilitate things in the film world. The extreme sectarian violence that has seized Iraq since the American invasion has become one of the major problems of Iraqi filmmaking (except for the Kurdish north), resulting in emigration and brain drain. Lack of general infrastructure, an absence of training opportunities, and heavy secu-rity problems have remained the prime obstacles for those filmmakers who insist on continuing to exercise their profession. The few post-2003 Arab-Iraqi films that have been produced and found their ways to festivals are either road movies or show signs of narrative fragmentation, resembling a patchwork of parallel actions dominated either by cryptic symbolism or by overt national allegories. It seems that, faced with defeat, national disintegration, destruction, occupation, and daily extremist violence, Arab-Iraqi stories are difficult to shape or parse.

This applies especially to *Underexposure* (Ghayr salih, 2005) by Oday Rasheed (ᶜUday Rashid), one of the first films to be made after Saddam's fall. It is a phantasmagorical accumulation of pri-vate and public observations and seemingly disconnected situations framed by the attempt of a filmmaker and his cameraman to shoot a film on expired film stock from a time before the embargo, reflecting the fact that Iraqi film was suffering from a complete ban on equipment, chemicals, and film stock after 1990. Rasheed, who received backing from the German director Tom Twyker, patron of Filmclub Berlin-Baghdad in 2004, was falsely reported to have directed the first Iraqi feature film in fourteen years.[25] Moreover, he was said to have been expelled from film school under Saddam Hussein and to belong to a post-invasion association of alternative artists called The Survivors (al-Nadjin).[26] In fact, the help Rasheed received from outside was less substantial than other Iraqi productions of the period that were directed by exiled Iraqis, such as *Zaman: The Man from the Reeds* (Zaman, radjul min qassab, 2003) by Amer (ᶜAmir) ᶜAlwan and *Dreams* (Ahlam, 2005) by Mohamed al-Daradji.

In fact *Zaman, the Man from the Reeds* took up earlier realist and socially committed traditions of Iraqi cinema. It follows a poor man who, because of the embargo, is forced to travel from the Shiite-inhabited marshes of southern Iraq to Baghdad in order to find a rare medicine for his ill wife. This journey is used as an opportunity to portray a country that has been economically devastated because of its corrupt regime and as a result of the international embargo. Seven years later *Son of Babylon* (Ibn Babil, 2010) by Mohamed al-Daradj offered the opportunity for a variety of human encounters and a means to discover more about the suppressed painful events of the past that entailed ferocious political persecution. The film's protagonist, a little boy, follows his grandmother—grudgingly at first—on a journey across Iraq as she is determined to find out more about the fate of the boy's disappeared father. In contrast, Kutaiba al-Janabi's (Qutayba al-Djanabi) docu-drama *Leaving Baghdad* (al-Rahhil min Baghdad, 2010) is set before the invasion in the early 2000s and pictures a man on his way to exile: Sadiq, a personal cameraman to Saddam Hussein, is on the run. He wants to join his wife in London. During his odyssey through several countries he is haunted by the fact of the disappearance of his son, who did not share his father's enthusiasm for the regime. The scenes allegedly shot by the fictional Sadiq— which are real-life footage from Saddam Hussein's archive—are no less tormenting for him than his private memories in the end.

The boldest attempt to tackle the situation in Iraq through the perspective of exile was certainly *Baghdad On/Off* (2003) by Saad (Sacd) Salman, a pre-invasion documentary shot undercover in 2000 that shows the filmmaker's clandestine and impossible journey from exile back to Baghdad, where his mother lies on her deathbed. It was followed by Maysoon Pachachi's *Return to the Land of Wonders* (al-cAwda ila balad al-cadja'ib, 2004). The director used her father's return to Iraq as a member of the first interim, United States-appointed Governing Council as an opportunity to visit her birthplace and the people of her childhood and to have a general look at the state of affairs in Iraq. Although the filmmaker was sheltered by her father's privileged position, the film still transmitted an urgent sense of imperilment.

Dreams (2005), in contrast, was shot under very difficult conditions. It capitalized on the post-colonial allegory of the raped nation or raped people (in this case, Shiites), even though inspired by real-life experiences of the filmmaker. Like *Underexposure*, the film is split into a number of diverse parallel actions with largely Shiite characters, framed by the story of Ahlam (literally, 'dreams'), a young woman whose bridegroom is dragged away by state security during their wedding, leaving her mentally disturbed and hospitalized. During the invasion, Ahlam's ordeal continues as her family is unable to prevent her from getting lost, raped, then trapped in a bombed-out building and eventually surrounded by American troops, the ultimate allegory of a devastated nation.

In fact, the invasion has affected Iraqi cinema on all levels, even in terms of memory. Twelve masters of the ninety-nine (Arab) Iraqi fiction films produced in Iraq since the country's first Egyptian-directed fiction film in 1946, *Son of the East* (Ibn al-sharq), were lost during the American invasion and many of the rest were damaged.[27]

Film students at the Fine Arts Academy have been suffering from a lack of material, equipment, and up-to-date practical training. The first Iraqi Film Festival, launched in the summer of 2006 and dedicated to past Iraqi production, was overshadowed by earlier bomb attacks on the National Theater. Moreover, the Independent Film and Television College, opened by Maysoon Pachachi and Kasim Abid (Qasim ᶜAbid) in 2004, was forced to close again in 2007. After a two-year hiatus the college tried to reopen and students were again attempting to make films until the situation became too difficult once more.[28] Some of the student films of that period bear witness to the challenges: *A Candle for the Shabandar Café* (Shamaᶜa li maqha al-Shahbandar, 2007) by Emad (ᶜImad) ᶜAli ᶜAbbas is an example. Abbas was shot and seriously wounded during the film shooting. The object of his film, a historic café, was itself bombed and destroyed. Kasim Abid's subsequent film tells a similar story. In *Life After the Fall* (Hayat ma baᶜd al-suqut, 2008) which was edited by Maysoon Pachachi, the director shows how his family tries to come to terms with the death of his brother, who was pulled out of his shop and murdered. Pachachi's and Abid's school was of course trying to make up for the deficiency of post-invasion public services.

After a certain consolidation of Shiite dominance under al-Maliki, the Ministry of Culture has started to show an interest in cinema. In 2013 it reportedly had eight full-length fiction and documentary films in the pipeline.[29] Judging by the earliest results, the outcome of state funding seems to run along traditionalist, sectarian, and tribal lines. *Silence of the Shepherd* (Samt al-raᶜi, 2014) by Raᶜd Mushatat was produced solely by the Ministry of Culture through the affiliated Film and Theater Foundation Baghdad (Da'irat al-sinima wa-l-masrah) and shot in al-Samawat southern Iraq, that is, in largely Shiite-inhabited territory. It deals with the disappearance of the daughter of a leading figure in the tribe who is believed to have run away with a neighbor's son, thereby disgracing her father for years to come. Only the shepherd of the village knows better, but for his own safety he discloses the secret much later, after the toppling of the dictator: the girl has been murdered by Saddam's officers, who catch her on the site where the killing and burial of Kurdish prisoners takes place. On the dramatic level the alluded to genocide serves merely as an excuse to explain the silence of the shepherd, who witnesses the innocent death of the female heroine but keeps the secret out of fear. At the same time the patriarchal, misogynist code of honor that has helped to dishonor her is never brought into question.

At this point it remains questionable whether state involvement will really help to solve the problems of Iraqi cinema, given the fact that it has already caused serious problems in the past, not only because of the numerous propaganda films produced under Saddam Hussein, but also for the reason that its regime has been responsible for severe ruptures in the free development of cinema. On the other hand, the case of Iraqi-Kurdish cinema shows that the state—or, in this case, local authorities—may play a crucial role in imagining the nation through film, particularly if they help produce films that high-light what may be considered unifying factors, such as language, geography, cultural preferences, and traditions.

The first-ever Iraqi-Kurdish film, *Narjis, Bride of Kurdistan* (Nardjis, ᶜarus Kurdistan) by Jaᶜfar ᶜAli, was filmed in northern Iraq in 1991, after the allied military operation against Iraq and the establishment of the no-fly zone, which resulted in greater auton-omy for the Kurdish north. The film was released in the city of Erbil but not shown in Baghdad.[30] Since then, most Kurdish productions have been realized abroad, like *A Silent Traveler* (see page 43) or more recent prominent films by the Iranian Kurd Bahman Ghobadi, *A Time for Drunken Horses* (2000), *Marooned in Iraq* (2002), *Turtles Can Fly* (2004), and *Half Moon* (2006), all shot in Iran. Similar to many Iranian post-revolution works, Ghobadi's films show deep humanism and a fascination with perilous nature. Crossing the border into Iraq is of special concern to his narratives, as if symbolically transgressing the artificial borders of the region's alleged nation-states.

The establishment of the Kurdistan Regional Government in Iraq after the American invasion in 2003 resulted in the creation of film-educational opportunities as well as several cultural institutions, including cinema departments under the Ministry of Culture. Kurdish satellite television and subsequently also locally based channels, for example MED TV and MEDYA TV, provided Kurds with professional training opportunities that helped improve the cinematic infrastructure.[31] The Kurdish-administered Iraqi north (or southern Kurdistan) has thus even succeeded in attracting Kurdish filmmakers from Iran, Syria, and the diaspora to shoot or receive financial support. Also, particularly the city of Erbil has developed into a cultural center that today possesses several operating and very up-to-date cinemas, including one multiplex that has more screens than the rest of Iraq together.[32]

As a consequence of this support, the situation of Kurdish cinema has improved significantly since 2003. Two of the subsequent Iraqi-Kurdish productions, *Kilomètre Zéro* (2005) by Hiner Saleem and *Narcissus Blossom* (Zaman al-nardjis, 2005)[33] by Mas^cud ^cArif Salih and Husain Hassan ^cAli, were shot in northern Iraq. In contrast to Ghobadi's films, they have an explicitly political character. *Narcissus Blossom*, in particular, is a typical national liberation film, set in the 1970s, with one central embattled male figure, a young student who avoids detention by escaping into the mountains and joining the *peshmergas*. Otherwise, the film is packed with the typical modernist repertory of post-colonial cinema, criticizing, among other elements, arranged marriage and patriarchal structures in traditional Kurdish society.

This particular critique was typical for post-colonial Arab film of the mid-twentieth century. Today it forms part of almost all Kurdish productions, for example, *Before Snowfall* (2013) by Hisham Zaman and *Memories on Stone* (Zikrayat manqushat ^cala hajar, 2014) by Shawkat Amin Korki. It is even voiced in Hiner Saleem's genre film *My Sweet Pepperland* (2013), which pays tribute to the American Westerns. Saleem is the most internationally recognized Kurdish filmmaker. Now based in France, the director left Iraqi Kurdistan as a teenager. He has been less interested in portraying armed resistance, preferring humane and humorous drama in order to highlight the absurdities of the inter-Kurdish and Kurdish–Arab situations. His films come the closest to European art house cinema.

The protagonist of his comedy *Kilomètre Zéro* is more concerned with how to leave with his family for Europe than with Saddam's constables. What really obstructs him is his wife's insistence on remaining with her bedridden father, rather than any political opponent of his homeland. This anti-heroic orientation is supported by the film's visual style and its understated acting. Nevertheless, the story offers a far-reaching panorama of the regime's atrocities and difficult Arab–Kurdish relations. Saleem not only received European funding for this, but was also supported by the Kurdish "government" (as stated in the credits) in northern Iraq and by Kurdish television. In a similar vein, *Crossing the Dust* (2006) by Shawkat Amin Korki uses the motif of a common journey, in this case of two *pershmerga*s with a little lost Arab boy called Saddam (!), in order to question the possibilities of peaceful coexistence. Set during the uncertain times of the American invasion, it follows the protagonists on their journey to the Kurdish cities that had not yet been liberated from central Iraqi control. Depicting the challenges of coexistence after the long years of discrimination and atrocities also lies at the core of Korki's subsequent film, *Kick Off* (Darbit al-bidaya, 2009). Its main character gets the idea of cleaning up a former football stadium to organize a game between Arab and Kurdish inhabitants of Kirkuk. To do this, he has to overcome numerous obstacles, and only partially succeeds in making the match work.

In general, Kurdish films are characterized by their spontaneous and vivid protagonists, largely due to the extensive use of non-professional actors, and reflect the particular warmth, sadness, and humor of a people embattled not only by the military forces of the formerly centralized, anti-democratic, hostile Iraqi government, but also by the harsh conditions of their native land, nature, climate, and way of life. They draw on the tradition of Yilmaz Güney (with the exception of *Kilomètre Zéro* and other films by Saleem, which tend to reduce the wild beauty and simultaneous cruelty of Kurdish topography to postcard beauty). Moreover, they stand out for their remarkable narrative linearity and coherence, particularly Ghobadi's films. More local in style and character studies, but no less poetic, are the works by Korki, who had to live in Iranian exile for several years before returning to his homeland.

In conclusion, northern Iraq has seen the emergence of an anti-colonial and sometimes unequivocally nationalist Iraqi-Kurdish cinema, rising from the ruins of the pre-1990 situation. Thus, while some more recent Arab film traditions, and particularly *auteur* films, have developed deep skepticism with regards to national heroism—or, in other words, have toppled the mythology of an ethnically, religiously, and ideologically undivided national body—the increase of publicly supported Kurdish productions seems symptomatic of the decentralized, if not disparaged, condition of the Iraqi state and its own self-understanding as a nation. The former hostile and exclusionist policy towards the Kurds and the Shiites has been replaced by a set of largely secessionist orientations.

Locked embrace: Syria

The current situation in Syria does not differ much from Iraq in terms of fragmentation, security, and infrastructure. Even though the Film Organization still exists in Damascus, the stronghold of Bashar al-Assad's regime, artists opposed to his regime on the one hand and to the Islamic State on the other have largely emigrated. Increasing dependency on foreign funding had already become the fate of Syrian film even before the outbreak of the revolt in 2011. The veterans of Syrian cinema Muhammad Malas and Usama Muhammad (or Oussama Mohammad, a more current spelling) had their fiction films *Passion* (Bab al-maqam, 2005) and *Sacrifices* (Sunduq al-dunya, literally, 'world box,' a type of magic lantern, 2002) coproduced with France as early as a decade ago. The reasons were only partially political; they were also rooted in the deep financial crisis of the Syrian National Film Organization, connected to the fact that film production has not been a priority for the Syrian state and just one more sign that the regime had opted for political isolationism for many years. Indirect censorship, combined with bureaucracy and inefficient distribution policies, resulted in the production of so-called 'cave films'—hundreds of exposed film rolls stored without ever being screened for a larger audience.[34]

In its early existence, the Film Organization was able to make ends meet by receiving its funding through the import and taxation of foreign films distributed in Syria, but audience numbers decreased because of the limited spending power of the country's middle class, which started to improve only in the course of the 1990s. Until the Arab Rebellion the country excelled in the production of television serials, but ended up with only one major film distributor, and the number of movie theaters has been reduced over the years to thirty-eight (with seventy-one no longer functioning).[35] In 1999 the Film Organization had a total budget of only 8 million francs (around US$1.5 million),[36] which jeopardized a production rate that even before 1995 did not exceed one or two films a year.[37] Not even the most prolific and accessible of Syrian film makers, ᶜAbd al-Latif ᶜAbd al-Hamid, was able to realize a film every year, as his filmography shows: *The Nights of the Jackal*, *Verbal Messages* (Rasa'il shafahiya, 1993), *Ascension of the Rain* (Suᶜud al-matar, 1995), *Breeze of the Soul* (Nasim al-ruh, 1998), *Two Moons and an Olive Tree* (Qamarayn wa zaytuna, 2001), *Listener's Choice* (Ma yatlubuhu al-mustamiᶜun, 2003), *Out of Coverage* (Kharidj al-taghtiya, 2007), *The Days of Boredom* (Ayam al-dadjar, 2009), *September Rain* (Matar aylul, 2010) and *The Lover* (al-ᶜAshiq, 2012). He at least had the opportunity to get films produced more frequently, most probably because of his contained political and social criticism, while others, like Malas or Muhammad, could not shoot for a decade or more and decided eventually to look for funding abroad. Others, like Raymond Boutros (Butrus), had severe problems with official censorship, for example with his first film *Algae* (al-Tahalib, 1991). He spent a whole year of editing trying to close the holes created by the censor's scissors in his cinematic account of the history of his hometown, Hama.[38] In contrast, his latest historical spectacle, *Hassiba* (2009), passed more easily, maybe because it dealt with the less controversial history of resistance under the French Mandate in the first half of the twentieth century.

A considerable number of committed Syrian filmmakers resorted to plainly political or socially guided narratives, against all odd resuming the tradition of Nabil Maleh's *The Extras* (1993). They featured embattled and besieged women, or showed couples in love, and include: *Dreamy Visions* (Ru'a halima, 2003) by the first Syrian woman filmmaker of full-length fiction, Waha al-Rahib; *Under the Ceiling* (Taht al-saqf, 2005) by Nidal al-Dibs; or, more prominently, *Land of Strangers* (Turab al-ghuraba', 1998) by Samir Zikra. Zikra's historical look at the beginning of the nineteenth-century Arab enlightenment *(nahda)* and the first signs of pan-Arabism focused on the life of thinker and writer Shaykh ᶜAbd al-Rahman al-Kawakibi (1852–1902) and his fight against obscurantism and the effects of five centuries of Ottoman rule in Syria.

State-supported Syrian cinema, despite its critical condition, produced a number of what can be classified as art house films during the 1990s and in the following decade. Like no other cinema, however, it also reflects the major problem of Arab *auteur* film, namely the difficult relationship with local audiences, which had either no chance or lacked the sensibility to watch and appreciate the Russian-inspired dark symbolism and hidden political allegory of, for example, *The Night* (1992) by Muhammad Malas or, even more so, Usama Muhammad's *Sacrifices*. The latter is a quasi-mythical story about an archaically structured family whose head dies before being able to pass on his name to one of his three grandsons. Growing up

Sacrifices (Sunduq al-dunya, 2002) by Usama Muhammad
(courtesy Institut du Monde Arabe, Paris)

nameless, each of the grandsons embraces a different attitude: the first submission, the second love, and the third power, violence, and cruelty, reflecting a dark vision of a deeply disturbed world dominated by absolute power.

Even the master of subtle comedy, ᶜAbd al-Hamid, fell into a similar vision in his *Two Moons and an Olive Tree*. Set in the Latakia Mountains, it focuses on two adolescent siblings and their friend, who are psychologically and physically tortured by the archaic cruelty of the adult world. In contrast, the "symbolical canticles of mourning" in *The Neighing of Directions* (also *The Journey*, Sahil al-djihhat, 1993) by Maher Keddo (Mahir Kiddu) and the "visual meditations" of *Refugees* (al-Ludjat, 1995) by Riyad Shayya, to use Salah Sermini's words, relied on the epic tropes of search and journey, but they still reflected a dark world.[39]

All this had led younger generation critics of Syrian film to accuse their colleagues of exaggerated individualism, exclusiveness, and elitism. One of these critics is Mayyar al-Roumi, whose

2000 documentary, *A Silent Cinema* (Sinima samita), presents the most outstanding directors of his country. In al-Roumi's view, because they are unable or unwilling to understand and meet the needs and preferences of local audiences, they represent a radical *cinéma d'auteur* that does not orient itself toward the homeland, but rather takes as its reference Western European and Russian art filmmakers such as Robert Bresson and Andrei Tarkovski.[40] To him, the "always announced contempt for commercial cinema reveals a form of fear of novelty, a selective acceptance of modernity."[41] Thus it seems that Syrian filmmakers have, on the one hand, internalized the lowbrow/highbrow schism between popular mainstream and committed film and, on the other, fallen prey to the all-too-dominant post-colonial modernist dogma of cultural 'progress' as embodied by the intellectual art film. At the same time, the isolationism and crypticism of the public-cinema generation was also forced on them from the outside by a state censorship that, with few exceptions, did not interfere directly as much as it simply drained away all film resources and distribution outlets, just as the regime's decades-old arbitrary rule paralyzed cultural life in Syria as a whole. In 2006 this dilemma prompted Usama Muhammad to draw the following comparison: "Our cinema is free but it is like a whisper in a closed room. . . . It is as if we sneaked into that closed room from the keyhole, and we grew inside it. In its turn, it sneaked inside us and grew. And we are stuck in this locked embrace."[42]

In fact, obliged by the system of state and self-censorship imposed by the autocratic and authoritarian regimes they exist in, cinematic works before the revolt in 2011 largely refrained from blaming the political system directly or depicting state-initiated torture. The alternative was to communicate instead with the bodies of their viewers, conveying the scope of general oppression by means of cinematic performativity similar to what the so-called body genres do. For example, the splatter film relies on audio-visual effects that produce a physical impact, built upon the relation of the viewer to the off-screen body and the viewer's physical interaction with what is presented. This is particularly evident in films like *Sacrifices* and cAbd al-Hamid's 2007 fiction *Out of Coverage* (Kharidj al-taghtiya).

In the latter film, the director chooses to tell the quite unsettling story of a middle-aged man who spends pretty much all of the film hovering madly between two jobs, two women, and two children, his own and his friend's, a leftist political prisoner for whose family he has decided to care until he loses control and falls desperately in love with his friend's wife. For a short moment he even feels tempted to denounce his friend to prevent him from being released and coming back to his family. The film's restless and panting rhythm is created by a chasing camera that follows the man's relentless and futile attempts to satisfy the needs of two families. It involves us in his constant running, driving, sweating, the mounting sexual tension that characterizes his desire for the woman he cares for just like his own wife, and his eventual roaming around a booth that is run by a state security agent who openly serves as a messenger and informant. The mere pace of action creates a strong effect of agitation.[43]

This panting rhythm has also been applied to a certain extent in *Sacrifices* and is reflected in the performance of the actors themselves. No wonder that Mayyar al-Roumi, who had criticized earlier the contempt of the older generation of filmmakers for its audience, chose a completely different style for his first feature-length film, *Round Trip* (Mishwar, 2012). It was shot shortly before the outbreak of the uprising and was only completed in 2012 as an Egyptian–French–German–Syrian coproduction. Like a road movie, the film follows a young couple, Walid and Suhair, on their train ride from Syria to Iran. Up to that point Walid's taxi had served as an insecure venue where they could exchange quick kisses; they decide to go to Tehran, where a friend of Suhair has an apartment which they can use to stay for a few days. However, as the long-awaited opportunity of solitude comes and the first exciting night has been spent in the sleeping car of the train, their interest in each other decreases sharply. The film plot is quite austere, with a few dialogue lines serving as a turning point when Suhair asks Walid about the affairs of his sisters and he explains they are different from her, more conservative and, not as open. She counters by saying he is just like all other men. The film ends with the two of them leaving the train, walking at a distance from each other. The simplicity of the film lies in the physical interaction of the couple, the sparseness of its dialogue, its long takes of observation of the changing landscape, the train, and the ambivalent presence of the train conductor, who is aware of their illicit relationship.

Today the serenity of *Round Trip* conveys an almost nostalgic vision, since the landscapes this film crosses are now war-riven and a trip of that sort has become unthinkable. Yet it is not only the geographic landscape that has changed. The same change applies to Syrian cinema and to Usama Muhammad's "locked embrace" in which the filmmakers were stuck. On 9 May 2011, after his invitation to the 64th Cannes Film Festival, Muhammad was forced to stay in France. The National Film Organization, his nominal employer, sacked him for his outspoken criticism of the Bashar al-Assad regime, turning him into a persona non grata at home. As Muhammad mentions later in his 2014 documentary *Silvered Water: Syria Self-Portrait* (Ma' al-fidda: Suriya sira zatiya), he was advised not to come back to Syria for his own safety. This happened at the very early stage of the Syrian insurgency that started in the provinces of Daraa and Homs. The insurgency quickly turned into a quasi-colonialist war in which the regime used not only the old methods of oppression, namely arbitrary arrests and torture, but also resorted to organized killing by the so-called *shabiha* militia and eventually used unrestrained military force to bomb the country's infrastructure into rubble. Muhammad's film shows that the war started at first between the national armed forces and the so-called Free Syrian Army, but was then extended to involve an increasing number of Islamist and Salafist militias, most prominently Nusrat

al-Sham and Daᶜish, or IS (Islamic State). The latter came to dominate more and more Syrian and Iraqi territory, competing with
Assad's forces and state security in inflicting unprecedented hardships on civilians.

The long and extraordinarily painful process by which the early
Syrian protests turned into a ferocious civil war that ripped the country and its people apart is reconstructed in an intellectually reflexive
and, at the same time poetic, way in the essay film *Silvered Water*,
directed, as it says in the credits, "by Oussama Mohammed, Wiam
Simav Bedirxan (Wi'am Simav Badr Khan), 1001 Syrians and me."
It relies mainly on iconic footage from the Internet that has documented pivotal events and inhumane practices. As the film progresses
it is complemented and eventually overlapped by fragmentary observations from besieged Homs provided by the young female Kurdish
documentary filmmaker Wiam Simav Bedirxan. She had contacted
Muhammad at the end of 2011 asking for his advice on filming after
she was able to smuggle a camera into the war zone.

Her material of the destroyed city radiates a strong intimacy, for
she not only documents the ruins but has an eye for the very small
details. Thus she collects haunting images of stray pets, dogs, cats—
injured, starving, or dying—victims of the shellings, and even more
heart-breaking, her portrait of little Omar, a four-to-five-year-old
whom she follows on one occasion to the grave of his father, as he
speaks about the flowers he has brought. Bedirxan's own dialogue
with the little boy and their common strolls through the rubble,
watching out for snipers, collecting flowers or mulberries, develop a
strong emotional intensity. This intensity is fostered by the dialogue
between mentor Muhammad and his virtual protégé, but also by the
former's comments, in which he questions the nature of film and
image, ruminating, for example, on the way the officers of the
regime stage torture sessions and how they thus become film directors in their own way.

Doubtless, the war has permitted the release of Syrian cinema's
creative forces, a release from the rule of oppression that has crept

inside bodies and minds. However, this liberation has been achieved at an unbelievably high price. The younger generation of filmmakers has finally found an outlet for their criticism and frustration with the acquiescence of the older generation, but as a result it has to carry the burden of the omnipresence of violence, destruction, and death. Most of the new directors who have started in the field of documentary or poetic essays—Soudade Kaadan (Suadad Kaᶜdan), Nidal Hassan, Mohamed Ali Attasi (Muhammad ᶜAli Atasi), Diana El-Jeroudi (al-Djarudi), Talal Derki (Darki), and Ziad Kalthoum (Kalthum), to name but a few—have fled the country. Their work is a world apart from the old Syrian cinema, as a brief comparison between Mohamed Malas's *Ladder to Damascus* (Sulum ila Dimashq, 2013) and Ziad Kalthoum's *The Immortal Sergeant* (al-Raqib al-khalid, 2014) may illustrate.

The two films were realized by directors from two different generations. Both are set in the same place and time: the Syrian capital, Damascus, during the uprising in 2012. The first is a fiction; the second documents in part the making of the first and is shocking in its bluntness and honesty. Malas's film is moreover quite cryptic in its storytelling. It focuses on a girl who is in a dark state, haunted by the shadow of another dead girl. A film student falls in love with her and invites her to join him and a group of young university students, intellectuals, and artists living together in an old Damascene house. There is no real narrative development here, just the different characters, giving brief glimpses into their convictions, thoughts, and shattered hopes as the uprising goes on. It is a beautiful, well-composed though dark images and imposing actors: the aesthetics add up to a Tarkowski-like elegy and the film stands in stark contrast to the mobile-phone and fly-on-the-wall style of Kalthoum's documentary.

Kalthoum's film starts with mobile-phone footage the young director captured clandestinely during his military service at the beginning of the revolt. Later, in his position as Malas's assistant director, he documents the extremely difficult shooting of the old master's film, which was punctuated by explosions, helicopters, a desperate passer-by obstructing film and sound recordings, and crew members traumatized or collapsing, having suffered detention themselves or lost loved ones. Amidst this havoc Malas seems somewhat remote and artificial, particularly when he answers in classical Arabic. Looking at *Ladder to Damascus* through the prism of *The Immortal Sergeant*, their directors are indeed worlds and epochs apart. No wonder *The Immortal Sergeant*, like *Silvered Water*, was programmed for Syria's Mobile Phone Film Festival that was held on 15 October 2014 in different cities: Aleppo, Atareb, Kafrnabel, Jabal al-Zawiya, and Deraa, and ironically enough, was called off for showing "indecent" imagery, that consisted, quite simply, of old film posters decorating the entrance of a Damascene movie theatre.

Lebanon: In search of a common denominator

The current presence, success, and larger visibility of Lebanese cinema in the international arena seems to indicate a consolidation of its film economy and production system. More than two decades after the end of the civil war, the Lebanese mediascape seems at first sight characterized by the cosmopolitanism of its elites, which goes hand in hand with an immense cultural diversity. Its numerous TV channels—some, such as LBC (Lebanese Broadcasting Corporation), profiting from petrodollars—have been catering to a transnational Arab entertainment industry, complemented by its advertisement, pop music, and beauty industries that have found their ultimate embodiment in female vamps such as Haifa Wehbe and Nancy ᶜAgram. Doubtless these fields have served as training grounds for film professionals as well.

One of the factors responsible for bringing Lebanese art cinema to life was certainly the creation of an alternative supporting network that offers training opportunities, most notably the Jesuits' film school, as well as film funding and independent screening

venues. This network, however, is based largely on private initiatives. In fact, with the closing of the last Studio Baalbek in 1994,[44]
Lebanese cinema was long characterized by a complete absence of
cinematic institutions, with the CNC or National Film Center
(which has existed since 1964) being run rather inefficiently by
alternating ministries. This has changed to a certain extent, with the
Ministry of Culture including a film commission for the financial
support of film culture and also backing Liban-Cinéma, a private
association that aims to improve the cinematic infrastructure and is
funded by the Ministry of Culture. In 2003, Liban-Cinéma succeeded in restoring a number of classic Lebanese films, most notably
Georges Nasr's *Where To?* (Ila ayn, 1957), the realist-oriented story
of a Lebanese immigrant to South America. Announcing the association's intention to facilitate Lebanese film production and
distribution further, the foundation's head, Aimée Boulos, proudly
proclaimed at the Cairo Film Festival in November 2004 that the
season had seen the preparation or shooting of a half-dozen full-
length feature films. In the year 2011 Lebanon achieved an
unprecedented peak, with nineteen coproductions in both categories, documentary as well as feature film.

Since then Lebanon has hosted an increasingly diverse production
including art house, mainstream, and documentary films made by a
new post-civil war generation: Ghassan Salhab, Khalil Joreige
(Djuraidj), Joana Hadjithomas, Philippe Aractingi, Nadine Labaki,
Ziad Doueiri (Duwayri), Dima El-Horr, Michel Kammoun, Mahmoud
Hojeij (Mahmud Hudjaidj), and, in the field of documentary,
Mohamed Soueid, Simon El-Habre (al-Habr), Wissam Charaf
(Sharaf), Zeina Daccache (Zayna Dakkash), Eliane Raheb, and Nadim
Mishlawi, among others. Some of these filmmakers were backed and
coproduced by local companies, such as Abbout Productions.

The explosive development of the creative documentary in particular is due to these new cultural initiatives. The first of these is
Beirut DC, which set up the Docmed program for training documentary producers from 2010 to 2013. It also runs a biannual film

festival, Ayam Bayrut al-Sinima'iya. The Beirut Screen Institute offers funding and training for creative documentaries as well. Furthermore, the Metropolis Association for Lebanese Art has created one of the first art house movie theaters, screens artistic films and regularly organizes retrospectives. In addition, Lebanon hosts AFAC (Arab Fund for Arts and Culture), a transnational Arab initiative that funds various film formats, among other projects.

These activities have certainly had a positive effect on creating an informed film culture, although it must be emphasized that they have a very limited effect on film economy as a whole. In other words, film production in Lebanon relies primarily on regional and international exchange on the non-commercial circuit. Looking more closely at film distribution in Lebanon, it becomes evident that local film culture, whether mainstream or innovative, is only weakly tied to the national economy. In 2010 the market share of Lebanese films in its homeland did not exceed 0.49 percent.[45] For the national market, like elsewhere in the world, is largely dominated by Hollywood productions.

Some Lebanese companies have been operating as distributors beyond its national borders for a long time, such as Georges Haddad Sons & Co., or the Empire Group, which was founded in 1956. Today the company has branches in almost all Gulf countries as well as in Jordan, Syria, and Egypt. The Empire Group has been expanding since 1992 in and outside of Lebanon. Empire International, for example, distributes, in particular, Columbia TriStar and Twentieth Century Fox films and has offices in Jordan, Dubai, Bahrain, Syria, and Egypt.[46] It has invested in multiplex cinemas as far away as Erbil in northern Iraq.[47] In Jordan, too, Empire has been very successful. In 2012 it achieved 25.86 percent of total market share in Jordan in terms of distribution, and thus ranked second after Selim Ramia & Co.[48] It has also signed contracts with Image Nation in Abu Dhabi for distributing their productions in the MENA region, even though it has primarily American movies in its repertoire.[49]

Lebanese cinema has produced a few films that achieved a certain popularity with Arab *and* Western audiences. Nadine Labaki's *Caramel* (Sukkar banat, 2007), for instance, received support at home and abroad alike, while blurring the line between art house and mainstream. Yet it needs to be asked whether this so far exceptional case really indicates progress and sustainability of national Lebanese production on the economic level, for it was produced by a French and not a Lebanese company. It was admitted to the prestigious Quinzaine des réalisateurs at the Cannes Film Festival and ended up distributed in numerous European countries. At the same time, however, it was also able to attract Arab presales through the local distributor Sabban Media as well as pay-TV-channel ART.[50]

Subsequently, Nadine Labaki's second feature, *Where Do We Go Now?*, earned in 2012 as much as one-third of what the most successful American film grossed in Lebanon.[51] With an Egyptian coproducer it was even released commercially in Egypt. Labaki's works are particular phenomena, though. *Caramel*, which deals with a group of women who meet in a beauty salon and their relation to men, capitalizes on gender conflicts, focusing on female bonding mixed up with some mainstream cock-of-the-walk fantasies. *Where Do We Go Now?*, Labaki's second feature is set in a religiously mixed Lebanese village and tackles the eruption of the sectarian conflict that ripped the country apart in 1973 through humor. As the tension between men rises, the women in the village come up with a trick: they invite a group of Russian prostitutes to divert their men from fighting.

No wonder Nadine Labaki's light and entertaining take on heavy subjects has sold better and in more countries than the usual Lebanese art house: films by Salhab, Aractingi, al-Horr, Joreige, and Hadjithomas have toured festivals but have otherwise been confined to the French art house circuit.[52] In fact, between 2006 and 2011 more than one-third (37 percent) of all Lebanese coproductions were undertaken with France. Another 20 percent were coproduced with the UAE, but the latter were predominantly documentaries. Some of the Lebanese feature film productions that relied on French support have exploited spectacular events, such as the Israeli war on Lebanon in 2007 and the presence of French stars, including *Under the Bombs* (Taht al-qasf, 2007), a docudrama by Aractingi, and *I Want to See* (Je veux voir, 2008) by Joreige and Hadjithomas, featuring Catherine Deneuve.

As a consequence, Lina Khatib has argued that Lebanese cinema lacks two fundamental characteristics for being labeled a national cinema: local funding and local distribution.[53] To her, the major common denominator of Lebanese film is the traumatic experience of war between the different factions of Lebanese society, particularly between Maronites, Sunnis, Shiites, and Druzes. Dealing with sectarianism and digesting the long-term effects of war has thus become a psychological necessity for the subsequent generation and at times also a political one, not least with regard to reconciliation.

Indeed, since Maroun Baghdadi's *Little Wars* (Hurub saghira, 1982), the civil war has been the major topic and common denominator of postwar Lebanese *auteur* cinema, with few exceptions. The social drama *When Maryam Spoke Out* (Lamma hikyit Maryam, 2001), shot on video by Assad Fouladkar, and *Bosta* (2005; literally, 'the bus'), by Philippe Aractingi (ᶜAraqtinji), belong to this category. *Little Wars*, whose breathless pace is dominated by a paranoid anti-hero, reflects like no other film the absurdity of a divided people caught in a war-torn country. The anti-hero, or the anti-heroine, is probably the most important legacy Baghdadi shares with the following generation.

The most popular and successful—but also criticized—work with respect to anti-heroes was *West Beirut* by Ziad Doueiri, which was released in 1999. Because it capitalized on popular genre elements, such as funny situations and a number of stylized comic characters, the film was questioned for its simplification and falsification of historical data. Its story focuses on two adolescent boys, ᶜUmar and Tariq, who at the very beginning are introduced using a Super 8 amateur camera, thoroughly observing their surroundings. They attempt to develop this footage throughout the rest of the film, hampered first by the outbreak of the war and then by the division of the city into West and East Beirut. Trying to reach a film laboratory, the boys even decide to cross the dangerous Green Line. In one of their attempts to get to the other side, they end up in Umm Walid's whorehouse, which turns out to be a safe haven, an El Dorado where all Lebanese factions are temporarily united by the power of sex and which disintegrates only toward the end of the film.

The integration of fictional elements in *West Beirut* into the actual historical framework was problematic. For the sake of dramatization, Doueiri chose to show the young protagonists witnessing a particular incident from the windows of their school—the deadly ᶜAin al-Rummana assault on a busload of Palestinian civilians on 13 April 1975, which was done in retaliation for the killing of four Christian Phalangists that same day. This incident is considered the spark that ignited the civil war. Yet the day it took place was a Sunday, when all schools were closed.[54] Other historical events appear strongly condensed in the film. Civil war is seen to affect daily life quickly, with schools and workplaces closing down. In no time at all, the boys—accidentally, almost for fun and without realizing the significance of the event—join the 1977 memorial march for the assassinated Druze leader Kamal Jumblat. By no means does the film signal the far-reaching effects this particular assassination had on the civil war. Yet with these temporal condensations on the one hand and political simplifications on the other, additionally endowed with a deep sense of comedy, the film was able to attract audiences in and outside Lebanon.

Human weakness and contradictions are also the most frequently shared characteristics of the quarrelsome inhabitants of the old villa in *Around the Pink House* (Bayt al-zahr, 1999); of Ghassan Salhab's disillusioned group of friends in *Terra Incognita* (al-Ard al-madjhula, 2002), who try to find a place for themselves in times of peace into which war continues to interject itself; and of Danielle ᶜArbid's

Terra Incognita (al-Ard al-madjhula, 2002) by Ghassan Salhab
(courtesy Institut du Monde Arabe, Paris)

nasty and treacherous bourgeois adolescent girl, whose betrayal in
In the Battlefields (Maᶜarik hubb, 2004) is her only means of survival and compensation in a world where adults can no longer be
role models and war has perpetuated social difference and exploitation. ᶜArbid's next film, *A Lost Man* (Un homme perdu, 2007),
about a French photographer who gets lost in the Middle East,
caused a stir mainly because of some sexually graphic scenes, but
seemed more interested in capitalizing on that transgression and
less in discussing the state of the nation in a serious manner.

A Perfect Day (Yaumun akhar, 2005) by Khalil Joreige and Joana
Hadjithomas in turn zooms right in on one of the dark spots of
Lebanese war history, namely the still unresolved issue of numerous
individuals who have disappeared without trace. Its plot unfolds in
a single day, a very special day when a young man takes his mother,
who has not accepted the disappearance of her husband fifteen years
ago, to declare him officially dead "in the absence of a body." In the
end, the day holds a chance of reconciliation for both. In contrast,
Eliane Raheb's (Rahib) documentary *Sleepless Nights* (Layali bila
nawm, 2013), the double portrait of a Maronite war criminal and a
woman whose son was abducted and disappeared, was much less

reconciliatory and radical in showing that, even twenty-five years after the end of the war, wounds have not healed and the fissures between factions are still deep.

Falafel (2006) by Michel Kammoun took a turn toward a more self-reflective mode, following a self-assured young man through his daily life, which reflects the spirit of the young postwar generation. A quite humorous account of the past was presented by Khalil Joreige and Joana Hadjithomas in their documentary *The Lebanese Rocket Society* (al-Nadi al-lubnani l-il-sawarikh, 2012). It tells the almost unbelievable story of the space program run by Lebanon in the 1960s, in which a rocket—named 'Cedar'—was being developed by students until the government-backed program was scrapped due to Western pressure and the beginning of the war. The highly poetic documentary *The One-man Village* (Sama^{c}an bi-l-day^{c}a, 2008) by Simon El-Habre depicts El-Habre's uncle, who returns to the deserted village of his ancestors. Similarly self-reflective and therapeutic is Bassem Fayad's documentary *Diaries of a Flying Dog* (Yaumiyat kalb ta'ir, 2014). In contrast, Mahmoud Hojeij's fiction *Stable Unstable* (Tali^c nazil, literally, 'up and down,' 2014) presents an ironic and cleverly constructed kaleidoscope of Lebanese society through patients who take turns in the consulting room of a psychologist. This recent tendency to combine social criticism, memory, and psychology is also found in *12 Angry Lebanese* (12 Lubnani ghadib, 2009) and *Shehrezade's Diary* (Yaumiyat Shahrazad, 2013) by Zeina Daccache (Zayna Dakash), both of which document the therapeutic effect of a theater workshop run with male and female prison inmates.

Dima El-Horr (al-Hurr), in turn, goes beyond any realist descriptions of psychological drama and uses the junk material of a memory that has been shattered by trauma. *Every Day is a Holiday* (Kull yaum ^{c}id, 2011) is the almost surrealistic road trip of three very different women who board a bus on the Lebanese Day of Liberation to visit their husbands in a remote jail. When the bus driver is hit by a stray bullet, the women are left in the middle of the arid mountainous nowhere full of sounds of muffled explosions, throngs of refugees, and rumors of massacres. The driver of a pickup filled with chickens who agrees to give them a ride has the air of a gangster and increases the sense of imperilment. The war is invisible but omnipresent. The slow-paced action often comes to a halt in beautifully arranged compositions, while neither clothes nor high heels seem affected by the rough, stony paths, underlining even more the impression of a dreamlike experience.

The most crucial aspect of this film is the subordination of the narrative to a specific spatio-temporal order or 'chronotope,' which transmits, more than anything else, a feeling of risk and identity loss. This sort of chronotope also recurs in other Lebanese *auteur* films and consists of a preference for long takes and long shots and, I would also add, the trope of roaming. Mikhail Bakhtin first introduced the notion of the chronotope with regard to the analysis of literary works. Among other uses, it was applied to describe the text's internal patterns created by the interrelated time–space dimensions that have even generic implications, such as epic length or eliptic condensations for the sake of suspense.

In cultural studies the chronotope has not only been instrumental in dissecting generic differences but also in identifying ideological orientations. In his study "DissemiNation" (1990), for instance, Homi Bhabha introduced the chronotope as a locus where national difference is constructed. Using Goethe's travel book *Italienische Reise*, he showed how the latter relied on the time–space nexus in order to differentiate home and host land. The use of specific narrative space–time configurations is also what Hamid Naficy identified in the work of exiled transnational filmmakers, like the Armenian-Canadian Atom Egoyan or Palestinian Elia Suleiman, whom he considers "interstitial authors," their work marked by the "configuration of claustrophobic spaces."[55]

Drawing on the work of Rick Altman, who sees genre cinema as ideologically infected and strongly related to national cinemas as marketing labels, Naficy suggests that transnational filming should be understood as a genre as well. There is no room to discuss this particular thesis here, but in Naficy's view, these thoroughly transnational *auteurs* live in post-industrial societies between different national borders and not within them. They "are constantly in the process of redefining themselves against encroaching abstraction and semiotic manipulation which the reduction to all life's spheres to sign systems promises. Under such circumstances, space becomes untrustworthy."[56] The cinematic strategies that they employ are moving between two poles: "it is the enclosed claustrophobic spaces, often in the form of prisons, which both express and encode the (melo)drama of transnational subjectivity. These phobic spaces are often played off of spaces of immensity. Space in transnational cinema, therefore, mediates between cosmos (order) and chaos (disorder)."[57]

I would suggest taking Naficy's argument a step further and applying it to Lebanese cinema as being exiled in its own homeland. This applies in particular to Ghassan Salhab, who was born as an expatriate Lebanese in Senegal and moved to Lebanon only as an adult. Interestingly, his films create a sort of Lebanese topography that moves between different urban and rural landscapes that are infested with obscured yet omnipresent signs of war. Just as in *Every Day is a Holiday*, these signs are not necessarily bound in a cause–effect chain. Instead, as detached elements they form an acoustic and visual inventory that can pop up at any time for no specific reason, creating in turn a strong effect of restlessness and looming danger. In *The Mountain* (al-Jabal, 2010), Salhab primarily uses the sound track to activate these associations. The extremely reduced plot focuses on the arrival of a man in a huge deserted hotel in the mountains where he wishes to isolate himself and write. He shuts himself up in his room where, as time passes, he finds himself surrounded by unsettling sounds, some of which come close to the noise of shooting and bombing. *The Mountain* forms part of a still unfinished geographic trilogy.

Less radical on the narrative level but still based on the same spatio-temporal principle is Salhab's second sequel, *The Valley* (al-Wadi, 2014). A man has a car accident on one of the lonely mountain roads and is struck by amnesia. He is saved by a group of men and women who take him to their estate. While they half-heartedly tend to his wounds, figure out his identity, and help him recover his memory, he finds himself more and more in the role of a hostage, for the estate is in reality a secret drug laboratory and its inhabitants fear its disclosure. Eventually, when all of a sudden explosions become visible on the horizon, army vehicles are retreating hastily and nearby villages are being deserted, the tension starts rising on the estate, so that the amnesic man becomes the projection screen for the fears and aggression of the other characters. Thus the film becomes an allegory of an oblivious present that covers only superficially the traumatic experiences of the past and a body of films. At the same time it proves once more that many Lebanese *auteur* films express brilliantly a sense of uneasiness and ambivalence without necessarily tackling its real sources, namely that the factors that led to the outbreak of the war are still unchanged.

One of the best reflections on this dilemma was presented in Wissam Charaf's (Sharaf) film essay *It's All in Lebanon* (Fi Lubnan, 2011), which deals precisely with the question that has preoccupied Lina Khatib: what kind of national identity does Lebanon have? The answer that Charaf finds goes beyond the omnipresence of war and extends to contradictions and paradoxes at the core of that identity. He analyzes the Lebanese mediascape, its visual and audio-visual practices as expressed in show business, prostitution, and cosmetic surgery as opposed to martyr ideology. He looks at religious radicalism, and pan-Arabism, condensed into the concepts of resistance and hedonism and, more importantly, of destruction and reconstruction. His conclusion: "It is all in Lebanon."

Palestine: National cinema without homeland

Like Jordanian and Lebanese cinema, Palestinian film enjoyed a considerable boom and astonishing international success on the festival circuit, despite the stalled peace process and continual deterioration of the social and political situation in the Occupied Territories under the Palestinian Authority since the second intifada in 2000. In early 2006, several full-length feature-film productions were shot in Palestine and Israel, all by a new generation of filmmakers: Hani Abu Asaad (Asʿad), Annemarie Jacir, Tawfik Abu Wael (Taufiq Abu Wa'il), Elia Suleiman, Rashid Masharawi, Najwa al-Najjar, and Muhammad Bakr. Between 2010 and 2012 a total of forty to forty-four films of all lengths and formats were produced in all the Palestinian territories.[58]

This led producer and documentary filmmaker Raed Andoni (Ra'id Anduni), during a discussion of one of his films, to sarcastically question why Palestinian cinema flourished while the country's crisis deepened. There is certainly no simple answer to his question. To begin with, most Palestinian features since Michel Khleifi (Khalifi)'s *Wedding in Galilee* may be loosely categorized as *auteur* or art house. But even if they were mainstream films, none of them can rely on local audiences to recuperate their investments. Since the first Intifada in 1989, under the pressure of uprisings, curfews, and military operations, the previous number of thirty-three movie theaters in the Occupied Territories has crumbled to three. Not a single one of them is located in Gaza.[59] Hence, most Palestinian spectators are left with a few festivals, cultural screenings, video tapes, DVDs, or the Internet for watching movies. This resulted in the more than absurd situation that some filmmakers themselves had never had a chance to watch a film in a movie theater, a circumstance that has been described in the documentary *Gaza 36mm* (2012) by Khalil al-Muzayen (al-Muzayin). Only in very exceptional cases, such as the works of Israel-based Nizar Hassan, do films by a Palestinian receive wider local exposure. In a personal interview with the author the filmmaker claimed to have had millions of spectators, with Israeli television having aired some of his self-critical and compromising documentaries.

It goes without saying that the lack of local distribution opportunities makes film production completely dependent on funding from Israel or other outside sources or on individual efforts. A temporary exception was Rashid Masharawi's Cinema Production Center in Ramallah, which was created before the Israeli incursion in 2002 to boost local production. It undertook mobile screenings through its Mobile Cinema initiative, and established an annual Kids Film Festival in the Occupied Territories. There have also been a number of other private initiatives, some of which are still operating, such as: the Palestinian Mobile Cinema Project, which also tries to organize mobile screenings; the A.M. Qattan Foundation, which has helped to fund a few films; and most importantly, Shashat, run by Alia Arasoughly (who also organizes the Annual Women's Film Festival), which offers debates, screenings, and publications and has produced dozens of shorts.[60] The Palestinian Authority's Ministry of Culture has also had its input. It created the Palestinian Cultural Fund, led by former Tunis PLO functionaries. However, it was blamed for not working hard enough to support local production. A few of the works it funded were shot by the minister's wife, Liana Badr, who also held the position of director of the film and television division of the Palestinian Ministry of Culture.

Yet despite the unfavourable conditions and limited resources there is an increasing number of Palestinians, particularly in the less privileged areas, who have been involved in filmmaking. This is also due to the more flexible and cheaper technology that has been available since the digital turn. This innovation has helped quite a few young, independent filmmakers from the Occupied Territories and even from Gaza to make their first steps. Moreover, production has generally increased in quantity and quality. This is certainly due to increased European interest and a hitherto unprecedented understanding of the virulence of the Palestinian question following the Oslo Accords. Funding opportunities from the Gulf have meanwhile played an additional positive role. Notwithstanding, Palestinian full-length film production and distribution continue to be almost completely detached from their homeland.

Unquestionably, one of the main problems of Palestinian cinema is displacement. Many of the more recognized Palestinian directors, whether born in Israel or abroad, have acquired other nationalities and are largely based outside the region. Palestinians of the 1948 generation, like Khleifi and Abu Asaad, chose the diaspora long ago; others, like Kamal Aljafari (al-Djaᶜfari) and Sameh Zoabi (Samih Zuᶜbi), have left Israel more recently. Masharawi and Suleiman's attempts to settle in Ramallah did not survive the massive Israeli military incursion in the spring of 2002. The renewed occupation left not only offices and homes, but also equipment and film material in ruins, as in the case of the documentary filmmaker ᶜAzza al-Hassan, who decided to move to Jordan at that point. Annemarie Jacir, May Masri, Cherein Dabis, and Mahdi Fleifel (Flayfil) were all brought up abroad.

Of course a few Arab-Israeli filmmakers, most notably Suha Arraf, Tawfik Abu Wael, and Nizar Hassan, still live in Israel, facing at times substantial psychological and political pressure. They rely in part on tolerant Israeli producers and technicians and on Israeli infrastructure. One prominent example is Tawfik Abu Wael, who originates from the small village of Umm al-Fahim and struggled hard to be able to study film at Tel Aviv University. His full-length feature, *Thirst* (ᶜAtash, 2004), found Israeli Avi Kleinberger as its producer; he had also produced Costa-Gavras, Elia Suleiman, and others. Abu Wael's film was realized with an almost exclusively Israeli staff. Yet in the case of his second full-length film, *Last Days in Jerusalem* (Tanathur, literally 'dispersal,' 2011), an adaptation of Ghassan Kanafani's *Returning to Haifa*, he had to compromise so extensively that the original story has become almost unrecognizable.

Of course the issues of assimilation and identity politics play a decisive role, as is quite evident in the case of Suha ᶜArraf's full-length fiction *Villa Touma* (2014). In Israel it made controversial headlines because its director had listed her film as Palestinian at the Venice Film Festival. The Israeli ministerial institutions that had funded the film objected to this, and pressured her to return the grant she had received—which she did in part. As a further consequence, the two leading funding agencies, the Israeli Film Fund and the Rabinovich Foundation, made it a condition for their future grantees to explicitly label their films "Israeli."[61] Relying on non-Israeli foreign funds does not necessarily save filmmakers from trouble either. Kamal Aljafari, director of the documentary *The Roof* (al-Sath, 2006), for example, had a legal dispute over his intellectual property with his producer, a German TV channel. The commissioning editor had tried to impose stylistic changes that would have altered the envisioned work beyond recognition.

Still, it must be stated that against all odds, Palestinian film, which started as an anti-colonial endeavor and since then has been roped into the Arab–Israeli conflict in different ways, has at last been able to develop into a sophisticated and cinematically conscious presence. It bears witness to the rocky path to imagining one's own community in the absence of an independent nation-state. It has given an ambivalent shape to the "dreams of a nation"[62] by representing and questioning a great variety of experiences and the very different living conditions of a dispersed and occupied "nation." For example, the struggle between martyr ideology and pragmatism that plays such a large role in the real-life Palestinian political arena has left its traces on the much-exposed fiction film as much as on Palestinian documentary. While positive images of martyrdom, as in *When You Were Paraded* (Lamma zaffuk, 2001) by Iyas Natur, for example, as well as cinematic techniques of emotional mobilization, most prominently applied in May Masri's and Muhammad Bakr's documentaries, were not completely abandoned, they have been complemented, if not opposed, by a large number of self-critical and deconstructive films in all formats.

Even if the era of exclusive unitary nationalism in Palestinian cinema has not passed (and could not face the immense Israeli military and political repression), films like Nizar Hassan's *Independence* (Istiqlal, 1994) have indicated that a more complex notion of cultural and political difference has been emerging.[63] Documenting the rituals and celebrations of the Israeli Independence Day, and the ambivalence it carries for Israeli Palestinians, allowed the filmmaker to reflect more generally on the complex ideas of nation and national belonging. This does not mean that earlier tropes related to culture, tradition, and resistance, including martyrdom, have been discarded, but they have been channeled into a more critical vision.

The first who paved the way for this development was certainly Michel Khleifi, today an almost neglected veteran in the Palestinian arena, despite his occasional reappearance with compelling documentaries such as *Forbidden Marriages in the Holy Land* (al-Zawadj al-mukhtalat fi-l-aradi al-muqadassa, 1995) or his subsequent *Route 181: Fragments of a Journey in Palestine-Israel* (2004). With him, Palestinian filmmaking moved away from the diaspora (that is, exiled filmmakers affiliated with different Palestinian political organizations) toward the soil of historical Palestine. He and the following generation of Palestinian fiction filmmakers, namely Hani Abu Asaad and Elia Suleiman—who, like Nizar Hassan, are also originally from Nazareth—and later Tawfik Abu Wael, changed the tropes of Palestinian film.

Nationalist and cultural self-assertion through images of resistance fighters, martyrs, and the different features of Palestinian cultural heritage gave way, as explained earlier in this book,[64] to helpless patriarchs, rebellious daughters, and aggressive young men, motifs still present in recent films, such as *Thirst* by Abu Wael. This trend also includes the trope of a spoiled wedding that appears from *The Wedding in Galilee* to *Rana's Wedding* (al-Quds fi yaumin akhar, 2002) by Hani Abu Asaad. It was complemented by the Israeli production *The Syrian Bride* (2004) by Eran Riklis and Najwa al-Najjar's short, *Yasmine's Song* (2005) and al-Najjar's second full-length feature, *Eyes of a Thief* (ᶜUyun al-haramiya, 2014). Along with al-Najjar's first full-length fiction *Pomegranates and Myrrh* (al-Murr wa-l-rumman, 2008) which was likewise pre-occupied with women's right to live an independent and self-sufficient life, these films offer a perfect dramatic pretext to negotiate change in correlation with oppression on both the personal and the political level.

Annemarie Jacir's two full-length fiction films, *Salt of This Sea* (Milh hadha al-bahr, 2008) and *When I Saw You* (Lamma shuftak, 2012), are likewise focused on women's stories, tackling two controversial political issues, refugees and the right of return. The first deals with a young American-Palestinian woman who visits Israel and stays after her visa expires. She manages to find the house of her grandfather in Jaffa, now inhabited by a young Israeli woman, whose friendly carelessness triggers the visitor's rage. In the end, she has to leave the country forcedly. Jacir's film

Rana's Wedding (al-Quds fi yaumin akhar, 2002) by Hani Abu Asaad
(courtesy Institut du Monde Arabe, Paris)

displays a complicated relationship between space and identity that was mirrored in an absurd way in real life. When Jacir tried to realize the film in Israel without an Israeli executive producer, it turned out to be very difficult for the production to get shooting permits. Eventually the director herself was denied re-entry to Israel for no evident reason, a fact that complicated the completion of the film. The parallels on- and off-screen are striking and engender the film's performative mode, as fictional and real trans- and regression (forced return to and renewed expulsion from the homeland) interacted and interfered during the making of the film. This became evident primarily through the solidarity campaign that took place in correlation with the banning.

In her next film, *When I Saw You*, Jacir depicted again the drama of refugees, turning to this history to present the story of a young mother and her little son who, as a consequence of the 1967 war, are separated from their husband and father. While the adults try to cope with and assimilate to life in the refugee camp, little Tariq has difficulties in adapting. One day he runs away and ends up accidently in a guerrilla fighters' camp. When his mother follows him there, her attitude starts changing as well. Yet her growing interest and silent admiration for one of the guerrilla fighters has no consequences, for she is still bound to her absent husband. Thus the film as well as its characters remain in limbo, something that describes quite accurately the situation of generations of Palestinian refugees to date.

While there is almost a sort of nostalgia in Jacir's depiction of the guerrilla of the 1960s (which in the end was part of the formation process of the PLO), armed resistance was qualified and critically examined in *The Wedding in Galilee*, or placed under scrutiny in Hani Abu Asaad's *Paradise Now* (al-Djanna al-an, 2005). The latter was even nominated for an Academy Award. It depicts the situation of two young, deprived, and sympathetic Palestinians who are roped in by an extremist group and groomed to become suicide bombers. While in this case the much more complex motivations for suicide bombing are reduced to the personal history of a young man who wants to whitewash his family's reputation because of his father's alleged past as an Israeli collaborator, Elia Suleiman's *Divine Intervention* (Yaddun ilahiya, 2002) is far more radical in its deconstruction of the notion of martyrdom.

This work, which was well received at the Cannes Film Festival in 2002, revolves around an allegorical love story between the male main protagonist from Nazareth (played by the director himself) and a beautiful woman from the Occupied Territory whom he can meet only in a car park at an Israeli checkpoint. The film displays its strength less through any rhetorical narrativity than through a number of highly ironic scenes that capitalize on and deconstruct the mass appeal of political agitation as a feature of a phantasmagorical popular culture that is, in the end, condensed in the image of the martyr. It allows a female Palestinian resistance fighter wrapped in the typical *kufiyah*, following the rules of electronic games, to miraculously transform into a virtual figure, a "ninja" who lifts herself high up into the air, equipped with extraordinary weaponry and supernatural powers.

Other productions may have moved away even more consciously from earlier revolutionary heroism and any open accusations of the Israeli Other. They tend to be inclusive, underlining differences and diversity within Palestinian society as well. ʿAzza al-Hassan, in her documentary *3cm Less* (3cm aqal, 2003), was not interested in praising the strength of Palestinian mothers or the courage of resistance fighters, but more eager to look behind the scenes. With her portrait of Hagar, a mother of ten children, who suffered constant emotional deprivation because of their mother's fight with Israeli authorities over the family's confiscated land, al-Hassan showed the price of 'heroism' — namely devastated families and maimed psyches. Like others, she does not shrink from including sympathetic Israelis. In one of her most subjective scenes, al-Hassan asks an Israeli actor to meet her second protagonist, Ra'ida — whose father lost his life hijacking a plane for the Palestinian cause—and pretend to have met her father.

Some filmmakers have displayed a strongly self-exploring and critical vein, particularly documentary directors such as Sobhi (Subhi) Zubaidi with *Looking Awry* (Shawwal, 2001), which focuses on racial difference in Palestinian society. Other examples are Najwa al-Najjar's *Quintessence of Oblivion* (Djawharat al-silwan, 2001), which explores the former local popular film culture, and Raed Andoni's *Improvisation: Samir and His Brothers* (Irtidjal, 2005), a gripping portrait of a musician family from Nazareth coming to terms with their art in the difficult conditions of occupation. In his next full-length documentary Andoni went one step further in radically personalizing his cinematic account to include his own private life. In *Fix Me!* (Sudaᶜ, 2009) he followed and investigated the reasons for his psychiatric treatment. In the process he exposed himself as a grumpy loner constantly struck by migraine, but without ever completely detaching his particular biography, nor his friend's and family's fates, from the more general impact of occupation.

Palestinian directors' self-critical pragmatism and deconstructive attitude have also been manifested in tropes of immobility and waiting, a recurrent motif primarily in Suleiman's last two fiction films, *Chronicle of a Disappearance* (Sidjil ikhtifa', 1996) and *Divine Intervention*. Both repeat almost identical images of elderly men sitting around and women engaged in senseless activities. A similar theme has also been brought up by Rashid Masharawi in his latest feature, *Waiting* (Intizar, 2005), and in Tawfik Abu Wael's documentary, *Waiting for Saladin* (Bi-intizar Salah al-Din, 2001). The major problem of the young men portrayed in these films is not violence or oppression, but boredom. This sense of stagnation has primarily been described by '1948 Arabs,' or Israeli Palestinians, and reflects these directors' feelings of belonging to a besieged culture, something that is cemented by the severely limited possibilities for Arab cultural activities in the Arab-Israeli 'metropolis' of Nazareth.[65]

Chronicle of a Disappearance (Sidjil ikhtifa', 1996) by Elia Suleiman
(courtesy Institut du Monde Arabe, Paris)

Most recently a trend toward black comedy may be observed in Palestinian productions. *Laila's Birthday* (ᶜId milad Layla, 2008) by Rashid Masharawi, or more recently Sameh Zoabi's *Man with a Cell Phone* (Bidun mobile, 2013), may serve as examples. In the latter, the main protagonist lives in an Arab-Israeli village and has eyes (and ears) only for girls with whom he keeps in contact over the phone. At the same time he is trying to avoid his constantly nagging father, who wants to mobilize people to keep the Israelis from erecting a cell-phone tower in the middle of their fields out of fear of radiation. The young man's *prise de conscience* starts only when he is detained and questioned because he was phoning a girl from Jenin.

Even more poignant in its absurdity is *Love, Theft, and Other Entanglements* (al-Hubb wa-l-sariqa wa mashakil ukhra, 2015) by Muayad Alayan (Mu'ayad ᶜAlyan), a black and white film that pays homage to the French *nouvelle vague*. Musa is an outright anti-hero. Constantly on the run from his father, who has acquired a work permit in Israel for him, the young man prefers to steal Israeli cars, sell them as pieces of junk, and spend the rest of his time roaming around his secretive lover, the mother of his little daughter who married a rich man early in her pregnancy to cover up their illicit relation. One day, however, he gets into real trouble and his situation becomes endlessly complicated. By accident he discovers an Israeli hostage in a stolen car, and is soon being chased by the Israeli secret service, as well as by the militants who want their hostage back. Desperately he tries to get an appointment for emigration to a Western country. Thus it is pragmatism and not martyr ideology or nationalist zeal that wins the day in this narrative.

Playing with genre cinema to confound the absurdity of a national entity and unity in view of the unresolved Israeli–Palestinian question is also the approach of the Israeli–Palestinian film *ᶜAjami* (2009), co-directed by Skandar Copti and Yaron Shani. Constructed in five chapters, the film uses thriller elements to tell the story of material need and violent Arab–Arab and Arab–Israeli encounters. Blood feuds, fighting, murder, drug dealing, and secret love relationships blend into strong emotional moments fostered by the improvised and therefore spontaneous acting style. The different strands of the story seem at first unrelated, and only at the end do they culminate in a violent dénouement that exposes the different links. The immediate message seems to be that whatever the protagonists, both Palestinians and Israelis, try to do, there is no way of escaping the tightly knit net of relationships and common entanglements.

Tunisia: The crisis of the auteur and the dogma of female liberation

At the outbreak of the revolution in 2010, film in Tunisia had passed its golden age and was caught in a crisis, despite the fact that the state still covers up to thirty percent of the budget of national film productions. On the structural level, Tunisian cinema's problem was intensified by the decomposition of the public SATPEC in 1992 and the technical deterioration and deficiencies of the

Gammarth production site, renovated and restructured by Tarek Ben Ammar into the LTC Gammarth only in 2006.[66] The footage of Selma Beccar's *Flower of Oblivion* (Khushkhash/Fleur d'oubli, 2006) had to be developed in the modern and well-equipped film laboratory of the Moroccan CCM in Rabat, rather than in Tunisia. A decade ago Tunisia used to produce an average of three to six movies per year (with an exceptional peak of nine films in 2006).[67] In 2007 and 2008, however, a total of only five films were produced.[68]

The highly experimental and emotionally intense chamber play *Her and Him* (Hiya wa huwwa, 2004) by Elyes Baccar (taking up the tradition of Jaibi's 1978 film, *The Marriage*), was given a surprisingly good reception at the box office. It was followed by Mohamed Zran's *The Prince* (al-Amir, 2005) and then by *Flower of Oblivion*. In addition, the emergence of a well-made and 'popular' love story like *The Prince*, which circulated in France on DVD, indicated a stronger mainstream orientation. But farce and comedy have also come more into vogue. In 2008 Ibrahim Letaïef (Latif), one of the few Tunisian directors who has turned to genre cinema, directed the comic thriller *Cinecitta*, about a film director who robs a bank, assisted by his crew, in order to get his film made. Letaïef did not change his stylistic orientation after the Tunisian revolution. His film *Flous Academy* (Hizz ya wiz/Affreux, cupides et stupides, 2013) is but another crook comedy in the style of the 1940s, dealing with a cheater who got cheated. A producer pretends to run a star academy to make money out of the aspirations of young talents, but gets robbed by a group of hedonistic Salafists. The script was denied public funding under the rule of Zine El-Abedine Ben Ali (Zain al-ᶜAbidin b. ᶜAli), most probably because of its negative representation of the police: the literal translation of the French title is 'the hideous' (the Salafists), 'the greedy' (the producer), and 'the stupid' (the police). The film made use of a number of Tunisian TV stars.[69]

Since the 1980s, Tunisian cinema has offered important components of popular film. Even if it has not developed a clear-cut star system, it has brought to light a set of highly capable actors and actresses who, due to their recurrent appearances, could develop star personae, such as Mouna Noureddine (Muna Nur al-Din), the eternal mother of Tunisian cinema (*Sama*); Hisham Rostom, the errant intellectual from *Golden Horseshoes* (Safa'ih min dhahab) and *Essaïda*; and sensual Amal Hdhili from *Silence of the Palaces* and *Bent Familia*. Tunisia has even exported its talents, most notably Hind Sabri, now a star in Egypt, who excelled as the adolescent girl in *Silence of the Palaces* and starred in, among other films, the prestigious Egyptian production *The Yacoubian Building* (ᶜImarat Yaᶜqubyan, 2006).

Yet there are also factors that have worked against box-office successes. As elsewhere, national television is reluctant to back the production of films meant for theatrical release. True, Tunisian television was ready to offer some financial support to fiction film, for example to *Summer Wedding* (Bab al-ᶜarsh/Noce d'été, 2004) by Mokhtar Ladjimi (Mukhtar Lᶜadjami). It was also able to boost the popularity of Selma Beccar's *Flower of Oblivion* through indirect promotion, namely interviews and reports. Yet earlier it had had an enormously negative effect on Tunisian film distribution. The banning of advertisements for new film releases on television, a regulation enacted after a 1992 agreement that allowed the private cable television channel, Horizons, launched in conjunction with French channel Canal +, to be transmitted in Tunisia, is believed to be one of the reasons why Tunisian audiences deserted their national cinema.[70]

At the same time, the type of art house film that had originally attracted audiences in Tunisia started losing its momentum. Tunisian *auteur* films between the mid-1980s and the 1990s, particularly those by Bouzid, Boughedir, and Moufida Tlatli, toured festivals, received numerous respected awards, and were even released in European art house film circuits. Works such as Nouri Bouzid's *Bent Familia* (Bint familya/Tunisiennes, literally, 'daughter of a good family,' 1997) and *Clay Dolls* (ᶜAra'is al-tin, 2002), or *The Magic Box* (Sunduq ᶜadjab, 2002) by Ridha Behi, were appealing because of their accomplished *mise en scène*, coherent scripts, and sensitivity. In contrast, more recent works by the same directors attracted less attention, even criticism. Boughedir's *Summer in La Goulette* (Halq al-wad, 1996) and Tlatli's *The Season of Men* (Musim al-ridjal, 2000) are two examples. Even widely praised films by newer directors, such as Mohamed Zran's (Mohamed al-Zran) *Essaïda*, about an adolescent boy from a deprived Tunisian shantytown, which won a larger number of prizes than its predecessors, obviously lack the finesse, poetry, and drive of previous Tunisian *auteur* films, such as Bouzid's *Man of Ashes*. In fact, some works have degenerated into mere plagiarism of earlier Arab *auteur* films, as can be noticed with *Summer Wedding* or Taieb Louhichi's *Child of the Sun* (Tifl al-shams, 2014).

Hence, in the late 1990s Tunisian cinema entered an era of stagnation and cinematic manierism. Ironically, one of its signs was a constant preoccupation with the question of women. Modernism, crystallized in the idea of female liberation, has been promoted by Tunisian film under Ben Ali's dictatorship to the extent that

The Season of Men (Musim al-ridjal, 2000) by Moufida Tlatli
(courtesy Institut du Monde Arabe, Paris)

Tunisian film scholar Sonia Chamkhi felt obliged to state that "the innovative ideas of today risk becoming the conformist ideas of tomorrow."[71] She continued: "From *Autumn Rain* by Ahmed Khèchine (1971) until *Bent Familia* by Nouri Bouzid (1997) and *Keswa, the Lost Thread* by Kalthoum Bornaz (1998), passing through *Honey and Ashes* by Nadia Farès (1998) and the recent short films by Nadia al-Fani, the same thing has been repeated over and over until stereotypes of men, and even more of subjugated women taken hostage by traditional and conservative structures, have been generated."[72]

Indeed, a large number of anti-colonial or merely feminist Tunisian films, from *Sejnane* (1974) and *cAziza* (1980) up to *Red Satin* or *Satin Rouge* (al-Sitar al-ahmar, literally, 'the red curtain,' 2002) by Raja Amari (cAmmari) and *The Season of Men* by Tlatli, express this orientation. Over the years it has become a source of pride for Tunisian cineastes, serving, in their eyes, as one of their national cinema's main trademarks. Ferid Boughedir, film historian and filmmaker, has become a spokesperson for this idea, emphasizing in a Ministry of Culture promotional booklet that the women's question is a preoccupation of almost every Tunisian film. To him, the emergence of 'women's cinema' and Tunisia's claim to have the highest participation of women in national Arab filmmaking have been facilitated by Tunisian law, which is considered the most liberal in all Arab Muslim countries in terms of gender equality.[73] In 1998, the film critic Abdelkrim Gabous even dedicated a whole book to his country's female cinematic activity, pointing out the high number of Tunisian women directors.

If, however, the proportion of Tunisian female directors is compared to that of other Arab countries with a similar limited total cinematic output, it turns out that Tunisia's self-portrayal is questionable. Seven Tunisian women filmmakers have managed to direct full-length fiction films to date; Lebanon, also a small country, has produced the same number. One of them, Randa Chahal-Sabbag, was able to direct four full-length films.[74] Yet

Lebanon did not generate a similarly canonized body of work on Arab society's alleged traditionalism in terms of gender relations, a fact that makes it even more necessary to qualify the discourse on Tunisian cinema's 'feminist' outlook and to examine the reason why it has become an established and evidently convenient means of positive self-portrayal.

The status of women has become one of the touchstones of modern Arab identity in relation to Europe and former colonizers. This shines through indirectly in one of Boughedir's analyses of the subject, which states that between 1967 and 1982 the image of women and "the family is in the heart of Tunisian cinema. . . . The family in this sense is often the microcosm representing the nation, and the generations which coexist in it are therefore as much appearances of the tradition–modernity confrontation."[75] Indeed, it was Boughedir's generation that took up the burden of the proof of modernity with its critique of gender inequality, a critique that has often been, for good reason, formulated in retrospect. In conjuring up an oppressive past, some of the most pivotal films, such as *Sejnane*, *Halfaouine*, *Silence of the Palaces*, *The Season of Men*, *Dance of Fire* (Habiba Msika/La danse du feu, 1994), Abdelatif Ben Ammar's *Melody of the Waterwheel* (Le chant de la noria, 2002), and *Flower of Oblivion*, either excluded the present or showed signs of insecurity when dealing with it, thus not always avoiding the trap of cultural essentialism.

The Season of Men is a good example of this tendency. The film is clearly divided into binary poles on the temporal as well as the spatial axis, moving between past and present, tradition and modernity, province (Djerba, in the south) and metropolis (Tunis, in the north), while negotiating the possibilities of change and emancipation for its female protagonists. The framing story shows cAisha living comfortably with her daughters in Tunis, but deciding for the sake of her handicapped little son to move back to their old house in Djerba. The dynamo of the action is clearly cAisha, who, after giving birth to two daughters, was unable to obtain her husband's consent to join him in the capital, sharing the fate of all the women of her family, who were separated from their men for eleven months a year. Later, she is brought into opposition with her mother-in-law on numerous issues, including the education of her two girls. The girls are portrayed as carrying the bitter seeds of the past into the present: once grown up, one daughter is unable to enjoy her sex life with her husband and the other is caught in a hopeless affair with a married man. Here the narration negates all present-time accomplishments: the fact that cAisha had separated from her husband after moving to Tunis to become the independent head of her household, bringing up two educated daughters who have the freedom to move around and choose their own men.

Indeed, with all the denouncing of oppression in Tunisian film, only rarely have the problems of 'modern' women been addressed, such as those of housewives, working women, and mothers (*Bent Familia* being a notable and insightful exception). Even when these problems are examined, strongly exceptional if not spectacular solutions are suggested, as in *Red Satin* by Raja Amari, in which a forty-year-old widow, housewife, and mother of an adult daughter discovers her own 'dark' side in a nightclub while worrying about her absent daughter. There, she makes friends with a belly dancer, becomes a performer herself, and starts an affair with the drummer, who also happens to be her daughter's boyfriend. Surprisingly, and even though he deserts her at the end, she agrees to give him her daughter's hand. What Raja Amari, a trained dancer herself, proposes as an outlet for bourgeois moral confinement, namely belly dancing, comes close to capitalizing on exotic Western visions of oriental dancing as a means of female self-exploration and sensuality, neglecting an immense variety of other possible local and global practices and lifestyles. As for the location, the director admits to having set foot in a Tunisian nightclub for the first time only for the purpose of shooting. This is not to deny that the film expresses the double standard of the filmmaker's society, where belly dancing has been morally stigmatized and sexual affairs in particular are usually covered up by silence.[76]

Three factors may have facilitated the predominance of the women's issue in Tunisian cinema and its eventual cinematic codification, which molded it into a 'national achievement': first, Third-Worldist post-colonial modernist ideology; second, limited political freedom; and third, European coproduction strategies based on the politics of cultural difference. The Tunisian preoccupation with the topic was originally heightened by the immediate legal and social liberalization of post-independence Tunisian society. There, like elsewhere in the region, Third-Worldist ideology, with its adherence to the modernist agenda, influenced governmental decisions and dominated intellectual life, leaving its traces on the cinephile cinema club movement in Tunisia, which gave rise to Boughedir and others of his generation.

Yet the free space Tunisian men and women directors have carved out from society and official censorship, particularly in the realm of sexuality that is one of the three corners of the Arab taboo triangle (sexuality, religion, and politics), has helped conceal the increasingly limited space for intellectual expression under the former regime of Ben Ali. This limitation is due to the despotic character of the country's political system at the time, which cemented its power by persecution and severe human rights violations; oppositional intellectuals were often subjected to travel controls, as happened to outspoken political dissidents like Moncef Marzouki (Munsif Marzuqi). Thus, while the Tunisian Ministry of Culture boasted about the liberal character of society and film on women-related issues, other social and political realms have remained untouched. A second and equally important factor, of course, is the undiminished interest of European coproducers, television channels, and cultural institutions in this particular topic.

Most Tunisian films that have dealt with this particular theme since the late 1980s have received substantial backing from European channels and institutions. Ironically, the country that worked hard to create the best conditions in the region for women is the one that puts the greatest blame on its society for discriminating against women, confirming one of the West's essential preconceived ideas about the Arab and Muslim world. This idea persists regardless of all the changes, contradictions, and negotiations in this arena and the fact that women's problems in the region are not simply related to Islam but also to class difference, social exploitation, and political injustice resulting from, among other sources, imbalanced North–South power relations.

This is by no means to say that pre-uprising Tunisian cinema merely degenerated into opportunism. In fact, it has simultaneously developed a set of tropes interrelated with the oppressed-woman motif which may be read as a response to political oppression: muted, passive, almost infantile characters, disturbed heterosexual relationships, and a tendency toward cryptic storytelling and stylized, burlesque *mise en scène*. This stands in stark contrast to the 1980s, when it was still possible to see Tunisian films that explicitly criticized state oppression. In his film *Golden Horseshoes* (1989), Nouri Bouzid, for instance, was quite graphic in his representation of abusive state practices. In the autobiographically inspired story, his main character, an intellectual just released from political imprisonment and torture, feels alienated from family and friends and is constantly haunted by the memories of his earlier physical abuse by state security.[77]

To get around the censorship, Bouzid had to cut out the most cruel torture scenes, but what remained in the finished film is still overt enough. Only three years later, however, when he scripted Moncef Dhouib's (al-Munsif Dhuwaib) *Sultan of the Medina* (*Sultan al-madina*, 1992), he chose to represent oppression and physical entrapment allegorically by elaborating some of the tropes of *Golden Horseshoes*. A good example of this is the nighttime roaming through the traditional *medina* with its small, crooked alleys, projecting the idea of a place for individual entrapment. This codification was certainly related to the fact that the regime of Ben

Ali, who came to power in 1989, had succeeded in substantially curtailing freedom of expression. Naturally, this may have added to the nightmarish dimensions of *Sultan of the Medina*. Ramla, a young girl from the countryside, is brought to the *medina*, the traditional urban neighborhood, to marry her cousin Bab, a gang leader, who is called Sultan of the Medina. His mother secludes the girl in a room to wait for her future husband, who is serving a prison sentence. The only person who is able to see the girl is Fraj, Bab's simple-minded brother, whose constant wandering through the old city makes Ramla wish to leave her confinement and go with him. However, the moment she escapes from her room it turns out that Fraj is too afraid to leave the *medina*. Ramla, now on her own, falls prey to Bab's gang, whose just-released boss does not recognize his bride. Subsequently the inhabitants of the *medina* interpret Ramla's disappearance as a miraculous evasion.

The quasi-mythical story speaks of double entrapment. The young girl who is supposed to be delivered soon to the holder of absolute power in the family is not the only one to suffer seclusion and isolation. Fraj, who enjoys the freedom to climb the terraces and mark the walls, turns out to lack the power to leave the *medina* and live in a different, more friendly and just environment. Shot mostly at night and placed in the strongly stylized setting of a traditional neighborhood consisting of myriads of terraces, old walls, dark alleys, and Bab's cramped house, the film radiates a paralyzing atmosphere and adds up to a profound sense of enclosure. Moreover, the centrality of the motif of rape reminds the spectator of classic melodrama's habit of presenting the sexual abuse of women as a metaphor for the arbitrariness of social injustice.

Rape as a dramatic turning point also figures prominently in *Tender Is the Wolf* (ᶜUrs al-dhib, 2006) by Jilani Saadi (Saᶜdi), the revenge story of a brutally abused prostitute whose rage is directed toward a kind-hearted bystander (Stoufa) instead of her abusers. Here again, the stylized *mise en scène* combines with a strongly confined location, a set of dark alleys and streets, to sublimate the film into an allegory of abusive power relations in which women figure as the most abused of all. Yet unlike *Sultan of the Medina*, the representation of people and locations is explicitly unaesthetic. This applies not least to the rape itself, which is depicted in a repulsive and explicit manner. The young woman is caught on the dark, deserted street by Stoufa's outcast friends. They bend her over the trunk of a car and leave her to one of the gang members, a Quasimodo-like character, to have fun with. This tremendously ugly albino rips off her pants with his silver-plated teeth and takes her from behind while the girl's underwear remains dangling from his mouth.

The narrative of *Tender Is the Wolf* circles around multiple treacheries. Stoufa fails to interfere on behalf of the girl. The same applies to the neighbors, who close their windows tightly to shut out her screams. The girl later punishes Stoufa emotionally by first attracting him, then depriving him of her love. Hence, according to the logic of the story, cruelty strikes randomly and victims' positions may shift according to circumstances and their readiness to join the game of cruelty. This in turn may be considered one of the main characteristics of tyranny and authoritarian rule, where the only law is that of striking arbitrarily.

Another satirical film that indulges even more in repulsive ugliness was realized as late as 2013, after the Arab uprising: *Bastardo* by Néjib Belkadhi (Nadjib Bilqadi). The story itself though was conceived as early as 2007. It deals with a poor neighborhood that is dominated by a strong man and his wife. However, one boy, who was found in the trash, grows up to challenge the despotic couple by monopolizing the telecommunications of the place. In the process the formerly shy and introverted bastard degenerates into an abusive beast himself. Main protagonists and locations are characterized by a strong degree of sordidness, coarse voices, deformed bodies, unkempt appearance, dirt, blood, and crawling insects.

If the above-described full-length fiction films have codified the arbitrariness of the political and social system into sordidness, some short films of the period are more frank about its abusive practices, such as *Anyone* (*Ayan kan*, 2010) by Rida Tlili and, to a certain extent, *Stadium* (2010) by Alaadin Selim (Alaᶜ al-Din Salim). *Anyone* starts with the failed suicide attempt of a young man and continues to follow the same person, who wanders through the nighttime city, to be caught by security forces during a random ID check. *Stadium* too is structured as a string of nighttime roamings, in which we see an elderly person moving through the city while a radio interview about a national football game that was held earlier that evening forms the acoustic backdrop of the event. The story told during the twenty-four minutes of the film is minimalist, nothing more than the man sitting in a café, getting drunk, walking, and eventually being beaten up by hooligans. The film's images seem to reveal a swamp-like environment in which the citizen may sink in violence at any time. An obviously dehumanized cityscape that starts with the stadium continues with filthy, wet streets and cumulates in endless, visually rich tracking scenes through a huge, scarcely lit industrial site. Interestingly, the trope of nighttime roaming is as present in these Tunisian short films as it is in the earlier mentioned full-length films. However, what is most crucial is the trope's dominance over any narrative linearity, to the extent that it becomes a basic structuring moment, a specific chronotope that expresses more than anything else a feeling of identity loss, humiliation, and physical vulnerability generated by an authoritarian system.

In 2010 Tunisia was the Arab country that started the uprisings, and is so far the only one where a democratic system could be established. As in Egypt, a considerable number of documentaries were produced in the first years, either presenting the ongoing events or selecting pressing social issues. At the same time an experimental spirit has become evident in some of the fiction films released after the rebellion. At times even a change of style from pre- to post-revolution can be observed, as in Jilani Saadi's case. His *Bidoun 2* (Bidun 2, literally, 'Without 2,' 2015) strongly resembles a cartoon in its stylization of characters and their weird actions. It seems, on the one hand, to breathe a sort of joyful anarchism; on the other, its ending is quite allegorical, with the two main protagonists, a man and a woman, being beaten up by a mob and a somnambulist old man with dark swimming goggles. The latter character opens the film, sitting in a dark apartment in front of a TV with a portrait of Ben Ali, the former president, hanging upside down on the wall. He reappears later as a hooker and crosses paths with the man and the woman as a quasi-dead body, while the two of them, homeless except for the car, with no place to go, drive aimlessly through the landscape. They quarrel at times, separate, sneak into a wedding, try to commit suicide, then rescue each other, but in the end they fall prey to the thugs led by the man with the goggles. It is quite evident that the film's dark humor depicts a period in transit.

Parody and an innovative style are the motor of another post-revolution film, a so-called mockumentary or fake documentary by Kaouthar (Kawthar) Ben Hania. Her *The Challat of Tunis* (Shallat Tunis, 2012) is actually based on Kamal al-Riyahi's novel *al-Mashrat* (The Razor) and uses the style of investigative documentaries for staging its action. It follows the filmmaker on her quest for an infamous criminal, Challat Tunis, who was supposedly arrested and sentenced for using a razor blade to slice open the backsides of girls wearing tight pants. Ben Hani, who is playing herself, manages to find him and some of his alleged victims, but soon discovers that none of her witnesses, including the man who claims to be the Challat, are really trustworthy. Thus, instead of deconstructing a masculine mythos, the film moves in precisely the opposite direction by participating in the process of its construction—and in doing so naturally pokes fun at Tunisia's macho culture. At the same time the film manages to capitalize on the pre-revolutionary feminist dogma of Tunisian cinema.

Algeria: History and national identity revised

In Algeria only ninety-one of the 458 movie theaters that existed in the colonial period are still operative.[78] State control and social-political factors, the same ones that have affected production, are to blame for that decline. At the turn of the millennium Algeria's cinematic output did not exceed two to three films per year, but around 2005 it started to increase considerably, thanks to a stronger involvement of public institutions. From 2007 to 2011, seven to ten full-length fictions per year were supported by the FDATIC (Fonds de développement de l'art, de la technique et de l'industrie cinématographique),[79] and an average of seven productions received financial support from the AARC (Agence algérienne pour le rayonnement culturel) in the years 2010 to 2013.[80] In contrast to the FDATIC, which has inherited some of the functions of the former CAAIC in offering substantial production funds, the AARC was founded only in 2005 and is more concerned with promoting Algerian cinema abroad, organizing screenings, and facilitating cooperation and coproductions.

Thus, after the long *années de plomb* or 'leaden years' of Islamist terror, it seems that conditions for film production have finally started to improve. Between 1994 and 2002 it was too dangerous to shoot in the Algerian capital. Some of the works produced during this period were set in the provinces, like the Tamazight-speaking *Machaho* (1995) by Belkacem Hadjadj and Mohamed Chouikh's *The Desert Ark* (al-cArsh, literally, 'the throne,' 1997). Other films were shot abroad, like Nadir Moknèche's (Muknash) *Harem of Madame Osmane* (2000), which was realized in Tunisia. Moknèche's next and quite successful film, *Viva Laldjérie* (2002), was one of the first to be shot in Algiers after the long years of terror. Quite a number of women directors focused on the precarious situation of women during the leaden years, including Yamina Bechir-Chouikh (Bashir Shuwikh) with *Rachida* (2002) along with Djamila Sahraoui's (Sahrawi) two films *Barakat!* (2005) and *Yema* (Yimma, 2012; literally: Mom). Merzak Allouache, who presented the French-language road movie *L'autre monde*, (literally: The Other World) in 2001, also skirted this same topic while tackling a number of other pressing issues, such as nepotism and the desperate situation of unemployed Algerian youth. On the latter theme, he returned in 2004 to his favorite Algiers neighborhood, Bab al-Wad (Bab el-Oued), with *Bab el web*. Allouache also underwrote *The Repentant* (al-Ta'ib, 2012), which, like *Yema*, represents a psychological drama of characters struggling with the aftereffects of terror on the fate of their closest family members.

With the grip of public monopoly on film production loosened, Algerian productions have naturally oriented themselves more toward European funding, since the biggest setback in the 1990s had been not only civil war but also the failed reform of state-run production. The major cinematic state enterprises had fallen apart. The Algerian public institution that kept up some support for fiction films during that time was Algerian Television (RTA), through its representative in the field of audio-visual production, the ENPA, which coproduced, among other films, *The Desert Ark*. Later, the RTA aided in the wider distribution of Mohamed Chouikh's 2005 production, *Hamlet of Women* (Duwwar al-nisa'/Douar de femmes), in the few remaining Algerian movie theaters after a big promotional campaign for the film. Some filmmakers also have been able to mobilize local cultural institutions to add to their film budgets, as in the case of Hadjadj for *al-Manara*.

Quite a number of the films made during this era deal more or less directly with the explosive social and political situation, particularly critiquing extremism and denouncing the latter's assaults on women, such as the aforementioned *Rachida*, *Barakat!*, *Yema* and *al-Manara* (2004). Some of the films not only blamed Islamist terror but attacked oppressive social structures as a whole, like *Bled Number One* (2006) by an Algerian director raised in France, Rabah Ameur-Zaïmèche. It tells the story of a young Algerian expelled from France who returns to the village of his parents at the same time as a young woman who has separated from her husband and is now blamed for dishonoring her family. Seen through the estranged eyes of the expat, the *bled* (*balad*, literally, 'country') or homeland is depicted as a perilous minefield where misogyny and extremism go hand in hand.

Another wave that started in the 1990s is represented by legendary stories set in seemingly archaic surroundings, like *The Desert Ark*, whose narrative unfolds in the deserts of the south. Its dissection of archaic patriarchal traditions, human cruelty, and injustice may of course be read as an allegory of Algeria's present inner turmoil. Interestingly, however, two more of these quasi-legendary narratives, namely *Machaho* by Belkacem Hadjadj and *Baya's Mountain* (La montagne de Baya, 1997) by Azzedine Meddour (ʿIzz al-Din Midawwar), have been linked to an important political change in the Algerian arena. Both are set in Kabylia's mountains and use Kabyle for their dialogue.

As mentioned earlier, until the mid-1970s Algerian films used a sort of sanitized and artificial colloquial Arabic for their dialogue, even for films explicitly set in Kabylia, such as the 1969 adaptation of Mouloud (Mawlud) Mammeri's novel *Opium and the Baton* (al-Afyun wa-l-ʿassa) by Ahmed Rachedi. In this case, not only the dialogue but also names had been exchanged for Arabic ones. For three decades, public film funding was denied to another screen adaption of one of Mouloud Mammeri's novels, *The Forgotten Hill* (La colline oubliée/Tawrirt yettwattun). Eventually it was directed by Abderrahmane Bouguermouh and released in 1997 with some public funding provided at the time by the CAAIC (which had assumed the tasks of the former ONCIC in 1987). The epic story unfolds during the Second World War in a remote Kabyle mountain village. It deals with the dreams and tragic moments of several young characters, including a student who has just returned from France.

Another quasi historical film, *Baya's Mountain* goes back further in history, to the end of the nineteenth century. It revolves around a combative and charismatic widow who, in the process of trying to avenge the death of her husband, becomes involved in the resistance against French colonialists and their rich Arab allies.[81] Belkacem Hadjadj's 2014 feature *Fadhma N'Soumer* likewise touches on a legendary Amazigh woman.

This unprecedented wave of Amazigh films rose ahead of the so-called Black Spring in 2001 which brought about massive protests in Kabylia. They were triggered by human rights violations and resulted in even more abusive practices, including the killing of protesters by central government forces. Eventually the conflict was resolved by reducing the police force in the region and admitting Kabyle as a 'national'—although not official—language in Algeria. In this context, the aforementioned Kabyle films are sending out a strong political message asserting Kabyle-Algerian national affiliation and identity without any reference to Arab Algerian culture. In linking their community simultaneously to anti-colonial resistance, like Arabic-speaking Algeria, the recoding of the nation as Kabyle and non-Arab works in both directions, toward the inside and the outside of the nation-state that surrounds them.

In the new millennium, Tamazight-language films continued to explore Amazigh history. One such film is *Si Mohand U M'Hand* (2006) by Rachid Benallel and Liazid Khodja. It pays tribute to a famous Kabyle poet whose family life was wrecked during the great Algerian revolt in 1871. The film was coproduced with the Moroccan TV channel 2M and the CCM (National Moroccan Film Center) at a time when Morocco was beginning to adopt a more inclusive policy toward its own Amazigh population. Other Tamazight-speaking films touch upon common daily-life stories using an observing realist style. *Ayrouen* (literally, 'Once upon a Time,' 2007), by Brahim Tsaki, was produced by Belkacem Hadjadj. It uses the Tergui language and depicts the relationship between a Tergui from the desert region and a young female European traveler, a relationship that is overshadowed by a tragic love story in the man's past. *The Yellow House* (La maison jaune, 2007) by Amor (ᶜAmr) Hakkar is set in present-time Aurès and pictures a family who tries to overcome sadness and depression after the loss of their adult son in an accident.

Like a number of other Algerian films, subsequent works by Amor Hakkar have turned away from the cruelty that had characterized the leaden years, and more toward social issues. *A Few Days of Respite* (Quelques jours de répit, 2011) recounts a homosexual love story, and *The Proof* (al-Dalil/La preuve, 2014) tells about an infertile taxi driver who ends up wrecking his personal life because of the social taboo surrounding male infertility. The first is set in France, and the second is set in the Aurès and uses the local Arabic dialect. The latter tackles a second taboo as well, namely illegitimate motherhood. The same topic had already been brought up some years earlier by Nadia Chraïbi (also spelled: Cherabi-Labidi for Sharabi Labidi) in a TV-style film: *The Other Side of the Mirror* (Wara' al-mir'a/L'envers du miroir, 2007). Another similarly pressing issue, illegal immigration, was at the center of *Harragas* ('harraga' is colloquial for illegal immigrant, 2009) by Merzak Allouache and *Rome Rather than You* (Ruma walla antuma, 2007) by Tariq Tegui.

Social interest, in combination with criticism of the current political system and the reevaluation of the historical national liberation phase, also came increasingly to the fore in all kind of formats and genres, often combined with the women's question. Some of them chose a rather comic or satirical representation. *Masquerades* (Maskhara, 2008) by Lyes Salem (Liyas Salim) received awards at all of the top Arab festivals for its originality. The story takes place in a provincial village and focuses on Munir, a kind-hearted but stubborn brother and husband who hardly can make ends meet for his family. Yet he insists on finding a prosperous match for his sister Reem. But this is not an easy task, for pretty Reem suffers from a strange disease, narcolepsy that makes her fall asleep at any likely or unlikely moment. Also, she is clandestinely in love with Munir's sidekick, good-for-nothing Khalifa. When a suitable groom fails to materialize, Munir simply invents one, a rich Australian. The rumor turns him suddenly into the most popular man in the village, until his fraud is discovered and Munir's dreams of prosperity crumble. In the end it is Khalifa who finds a cure for his beloved Reem and her brother has to accept their alliance grudgingly.

Masquerade's humor sticks out among the numerous bleak and tragic cinematic approaches from Algeria. Nonetheless, according to filmmaker Salem, the film has a political undertone. "I wanted her to symbolize Algeria," Salem said about the heroine of his movie. She "is torn between her brother and lover: the former still clings to the past and seeks to impose his will, even if through lies. As to her lover, he is open and looks to the future with an open mind, but he is hesitant."[82] Not only Salem, but also Nadir Moknèche uses his female protagonists as an allegory either of the nation or of the degenerated political system of his homeland, most evidently in his *Délice Paloma* (2006), which was promptly denied a screening license in Algeria. It features Mme Aldjéria, who is a perfect facilitator for whatever her clients plan or wish for. As she becomes more and more self-confident about her business and her powerful contacts, she works for the acquisition of the touristic Caracalla Baths. But her influential "friends" let her down at the last moment and she has to watch helplessly as her empire disintegrates.

Moknèche, who was born and is based in France but who spent his childhood in Algeria, refrains from using Arabic for his film dialogues. Dubbed "the Algerian Almodóvar," he has often shown a preference for dominant if not hysterical mother figures.[83] His satire *Haram of Madame Osmane* (Le Harem de Madame Osmane, 1999) became an unexpected hit in France upon its release. The mother figure here is embodied by a retired female freedom fighter presiding strictly over a female household composed of two young women, her daughter and her niece, whose freedom she constantly tries to curtail.

Moknèche's second film, *Viva Laldjérie* (2003), was less satirical, with a stronger tragic overtone. Set in the immediate post-leaden years in Algiers, it presents another female triangle: Papicha, a withdrawn mother and former belly dancer; Goucem, a hedonistic daughter in love with a married man; and Fifi, a kind-hearted prostitute and Goucem's friend. They try to meet their needs against all odds until Fifi is hunted by a client, evidently a state official, who has lost his gun. The girl disappears and she is found dead. Ironically, the entire scope of the tragedy is never fully grasped by the film's protagonists: it was Goucem who had stolen the client's gun, and she will remain unaware of the fact that her deed was the reason for her friend's abduction. The political system as allegorically represented by the owner of the gun remains obscure, with the air of a frightening, unpredictable presence.

In *Goodbye Morocco* (2013), Nadir Moknèche's most recent film, he finally departs from the trope of hysterical mothers and lascivious daughters and ventures into an entirely different genre with a changed constellation of characters. Moreover, his thriller takes place not in Algeria but in Tangier, Morocco, because the director had not set foot in Algeria since 2006, after he was denied the screening license for *Délice Paloma*.[84] This film features Lubna Azabal as an architect and single mother who fights for the custody of her child. Her success is imperiled by her illicit relationship with her business partner, a Serb, who is clandestinely involved in the smuggling of ancient Roman artifacts. In the end, her world falls apart. What appears in the core of this film, as in other films by Moknèche, is a violent, unrelenting social and political system confronted with hard-to-crack women.

Not everyone shares this criticism of the system and its history, though. On the contrary, there has been, it seems, a remarkable resurgence of anti-colonial patriotic films similar to the immediate post-independence era. For example, *Journey to Algiers* (al-Saffar ila al-Djaza'ir/Voyage à Alger, 2010) by Abdelkerim Bahloul (ᶜAbd al-Karim Bahlul), which is said to be based on a true story, takes a much more conciliatory tone even though it likewise deals with corruption. It tells the story of the widow of a martyr who, with her children, is sent to live into the beautiful house of a *pied-noir* who has fled to France. As time goes by and the FLN party becomes more established, she is pressured to evacuate the house. She decides to travel to the capital to make a complaint to the president himself (supposedly Boumedienne), who eventually ensures justice. Thus the film ultimately returns to the nationalist heroic model, which other Algerian films have continued to promote. *Zabana* (2012) by Said Ould-Khelifa, for example, depicts the events that surround the execution of the FLN leader Ahmad Zabana in 1956 as the starting point of the Algiers revolt. *Mostefa Ben Boulaid* (Mustafa b. Bu Lᶜayd, 2008), by film veteran Ahmed Rachedi, is a bluntly laudatory piece reminiscent of the national liberation films of the 1970s. Its male protagonist is a straight hero who speaks polished almost-classical Arabic and loses his life for his homeland in the end.

Lyes Salem, in contrast, tried in his latest film to demystify this most highly mythologically charged epochs of Algerian history, namely national liberation and its aftermath, though it proved to be far less original than *Masquerades*. In his only even mildly humorous historical spectacle, *al-Wahrani* (L'Oranais, literally, 'the man from Oran,' 2014), he shows the gradual corruption of a former freedom fighter and FLN squad following independence, to the point where he betrays his former friends and comrades to persecution and death. When Salem was asked why he chose a narrative set in the first years after independence, he answered that Algerian cinema had hardly explored this particular epoch, in which national identity was in the process of taking shape.[85] That this process was charged with ambiguities and contradictions goes without saying. Yet the film ventures to depict even the degeneration, corruption, and personal betrayal of the original revolutionary ideas that came along with the war of liberation. Surprisingly, the film received quite extensive public financial support at home, not a matter to be taken for granted given the authoritarian tendency of the current Algerian ruling system.

Genuinely critical assessment of the liberation war was brought up in other formats as well as in formally innovative films. For example, *Fidaï* (Algeria, 2012) by Damien Ounouri, is a personal multi-layered documentary about the filmmaker's uncle, who in his youth participated in armed resistance in France and committed, upon orders, a politically motivated assassination. Ounouri goes back to his uncle's village, speaks with members of the extended family who are almost completely unaware of the details of their father's and grandfather's history, traces the places of his humiliation and repression through the colonists and French soldiers, restages the assassination in France, and silently observes the long-term effects on the health and psychological well-being of his uncle. It opens up a number of questions, mainly on the fragility of heroism but also on culpability and shame.

Another example is *Bloody Beans* (Lubiya hamra, 2013) by Narimane Mari, which depicts a group of children who playfully improvise the different stages of Algeria's colonization and national liberation war on a beach. The director seems to bring together two film-theatrical traditions, Peter Brook's *Lord of the Flies* (1963) and Fernando Arrabal's *Viva la muerte* (1970), into an original experimental film characterized by hand camera and improvised acting. In this way it presents rebellion and liberation as a children's game governed by dynamics that are practically a force of nature, and avoids any heroization.

Like another recent Algerian film *Bloody Beans* sits uncomfortably within any kind of categorization. Tariq Teguia's *Zanj Revolution* (Thawrat al-Zandj, 2013) seems much better labeled as international art house, resembling works by Jim Jarmush or Wim Wenders. *Zanj Revolution* does not transcend the national into the transnational or even global simply because it is an Algerian–French–Lebanese–Qatari coproduction—this it shares with so many other films—but rather because it contains a variety of film-historical references and is set in different locations, from Algeria to Greece and from Lebanon to Iraq (the scenes in the latter were actually shot in Egypt). In style it pays tribute to the French *nouvelle vague* as represented in the works of Chris Marker and Jean-Luc Godard, and at the same time it pays tribute to *Nahla*, the iconic art film of Algerian director Farouk Beloufa.[86]

The film's constantly changing color scheme is one of those references. It alters between black and white, color, and monochromatic images depending on the mood of the characters and the events—

Zenj Revolution (Thawrat al-Zandj, 2013)
by Tariq Teguia *(courtesy Tariq Teguia)*

quite unconventionally, at times, within one scene. Its main character is transnational herself: Nahla is a young Palestinian whose
parents live in Greece. She attracts the attention of an Algerian journalist, Battuta, who has arrived in Beirut in search of historical
material that may shed light on the truth of the black slaves' revolution that supposedly took place in southern Iraq in the ninth
century AD under Abbasid rule. Their paths cross for a short while
in Beirut; she continues into Greece with a friend while he travels
farther south to the Iraqi swamps to find the last traces of the revolt
imprinted on the black skin of a local inhabitant. Their brief
encounter is constantly intercut with images of a group of Greek
activists who at night fill the streets of their hometown with revolutionary graffiti.

Morocco: Diversity and changed rhythm

Morocco has recently become one of the largest film-producing
countries on the African continent. While its overall output was only
forty-three films between 1991 and 2000,[87] in 2013 it was the third
biggest film-producing country in Africa, after South Africa and
Egypt, with an output of approximately twenty full-length feature

films a year.[88] According to Sahar Ali, the authorities issued permissions for the shooting of seventeen full-length feature films for cinema in 2010, nineteen in 2011, and eighteen in 2012. There is a similar number of video film productions per year.[89]

Morocco has also managed to attract a considerable number of high-profile foreign productions shooting in Ouarzazate, in the southern desert, a fact that helped to improve the country's cinematic infrastructure and technical know-how.[90] Morocco's film industry was buoyed by the modernization of the technical equipment of the national CCM: television channel Maroc 2 began to show a strong interest in investing in films around the turn of the millennium. The other major reason for Morocco's success in increasing and stabilizing production rates is that it modified its film funding system in 2004, introducing the French *avances sur les recettes* system that redirects a certain percentage of the total box office income to national productions.[91] Like other film-producing countries in the region, its art house productions still cannot do without external funds—38 percent of Moroccan films rely on coproduction[92]—but the ability to secure a considerable proportion of their budget at home puts productions in a much better starting position.

As a consequence, there is a considerable number of Moroccan directors who have managed to direct more than ten films each, a fact that is quite exceptional on the African continent.[93]

Jamal Bahmand, who strongly disputes the notion of New Moroccan Cinema, asserts that "around the early 1990s a popular movement of urban cinema revitalized the Moroccan film scene, which had until then been dominated by paradigms that failed to establish an indigenous tradition of cinema veritably popular with its postcolonial public."[94] He proposes instead the label "New Urban Cinema" due to the immense diversity of its makers. He groups Moroccan directors into three strands based on their age, geographic location, and social affiliation, which he sees as directly related to the kind of cinema they make and the response they receive from

Moroccan audiences. First, there are the Casablanca- or Moroccan-based directors, who are relatively consistent with the 1990s style and orientation, among whom are Hakim Nouri, Abdelkader Lagtaa (ᶜAbd al-Qadir Laqtaᶜ), Moustapha Derkaoui (Mustafa Darqawi), Saad Chraïbi (Saᶜd Sharabi), Mohamed Asli (Muhammad ᶜAsali), and Farida Ben Lyazid. Second are the directors from the diaspora or second-generation immigrants, most notably Nabil Ayouch, Narjiss Nejjar (Nardjis Nadjar), Laïla Marrakchi (Layla Marakishi), Faouzi Bensaïdi (Fawzi Bin Saᶜidi), Noureddine (Nur al-Din) Lakhmari, and Ali Benkirane (ᶜAli Bin Kiran). Third, and youngest, are Hicham Lasri, Mohammed Achaour, and the brothers Swel (Suhail) and Imad Noury (ᶜImad Nuri), who all produce an "unapologetically subjective cinema of globalization."[95]

Unquestionably exceptional among Moroccan directors of the second strand are Nabil Ayouch and Laila Marrakchi, who have attained the strongest visibility on the international mainstream film market with *Whatever Lola Wants* (2008) and *Rock the Kasbah* (2012). Both were coproduced by French Pathé Production. In contrast to Ayouch's *Whatever Lola Wants*, which suffered from a lack of authenticity, particularly because it did not represent regional locations and behavior realistically, *Rock the Kasbah* is well crafted in terms of *mise en scène* and based on a witty script. In terms of genre, it places the typical American wedding and funeral family-gathering plot into a Moroccan setting, depicting a family being rocked by internal conflicts and a long-disguised secret in the aftermath of its patriarch's death. Thus it manages to come close to the international mainstream while flavored with home-grown glamour, featuring some of the most internationally recognized Arab film stars: the Moroccan Lubna Azabal, the Lebanese Nadine Labaki, the Palestinian Hiam Abbas, and even, in a guest appearance, the Egyptian Omar Sharif.

No wonder the development of the film industry has become the object of national interest. In October 2012, King Muhammad IV asserted that cinema is at the heart of the country's cultural agenda, that the crown has "always taken a special interest in the question of cinema," and that "film production must accompany the changes and achievements taking place in our country." He went on to guarantee the freedom of creation.[96] In 2006 the CCM had commissioned a diagnostic and strategic study of the film sector. Its ambitious recommendations were adopted as a national strategy plan in 2007, with the aim of pushing production rates up to thirty films a year, among others goals.[97]

But this is just one side of the picture as Sahar Ali has observed, for "despite the dominant role of the state in developing the domestic film industry, Moroccan cinema is caught in a sort of paradox: an increase of the number of films produced (many of which gained international recognition) and a sharp and consistent decline of the number of cinemas. Piracy, combined with audience disinterest, contribute to exacerbating the problem: an increasing production versus a distribution and operating sector in difficulty. Dominant state funding faces a near absence of the private sector."[98]

Indeed, the issue of distribution is crucial in assessing the vitality of the film industry. At first it seemed that Moroccan films were able to reach very large audiences, an achievement that has become more regular since the late 1990s. Abdelkader Lagtaa's *A Love Affair in Casablanca* (Hubb fi-l Dar al-Bayda', 1991) was an unprecedented national box-office hit upon its release in 1992, drawing over 400,000 spectators.[99] Some other successes were the comedy *The Bandits* (al-Bandiya, 2003) by Said Naciri (Saᶜid al-Nasiri), the hotly debated and exceptional (for being a French production) Jewish–Muslim love story *Marock* (2004) by Laïla Marrakchi, and *The Moroccan Symphony* (al-Sinfuniya al-maghribiya, 2006) by Kamal Kamal, which stayed in theaters for five consecutive weeks.[100] In the first half of the 2000s around 300,000 to 500,000 viewers were counted for national productions. Yet a significant drop in overall admissions followed, a problem that has been further aggravated by piracy and the lack of any investment in movie theaters, particularly in the new digital systems.

In 2011 the country had only sixty-eight screens left and two multiplex cinemas in Marrakesh and Casablanca.[101] In 2012 the highest admission for a Moroccan film had fallen to 230,519[102]; in the year before it was even less, only 75,307.[103] Still, the local market share was nearly 18 percent (American films 48 percent and Egyptian 13 percent). It must also be noted that Moroccan films do much better at home than Lebanese films, for example. Remarkably enough, in 2011 two Moroccan films, the comedy *The Day Tzad Switched Off the Light* (Nahar Tzad taffa al-daw) by Mohamed Karrat and *Wings of Love* (Djinah al-hawa/Les ailes de l'amour) by Abdelhai Laraki (Abd al-Hay al-ʿAraqi), grossed best at the box office, ahead of foreign productions. In 2012 as well, two Moroccan comedies had the highest admissions, *Road to Kabul* (al-Tariq ila Kabul) and *A Moroccan in Paris* (Marukki fi Paris) by Said Naciri.[104]

One of the first comedies to attract Moroccan audiences' interest was *The Search for My Wife's Husband* (1994) by Mohamed Ben Abderahmane Tazi. The fact that the film is a comedy that tackles gender issues was certainly one reason for its success. In fact, several of the most popular films in the following years were centered on gender relations within the family, gender equality, female liberation, and love affairs, such as *Women . . . and Women* (Nisa' . . . wa nisa', 1998) by Saad Chraïbi (Saʿd Shraybi), *Closed Door* (al-Bab al-masdud, 1998) by Abdelkader Lagtaa, Hakim Nouri's *Love Story* (Qissat hubb, 2002), Moustapha Derkaoui's *Casablanca by Night* (al-Dar al-bayda' by night, 2003), and *Samira's Garden* (Samira fi-l-Day'a, 2007) by Nabil Lahlou.

These topics were often combined with humor or staged as a comedy, most notably *Art of Love* (Fann al-hubb, 2001) by Said Naciri and *She's Diabetic, Has Hypertension but Refuses to Kick the Bucket* (Fiha al-maliha wa-l-sukkar wa ma baghatsh tamut, 2000) by Hakim Nouri. The latter plays on all kind of stereotypes, as the young husband and timid son of a domineering mother gets lured into a relationship with a beautiful neighbor. Some films on gender equality became more outspoken after the Mudawanna (the new Family Code) was ratified in 2004, stressing the shared responsibilities of men and women and putting stronger restrictions on men's rights with respect to divorce and polygamy. Zakia Tahri (al-Tahiri; lead player of Ben Lyazid's *A Door to the Sky*) directed in 2009 *Number One* (Arabic title is the same), a social comedy on the gradual awakening of a young woman who is dominated by her elderly white-collar husband. Some films did not shy away from pointing out extreme grievances, such as *Behind Closed Doors* (Khalf al-abwab al-mughlaqa, 2014) by Mohammed Ahd Bensouda (Muhammad cAhd Bin Sawda), a top-selling film that addresses the problem of sexual harassment.

The most popular recent comedies, however, present socially or politically colored issues. *Road to Kabul* by Brahim Chkiri (Ibrahim al-Shukayri), for instance, is a buddy film with farce elements about four Moroccans searching for a friend who disappeared on the way to Amsterdam. The young man had planned to immigrate clandestinely to the Netherlands to find employment, but ended up instead as a hostage in Afghanistan. Coming to his rescue, the friends set out on a dangerous journey and take turns falling prey to bloodthirsty Islamists, on the one hand, and ruthless American army personnel, on the other. The second main topic of Moroccan cinema has remained poverty and social inequality, as expressed in more realist dramas such as *Majid* (Madjid, 2011), a road movie by Nassim cAbassi about a little boy searching for a trace of his deceased parents, or—what Dwyer has termed "neo-realist films"—*Casanegra* (Casa negra, 2008) and *Zero* (2012), both by Nour-Eddine Lakhmari, and *Death for Sale* (Mawt li-l-bayc, 2011) by Faouzi Bensaïdi. These male-centered and action-oriented dramas have much of the air of American film noir, with the heroes hovering on the edge of criminality, often doomed to failure. The Moroccan film industry has also started to experiment with genre films other than the action film. Jérôme Cohen-Olivar underwrote a French–Moroccan coproduction, the horror movie *Kandisha* (2008), featuring the internationally acclaimed Palestinian actress Hiam Abbas, based on a local legend.

At the same time a sensitive topic, namely Morocco's so-called 'leaden years' has emerged in less mainstream-oriented films. As a result, some films took it upon themselves to speak either in passing or outright of the ferocious political prosecution, human rights violations, and disappearances that took place during that period. In the Moroccan context, of course, the leaden years denote different events than in Algeria. They refer to the period that started with the leftist movement after independence and continued with heavy crackdowns on political protests in 1981 and 1990 under the reign of King Hassan II between 1961 and 1999. With the ascent of the new heir, Mohammed IV, to the throne, the relative relaxation with regard to freedom of expression that had started in the course of the 1990s has increased.

Examples of films that address political persecution and human rights violations are *The Black Room* (Darb Maulay al-Sharif/La chambre noire, 2004; literally, 'Maulay al-Sharif Alley') by Hassan Ben Jelloun (Bin Jalun), *Memory in Detention* (Zakira muᶜtaqala, 2004) by Jillali Ferhati, and Leïla Kilani's documentary *Our Forbidden Places* (Amakin mamnuᶜa, 2008). *A Thousand Months* (Alf shahr, 2003) by Faouzi Bensaïdi is one of those that touches on the topic only in passing, in combination with the issue of religious fundamentalism. It is set in the magnificent Atlas Mountains scenery during the holy month of Ramadan. A village, its people, and the social and ideological tensions between them are portrayed through the eyes of a little boy, for instance the fuss created around a young rebellious girl who is stigmatized morally for listening to modern music and adopting a modern dress style. One basic thread in the story is the secret of the young boy's family; he is unaware of the fact that his father is a political detainee, but thinks he has emigrated.

A Thousand Months also shows the rising interest in Morocco's countryside and its diverse cultures. Mohamed Asli set his *Angels Don't Fly above Casablanca* (Fauq al-Dar al-bayda' al-mala'ika la tuhalliq, 2004) in the Amazigh-inhabited Atlas Mountains. It traces the struggle of a have-not to make a living between the city of Casablanca and his home village. The interest in the region has not confined itself to a representation of living conditions, but has reached out to explore Amazigh mythology, as in Hakim Belabbes's (Bilabis) original docu-drama *Defining Love: A Failed Attempt* (Muhawala fashila li-taᶜrif al-hubb, 2012). At the same time a number of filmmakers started using the Amazigh language for their dialogue.

The first Amazigh-speaking films meant for theatrical release appeared in 2006. Some of them enjoyed a career in festivals, most notably *Heart Edges* (Amazigh title: *Tizza Woul*) by Hicham Ayouch (Hisham ᶜAyush) and *Skeleton* (Amazigh title: *Taghssa*) by Yassine Fanane (Yasin Fanan). Already in the late 1990s a wave of Amazigh video films had started to surface, particularly in the south.[105] As Daniela Merolla has pointed out, most of these cheaply made and market-oriented but nevertheless socially committed videos were produced by Chleuh Berbers. They have been widely distributed through legal sales or piracy—even abroad— and their narratives "tend to reproduce the conventional social discourse of the community addressed and in particular of the Chleuh lower-middle urban class and its perspective on life."[106] Meanwhile, Moroccan television has Amazigh-speaking channels and airs Amazigh films on a regular basis. This opening to depart from the original Arabization policy that was adopted after independence started gradually around the turn of the millennium and may certainly be regarded as an attempt to ease social and political tensions. The Amazigh language has even become part of the primary-school curriculum.

Thus Moroccan cinema in general is becoming more strongly marked by an inclination to diversity and greater inclusiveness (except for the Sahrawi issue), not only on the ethnic and cultural level, but also in terms of sexual representation and with regard to individual film language. For instance, *The Wretched Life of Juanita*

Narboni (Juanita, bint Tandja/La vida perra de Juanita Narboni, 2005) a Spanish–Moroccan coproduction by Farida Ben Lyazid presented a sort of nostalgic multiculturalism. It used the life story of a Tangier-born Spanish woman as a pretext to revive and deplore the city's former multiculturalism in the colonial era. The myth of liminal yet diverse Tangier—likewise a trope in Western cinema and literature—has persisted and emerged in works of the new generation. *Fissures* (Shuquq, 2009) by Hicham Ayouch is the story of a love triangle that involves three socially marginalized characters: a sensitive older architect, his macho young friend who has just been released from prison, and a suicidal Brazilian woman. They live on the limits of everything: society, emotions, sensuality, fantasy, and existence itself. The appeasing elegies of Ben Lyazid stand in stark contrast to the rough and dynamic *mise en scène* of Ayouch. Even though both films are set in the same city, their cinematic and ideological approaches are absolutely different, indicating a clear generational shift in Moroccan *auteur* cinema.

They Are the Dogs (Humm al-kilab, 2013) by Hicham Lasri is a similarly 'rough' film that, in the midst of the Arab Spring uprising, takes the opportunity to examine Morocco's leaden years. It uses the fake documentary format and hand camera to follow a TV crew that is shooting a report on the rebellion. Among the people gathered on the streets they run into an elderly man, strangely disoriented as to time and place. Spontaneously, the crew decides to follow him, and discovers that the man has just been released after having spent twenty years in jail as a political prisoner. They document his quest for his family, friends, and past life, and get sucked into a spiral of deceptions and disappointments surrounding their ambiguous hero.

Ambiguity also surrounds the hero of Hicham Lasri's last film, *The Sea is Behind* (al-Bahr min wara'akum, 2014). The title alludes to the famous statement of Tariq b. Ziad, with which the legendary Arab military leader encouraged his men to conquer Iberia after crossing Gibraltar: "The sea is behind you and the enemy in front of you!" indicating that they have no other choice but to fight. This message stands in ironic opposition to Lasri's hero Tariq, a desperate and broken man who wears makeup and female dresses. For he earns his living by dancing on a cart, disguised as a woman. Yet the horse that usually draws the cart, and that belongs to his father, is dying and Tariq's life is in tatters anyway. A policemen has taken his place in the relationship with his wife and sons, while his father is only interested in the ailing horse. The film is shot in black and white and the plot appears fragmented, divided into absurd stylized sketches punctuated by rhythmic electronic music.

It seems that a substantial proportion of younger Moroccan *auteurs* have discovered motion and mobility as a new form to communicate the ambivalences and contradictions of their society. These are films that often touch on taboos, such as violence or sexuality, using a fast-paced rhythm—whether in music, camera, editing, or acting—and rely strongly on dramatic catharsis. It should be noted that according to film theory action-style *mise en scène* is believed to have a direct physical impact on the viewer in reproducing a masculine structure of feeling that crystallizes in the body's contact with the world, its rush, its expansiveness.[107] It can "promote an active engagement with the world, going out into it, doing to the environment; yet the enjoyment of them means allowing them to come to you, take you over, do you."[108]

Rush and expansiveness, a panting rhythm that "comes to you," has not remained a strictly male domain. Leïla Kilani's *On the Plank* (ᶜAla al-haffat, literally, 'on the edge,' 2011), for example, is punctuated by staccato-like scenes of the two young female protagonists, Badiᶜa and Iman, both workers in a Tangiers shrimp factory. But this is not just the editing, it is also the actresses' performance. There is the moment when Badiᶜa violently soaps and scrubs her whole body in an effort to rub off the odor of her work, or later, when she and her friend Iman, in another long and sleepless night, rush through the busy streets of the city in search of adventures. They run into two other girls who take them to a group

On the Plank ('Ala al-haffat, 2011) by Leïla Kilani
(courtesy Fortissimo Films)

of small-time gangsters and opportunists. They discover that their new acquaintances work in the Free Zone, inaccessible without a permit. Iman and Badiᶜa find a way to sneak into the space, and explore it until dawn. Always busy looking for new opportunities that may help improve their economic and private situations, the girls are constantly in motion and rarely enjoy a moment of silence or contemplation.

An inclination toward diversity in representation has seized Moroccan genre cinema as well, particularly the action film, usually centered on male heroes. *One Minute of Sun Less* (Lahzat zalam/Une minute de soleil en moins, 2003) by Nabil Ayouch, a highly cinematic TV film produced by the German–French channel Arte, uses a typical police film plot to tell a disturbingly deconstructive story. The director revives old Moroccan tropes of social deprivation and exploitation by portraying the investigation of a murder in a style that strongly contradicts the usual soothing, poetic Moroccan *auteur* film style.

Beautiful Turia, who lives with her handicapped little brother in the villa of the victim, a known Tangiers drug trafficker, is placed under police scrutiny as the main murder suspect. Things become

One Minute of Sun Less (Lahzat zalam, 2002) by Nabil Ayouch
(courtesy Institut du Monde Arabe, Paris)

increasingly complicated as the victim turns out to be homosexual, as does the investigating captain, Kamil. The latter takes in Turia, only to get involved with her in a sexual affair in which she is the active agent. Handheld camera and the stark contrasts of a conscious video aesthetic, combined with the captain's personal fantasies popping up (a stylistic method used in horror movies or or popular American televised detective series like *Crossing Jordan)*, merge into a kind of globalized but unsatisfying postmodern conflation, leaving far behind the vision of cultural gaps and difference.

In the same vein, the already mentioned *Casanegra* (2008) and *Zero* (2012) by Lakhmari appropriate the usual action and thriller repertory in presenting the typical male embattled hero. What still comes across as a buddy film in *Casanegra*, combined with the typical Moroccan trope of the deprived and jobless male youth, develops in *Zero* into a straightforward film noir thriller telling the typical 'one man against the world' story. The hero is an insignificant corrupt policeman, nicknamed Zero, who is going through difficulties on every level. He gets smacked around by his superiors, who want their share in the little profits Zero makes as a would-be pimp, as well as by his tyrannical veteran father, who is in a wheelchair. However, one day Zero is struck by the pleas of a mother who has been looking for her lost teenage daughter everywhere in the big city of Casablanca. Slowly but surely turning into an angel of retribution, he takes up the mission until he finds the girl in a high-class brothel. During the ensuing showdown he finds himself confronted by his boss and takes him down, only to be eradicated himself in the end.

Lakhmari's films created controversy in Morocco and were even questioned with regard to their Moroccan identity.[109] This is not surprising given the fact that they touch on the taboo of homosexuality and display linguistic vulgarity and graphic violence, particularly in the bloody ending of *Zero*. They stand, moreover, in stark opposition to the usual sense of alienation and victimization expressed in the plots and film style of early Moroccan *auteur* cinema and that still reappears today, even in films that touch on cultural and religious taboos. The autobiographically inspired gay life story *Salvation Army* (Djaysh al-tahiya, 2014) by Abdallah Taia (ᶜAbd Allah al-Tayiᶜ) is an example, as are the previously mentioned films by Jilali Ferhati.[110] Slow and silent action, as well as a tendency to lengthy scenes and long shots, are some of the characteristics of this style of filmmaking. Like Lebanese 'exilic' *auteur* films, they seem to invite the viewer to distanced observation if not voyeurism. Examples abound, such as Yasmine Kassari's (Yasmin al-Qassari) *L'enfant endormi* (al-Raqid, literally, 'the sleeping child,' 2004), about a local habit of women putting the fetuses in their wombs to sleep for years until the father returns. It is not just the slow pace but also the trope of roaming that recurs in these films, such as in Tazi's *The Big Journey* (1981). More recently it is found in *The Wind Horse* (ᶜAwd rih, 2001) by Daoud Aoulad Syad (Dawud Awlad Syad), a road movie that tells the story of two men from two different generations traveling through the country in search of things that may enrich their life. The grappling with meaning and identity is the motor of the cinematic obsession with space. The attempt to get lost in the immensity of one's surroundings may be a symptom of what Naficy has labelled "liminal panics." If we follow his argument, this attempt is triggered by displacement.[111] It seems that this notion of literal physical displacement can be extended to the mental displacement of the modern intellectual, who is confronted with the contradictions that are produced by traditional or underdeveloped societies in today's globalized context and is forced to deal with his or her inner alienation in view of these ambiguities.

In this respect, the satire *Waiting for Pasolini* (Fi intizar Pasolini, 2007) by Daoud Aoulad Syad can be read as an allegory of the contested position of the Moroccan artist or intellectual in his society. Thami is a satellite-dish salesman and a former film extra. He befriended the great director Pier Paolo Pasolini during the shooting of *Oedipus Rex* in Ouarzazate in 1966. Forty years later, an Italian crew comes back to Ouarzazate to prepare the shooting of a film about the Bible. Thami is convinced that his friend Pasolini is back in

The Wind Horse ('Awd rih, 2001) by Daoud Aoulad Syad
(courtesy Institut du Monde Arabe, Paris)

WWW. What a Wonderful World (2006) by Faouzi Bensaïdi
(courtesy Faouzi Bensaïdi)

town, thus triggering cinema fever in the whole village. Soon, however, he learns that his beloved director died years ago—something he cannot admit to the others, for now his compatriots' expectations lie heavily on his shoulders. Everybody thinks he can speak on their behalf and get them well-paid jobs in the production. Syad's representation of the fundamentally negative worldview and vision of the villagers, their desire for prosperity, and the Italian crew for whom the locals are just visual material, not only opens questions about the relationship of Third and First World cultures. Using the image of an idealized Pasolini as the embodiment of a more compassionate and egalitarian approach to representing the Other exceeds the issue of representation and power toward the relation of art and society in general in the presence of social and political inequalities. Given the pragmatism displayed by both the needy villagers and the materialist, business-as-usual Italian crew, Pasolini stands quite emblematically, if not nostalgically, for a long-bygone committed artistic expression as it existed in the heart of post-colonial Third-Worldist film culture.

However, this 'old-fashioned' concept of film has been overtaken in other Moroccan productions by a more postmodern conceptualist and deconstructive vision of cinema. *WWW: What a Wonderful World* (2006) by Faouzi Bensaïdi is a witty, stylized film, simultaneously slow- and fast-paced, with amazing framings and orchestrated audio-visual compositions that resemble music clips. At the center of these scenes is Kinza, a female traffic cop. Under her regime, the traffic light she supervises turns into real choreographies. She lives in the same grey and insignificant Casablanca *bidonville* (slum) as her friend Su^{c}ad, a prostitute, and Kamil, a cold-blooded contract killer who is Su^{c}ad's favorite customer. Kamil's world falls apart because of the interference of a hacker who stumbles upon the site where Kamil receives his orders, but also because of Kinza's voice, as she rents her mobile phone to customers in the neigborhood for some extra cash. With this crude mixture of ultra-modern props and activities set in the downtrodden, dusty outskirts of Casablanca that would normally stand for social deprivation and underdevelopment, Bensaïdi achieves a recoding of the place and related tropes toward a deconstructive representation that refutes the common temporal and cultural binaries, caught between progress and tradition, of the common modernist representations.

6

CONCLUSION

Launching a program of industrial film production was considered a national achievement in the former Arab colonies and protectorates. The acquisition of cinematic techniques was a sign of progress, and offered a real opportunity to expand economically. On the political level, cinema was believed to create a platform for counter-representations, giving the formerly colonized a chance to challenge Western dominance, at least on the screen.

However, despite the great efforts that were made, particularly in the immediate post-independence era, Arab filmmaking was only partly able to compete with 'First World' cinema. It has remained greatly dependent on Western imports, technical know-how, evaluation, and partly even on Western financial support. The so-called Third-Worldist anti-colonial cinema did not succeed in resolving the contradiction between cultural promotion, political commitment, and rentability, and was soon eclipsed either by an entirely mainstream-oriented cinema or by the rather anti-authoritarian, deconstructive, and stylistically innovative, yet regionally marginalized, *cinéma d'auteur*.

Nonetheless, mainstream as well as individualist cinema was able to convey elements of native art and culture, and became actively involved in the creation of specific national or cultural identities. Although the medium became part of a mass-mediated culture, and functioned as a means of mass entertainment, commercialism, the obligation of profitability, and competition with Western products, it did not result in a complete imitation of Western cinema, but initiated the reformation of the imported film language according to the needs of local audiences. Artistic means of representation originating in the West have thus been modified by native artistic forms.

The influence of traditional arts on Arab cinema was particularly strong at the time of its foundation. This applies first of all to the post-colonial Egyptian film industry. Local music was worked into films, as were the different popular performing arts and, last but not least, traditional, primarily popular, narrative forms. The regional dialect functioned as a mediator, transforming the Egyptian dialect into a sort of cinematic *lingua franca* understood in many Arab countries, and also contributed to the creation of an Egyptian cultural hegemony, which was later challenged by the development of other regional Arab film industries.

In general, the regional dialects have functioned as agents of the popular arts in Arab cinema. Yet elitist arts, such as classical Arabic poetry, have also been incorporated, though not extensively, into commercial cinema, for example in the musical. In contrast, Islamic visual arts have hardly been utilized. The lack of widespread traditional, figurative, and symbolic modes of representation encouraged the dominance of linguistic means of expression particularly in the beginnings of Arab filmmaking. The ambiguity of the image has often been reduced and geared to a plain legibility via linguistic metaphors and symbols.

The use of native arts in mainstream cinema has, like everything else, been subjected to the mechanisms of supply and demand. Some of these arts have been transformed, just like cinema itself, into a trans-regional mass commodity. Some genres of Arab music, for example, lost their specific local character during this process of constant mixing and reproduction. Despite this fact, some structures and elements of the popular arts which preceded mass-mediated culture have survived in commercial cinema, including the predilection for musical performance, the use of anecdotal inserts, verbal comedy, and character typologies.

In the era of decolonization, Arab *cinéma d'auteur* has attempted to revive indigenous formative artistic means by a conscious utilization of them. It discovered the cultural heritage as a means of formal, or even spiritual, innovation, indicating a new search for cultural identity. However, it has not always been successful in erasing binary antagonisms, such as past and present, tradition and modernity, East and West. Instead, its endeavors have sometimes been led astray by empty aestheticism or eclipsed by the representation of an oppressive sociopolitical reality. The intellectual efforts of this type of filmmaking have been addressed primarily to Western audiences. Its success at Arab box offices has remained limited.

The lack of authenticity imputed to commercial Arab cinema has to be qualified. Not only on the level of formal creation, but also on all the other levels of cinematic production, mixing and mutual penetration between the foreign and the native has taken place, often leading to a cultural revaluation and repackaging of the imported elements. The presentation, for example, of Western dress, habits, and lifestyle does not necessarily mean that traditional ideas have been abandoned. On the contrary, they have sometimes been used to confirm conservative concepts and perceptions. Moreover, certain genres, such as the historical and the religious film, have contributed to the creation of a national consciousness dissociated from the West, and have reinforced traditional values by reinterpreting and mythologizing Arab-Islamic history. A similar function has been allocated to realism, which appeared in most Arab countries immediately after national independence.

Because of its sociopolitical commitment and anti-colonialist attitude, in the early post-colonial era realism was considered, more than other genres, as an expression of national culture. It is true that realism has been concerned with the representation of the indigenous population and the daily life of the underprivileged classes,

which had been neglected during colonial times. However, realism
has only exceptionally achieved an authenticity in the sense of a
pluralist, multiple, and contradictive representation. The visually
and topographically realistic approach has often been subordinated
to state doctrines or political utopias. Realism is measured according to its *iltizam* and not its 'authentic' representation, because, in
Lizbeth Malkmus's words, "a message about reality is mixed up
with cinematic realism."[1] Much more than popular genres—particularly the farce, which tends to evade the production of
meaning—realism has produced clear causal relations as well as
binarisms and antagonist conflict, thus becoming one of the most
faithful supporters of conventional Western drama.

However, this is not to suggest that the development of realism in
the Arab countries is due only to the temporary spread of socialist
ideologies or a result of the encounter with colonialism and Western
art forms, such as realist literature. As in nineteenth-century
Europe, the changed living conditions of the industrial age brought
about a new consciousness of reality in the Arab world. Hence, as
Auerbach states, the big movements of modern times, such as revolutions and wars, in which huge masses of people are involved,
together with modern transportation and the fast transmission of
news, constantly move the world closer together. More and more
people are affected at the same time by the same events.[2] This
development sharpens the consciousness of larger contexts and promotes realist views.

Furthermore, in times of great social change, realism offers handy
models to explain reality. Contrary to traditional or modern epic narrative forms, realist cinematic conventions allow the viewer to enter
into a 'panopticon,' a closed universe that suggests a completely
comprehensible and explicable world. It is no accident that realism
appeared at a time when many Arab countries were attaining national
independence. Realism performs a conserving and reflective function
that is immensely important for the formerly colonized, who were
deprived even of their own image.

"In the contemporary Arab world conserving realism reacts to a double aggression: with the social changes starting after independence under the slogan of a demanding and ambitious modernity the merely external aggression of colonial times turned into an internal aggression."[3] Self-reflection and self-affirmation enabled by realism are not only the result of this aggression, but also help to absorb it.

In the same way as the historical and religious film, realism has contributed to confirming a unitary national identity by creating myths and forming affirmative, often uncritical, self-reflections. On the ideological level, it has varied between the loud demand for cultural revolution and latent attempts at restoring traditional conservative values.

A more subjective, self-critical, and pluralist representation of Arab realities is offered not by realism, but by the *cinéma d'auteur*, which has been encouraged by the failures of the first post-colonial national regimes and the sociopolitical disillusionments summarized to a certain extent in the 1967 defeat. Arab *cinéma d'auteur* strives for more economic and ideological independence, and also attempts to abandon ethnocentrism. Visually and linguistically, it has brought the history of individuals, regions, and marginalized groups increasingly to the fore, thereby underlining regional and hybrid identities.

It has also been at pains to deconstruct dominant nationalist and patriarchal myths and discourses. Personal stories of men and women have gained priority over the collective unitary national history. This is the reason why the *cinéma d'auteur*, much more than any other genre, simultaneously questions both modernist concepts of development and progress and conservative, traditionalist views, without necessarily abandoning a secularly oriented image of mankind. It has mediated the notion of the 'problematic' individual who comes into conflict with his or her surroundings or with his or her self, rather than being a passive creature guided by providence, fate, or social conditions.

Individualist non-conformism has also been expressed on the formal level. Male and female directors increasingly use epic, nonlinear types of narration instead of conventional drama. The omniscient realist discourse has been abandoned in favor of a variety of subjective perspectives. Juxtaposed with individualism, specific, more regional characteristics have entered these art movies. They become visible, for example, in the use of language and topography, in a completely new relation to space. In some works space was even given an essential, contextually structuring function.

The ideas of individuality and originality that define the formal and ideological concepts of the genre correspond to the elitist Western comprehension of arts, automatically pushing the film maker into the position of an unadapted outsider who speaks not for the masses but only for a small, often intellectual or elitist, group. This concept marginalizes the *auteur* film considerably and restricts its influence on native audiences, who still interact primarily with the Egyptian, or Western, mass product.

During the last two decades, however, the latter has witnessed a certain decentralization, curbing the Egyptian monopoly in some places because of the thriving of regional competition, as in Morocco for instance, and because of the introduction of transregional Arab television as well as new media. At the same time, the emergence of different forms of cooperation in production and distribution, as well as some pan-Arab funding opportunities between certain Arab countries, most notably Morocco, Egypt, Tunisia, Lebanon, and the Gulf states, opened new possibilities. However, it also reinforced the interdependence of national and transnational Arab film culture(s) regionally as well on the international level, particularly with Europe. Hence, the Arab—or, better, the MENA (Middle East and North Africa)—film market has, despite all efforts remained marginal to the global film market, with only a few exceptions of individual films that may be considered international productions. Doubtless the hegemony of the big industries, mainly the American, followed by regionally powerful industries such as the Indian, is still defining the overall picture. The same applies to the general dichotomy between the Egyptian and Moroccan main-streams, on the one hand, and European-financed and -distributed Arab art house films, on the other.

Since the turn of the new millennium, Arab cinema has diversi-fied and been put in jeopardy at the same time, for a multitude of reasons. The last two decades have been charged with a number of epoch-making events and sweeping changes for both good and bad. The most important of these is the so-called Arab Spring or Rebellion that started in December 2010, and which brought first hope and then counter-revolution and war, sometimes with unbe-lievable chaos and extreme suffering, to the affected countries, first and foremost Tunisia, Egypt, Yemen, Libya, and Syria. These changes have made previous decisive historical events seem increasingly remote or irrelevant, including the most drastic ones, such as the al-Aqsa Intifada in 2000, the 9/11 attack, the allied inva-sion of Afghanistan and Iraq in 2001 and 2003, the subsequent failure of the Oslo Accords, the construction of the Israeli security wall, and the military strike on culturally vibrant Lebanon in 2006.

Thus, the former political and economic stagnation common to the autocratic Arab regimes that preceded the rebellion has received a strong blow, affecting film culture(s) as much as society in gen-eral. While some Arab 'nations,' like Morocco, have either continued or started discovering 'national' filmmaking, and the idea of a film industry as a source of national pride, others have used it as means to cover up for the failures of their homeland's authoritar-ian regime to provide full civil rights to their citizens, as in Tunisia and Syria before the Arab uprising. At the same time it became evi-dent that even European-financed, individualized Arab filmmaking continued to recycle specific national dramas, for instance the Palestinian or Lebanese search for a homeland and for a national and cultural identity.

In Syria a new exiled generation has started challenging the ear-lier state-monopolized art house cinema. At the same time Algeria and Morocco have witnessed the appearance of Amazigh-speaking films that have gone hand in hand with a cultural awakening of this large indigenous minority. Meanwhile, extreme political changes have led, in the case of Iraq, to a sort of cinematic secession that allowed the collapse of national cinema and the emergence of a genuinely Kurdish cinema based in and funded by northern Iraq.

In addition, the so-called digital turn initiated by the introduction of new technologies, and the profound shifts in production and distribution due to the advent of new players in the field of cinema, among other factors, particularly in the Arab Gulf region, have left a distinctive mark on local film culture. Young talents with innovative ideas and styles have been brought to the fore, while some of the older market structures have changed, rendering national borders more permeable, such as in Saudi Arabia, where a number of female filmmakers have offered insights into a hitherto strongly protected and secluded society. It is primarily also new media that have offered a hand in creating new spaces for national and transnational exchange. Collectively produced films from all over the Arab world, including the Gulf countries, that are rarely or never theatrically released have made use at times of online platforms to access audiences or have merged with other forms of artistic expressions, such as video art presented in galleries and museums. All this has and will continue to influence the sort of cultural and national identity displayed and produced by Arab filmmaking.

ACKNOWLEDGMENTS

The initial research that led to this book could not have been accomplished without the financial support of the Studienstiftung des Deutschen Volkes. I am also very grateful to the Cinématheque Algérienne, the Algerian Cultural Institute, and the Institut du Monde Arabe in Paris.

For their professional support and advice, I would like to thank Ibrahim al-Ariss, Marie Claude Behna, Gabriele Braune, Joachim Colmant, Karin Hörner, Boudjemaa Kareche, Verena Klemm, Albrecht Noth, Muhammad Kamil al-Qalyuni, Kamal Ramzi, Ella Shohat, Robert Stam, and Magda Wassef. My thanks go also to the many filmmakers and cineastes who gave me their time for interviews or provided information when preparing the first edition.

I would also like to thank those who shared their books, materials, time, knowledge, and experience for the second and third edition: Akram Zaatari, Alia Yunis, cAzza al-Hassan, Arsenal Filmverleih (Tübingen, Germany), Ferid Boughedir, Hady Zaccak, Irit Neidhardt, Khalil Benkirane, Laura Marks, Marie-Claude Behna, Mohamed Soueid, Mustafa al-Masnaoui, Magdy Ahmad Ali, Ali'N Productions (Nabil Ayouch), Najwa Najjar, Nizar Hassan, Raed Andoni, Stefan Pethke, Talal al-Muhanna, and many others.

I am also grateful to Ella Shohat and Robert Stam for organizing the conference "The Cinema, the Middle East, and the Transnational Imaginary" in May 2014 at NYU Abu Dhabi that has been particularly inspiring for the leading questions in the updates to this book. Thanks go also to Karima Laachir and Saeed Talajooy for asking me to contribute the article "Resisting Pleasure?" to their volume *Resistance in Contemporary Middle Eastern Cultures. Literature, Cinema, and Music* which laid the groud work for some passages in this book.

My special thanks go as always to my family, my husband Onsi Abou Seif for his precious comments, my son Ani Abou Seif for his patience and humor, my sisters-in-law Nawal and Busayna (Souheir) Abou Seif, my aunt and uncle Irmgard and Karl Schlumberger for their constant and loving support, as well as to my life-long friends: Angelika Bartsch, Angela Kandt, Anna Hoffmann, Daoud Abd El-Sayed, Karima Kamal, Vivian Fouad, Yuergen Lingg.

NOTES

INTRODUCTION

1   Many articles and works on the film making of the Maghreb have been published in France, as a result of its close historical relationship with North Africa. Publications on Iraq and Egypt and even a dictionary, Claude Michel Cluny's *Dictionnaire des nouveaux cinemas arabes* (Paris, 1978) have appeared in French. In the anglophone and German-speaking countries only a few works on Arab cinema have appeared. Erika Richter's *Realistischer Film in Ägypten,* published in 1974 in East Berlin, is more or less a 'classic.' It contains a description and analysis of Egyptian realism, as does Michael Lüder's *Gesellschaftliche Realität im ägyptischen Kinofilm. Von Nasser zu Sadat.* Cairo-based journalist Kirstina Bergmann's *Filmkultur und Filmindustrie in Ägypten* is a popular work on Egyptian Cinema that gives a detailed but rather descriptive presentation of films produced by the Egyptian film industry. Michael Lüders's M.A. thesis *Film und Kino in Ägypten. Eine historische Bestandsaufnahme 1896–1952* contains a mine of precious information about early Egyptian film making.

2   Hashim al-Nahas published his article from this volume as a book: *al-Hawiya al-qawmiya fi-l-sinima al-ᶜarabiya* (Cairo, 1986).

3   *Les 2 écrans* 31, February 1981.

4   Robert Stam, p. 52.

5   Cf. Edward Said, *Orientalism.*

6   Claude Michel Cluny, "al-Sinima al-maghribiya," in Muhammad Kamil al-Qalyubi et al., *al-Sinima al-ᶜarabiya wa-l-ifriqiya,* p. 46.

7   Mostefa Lacheraf, "Du 'Voleur de Bagdad' à 'Omar Gatlato,'" in Guy Henebelle, ed., *Cinémas du Maghreb,* p. 26.

8   Sami Zubaida, "Components of Popular Culture in the Middle East," in Georg Stauth and Sami Zubaida, eds., *Mass Culture, Popular Culture, and Social Life in the Middle East,* p. 155.

9   Ibid.

10 Georg Stuath, "Local Communities and Mass Culture," in Georg Stauth, Sami Zubaida, p. 66.

11 Ibid., p. 67.

12 Michael R. Real, *Mass-Mediated Culture,* p. 209.

13 Mike Featherstone, "Consumer Culture, Symbolic Power, and Universalism," in Georg Stauth, Sami Zubida, p. 35.

CHAPTER 1

1   Mauritania may be included in this category, as the only significant Mauritanian director, Med Hondo, shot his films mainly in France.

2   ᶜAdnan Madanat, "al-Urdun," in *al-Turath al-sinima'i fi-l-watan al-ᶜarabi,* an unpublished study for *al-Ittihad al-ᶜamm li-l-fananin al-ᶜarab* during the 17th International Cairo Film Festival, Cairo, 6–9 December 1993.

3   According to Ibrahim al-ᶜAriss (*Rihla fi-l-sinima al-ᶜarabiya,* p. 44), 161 films had been produced by the mid-1970s.

4   Saudi Arabia was not affected by this agreement due to its unimportance at the time; nor was Libya, which belonged to the Italian sphere of influence. France dominated north-west Africa (the Maghreb) and Syria and Lebanon, while the remaining eleven countries were politically and economically dependent on Great Britain.

5   Ahmad al-Hadari, *Tarikh al-sinima fi Misr,* p. 32.

6   Abdelghani Megherbi, *Les Algériens au miroir du cinéma colonial*, p. 15.

7   Guy Henebelle, *Les cinémas africains en 1972*, p. 177.

8   Ella Shohat, *Israeli Cinema*, p. 15.

9   Megherbi, *Les Algériens*, p. 15.

10 al-Hadari, *Tarikh*, pp. 35 and 64.

11 Ibid., p. 77.

12 Henebelle, *Les cinémas africains*, p. 177.

13 Shohat, *Israeli Cinema*, p. 15.

14 Megherbi, *Les Algériens*, pp. 19–20.

15 Galal Al-Charkawi, *Risala fi tarikh al-sinima al-ᶜarabiya*, p. 16.

16 al-Hadari, *Tarikh*, p. 92.

17 The introduction of television was justified as a means of communication controlled by the state. As with video films, television was watched privately in the family circle, and the threat to morals of a visit to a dark cinema was thus excluded. See Monika Mühlböck, *Die Entwicklung der Massenmedien am Arabischen Golf*, p. 178.

18 Ibid., p. 177.

19 Georges Sadoul, *Cinema in the Arab Countries*, p. 190.

20 Shohat, *Israeli Cinema*, p. 15.

21 al-Hadari, *Tarikh*, p. 75.

22 Henebelle, *Les cinémas africains*, p. 177.

23 al-Hadari, *Tarih*, p. 96.

24 Ibid., p. 120.

25 Muhammad K. al-Qalyubi, "al-Sinima al-ᶜarabiya wa-l-ifriqiya," p. 13, and al-Hadari, *Tarikh*, p. 143.

26 Michael Lüders, *Film und Kino*, p. 13.

27 al-Hadari, *Tarikh*, p. 139.

28 Ibid., p. 148; al-Charkawi, *Risala*, p. 21. Al-Charkawi gives 1922 as the year of production.

29 al-Hadari, *Tarikh*, p. 181.

30 Henebelle, *Les cinémas africains*, p. 146.

31 Jean Aliksan *Tarikh al-sinima al-suriya*, p. 23 ff.

32 Lucienne Khoury, "History of the Lebanese Cinema," in Sadoul, ed., *Cinema*, p. 120. Taking into consideration the contemporary

confessional and ethnic fragmentation of Lebanon, the Lebanese film
critic Mohamed Soueid challenges the categorization of films according to the ethnic origins of each film maker. He sees no reason for
negating the achievements of non-Arab emigrants. Therefore the
works that stem from integrated minorities or individuals are considered in the following as a part of Arab film making unless they are
products of colonial European cinema. Cf. Mohamed Soueid, *al-
Sinima al-mu'adjala*, p. 11 ff.

33 Sunduq da^cm al-sinima, ed., *Banurama al-sinima al-misriya* 27–82.

34 Lüders, *Film und Kino*, p. 40.

35 Sadoul, ed., *Cinema*, p. 287. During the 1980s Egypt produced an
average of sixty films a year.

36 Al-Charkawi, *Risala*, p. 45.

37 Gudrun Krämer, "Studien zum Minderheitenproblem," *Islam 7,
Minderheit, Millet, Nation? Die Juden in Ägypten 1914–1952*,
Wiesbaden, 1982, p. 402 ff.

38 Ibid., p. 31.

39 Samir Farid, "al-Baniya al-asassiya li-l-sinima fi Misr," estimates that
over 100 cinemas existed in 1936.

40 Megherbi, *Les Algériens*, p. 63.

41 Jacob Landau, *Studies in Arab Theater and Cinema*, p. 61.

42 Salah Dehni, "History of the Syrian Cinema," in Sadoul, ed., *Cinema*,
p. 99.

43 Ibid., p. 100.

44 Landau, *Studies*, p. 39.

45 Megherbi, *Lex Algériens*, p. 34.

46 Ibid., p. 264.

47 Henebelle, *Les cinémas africains*, p. 177, gives Luitz Morat and A.
Vercourt as directors of this film and 1923 as the year of production;
Hala Salmane, *Algerian Cinema*, p. 9, gives Georges Bourgeois as
director and 1922 as the year of production, Ahmad Sidjilmasi Idris,
"Filmughrafyat al-sinima al-maghribiya al-aflam al-riwa'iya
(1912–1986)," in *Dirasat sinima'iya* 8, p. 16, gives Luitz Morat as
director and the year of production as 1922.

48 Henebelle, p. 177.
49 Salmane, *Algerian Cinema*, p. 9.
50 Ibid.
51 Ibid., p. 10.
52 P. Murati, quoted in Megherbi, *Les Algériens*, p. 47.
53 Megherbi, *Les Algériens*, p. 47 ff.
54 Ibid., p. 53.
55 Ibid., p. 55 f.
56 Ibid., p. 42.
57 Henebelle, *Les cinemas africains*, p. 178.
58 Ibid., p. 146.
59 Megherbi, *Les Algériens*, p. 57.
60 Ibid., p. 65.
61 Henebelle, *Les cinémas africains*, p. 178.
62 Megherbi, *Les Algériens*, p. 49.
63 Ibid., p. 62 ff.
64 Henebelle, *Les cinémas africains*, p. 178.
65 Guy Henebelle and Khemais Khayati, *Le Palestine et le cinéma*, p. 229 ff.
66 Shohat, *Israeli Cinema*, p. 21 ff.
67 Lotfi Maherzi, *Le cinéma algérien*, p. 62.
68 Ibid., p. 63.
69 Henebelle and Khayati, *Le Palestine et le cinéma*, p. 26.
70 Sadoul, ed., *Cinema*, p. 271 ff.
71 Salah Dehni, "Tadjribat al-sinima fi Suriya," in *al-Ma^criffa* (Damascus) 131 (January 1973), p. 36.
72 Henebelle, pp. 150 and 179.
73 Ibid., p. 150.
74 Neila Ghabri, "La gestion de la SATPEC," p. 14 (Thesis for the Institut de presse et des sciences de l'information, Tunis, 1980).
75 Maherzi, *Le cinéma algérien*, p. 199 f.
76 In Syria unqualified bureaucrats and the private ownership of cinemas cause mainly minor films to be projected (V. Shafik, *Zensierte Träume. 20 Tahre syrischer Film* , p. 29). In Algeria a chronic lack of

foreign currency lead to a decrease of standards. In 1991 for example, the highly indebted public distribution company ENADEC was able to import only fifty-five films. Nationalization also had disadvantages for the management of theaters, in Egypt as well as in Algeria. Some cinemas even had to be closed down (K.Z., "On va au ciné ce soir?" Cinématheque Algérienne, Dossiers, Parc des Salles, p. 14.) Reprivatization of theaters has now started in both countries.

77 Henebelle, *Les cinémas africains,* p. 147 ff.

78 Shafik, *Zensierte Träume,* p. 28.

79 The name is not clear. Boshko Vochinitch is another possibility; see Diana Jabbour, "Syrian Cinema: Culture and Ideology," in Alia Arasoughly, ed., *Critical Film Writing from the Arab World,* p. 44.

80 Maherzi, *Le cinéma algérien,* p. 86.

81 Salmane, *Algerian Cinema,* p. 23.

82 Mouny Berrah, "Algerian Cinema and National Identity," in Arasoughly, *Critical Film Writing,* p. 65.

83 Author's interview with Taufik Salih, Cairo, 12 July 1993.

84 ᶜAbd al-Munᶜim Saᶜd, *al-Mukhridj Ahmad Badr Khan uslubuh min khilal aflamih,* p. 154.

85 The second Syrian silent long feature film, *Under the Sky of Damascus* by ᶜAtta Makka, appeared in 1932, by which time the first Egyptian musical, *The Song of the Heart* (Unshudat al-fu'ad) by Mario Volpi, was ready for distribution.

86 Lizbeth Malkmus states, erroneously, that the notion of *muqawalat,* since it derives from the root *qal* (to speak), expresses the peculiar dependence of Egyptian cinema on language (Lizbeth Malkmus and Roy Armes, *Arab and African Filmmaking,* p. 114).

87 al-Qalyubi, "al-Sinima al-ᶜarabiya," p. 19.

88 Moulay Driss Jaïdi, *Le Cinéma au Maroc,* p. 61.

89 al-Qalyubi, "al-Sinima al-ᶜarabiya," p. 24.

90 Shakir Nouri, *A la recherche du cinéma Iraqien 1945–1984,* 53 ff.

91 Ibid., p. 123.

92 Ibid., p. 122.

93   Wassyla Tamzali, *En attendant Omar Gatlato*, p. 177.

94   Ferid Boughedir, "Les quatre voies du cinéma marocain;" in Guy Henebelle, "Cinémas du Maghreb," p. 208.

95   Ibrahim al-ᶜAriss, *Rihla fi-l-sinima al-ᶜarabiya*, p. 44. Al-ᶜAriss's figure differs from that quoted by Zahir Henry Azar in *Malaf al-sinima al-Lubnaniya*, Beirut (probably late 1970s), where the figure given is sixty-five films for the same period. Al-ᶜAriss's figure may include films by Lebanese directors produced and shot abroad.

96   Ibid., p. 45.

97   Ibid., p. 48.

98   Soueid, *al-Sinima al-mu'adjala*, p. 52 ff.

99   See Ella Shohat, "Post-Third Worldist Culture: Gender, Nation, and the Cinema," in M. Jacqui Alexander, ed., *Feminist Genealogies, Colonial Legacies, Democratic Futures*.

100 Khemais Khayati, *Salah Abou Seif Cinéaste Egyptien*, p. 179.

101 Ibid. p. 183.

102 Abdou B., "Entretien avec Ahmed Rachedi," p. 16.

103 Maherzi, *Le cinéma algérien*, p. 278.

104 Salmane, *Algerian Cinema*, p. 29.

105 This boom ended abruptly in 1979 and production fell to the same level as in the 1960s. This may have been due to the breakdown during the Civil War of the Lebanese film industry, whose studios and distribution companies were bases for Syrian producers.

106 Acrame, "Denationaliser le cinéma," *Les 2 écrans* 7 (November 1978), p. 38.

107 al-Qalyubi, "al-Sinima al-ᶜarabiya," p. 26.

108 Nouri, *A la recherche du cinéma Iraqien*, p. 60.

109 Ibid., p. 70

110 Ibid, p. 165.

111 Ghabri, "La gestion de la SATPEC," p. 14.

112 Author's interview with Ahmed Attia (producer), Tunis, 30 October 1990.

113 Jaïdi, *Le Cinéma au Maroc*, p. 140.

114 Ibid., p. 116.

115 Viola Shafik, "Realität und Film im Ägypten der 80er Jahre," p. 74.

116 Nouri Bouzid and Youssef Chahine were accused of zionism by some critics after having presented a positive image of Jews in *The Man of Ashes* and *Alexandria Why?*

117 Soueid, *al-Sinima al-mu'adjala*, p. 85.

118 Nouri, *A la recherche du cinéma Iraqien*, p. 118.

119 Berrah, *Algerian Cinema*, p. 75; see also Abdou B., "Le dernier tabou," *Les 2 écrans* 44, April 1982, p. 20.

120 Although the director makes the young girl show her breasts, he generally avoids any erotic allusions in the gender relations.

121 Author's interview with Nouri Bouzid, Tunis, 6 November 1992.

121 Nouri, *A la recherche du cinéma Iraqien*, p. 118.

123 Berrah, *Algerian Cinema*, p. 63.

124 Maherzi, *Le cinéma algérien*, p. 209 ff.

125 Salmane *Algerian Cinema*, p. 41.

126 Jaïdi, *Le Cinéma au Maroc*, p. 120,, and Abdelghani Megherbi, *Le miroir apprivoisé*, p. 95.

127 Cf. Shafik, "Realität und Film," p. 74.

128 Jaïdi, *Le Cinéma au Maroc*, p. 142.

129 See Henebelle, *Les cinémas africains*, p. 182.

130 Jaïdi, *Le Cinéma au Maroc*, p. 115.

131 Ibdi, p. 127 f.

132 Ibid., p. 124.

133 Nouri, *A la recherche du cinéma Iraqien*, p. 82.

134 Megherbi, *Le miroir apprivoisé*, p. 15 Cinemas only equipped with 16 mm projectors are not included.

135 The Documentation Center for Cultural Development of the Tunisian Ministry of Culture (Markaz al-dirasat wa-l-tauthiq li-l-tanmiya al-thaqafiya).

136 Ghabri, "La gestion de la SATPEC," p. 73.

137 Hans Gunther Pflaum, *Film in der Bundesrepublik Deutschland*, Bonn, 1985, p. 129.

138 Samir Farid, "al-Baniya al-asassiya li-l-sinima fi Misr," p. 2.

139 Jaïdi, *Le Cinéma au Maroc*, p. 154.

140 Ibid., p. 122.

141 Monique Henebelle, "La nouvelle vague du cinéma tunisien," *L'afrique litteraire et artistique* 25 (October 1972), p. 81.

142 Documentation Center for Cultural Development of the Tunisian Ministry of Culture.

143 See Viola Shafik, "Variety or Unity: Minorities in Egyptian Cinema," forthcoming in *Orient* I/98, Hamburg, 1998.

CHAPTER 2

1 "Fotografien betrachten," in Friedrich Knilli, ed., *Semiotik des Films*, p. 251.

2 Egyptian television started its first transmission in July 1960.

3 Mohamed Aziza, *L'Image et l'Islam*, p. 126.

4 Lacheraf, "Du 'Voleur de Bagdad' à 'Omar Gatlato,'" p. 26. Lacheraf's formulation is rather too categorical since visual representation was not entirely absent from Arab culture.

5 Richard Ettinghausen, "The Man-Made Setting," in Bernard Lewis, *The World of Islam*, p. 62.

6 Ibid., p. 57 and Oleg Grabar, *The Formation of Islamic Art*, p. 74.

7 Van Reenen, *Das Bilderverbot*, p. 56.

8 Grabar, *The Formation of Islamic Art*, p. 83.

9 Ibid., p. 86.

10 Ibid., p. 82.

11 Aziza, *L'Image et l'Islam*, p. 38.

12 Ettinghausen, "The Man-Made Setting," p. 62.

13 Middle Eastern Christians developed figurative modes of representation used mainly in the religious context. Although theoretically accessible to everybody, this art has been culturally marginalized.

14 al-Charkawi, *Risala fi tarikh al-sinima al-ᶜarabiya*, p. 27 ff.

15 Landau, *Studies*, p. 164.

16 In 1986 the representation of all prophets mentioned in the Quran was prohibited.

17 Landau, *Studies*, p. 164 ff.

18 Monika Mühlböck, *Die Entwicklung der Massenmedien am arabis-chen Golf*, p. 178. See Chapter 1, n. 17.

19 ᶜAbd al-Munᶜim Fuda, *al-Fatawi*, p. 1555.

20 Wadjih Khayri, "al-Haram wa-l-halal fi-l-sinima."

21 Mühlböck, *Die Entwicklung der Massenmedien*, p. 95.

22 Shaukat al-Rabiᶜi, *al-Fann al-tashkili al-muᶜasir fi-l-watan al-ᶜarabi 1885–1985*, p. 19.

23 Ettinghausen, "The Man-Made Setting," p. 57.

24 See Mohamed Scharabi, "'Islamische' Architektur und darstellende Kunst der Gegenwart," in Werner Ende and Udo Steinbach, eds., *Der Islam in der Gegenwart*, p. 626 ff.

25 Ettinghausen, "The Man-Made Setting," p. 68.

26 Ibid., p. 69.

27 François Guérif, Entretien avec Nacer Khemir, p. 17.

28 Ibid., p. 16.

29 Ibid., p. 16.

30 Grabar, *The Formation of Islamic Art*, p. 193.

31 Ibid., p. 187 ff.

32 Ibid., p. 179.

33 Ibid., p. 191.

34 I. M. Peters, "Bild und Bedeutung," in Knilli, ed., *Semiotik des Films*, p. 56.

35 Daniel Dayan, "The Tutor-Code of Classical Cinema," in Bill Nichols, ed., *Movies and Methods (I)*, p. 444.

36 Stefano Bianca, *Architektur und Lebensform im islamischen Stadtwesen*, p. 126.

37 Cf. Roland Barthes, "Rethorik des Bildes," in Wolfgang Kemp, *Theorie der Fotografie III*, p. 138–48.

38 Gerhard Kurz, *Metapher, Allegorie, Symbol*, p. 83.

39 Charles Pellat, "Jewellers with Words," in Bernard Lewis, *The World óf Islam*, p. 145.

40 Hamilton A. R. Gibb, *Studies on the Civilization of Islam*, p. 154 ff.

41 Salma Jayushi, *Trends and Movements in Modern Arabic Poetry II*, Leiden, 1977, p. 475.

42 Hanan Mikhail-Ashrawi, *The Contemporary Literature of Palestine,* Ann Arbor, 1983, p. 15.

43 Roger Allen, *The Arabic Novel. A Historical and Critical Introduction,* p. 71.

44 Kurz, *Metapher, Allegorie, Symbol,* p. 83.

45 Christian Metz, "Current Problems of Film Theory," in Nichols, ed., *Movies and Methods (I),* p. 571.

46 *Sunduq al-dunya* means literally 'world box.' It is a long wooden box with peepholes, through which images can be watched.

47 Curt Prüfer, *Ein ägyptisches Schattenspiel,* p. xiii.

48 Ibid., p. vff.

49 Landau, *Studies,* p. 9.

50 Ibid. p. 9 ff.

51 See ᶜAdil Abu Shanab, *Masrah 'arabi qadim. Karakuz,* p. 197–98.

52 Ibid., p. 174.

53 Ibid., p. 22.

54 ᶜAli al-Raᶜi, *al-Masrah fi-l-watan al-ᶜarabi,* p. 40.

55 Landau, *Studies,* p. 2 ff.

56 ᶜAbd al-Muᶜti Shaᶜrawi, *al-Masrah al-misri al-muᶜasir,* p. 31.

57 Ibid., p. 46.

58 ᶜAli al-Raᶜi, *Finun al-kumidiya. Min khayal al-zil ila Nagib al-Rihani,* p. 81.

59 Mohamed Aziza, *al-Islam wa-l-masrah,* p. 22 ff.

60 Shaᶜrawi, *al-Masrah al-misri al-muᶜasir,* p. 34.

61 Ignace Goldziher, *A Short History of Classical Arabic Literature,* p. 87 ff.

62 Cf. al-Raᶜi, *Finun al-kumidiya,* p. 10 ff.

63 Cf., among others, al-Raᶜi, *Finun al-kumidiya,* p. 174.

64 Landau, *Studies,* p. 85.

65 Ibid., p. 94.

66 Ibid., p. 98.

67 Cf., among others, al-Raᶜi, *al-Masrah,* p. 545.

68 Landau, *Studies,* p. 101 ff.

69 al-Raᶜi, *al-Masrah,* p. 511.

70 Landau, *Studies*, p. 91.

71 This term signifies a non-Arabic speaking Nubian or Sudanese person.

72 It means 'foreigner' but is mainly attributed to Europeans.

73 Coptic bookkeepers were unpopular due to their traditional role as tax collectors since the Islamization of Egypt.

74 See Prüfer, *Ein ägyptisches Schattenspiel* p. xiii.

75 al-Raᶜi, *Finun al-kumidiya*, p. 46 ff.

76 See Landau, *Studies*, p. 51.

77 al-Raᶜi, *Finun al-kumidiya*, p. 270.

78 See C. Prüfer, p. xiv, and Abu Shanab, *Masrah ᶜarabi qadim*, p. 179.

79 Dehni, *Tadjiribat al-sinima fi Suriya*, p. 36.

80 Not to be confused with an Egyptian film of the same name by Daoud Abd El-Sayyed, released in 1983.

81 Unpublished interview by the critic Kamal Ramzi during the Damascus Film Festival in November 1991.

82 Similar things are reported about Tunisian shadow plays: "While Muslims were hardly ever reviled by Karagöz, Jews often were. The latter tried to get the better of Karagöz, who however, saw through their devices. The Maltese were treated even more execrably in those plays, the spectator probably, in their derision, identifying the Maltese scapegoat with all European Christians in Tunis." (Landau, *Studies*, p. 41).

83 Cf. Landau, *Studies*, p. 35 ff.

84 Anneliese Novak, *Die amenikanische Filmfarce*, p. 28 ff.

85 See Mikhail Bakhtin, *Literatur und Karneval*.

86 Ibid., p. 16.

87 Because of the 'nauseating excess' and 'frankly sexual expressions,' ᶜAdil Abu Shanab made considerable abridgements. (Abu Shanab, Masrah ᶜarabi qadim, p. 75).

88 Landau, *Studies*, p. 41 ff.

89 Ibid., p. 41, and Abu Shanab, *Masrah ᶜarabi qadim*, p. 57.

90 Nouri, *A la recherche du cinéma iraqien*, p. 18 ff.

91 See Novak, *Die amerikanische Filmfarce*, p. 30.

92 Ferid Boughedir and Mustapha Nagbou, "Le 'Nouveau Théâtre,'" in Guy Henebelle, *Cinémas du Maghreb*, p. 192.

93 Berrah, *Algerian Cinema*, p. 40.

94 Mouny Berrah, Interview du collectif "Nouveau Théâtre," p. 38.

95 Boughedir and Nagbou, "Le 'Nouveau Théâtre,' " p. 192.

96 Berrah, *Algerian Cinema*, p. 40.

97 Boughedir and Nagbou, "Le 'Nouveau Théâtre,' " p. 190.

98 Mohamed Soueid, *al-Sinima al-mu'adjala*, p. 15 ff.

99 Ibid., p. 123.

100 Robert Stam, *Subversive Pleasures. Bakhtin, Cultural Criticism, and Film*, p. 79.

101 The distribution title is *Dananir*, but the film was originally entitled *Harun, al-Rashid—The Story of Dananir* (Harun al-Rashid—qissat Dananir).

102 Reda Bensmaïa, *Cinéma algérien et "caractére national"*, p. 16.

103 Hamilton A. R. Gibb and Jacob Landau, *Arabische Literaturgeschichte*, p. 234 ff.

104 Bensmaïa, *Cinéma algérien*, p. 14.

105 Ibid., p. 14. "Ouach" derives from Berber, "rak" from Arabic, and "bian" from French.

106 Frantz Fanon, *Schwarze Haut, weiße Masken*, p. 15.

107 John P. Entelis, *Algeria. The Revolution Institutionalized*, p. 93 ff.

108 G. Rahat, "Quel avenir pour le cinéma algérien?" in *al-Moudjahid* 22.

109 Berrah, "Algerian Cinema," p. 70.

110 Bensmaïa, *Cinéma algérien*. p. 21.

111 Kamel Benabdessadok, "Culture orale et cinéma," *Les 2 écans* 25, p. 25.

112 "A'dar a'ul saᶜit ma infak zurar il-djakitta?"

113 "La, la, zurar djakittit ih! Biy'ulu man fac Zayd yamshi yaᶜni fidil Zayd yimshi lihad ma hifyit riglih, man fak ᶜUmar ya'kul yaᶜni ᶜUmar ᶜagebu al-akl fidil yiruss fi-illi-'uddamuh wi balatt ᶜala al-siniya wi lizi' fi kursi al-sufra."

114   In the same film, the representative of power, a pasha and amateur gardener, is symbolically overthrown and humiliated when the teacher Hamam derides him, not knowing his real position.

115   Stam, *Subversive Pleasures,* p. 68.

116   Ibid., p. 59.

117   Joachim Paech, *Literatur und Film,* p. 141.

118   Stam, *Subversive Pleasures,* p. 69.

119   See Ives Thoraval, *Regards sur le cinéma égyptien, Beirut,* 1975, p. 87 ff.

120   See Kurz, *Metapher, Allegorie, Symbol,* p. 9.

121   *Hadafni bi-l-kubbaya ^cayiz yihdifni dilwa'ti bi-l-talaga?*

122   *La hadd Allah ya si Ghadab Allah ib^cid ^can sitt Masha' Allah!*

123   *Dah inti ma tikayifhush ila ahwittik, ma tirawa'hush ila dihkittik— yib'a tibalaghih il-khabbar shughlanit hadrittik!*

124   Pellat, "Jewellers with Words," p. 142.

125   Hugo von Hoffmannsthal, in Stefano Bianca, *Architektur und Lebensform im islamischen Stadtwesen,* p. 86.

126   This served for intellectual instruction.

127   Cf. Heinz und Sophia Grotzfeld, *Die Erzählungen aus "Tausendundeiner" Nacht.*

128   Cf. Abderrahmane Djelfaoui, "Le mystère sans demesure," Les 2 écrans 53, p. 35.

129   Ibid., p. 35.

130   Georg Seeßlen, *Kino der Gefühle,* p. 23.

131   Cf. Mohammed Aziza, *al-Islam wa-l-masrah.*

132   The notion of Middle Cinema is used by Indian film critics to describe directors who work under commercial conditions but try to address relevant social or political topics. In my view, this is a constructive definition to apply to Egyptian cinema because not all committed Egyptian directors since the late 1970s can be assigned to genre categories such as New Realism.

133   Literally, the title means 'who comes from the East.' It refers to the East wind.

134   See Ferid Boughedir, "Panorama des cinémas maghrébins," in

Mouny Berrah, Jacques Lévy, Claude-Michel Cluny, *Les cinémas arabes*, CinémAction 43, pp. 59–71.

135 The word 'Gatlato' *(qatlatu)* is a colloquial variant of the classical Arabic *qatalathu* (she killed him) and was introduced by the French title of the film ("Omar Gatlato"). It abbreviates the expression *ᶜUmar, qatalathu al-rudjula,* meaning 'Omar, who was killed by virility.' However, as Mouny Berrah points out, the colloquial *rudjula* "is too quickly reduced to machismo by Western critics, when in fact the subject is gang values, of which dignity is the center-piece—a value system that constitutes the base of popular music, and codifies the everyday life of young people around the respect of others, the given promise, faithfulness in love, and unbreakable friendships. These values are supported by a special, precise vocabulary that only the 'initiated,' and particularly the masters of popular music, possess," (In Alia Arasoughly, ed., *Crtical Film Writing,* p. 77).

136 *Chaabi (shaᶜbi)* means 'popular'—of the people—and describes here an Algerian musical genre.

137 Michael Lüders, *Film und Kino in Ägypten,* p. 52.

138 Salah Ezz Eddine, "La Role de la Musique dans le Film Arabe," in Sadoul, ed., *Cinema,* p. 157.

139 Ibid., p. 159.

140 Ibid., p. 160 ff.

141 There are no 'Bedouin' rhythms. According to Dr. Gabriele Braune from the Institut for Music Ethnology in Berlin, in Egypt this notion describes Arab rhythms, those from the Arab peninsula. (Personal correspondence, 2 July 1992).

142 Ezz Eddine, "La Rôle de la Musique," p. 162.

143 Muhammad al-Sayyid Shusha, *Ruwwad wa ra'idat al-sinima al-mis-riya,* p. 72.

144 al-Charkawi, *Risala fi tarikh al-sinima al-ᶜarabiya,* p. 164.

145 *Djariya (plural, djawari)* means literally maid or slave.

146 Soueid, *al-Sinima al-mu'adjala,* p. 21.

147 Richter, *Realistischer Film in Ägypten,* p. 39.

148   Ezz Eddine, "La Rôle de la Musique," p. 158.

149   Lacheraf, "Du 'Voleur du Baghdad' à 'Omar Gatlato,'" p. 31.

150   Mustapha Chelbi, *Culture et mémoire collective au Maghreb*, p. 156.

151   Teshome Gabriel, "Towards a Critical Theory of Third World Films." In Jim Pines and Paul Willemann, eds., *Questions of Third Cinema*, p. 31.

152   ᶜAli al-Raᶜi, *al-Kumidiya al-murtadjala*, p. 19.

153   Landau, *Studies*, p. 71.

154   Ibid., p. 91.

155   Cf. Helga de la Motte-Haber, *Filmmusik*.

156   de la Motte-Haber, p. 144.

157   Both examples were suggested by G. Braune, personal correspondence.

158   Cf. A. Shiloah, "The Dimension of Sound," in Bernard Lewis, ed., *The World of Islam*, p. 162 ff.

159   Habib Hassan Touma, *Die Musik der Araber*, p. 21.

160   Braune, personal correspondence.

161   Ibid.

162   According to legend, in spite of the Caliph's prohibition a slave of Djaᶜfar wrote a lament in vernacular Arabic that is supposed to be the first mawwal. However, the poem Umm Kulthum sings in this place is not a *mawwal*, but a classical Arabic poem set to music. (See Mohamed Bencheneb, "Mawaliya, Mawwal," in *Enzyklopädie des Islam*, Leipzig, 1913, p. 484).

163   *Rahalat ᶜank sadjiᶜat al-tuyyur / wa dhawat fik yaniᶜat al-zuhhur / ah ya qasr wa-l-hayatu suttur / [...] / mat fik al-hawa' wa daᶜat fik amani / kunna ahla min ibtisam al-zuhhur.* The square brackets indicate a verse that could not be reconstructed from listening.

164   Braune, personal correspondence.

165   Abbas Fadhil Ibrahim, "Trois mélos égyptiens observés à la loupe," in Mouny Berrah and Jacques Lévy, *Les cinémas arabes et Grand Maghreb*, p. 122.

166   Shiloah, "The Dimension of Sound," p. 170.

167   Not to be confused with an Iraqi musical genre of the same name.

168 Touma, *Die Musik der Araber,* p. 66.

169 Ibid., pp. 71–72.

170 al-Charkawi, *Risala fi tarikh al-sinima al-ᶜarabiya,* p. 171.

171 ᶜAbd al-Munᶜim Saᶜd, *al-Mukhridj Ahmad Badr Khan uslusbuh min khilal aflamuh,* p. 144.

172 Ibid., p. 45.

173 Lüders, *Film und Kino in Ägypten,* p. 46. Badrakhan even sets up the rule that the instrumental introduction announcing the general mood of the song should not exceed ten seconds. The intermezzo is limited to five seconds. (Saᶜd, *al-Mukhridj Ahmad Badr Khan,* p. 44).

174 al-Charkawi, *Risala fi tarikh al-sinima al-ᶜarabiya,* p. 64.

175 Shusha, *Ruwwad wa ra'idat al-sinima al-misriya,* p. 69.

176 Braune, personal correspondence.

177 Shusha, *Ruwwad wa ra'idat al-sinima al-misriya,* p. 72.

178 al-Charkawi, "History of the U.A.R. Cinema 1896–1962," in Sadoul, ed., *Cinema,* p. 89.

179 Ezz Eddine, "La Role de la Musique dans le Film Arabe," p. 166.

180 Chelbi, *Culture et mémoire collective au Maghreb,* p. 155.

181 Author's interview with Assia Djebar, Paris, October 1991.

182 Ibid.

183 Later, Djebar introduced a similar principle of structuring to her literature, for example in her novel *Fantasia* (1985).

184 H. G. Farmer, "Nawba," in *Enzyklopädie des Islam,* Leipzig, 1913, p. 957 ff.

185 As this text is a quotation, the French terms have been kept. The correct description used by Farmer are in brackets.

186 Wassayla Tamzali, "*La nouba des femmes de Mont Chenoua.* Notes prisant pendant le tournage, Tipasa, Mars 1977," p. 46.

CHAPTER 3

1 See Paech, *Literatur und Film,* p. 27 ff.

2 Ibid., p. 30.

3 This is an originally Arab subject.

4 Kamal Ramzi, *al-Masadir al-adabiya fi-l-aflam al-misriya*, p. 122 ff.

5 Elisabeth Frenzel, *Stoff-, Motiv- und Symbolforschung*, p. 49.

6 Ibid., p. 49.

7 Ibid., p. 47.

8 See Elisabeth Frenzel, *Motive der Weltliterature*, Stuttgart, 1976, p. 450.

9 Ibid., p. 439 ff.

10 Al-Charkawi, *Risala fi tarikh al-sinima al-ᶜarabiya*, p. 109.

11 The of temporary rebellion against the father's reign may American melodrama (cf. SeeBlen, *Kino der Gefuhle*), similarities are less the result of plagiarism than of comparable social conditions.

12 Abdou B., "Der algerische Film: Thema und Ausführung," in *Film in Algerien ab 1970, Kinemathek* 57, p. 4.

13 Saᶜid Murad, "Malamih al-waqiᶜiya fi-l-sinima al-suriya," in al-Djamiᶜa al-tunisiya li-nawadi al-sinima, ed., *al-Waqiᶜiya fi-l-sinima al-ᶜarabiya*, p. 42.

14 Al-ᶜAriss, *Rihla fi-l-sinima al-ᶜarabiya*, p. 46.

15 Nouri, *A la recherche du cinéma iraqien 1945–85*, p. 134 ff.

16 Colin MacCabe, "Realism and the Cinema," *Screen*, Vol. 15, No. 2, 1974.

17 Christopher Williams, *Realism and the Cinema*, p. 157.

18 See Paech, *Literatur und Film*, p. 79.

19 André Bazin, *What is cinema?*, p. 22 ff, p. 32.

20 Raymond Williams, *A Lecture on Realism*, p. 64 ff.

21 Terry Lovell, *Pictures of Reality*, p. 66.

22 Ibid., p. 68.

23 Ibid., p. 76 ff.

24 See Sunduq daᶜm al-sinima, ed., *Banurama al-sinima al-misriya* 2782.

25 The circumscription of realist films is not simple, because some works constantly make use of stylistic means of other genres, like comedy, melodrama, and police film. Films of this sort are for example *The Beast* by Abu Seif and *Struggle in the Valley* by Chahine.

26 See Viola Shafik, "Realität und Film," p. 93.

27 al-Charkawi, *Risala fi tarikh al-sinima al-ᶜarabiya*, p. 78.
28 Cited in Samir Farid, *Nahw manhadj ᶜilmi li-kitabat tarikhuna al-sinima'i*, p. 152.
29 Erich Auerbach, *Mimesis. Dargestellte Wirkichkeit in der abendländischen Literatur*, p. 25.
30 Lüders, *Film und Kino*, p. 63.
31 Farid, *Nahw manhadj ᶜilmi li-kitabat tarikhuna al-sinima'i*, p. 152.
32 Gibb, *Studies on the Civilization of Islam*, p. 273.
33 Ibid., p. 292.
34 Hilary Kilpatrick, The Modern Egyptian Novel, p. 23.
35 Lüders, *Film und Kino*, p. 31.
36 Hashim al-Nahas, *Nagib Mahfouz ᶜala al-shasha*, p. 13.
37 Ibid., p. 28 ff.
38 Ibid., p. 16.
39 Ibid., p. 28.
40 Claude-Michel Cluny, *Dictionnaire des nouveaux cinémas arabes*, p. 239.
41 Author's interview with Salah Abu Seif, Cairo, 2 March 1988.
42 Youssef Chahine also adapted two scripts by Mahfouz in his films *Djamila Bouhreid* (1958) and *Saladin* (al-Nasir Salah al-Din, 1963). These works do not belong to the realist genre (al-Nahas, *Nagib Mahfouz*, p. 28 ff).
43 Egyptian television, Channel 1, *Dhakirat al-sinima*, 4 September 1992.
44 Bazin, *What is cinema?*, p. 33.
45 Shooting on location is affected by inconveniencies such as noise and crowds of curious observers. Technical conditions for camerawork and lighting are far from ideal.
46 Thomas Geidel, "Ägypten wie es leibt und lebt," in *Die Tageszeitung*, Berlin, January 27, 1986.
47 Author's interview, Cairo, 20 January 1988.
48 Kilpatrick, *The Modern Egyptian Novel*, p. 126 ff.
49 Khémais Khayati, *Salah Abou Seif Cinéaste Egyptien*, p. 180.
50 Ibid., p. 118.

51 Mustafa Badawi, "The concept of Fate in Modern Egyptian Literature," in Hartmut Fähndrich, *Die Vorstellung vom Schicksal,* Bern, 1983, p. 63.

52 Shafik, "Realität und Film," p. 104.

53 Ibid., p. 94.

54 Ahmed Bedjaoui, "Silences et Balbutiements," in Miloud Mimoun, ed., *France-Algérie,* p. 30 ff.

55 Maherzi, *Le Cinéma Algérien,* p. 263.

56 Abdou B., "Der algerische Film: Thema und Ausführung," p. 9.

57 Maherzi, *Le Cinéma Algérien,* p. 281.

58 Stephen Heath, "Film: the Art of the Real," p. 18.

59 *Khammas* peasants are leaseholders who are allowed to keep one fifth of the harvest.

60 Interview with A. Tolbi, in *Cahiers du cinéma,* No. 266–67, May 1976, and Maherzi, *Le Cinéma Algérien,* p. 250.

61 According to Mouny Berrah, Zinet's unusual choice of style and location, i.e., the streets of Algiers, was mainly due to the fact that his film was commissioned by the mayor of Algiers and not by the ONCIC (in Arasoughly, ed., *Critical Film Writing,* p. 76).

62 Lacheraf, "Du 'Voleur du Baghdad' à 'Omar Gatlato,'" in Henebelle, *Cinémas du Maghreb,* p. 34.

63 Murad, "Malamih al-waqiⁿiya fi-l-sinima al-suriya," in al-Djamiⁿa al-tunisiya li-nawadi al-sinima, ed., *al-Waqiⁿiya fi-l-sinima al-ⁿarabiya,* p. 42.

64 Munir al-Saⁿidanni, "al-Ishkaliya al-djamaliya fi-l-sinima al-waqiⁿiya al-ⁿarabiya," in al-Djamiⁿa al-tunisiya li-nawadi al-sinima, ed., *al-Waqiⁿiya fi-l-sinima al-ⁿarabiya,* p. 82.

65 According to Taufik Salih the notion *al-sinima al-badila* was coined at the first hand by the Egyptian film critic Samir Farid who was a founding member of the Egyptian New Cinema Society himself. (Author's interview with Taufik Salih, Cairo, 12 July 1993.)

66 Al-Saⁿidanni, op. cit., p. 82.

67 Soueid, *al-Sinima al-mu'adjala,* p. 41.

68 Cf., Aliksan, *Tarikh al-sinima al-suriya,* p. 55 ff.

69 Moshe Ma'oz, "The emergence of Modern Syria" in Moshe Ma'oz and Avner Yaniv, eds., *Syria under Assad*, p. 30.

70 Murad, op. cit., p. 47.

71 Allen, *The Arabic Novel*, pp. 49 and 74.

72 The literal translation of the novel's title is "Men in the Sun" (Rigjal fi-l-shams).

73 Cluny, *Dictionnaire des nouveaux cinémas arabes*, p. 109.

74 Murad, op. cit., p. 43.

75 Nouri, *A la recherché du cinema iraqien*, p. 137.

76 *Alyam* is a vernacular version of *al-ayam*, 'the days.'

77 Jaïdi, *Le Cinéma au Maroc*, p. 114.

78 Henebelle, "Les cinémas africains en 1972," p. 181.

79 Cf. Peter von Oertzen, "Geschichte und politisches Bewußtsein," in Malte Ristau, ed., *Identität durch Geschichte*, p. 16.

80 Detlef Hoffmann, "Geschichtsbewußtsein – Identitätsfindung," in Ristau, ed., p. 30.

81 Alfred Georg Frei, "Alltag – Region – Politik," in Ristau, ed., p. 85.

82 Cf. Gibb and Landau, *Arabische Literaturgeschichte*.

83 Kamal Ramzi, "al-Shakhsiyat al-tarikhiya fi-l-sinima al-ᶜarabiya," in *Shu'un ᶜarabiya* 26, p. 81.

84 Ignace Goldziher, *A Short History to Classical Arabic Literature*, p. 74.

85 Charles Pellat, "Jewellers of Words," in Lewis, ed., *The World of Islam*, p. 145.

86 Bencheneb, "Mawaliya, Mawwal," in *Enzyklopädie des Islam*, Leipzig, 1913, p. 867.

87 Goldziher, *A Short History of Classical Arabic Literature*, p. 73.

88 Reinhard Hesse, "Adieu Bonaparte," in *Die Tageszeitung, Berlin*, 21 May 1985.

89 Cf. Natalie Zemon Davis, "'Jede Ähnlichkeit mit lebenden oder toten Personen...': Der Film und die Herausforderung der Authentizität," in Rainer Rother, *Bilder schreiben Geschichte: Der Historiker im Kino*, p. 56.

90 Cf. Said, *Orientalism*.

91   Cf. Soumaya Ramadan, "al-Hamla al-firinsiya ᶜala Misr: qira'a min mandhur nasawi," in Multaqa al-mar'a wa-l-zakira, ed., *Zaman al-nisa'*, Cairo, 1998.

92   Cf. Viola Shafik, "Youssef Chahine: Barocke Obsessionen."

93   Cf. Ramzi, "al-Shakhsiyat al-tarikhiya fi-l-sinima al-ᶜarabiya," p. 79 ff.

94   Hadiths are documented utterances of the Prophet.

95   *al-djanna li-man ataᶜanni wa law kana ᶜabdan habashiyan; al-nar li-man ᶜasani wa law kana sharifan qurayshiyan.*

96   *al-Tawhid* is the central Muslim confession affirming Allah's attribute as the One and Only.

97   Reynold A. Nicholson, *A Literary History of the Arabs*, p. 234.

98   Ironically, this concept corresponds to a French political strategy during the Algerian war that tried to assimilate native Algerians by defining them as 'Francais Musulman' (French Muslims) (see Abdelghani Megherbi, *Les Alériens au miroir du cinéma colonial*, p. 53).

99   Issam A. Sharif, *Algerien vom Populismus zum Islam*, p. 121.

100 Maherzi, *Le Cinéma algérien*, p. 28.

101 Ibid., p. 279.

102 Ibid., p. 235.

103 Roland Barthes, *Mythen des Alltags*, p. 130–31.

104 Maherzi, *Le Cinéma algérien*, p. 263.

105 *Zerda* in the Algerian vernacular is a celebration at which numerous guests are honored with generous hospitality, dance, and music.

106 Freunde der deutschen Kinemathek Berlin, ed., 13. *Internationales Forum des jungen Films* 31, Berlin, 1983.

107 Ibid.

108 Marc Ferro, "Gibt es eine filmische Sicht der Geschichte?" in Rother, *Bilder schreiben Geschichte*, p. 22.

109 Andrew Tudor, "Genre and Critical Methodology, in Bill Nichols, ed., *Movies and Methods I*, p. 123.

110 Thomas Elsaesser, *New German Cinema*, p. 41.

111 Ibid., p. 43.

112 This notion was introduced in 1948 by the French film maker Alexandre Astruc (Cf. Claude Beylie, *Les Maîtres du cinéma français,* Paris, 1990, p. 141).

113 Elsaesser, *New German Cinema,* p. 43.

114 Andrew Sarris, "Towards a Theory of Film History," in Nichols, ed., *Movies and Methods I,* p. 244.

115 Ibid., p. 247.

116 Ibid.

117 Elsaesser, *New German Cinema,* p. 42.

118 Cf. Manthia Diavara, *African Cinema,* Bloomington, 1992.

119 Cf. Mouny Berrah, ed., *Les cinémas arabes et Grand Maghreb,* and Claude-Michel Cluny, *Dictionnaire des nouveaux cinémas arabes.*

120 Nouri Bouzid, "Sinima al-waᶜy bi-l-hazina," in al-Djamiᶜa al-tunisiya li-nawadi al-sinima, ed., *al-Waqiᶜiya fi-l-sinima al-ᶜarabiya,* and Samir Farid, "Min al-sinima al-djadida ila al-waqiᶜiya al-djadida."

121 Abdou B., "Der algerische Film," p. 9, and Berrah, "Algerian Cinema: Five Landmarks between Hollywood and Cairo," p. 34.

122 Samir Farid, "al-Zilal ᶜala al-djanib al-akhar wa tatawwur sinima al-shabab fi Misr."

123 Saᶜid Murad, "Malamih al-waqiciya fi-l-sinima al-suriya," p. 42.

124 Working title of *The Niht* (al-Layl, 1992).

125 Viola Shafik "Mohammed Malas. Traum un Erinnerung," in *Journal Film* 22, Freiburg, fall 1990, p. 15.

126 Author's interview with Ghaleb Chaath, Cairo, 14 January 1988.

127 Cf. Viola Shafik, *Realität und Film,* p. 68.

128 Bouzid, "Sinima al-waᶜy bi-l-hazima," p. 54.

129 Author's interview with Ghaleb Chaath, Cairo, 14 January 1988.

130 Ibid.

131 The films considered in the following as autobiographic generally juxtapose fictional parts with more or less strongly accentuated elements of the film maker's life.

132 Shafik, "Youssef Chahine," p. 53.

133 Samir Farid, "Hadith maᶜa Yusuf Shahin," in *Nashrat nadi al-sinima.*

134 *Rih al-sadd* means literally 'the dam wind, and has the the locu-
tionary force of "go to hell!" It derives from an idiomatic
Tunisian expression: "The wind on the dam takes away but does
not bring back" *(rih al-sadd ya'khudh wa la yarudd).*

135 Author's interview with Nouri Bouzid, Tunis, 6 October 1992.

136 Werner Kobe, "Nouri Bouzid," p. 19.

137 Author's interview.

138 ᶜAdnan Medanat, "Liqa' maᶜa al-mukhridj al-tunissi Mahmud b.
Mahmud," p. 30.

139 Bruno Jeaggi and Walter Ruggle, eds., *Nacer Khemir. Das verlorene Halsband der Taube,* p. 120.

140 The fate of an acquaintance inspired the director to write the
screenplay. During the Nasser era he was caught in the state security net and detained without charge for several years.

141 François Guérif; "Noce en Galilée," interview with Michel
Khleifi, F. Sabourand, S. Toubiana, A. de Baecque, *Cahiers du
Cinéma,* No. 77, November 1987, p. III.

142 Ibid.

143 Aziz Krichen, "*Le Syndrome Bourguiba,* p. 21.

144 Ibid., p. 32.

145 Ibid., p. 42 f.

146 Cf. Samir Farid, "Surat al-mar'a fi-l-sinima al-ᶜarabiya."

147 Werner Kobe, "Néjia Ben Mabrouk," p. 17.

148 The title alludes ironically to the Egyptian film of the same title
by Anwar Wagdi.

CHAPTER 4

1 Andrew Higson, *Waving the Flag: Constructing a National
Cinema in Britain,* p. 4; cf. Lina Khatib's discussion of Lebanese
cinema: *Lebanese Cinema: Imagining the Civil War and Beyod,* p.
186.

2 Stephen Crofts, "Conceptualising National Cinemas," in Valentina
Vital and Paul Willemen, eds., *Theorising National Cinema,* p. 44.

3 See Shafik, *Popular Egyptian Cinema*, for an extensive analysis of Egyptian genres.

4 Cf. Shafik, *Popular Egyptian Cinema*, p. 247.

5 Crofts, "Conceptualising National Cinemas," p. 44.

6 Thomas Elsaesser as quoted in Crofts, ibid.

7 Ibid.

8 Sahar Ali, "Statistical Data Collection Project on Film and Audio-visual Markets in 9 Mediterranean Countries. Country Profile: 1. Egypt," p. 63.

9 Cf. page 76.

10 Cf. Shohat and Stam, *Unthinking Eurocentrism*, pp. 283, 307. The authors understand the hybrid and parodic stylistic means applied by some "Third World" filmmakers, like Youssef Chahine for instance, as a "cannibalistic" devouring and digesting of First World Culture.

11 Arjun Appadurai, *Modernity at Large: Cultural Dimensions of Globalization*.

12 Ali, "Country Profile: 1. Egypt," p. 56.

13 Ibid., p. 57.

14 Ibid., p. 63.

15 Ibid., p. 68.

16 Ibid., p. 69.

17 al-Naggar, "Sina'at al-sinima fi Misr," p. 320.

18 18th Egyptian National Film Festival, 5–12 December 2014, *Sunduq al-tanmiya al-thaqafiya*, pp. 145–48.

19 Ali, "Country Profile: 1. Egypt," p. 61.

20 Ibid., p. 56.

21 Ibid., p. 52.

22 Ibid.

23 al-Naggar, "Sina'at al-sinima fi Misr," p. 308.

24 Reem Shawkat, "The Struggle of Young Egyptian Artists in Natural Colors," *Menassat* (Beirut), 22 January 2010

25 Kevin Dwyer, *Beyond Casablanca: M.A. Tazi, Moroccan Cinema, and Third World Filmmaking*, p. 32.

26 Laura Marks, "What Is That *and* between Arab Women and Video?" pp. 41–69.

27 Presented also at the Eighth Biennale of Arab Cinema, Paris, 22–30 July 2006.

28 Narjès Torchani, "Tunisie: Centre national du cinéma et de l'image—Du retard à rattraper," *Allafrica* (Cape Town), 20 November 2012.

29 See Abounaddara's website: http://www.abounaddara.com; Sonja Mejcher-Atassi, "Abounaddara's Take on Images in the Syrian Revolution: A Conversation between Akram Zaatari and Charid Kiwan," *Jadaliyya*, Washington DC, 8 July 2014.

30 Ali, "Statistical Data Collection Project," p/ 74. The data provided by Ali may be imprecise. For she mentions that Hamas has allocated funds for the production of a movie on the abduction of Shalit in September 2013. If it is *The Dispersion of Illusion*, there is evidence it was already online a year earlier.

31 Lucas Rosant, "Census and Analysis of Film and Audiovisual Co-productions in the South Mediterranean Region 2006–2011," *Euromed Audiovisiual III CSU*, p. 15.

32 Irit Neidhardt, *Untold Stories*, Westminster Papers in Communication and Culture 7, no. 2 (2010), p. 44.

33 Shafik, "Der belagerte Film oder Europas arabisches Filimschaffen," p. 133.

34 Leila Ahmed, *Women and Gender in Islam*, p. 151.

35 Crofts, "Conceptualising National Cinemas," p. 45.

36 Ibid.

37 Elsaesser, *New German Cinema: A History*, p. 108.

38 Rick Altman, *Film/Genre*, p. 156.

39 Bill Nichols, *Introduction to Documentary*, p. 1.

40 Shohat and Stam, *Unthinking Eurocentrism*, p. 302.

41 Shafik, "Egyptian Cinema," in O. Leaman, ed., *Encyclopedia of Middle Eastern Cinema*, p. 76.

42 Stuart Hall, "Notes on Deconstructing 'the Popular,'" in R. Samuel, ed., *People's History and Socialist Theory*, pp. 227–40.

CHAPTER 5

1 These notions are discussed by Elsaesser, *New German Cinema*, p. 44.

2 For more information, see the Sudanese Film Group's website: http://www.sudancineast.com/index.php?option=com_content&view=article&id=91&Itemid=18

3 An extensive analysis of this film is offered by Andrea Flores Khalil, "*Insan* (Human Being) and the Challenges to Personhood," paper for "Crossing Borders: Sudan in Regional Contexts," 22nd Annual Meeting of Sudan Studies Association.

4 Amal Sulayman Mahmoud al-ᶜUbaydi, "Cinema in Libya," pp. 413–17.

5 Sami Zaptia, "Libya Movie Awards Come to Successful Conclusion," *Libya Herald* (Tripoli), 10 November 2013.

6 For more details, see Sahar Ali, "Statistical Data Collection Project on Film and Audio-visual Markets in 9 Mediterranean Countries. Country Profile: 4. Jordan," p. 59.

7 Ibid., p. 60.

8 Ibid., pp. 66–67.

9 Ibid., pp. 78–81.

10 Victoria Scott, "DFI Postpones New Festival after Laying Off Dozens of Employees," *Doha News* (Doha), 12 January 2014.

11 Alex Ritman, "Whatever Happened to the Qatari Film Industry?" *The Guardian* (London), 6 March 2014.

12 Ibid.

13 Phil Hoad, "The Disappearance of *Jinn*, the United Arab Emirates' First Horror Film," *The Guardian* (London), 12 December 2012.

14 Y. Admon, "Revival of Cinema Sparks Debate in Saudi Arabia," in MEMRI Report No. 595 (Washington DC), 11 March 2010.

15 Samir Farid, "The Stakes of Representation," Al-Ahram Weekly, no. 797 (Cairo), 1–7 June 2006.

16 Cornpone, "Rare Saudi Film Vies for Prize at Rome Film Festival," Free Republic (blog), 18 April 2007.

17 Donna Abu Nasr, "*Menahi*: Saudi Movie Screened in Riyadh First Time in 30 Years," *The World Post*, US online edition, 9 July 2009.

18 "Madjmu^cat talashi al-sinima'iya tusharik fi mihradjan Abu Dhabi al-sinima'i bi sab^cat aflam," *Riyadh*, no. 50 (Riyadh), 5 April 2009.

19 Sermini, "Cinema in the Arab Mashriq (East)," p. 72.

20 Yusuf al-^cAni, *al-Sinima: istidhkarat bayn al-ẓalam wa-l-daw'*, p. 157.

21 Kiki Kennedy-Day, "Cinema in Lebanon, Syria, Iraq, and Kuwait," p. 32.

22 The title of this film is translated by Rebecca Hillauer as *20/20 Vision*.

23 Sermini, "Cinema in the Arab Mashriq (East)," p. 73.

24 Bob Skorodinsky, "Iraqi Cinema," http://www.ac.wwu.edu/~skorodr/Cinema/ (last updated 10 June 2003).

25 *Der Tagesspiegel Online*, "Ein Berliner Filmclub für Bagdad," 19 August 2004.

26 Silke Kettelhake, "Oday Rasheed's 'Underexposure': Blinking Incredulously at the Sun," Qantara.de, 2005.

27 According to Qassim Muhammed, head of the current Ministry of Culture cinema department. See Sam Dagher, "Iraqis Cling to Shreds of Movie Nostalgia," Agence France Press, *Middle East Times*, 3 July 2006.

28 Cath Clark, "Heroes and Handycams," *The Guardian* (London), 1 May 2009.

29 Ali Abdulameer, "Iraq's Film Industry Hits Bottom," *al-Monitor*, 24 October 2013.

30 Sermini, "Cinema in the Arab Mashriq (East)," p. 73.

31 Mustafa Gündoğu, *An Introduction to Kurdish Cinema*, n.d., p. 8.

32 Abdulameer, "Iraq's Film Industry Hits Bottom."

33 Kurdish titles will not be added, for lack of consistent transliterations.

34 Mayyar al-Roumi and Dorothée Schmid, "Le cinéma syrien," p. 17.

35 Euromed Audiovisual II Programme, MEDA Countries' Fact Sheets.

36 al-Roumi and Schmid, "Le cinéma syrien," p. 11.

37 Ibrahim, *Ru'a wa mawaqif fi-l-sinima al-suriya*, p. 177.

38 Khalil Sweileh, "Raymond Boutros: The Last Communist," *Al-Akhbar English* (Beirut), 2 August 2012.

39 Salah Sermini, "Cinema in the Arab Mashriq (East)," Filmmuseum Frankfurt, *Panorama of Arab Cinema, 1954–2004*. Frankfurt am Main (2004): 70–74.

40 al-Roumi and Schmid, "Le cinéma syrien," p. 16.

41 Ibid., p. 22.

42 As quoted in Salti, *Insights into Syrian Cinema*, p. 162.

43 Cf. Viola Shafik, "Resisting Pleasure? Performativity and Political Resistance in Arab Cinema," in Karima Laachir and Saeed Talajooy, eds., *Resistance in Contemporary Middle Eastern Cultures*, p. 126.

44 Zaccak, *Le cinéma libanais*, p. 374.

45 Sahar Ali, "Statistical Data Collection Project on Film and Audiovisual Markets in 9 Mediterranean Countries. Country Profile: 3. Lebanon," p. 91.

46 Ibid., p. 82.

47 Ahmed Abdel Hamid Zebari, "Iraqi Kurdistan Seeks Cinema Revival," *al-Monitor*, 1 July 2013.

48 Ali, "Country Profile: 4. Jordan," p. 72.

49 Ali, "Country Profile: 3. Lebanon," p. 82.

50 BFI, "*Caramel*—A Lebanon You Don't See in the News."

51 Ali, "Country Profile: 3. Lebanon," p. 93.

52 Ibid., p. 97.

53 Khatib, *Lebanese Cinema. Imagining the Civil War and Beyond*, p. 186.

54 Zaccak, "Regard sur le cinéma libanais," p. 188.

55 Hamid Naficy, "Phobic Spaces and Liminal Panics: Independent Transnational Film Genre," in Ella Shohat and Robert Stam, eds., *Multiculturalism, Postcoloniality, and Transnational Media*, p. 203.

56 Ibid., p. 222.

57 Ibid., p. 211.

58 Sahar Ali, "Statistical Data Collection Project on Film and Audiovisual Markets in 9 Mediterranean Countries. Country Profile: 5. Palestine," pp. 86–88.

59 Ibid., pp. 96, 98.

60 Ibid., p. 75.

61 Nirit Anderman, "Israeli Film Fund Closes Palestinian Loophole: Creators Must Pledge to Be 'Israeli,'" *Haaretz* (Tel Aviv), 27 January 2015.

62 Cf. Hamid Dabashi, ed., *Dreams of a Nation: On Palestinian Cinema*.

63 Shafik, "Palestinian Cinema," pp. 130–49.

64 See page 199.

65 Nizar Hassan, personal interview with the author, Cairo, 17 March 2002.

66 Ministry of Culture, *Le cinéma en Tunisi*, p. 11.

67 Ibid.

68 "Tunisia," in *The Mediterranean Audiovisual Landscape*, p. 63.

69 Hayet Gharbi, "Les salafistes veillent au grain," *Turess*, 24 April 2013.

70 Ferid Boughedir, personal interview, Paris, 26 July 2006.

71 Chamkhi, *Cinéma tunisien nouveau*, p. 221.

72 Ibid., p. 220.

73 Ministry of Culture, *Le cinéma en Tunisie*, p. 5.

74 Rebecca Hillauer, *Encyclopedia of Arab Women Filmmakers*, p. 372.

75 Gabous, *Silence, ells tournent!*, p. 174.

76 Hillauer, *Encyclopedia of Arab Women Filmmakers*, pp. 147–56

77 See page 194.

78 Sahar Ali, "Projet de collecte de données statistiques sur le marches cinématographiques et audiovisuels dans 9 pays méditerranéens. Monographies nationales: 6. Algérie," p. 96.

79 Ibid., p. 83.

80 Ibid., p. 89.

81 Omar Idtnain, "Le cinéma Amazigh au Maroc: Eléments d'une naissance artistique," *Africultures* (Les Pilles), 20 October 2008.

82 Jordan Elgrably, "Lyes Salem's Debut, *Masquerades*, Gently Ribs Algeria," *Levantine Review* (Los Angeles), 6 October 2010.

83 Lisa Nesselson, "Review, *Viva Laljérie*," *Variety* (Los Angeles), 11 May 2004.

84 Benjam Stora, "Eih dunkler Thriller," *Qantara* (Bonn), 14 August 2013.

85 Hamdi Baala, "Avant-première de *L'Oranais*: Une fresque historique à caractère politique," *Al Huffington Post* (Algiers), 7 September 2014.

86 See page 99.

87 al-Masnaoui, *Abhath fi-l-sinima al-maghribiya*, p. 135; personal interview with the author, Paris, 25 July 2006.

88 See Euronews report, December 2013, https://www.youtube.com/watch?v=odXhjgG6E7Q

89 Sahar Ali, "Statistical Data Collection Project on Film and Audiovisual Markets in 9 Mediterranean Countries. Country Profile: 2. Morocco," pp. 107–109.

90 Ibid., p. 99.

91 al-Masnaoui, personal interview.

92 Lucas Rosant, "Census and Analysis of Film and Audiovisual Co-productions in the South Mediterranean Region 2006–2011," p. 103.

93 Kevin Dwyer, "Morocco: A National Cinema and Large Ambitions," in Josef Gugler, ed., *Film in the Middle East and North Africa*, p. 328.

94 Jamal Bahmand, "Casablanca Unbound: The New Urban Cinema in Morocco," *Francosphères* 2, no. 1 (2013), p. 75.

95 Ibid., p. 79.

96 Martin Dale, "Comedies, Social Dramas and Neo-realist Dramas Challenge Social Mores," *Variety* (Los Angeles), 6 December 2014.

97 Dwyer, "Morocco: A National Cinema with Large Ambitions," pp. 333–34.

98 Ali, "Country Profile: 2. Morocco," p. 132.

99 Bahmand, "Casablanca Unbound: The New Urban Cinema in Morocco," p. 73.

100 al-Masnaoui, personal interview.

101 Ali, "Country Profile: 2. Morocco," p. 111.

102 Ibid., p. 123.

103 Ibid., p. 120.

104 Ibid., pp. 119–22.

105 al-Masnaoui, personal interview.

106 Merolla, "Digital Imagination and the 'Landscapes of Group Identities,'" p. 128.

107 Richard Dyer, *Only Entertainment*, p. 66.

108 Ibid., p. 69.

109 Yassmine Zerrouki, "From *Casanegra* to *Zero*: A Story of Casablanca," *Morocco World News* (Rabat), 19 January 2012.

110 See page 202.

111 Ibid. cf. Naficy, "Phobic Spaces and Liminal Panics."

CHAPTER 6

1   Malkmus and Armes, *Arab and African Film Making*, p. 115.

2   Auerbach, *Mimesis*, p. 426.

3   Aziza, *L'image et l'Islam*, p. 67.

BIBLIOGRAPHY

Abdulameer, Ali. "Iraq's Film Industry Hits Bottom." *al-Monitor*, 24 Oct. 2013. http://www.al-monitor.com/pulse/originals/2013/10/iraq-cinema-movies-industry-decline.html

Abu Nasr, Donna. "*Menahi*: Saudi Movie Screened in Riyadh First Time in 30 Years." *The World Post*, US online edition, 9 July 2009. http://www.huffingtonpost.com/2009/06/08/menahi-saudi-movie-screen_n_212626.html

Abu Shanab, ʿAdil. *Masrah ʿarabi qadim: Karakuz*. Damascus: Wizarat al-Thaqafa, [1963?].

Acrame. "Egypte: Dénationaliser le cinéma." *Les 2 écrans* (Algiers) 7 (Nov. 1978): 37–42.

Admon, Y. "Revival of Cinema Sparks Debate in Saudi Arabia." In MEMRI Report No. 595. Washington DC, 11 March 2010. http://www.memri.org/report/en/0/0/0/0/0/0/4027.htm

Afya, Muhammad Nur al-Din. "Mishal Khalifi (Michel Khleifi) wa khitabuh al-sinima'i." *Dirasat sinimia'iya* (Qunaitara, Morocco) 1 (June 1985): 16–20.

Ahmed, Leila. *Women and Gender in Islam*. New Haven, 1992.

Ali, Sahar. "Statistical Data Collection Project on Film and Audio-visual Markets in 9 Mediterranean Countries. Country Profile: 1. Egypt." *Euromed Audiovisual III CSU*. Strasbourg, 2013. http://euromedaudiovisuel.net/p.aspx?t=general&mid=157&l=en

_____. "Statistical Data Collection Project on Film and Audio-visual Markets in 9 Mediterranean Countries. Country Profile: 2. Morocco." *Euromed Audiovisual III CSU*. Strasbourg, 2012.

_____. "Statistical Data Collection Project on Film and Audio-visual Markets in 9 Mediterranean Countries. Country Profile: 3. Lebanon." *Euromed Audiovisual III CSU*. Strasbourg, 2013.

_____. "Statistical Data Collection Project on Film and Audio-visual Markets in 9 Mediterranean Countries. Country Profile: 4. Jordan." *Euromed Audiovisual III CSU*. Strasbourg, 2013.

_____. "Statistical Data Collection Project on Film and Audio-visual Markets in 9 Mediterranean Countries. Country Profile: 5. Palestine." *Euromed Audiovisual III CSU*. Tunis, 2013.

_____. "Projet de collecte de données statistiques sur les marchés cinématographiques et audiovisuels dans 9 pays méditerranéens. Monographies nationales: 6. Algérie." *Euromed Audiovisual III CSU*. Tunis, 2014.

Aliksan, Jean. "al-Sinima al-suriya fi khamsin ᶜaman." *Al-hayat al-sinima'iya* (Damascus) 1 (1978).

_____. *al-Sinima fi-l-watan al-ᶜarabi*. Kuwait, 1982.

_____. *al-Sinima wa-l-qadiya al-filastiniya*. Damascus, 1987.

_____. *Tarikh al-sinima al-suriya*. Damascus, 1987.

Allen, Roger. *The Arabic Novel: An Historical and Critical Introduction*. Manchester, 1982.

Aloudat, Hussein (al-ᶜAwdat, Husain). "al-Qadiya al-filastiniya fi-l-sinima al-ᶜarabiya al-suriya." In *Ayam Filastin al-faniya wa-l-thaqafiya*. Cairo, 1990.

Altman, Rick. *Film/Genre*. London, 1999.

Anderman, Nirit. "Israeli Film Fund Closes Palestinian Loophole: Creators Must Pledge to Be 'Israeli.'" *Haaretz* (Tel Aviv), 27 Jan. 2015. http://www.haaretz.com/life/movies-television/.premium-1.639252

Anderson, Benedict. *Imagined Communities*. New York, 1991.

al-ᶜAni, Yusuf. *al-Sinima: istidhkarat bayn al-zalam wa-l-daw'*. Beirut, 2003.

Appadurai, Arjun. *Modernity at Large: Cultural Dimensions of Globalization*. Minneapolis, 1996.

Araib, Ahmed. "Structure du film politique chez Souheil Ben Baraka." *Dirasat simima'iya* (Qunaitara, Morocco) 6 (April 1987): 58–62.

Arasoughly, Alia, ed. *Critical Film Writing from the Arab World*. Quebec, 1996.

al-ᶜAriss, Ibrahim. *Rihla fi-l-sinima al-ᶜarabiya*. Beirut, 1979.

Armes, Roy. *Postcolonial Image: Studies in North African Film*. Bloomington, 2005.

_____. *Third World Film Making and the West*. Berkeley, 1987.

al-Aᶜsad, Asᶜad. "al-Thaqafa al-filastiniya fi muwadjahat al-ihtilal." *al-Katib* 73 (1986).

Auerbach, Erich. *Mimesis: Dargestellte Wirklichkeit in der abendländischen Literatur*. Bern, 1988.

Aulas, M.-C. "Ecrans et caméras en Egypte." In *L'Egypte d'aujourd'hui: Permanence et changements 1805–1976*. Paris: Groupe de Recherches et d'Etudes sur le Proche Orient, 1977.

ᶜAwad, Djibril. "al-Sinima fi-l-djabha al-shaᶜbiya li-tahrir Filastin." *Al-Hadaf* (Damascus), 23 Dec. 1985: 254–58.

Aziza, Mohamed (ᶜAziza, Muhammad). *L'image et l'Islam*. Paris, 1978.

_____. *al-Islam wa-l-masrah*. Cairo, 1990.

B., Abdou. "Der algerische Film: Thema und Ausfürung." *Film in Algerien ab 1970. Kinemathek* (Berlin) 57 (Dec. 1978): 4–12. French version: "Le cinéma algérien: Thème et version." *Les 2 écrans* (Algiers) 1 (March 1978): 10–19.

_____. "Le dernier tabou." *Les 2 écrans* (Algiers) 44 (April 1982): 20–25.

_____. "Entretien avec Ahmed Rachedi." *Les 2 écrans* (Algiers) 13 (May 1979): 15–17.

_____. "Farouk Beloufa." *Les 2 écrans* (Algiers) 13 (May 1979): 38–44.

B., Abdou, and Moulay Brahimi. "Entretien avec Djilali Ferhati." *Les 2 écrans* (Algiers) 47–48 (July–Aug. 1982): 25–27.

B., R. CAAIC. "Le temps des vaches maigres." *Soir d'Algérie* (Algiers), 30 June 1991.

Baala, Hamdi. "Avant-première de *L'Oranais*: Une fresque historique à caractère politique." *Al Huffington Post* (Algiers), 7 Sept. 2014. http://www.huffpostmaghreb.com/2014/09/06/loranais-film-lyes-salem_n_5777292.html

de Baecque, Antoine. "L'architecture des sens: *Noce en Galilée*." *Cahiers du cinema* (Paris) 77, no. 401 (Nov. 1987): 45–47.

———. "La force du faible: 'Noce en Galilée,' entretien avec Michel Khleifi." *Cahiers du cinema* (Paris) 77, no. 401 (Nov. 1987): 3.

Bahmand, Jamal. "Casablanca Unbound: The New Urban Cinema in Morocco." *Francosphères* 2, no. 1 (2013): 73–85.

Bakhtin, Mikhail. *Literatur und Karneval*. Munich, 1985.

Barthes, Roland. *Mythen des Alltags*. Frankfurt am Main, 1964.

Bazin, André. *What Is Cinema? (II)*. Berkeley, 1971.

Benabdessadok, Kamel. "Culture orale et cinéma." *Les 2 écrans* (Algiers) 25 (June 1980): 25–27.

Bennoune, Mahfoud. *The Making of Contemporary Algeria*. Cambridge, 1988.

Bensaleh, Mohamed. *Cinéma en méditerranée: Une passerelle entre les cultures*. Aix-en-Provence, 2005.

Bensmaïa, Réda. "Cinéma algérien et 'caractère' national." *Les 2 écrans* (Algiers) 31 (Feb. 1981).

———. "La Nouba des femmes du Mont Chenoua." *Les 2 écrans* (Algiers) 17 (Oct. 1979): 52–60.

———. "Qui parle Nahla: Notes sur l'esthétique de deux films algériens." *Les 2 écrans* (Algiers) 46 (June 1982): 18–29.

———. "Soleil des Hyènes de Ridha Behi." *Les 2 écrans* (Algiers) 5 (July 1978): 40–44.

Bergmann, Kristina. *Filmkultur und Filmindustrie in Ägypten*. Darmstadt, 1993.

Berrah, Mouny. "Abdelhamid Benhadouga: 'Le cinéma m'offre la possibilité de communiquer avec ceux pour lesquels j'écris.'" *Les 2 écrans* (Algiers) 11 (March 1979): 44–48.

———. "Algerian Cinema: Five Landmarks between Hollywood and Cairo." In August Light Productions, ed., *Liberation and Alienation in Algerian Cinema*, 29–36. Cambridge, 1991.

————. "Interview du collectif 'Nouveau Théâtre.'" *Les 2 écrans* (Algiers) 9 (Jan. 1979): 37–40.

————. "Interview M. Allouache." *Les 2 écrans* (Algiers) 7 (Nov. 1978): 17–19.

————. "Nahla ou le nécessaire détour de Larbi." *Les 2 écrans* (Algiers) 13 (May 1979): 34–38.

————. "La zerda." *Les 2 écrans* (Algiers) 49 (Oct. 1982): 39–42.

Berrah, Mouny, Jacques Lévy, and Claude Michel Cluny, eds. "Les cinémas arabes et Grand Maghreb." *CinémAction* (Paris) 43 (1987).

Beylie, Claude. *Les Maîtres du cinéma français*. Paris, 1990.

Bianca, Stefano. *Architektur und Lebensform im islamischen Stadtwesen*. Zurich, 1979.

Bosséno, Christian. "Le cinéma tunisien." *La revue du cinéma* (Paris) 382 (April 1983): 49–62.

————. "Youssef Chahine, l'Alexandrin." *CinémAction* (Paris) 33 (1985).

Bouchefirat, A. "Rachid Boudjedra." *Les 2 écrans* (Algiers) 22 (March 1980): 32–37.

Boudjedra, Rachid. *Naissance du cinéma algérien*. Paris, 1971.

Boughedir, Ferid. "Cinema in the Maghreb: An Experimental Laboratory for 'New Arab Cinema.'" Filmmuseum Frankfurt. *Panorama of Arab Cinema, 1954–2004*. Frankfurt am Main (2004): 47–50.

Boukella, Djamel. "Remous." *Algérie Actualité* (Algiers) 1043 (10–16 Oct. 1985).

Brace, Richard M. *Morocco, Algeria, Tunisia*. Englewood Cliffs, 1964.

Brahimi, Denise. *Cinémas d'Afrique francophone et du Maghreb*. Paris, 1997.

Bresson, Charles. "Que veux-tu de moi?" Conference: La Création cinématographique du Sud face au marché du Nord. *Journées Cinématographiques de Carthage*, Tunis, 5–6 October 1992.

Bughaba, Ahmad. "Hiwar maᶜa Djilali Farhati." *Dirasat sinima'iya* (Qunaitara, Morocco) 6 (April 1987): 21–25.

Burdjawi, Darwish. *Aflam ᶜarabiya: mutaghayyirat al-infitah fi sinima al-shabab 1980–1985*. Cairo, 1986.

Burton, Julianne. "Marginal Cinemas and Mainstream Critical Theory." *Screen* 26, no. 3–4 (May–Aug. 1985): 2–20.

"Caramel—A Lebanon You Don't See in the News." BFI (British Film Institute). London, n.d. http://www.bfi.org.uk/sites/bfi.org.uk/files/downloads/uk-film-council-caramel-case-study.pdf

Chakravarty, Sumita S. "National Identity and the Realist Aesthetic: Indian Cinema of the Fifties." *The Quarterly Review of Film Studies* (Spring 1987).

Chamkhi, Sonia. *Cinéma tunisien nouveau.* Tunis, 2002.

al-Charkawi (al-Sharqawi), Galal. *Risala fi tarikh al-sinima al-ᶜarabiya.* Cairo, 1970.

Chelbi, Mustapha. *Culture et mémoire collective au Maghreb.* Paris, 1989.

Chelfi, Mustapha. "Le dit et le non-dit." *Algérie Actualité* (28 March–3 April 1985).

Chmait, Walid. "Le cinéma arabe d'alternative." *Les 2 écrans* (Algiers) 19 (Dec. 1979): 6–13.

Chouika, Driss. "Le cinéma au Maroc." *Dirasat sinima'iya* (Qunaitara, Morocco) 7 (Sept. 1987): 62–60.

———. "Entretien avec S. Ben Baraka." *Dirasat sinima'iya* (Qunaitara, Morocco) 8 (Feb. 1988): 53–62.

Ciné Club Jean-Vigo Cinéma Méditerranéen, ed. "Egypte: Redécouverte et confirmation." In *Actes du 8e Rencontre de Montpellier.* Montpellier, 1987.

Clark, Cath. "Heroes and Handycams." *The Guardian* (London), 1 May 2009. http://www.theguardian.com/film/2009/may/01/maysoon-pachachi-iraq-baghdad-film

Cluny, Claude Michel. "Actualité du cinéma arabe." *Cinéma* (Paris) 77, no. 222 (June 1977): 31–40.

———. *Dictionnaire des nouveaux cinémas arabes.* Paris, 1978.

Cornpone. "Rare Saudi Film Vies for Prize at Rome Film Festival." Free Republic (blog), 18 April 2007. http://www.freerepublic.com/focus/f-news/1819024/posts

Crofts, Stephen. "Conceptualising National Cinema/s." In Valentina Vital and Paul Willemen, eds., *Theorising National Cinema.* London, 2006.

Dabashi, Hamid, ed. *Dreams of a Nation: On Palestinian Cinema.* London, 2006.

Dagher, Sam. "Iraqis Cling to Shreds of Movie Nostalgia." Agence France Press. *Middle East Times*, 3 July 2006.

Dale, Martin. "Comedies, Social Dramas and Neo-realist Dramas Challenge Social Mores." *Variety* (Los Angeles), 6 Dec. 2014. http://variety.com/2014/film/news/moroccan-cinema-continues-to-challenge-taboos-1201370163/

Darwish, Mahmud. "Mishal Khalifi wa khitabuh al-sinima'i." *Dirasat sinima'iya* (Qunaitara, Morocco) 1 (June 1985): 16–20.

Darwish, Salah. "al-Sinima'iyun yunaqishun humum al-film al-misri: udjur al-nudjum wa-l-dara'ib wa-l-muwazzi^c al-kharidji tuhaddid sina^cat al-sinima." *al-Djumhuriya* (Cairo), 6 September 1987.

Dehni (Duhni), Salah. "Tadjribat al-sinima fi Suriya." *al-Ma^criffa* (Damascus) 131 (January 1973). French: "L'expérience du cinéma en Syrie." *Cinéma* (Paris) 75, no. 197 (1975).

Diavara, Manthia. *African Cinema*. Bloomington, 1992.

al-Dissuqi, Ibrahim. "al-Mukhridjun al-shabab." *al-Sinima al-fann al-sabi^c* (Cairo) 2 (1979).

Djaider, Mireille. "Les aventures d'un héros." *Les 2 écrans* (Algiers) 7 (Nov. 1978): 14–17.

al-Djami^ca al-Tunisiya li-Nawadi al-Sinima, ed. *al-Waqi^ciya fi-l-sinima al-^carabiya*. Tunis, 1988.

Djebar, Assia. "Sedjnane de A. Ben Ammar." *Les 2 écrans* (Algiers) 3 (May 1978): 24–27.

Djelfaoui, Abderrahmane. "Le mystère sans démésure." *Les 2 écrans* (Algiers) 53 (Feb. 1983): 33–39.

al-Duman, Khalil. "al-Film al-maghribi: al-qira'a al-thaniya." *Dirasat sinima'iya* (Qunaitara, Morocco) 1 (June 1985): 5–7.

———. "Qira'at fi-l-film al-maghribi: ^cara'is min qasab." *Dirasat sinima'iya* (Qunaitara, Morocco) 3 (March 1986): 4–6.

Dwyer, Kevin. *Beyond Casablanca: M.A. Tazi, Moroccan Cinema, and Third World Filmmaking*. Cairo, 2004.

———. "Morocco: A National Cinema with Large Ambitions." In Josef Gugler, ed., *Film in the Middle East and North Africa*. Austin, 2010.

Dyer, Richard. *Only Entertainment*. London, 2002.

Eichenberger, A. "Hollywood des Nahen Ostens? 50 Jahre ägyptischer Film: ein Interview mit Salah Abu Seif." In *Filmkorrespondenz* 11 (Bonn), 2 Nov. 1977.

Elgrably, Jordan. "Lyes Salem's Debut, *Masquerades*, Gently Ribs Algeria." *Levantine Review* (Los Angeles), 6 October 2010. http://www.levantinecenter.org/levantine-review/film/lyes-salems-debut-masquerades-gently-ribs-algeria

Elsaesser, Thomas. *New German Cinema: A History*. New Brunswick, 1989.

Ende, Werner, and Udo Steinbach, eds. *Der Islam in der Gegenwart*. Munich, 1984.

Entelis, John P. *Algeria: The Revolution Institutionalized*. Boulder, 1986.

Euromed Audiovisual II Programme. *MEDA Countries' Fact Sheets*. Distributed at Berlin conference, 10–11 February 2007.

Faath, Sigrid. *Tunesien: Die politische Entwicklung seit der Unabhängigkeit 1956–1986*. Hamburg, 1986.

Fähndrich, Hartmut. *Die Vorstellung vom Schicksal*. Bern, 1983.

Fanon, Frantz. *Schwarze Haut, weiße Masken*. Frankfurt am Main, 1980.

Farid, Samir. "al-Bunya al-asasiya li-l-sinima fi Misr." Study for the 5th Damascus Film Festival, 1987.

_____. "al-Bari' ... namudhadj ᶜalami li-l-tafaᶜul maᶜ al-waqiᶜ al-hay." *al-Djumhuriya* (Cairo), 16 March 1987.

_____. "al-Bari' simfuniya fi arbaᶜ harakat." *al-Djumhuriya* (Cairo), 22 March 1987.

_____. "al-Fidiyu." In *Sinima 84–86*. al-Thaqafa al-Djamahiriya, 1987.

_____. "Hadith maᶜa Yusuf Shahin." *Nashrat nadi al-sinima* (Cairo) 20 (1971).

_____. *Hawiyat al-sinima al-ᶜarabiya*. Beirut, 1988.

_____. "L'image de Abdenasser dans le cinéma égyptien." *Les 2 écrans* (Algiers) 28 (Nov. 1980): 25–27.

_____. "*al-Liss wa-l-dahiya* fi suq al-sinima al-misriya." *al-Djumhuriya* (Cairo), 23 March 1984.

_____. "Min al-sinima al-djadida ila al-waqiᶜiya al-djadida." *al-Djumhuriya* (Cairo), 10 March 1987.

———. "Mu'assasat al-sinima am al-sinima'iyun?" *al-Djumhuriya* (Cairo), 4 Feb. 1971.

———. "Nahw manhadj ^cilmi li-kitabat tarkhuna al-sinima'i." *al-Tali^ca* (Cairo) 3, no. 73 (1973).

———. "Sikat saffar wa djudhur al-tadjdid fi-l-sinima." *al-Djumhuriya* (Cairo), 3 March 1987.

———. "The Stakes of Representation." *Al-Ahram Weekly*, no. 797 (Cairo), 1–7 June 2006. http://weekly.ahram.org.eg/2006/797/cu1.htm

———. "Surat al-mar'a fi-l-sinima al-^carabiya." *al-Hayat al-sinima'iya* (Damascus) 21 (Spring 1984): 4–15.

———. "al-Zilal fi-l-djanib al-akhar wa tatawwur sinima al-shabab fi Misr." *al-Djumhuriya al-^cadad al-usbu^ci* (Cairo), 1 April 1975.

Farzanefar, Amin. *Kino des Orients: Stimmen aus einer Region*. Marburg, 2005.

"Film Ma^craka." *al-Hayat al-sinima'iya* (Damascus) 28 (Winter 1986): 59–62.

Flores Khalil, Andrea. "*Insan* (Human Being) and the Challenges to Personhood." Paper for "Crossing Borders: Sudan in Regional Contexts," 22nd Annual Meeting of Sudan Studies Association, n.d. http://www.sudanstudies.org/khalil03.pdf

Frenzel, Elizabeth. *Motive der Weltliteratur*. Stuttgart, 1976.

———. *Stoff-, Motiv- und Symbolforschung*. Stuttgart, 1963.

Fuda, ^cAbd al-Mun^cim. "al-Fatawi." *al-Azhar* 10, no. 65 (April 1993): 1555–57.

Gabous, Abdelkrim. *Silence, ells tournent! Les femmes et le cinéma en Tunisie*. Tunis, 1998.

Gallaoui, Mohamed. "Le film marocain des années quatre-vingt." *Vision* (Rabat) 21 (April 1992): 44–46.

Geidel, Thomas. "Ägypten, wie es liebt und lebt: Gespräch mit dem ägyptischen Filmemacher Salah Abu Seif." *Die Tageszeitung* (Berlin), 27 Nov. 1986.

Ghabri, Neila. "La gestion de la SATPEC." Thesis for the Institut de presse et des sciences de l'information, Tunis, 1980.

Ghali, Noureddine (Nur al-Din). "Reflets et mirages du cinéma égyptien." *Jeune cinéma* (Paris) 83 (Dec. 1974–Jan. 1975).

Ghanima, Hasan. "Ghalib Sha^cth wa-l-iskan al-filastini." Interview in *CinémArabe* (Paris) 4–5 (Oct.–Nov. 1976): 11–12.

Gharbi, Hayet. "Les salafistes veillent au grain." *Turess*, 24 April 2013. http://www.turess.com/fr/letemps/75641

Gibb, Hamilton A.R. *Studies on the Civilization of Islam*. Boston, 1962.

Gibb, Hamilton A.R., and Jacob Landau. *Arabische Literaturgeschichte*. Zurich, 1968.

Goldziher, Ignace. *A Short History of Classical Arabic Literature*. Hildesheim, 1966.

Grabar, Oleg. *The Formation of Islamic Art*. New Haven, 1987.

Grotzfeld, Heinz, and Sophia Grotzfeld. *Die Erzählungen aus Tausendundeiner Nacht*. Darmstadt, 1984.

Guérif, François. "Entretien avec Nacer Khemir." *La revue du cinéma* (Paris) 417 (June 1986): 16–17.

———. *"Noce en Galilée."* Interview with Michel Khleifi, F. Sabourand, S. Toubiana, A. de Baecque. *Cahiers du Cinéma* 77 (Nov. 1987).

Gündoğdu, Mustafa. *An Introduction to Kurdish Cinema*, n.d. http://www.academia.edu/5773023/An_Introduction_to_Kurdish_Cinema

H., G. "Ciné-Maleurs." *Alger-Republicain* (Algiers), 23 Feb. 1991.

Habib, Mustafa. "Theater and Cinema." In *Cultural Life in the United Arab Republic*. Cairo: UNESCO, 1968.

al-Hadari, Ahmad. *Tarikh al-sinima fi Misr*. Cairo, 1989.

Hafez, Sabry. "Shifting Identities in Maghribi Cinema: The Algerian Paradigm." *Alif* (Cairo) 15 (1995): 39–80.

Hall, Stuart. "Notes on Deconstructing 'The Popular.'" In R. Samuel, ed., *People's History and Socialist Theory*. London, 1981.

Hamzaoui, Hamid. *Histoire du cinéma égyptien*. Paris, 1997.

Harib, Ihsan. "al-Sinima al-^ciraqiya bayn al-ams wa-yaum." *al-Hayat al-sinima'iya* (Damascus) 3 (July 1979): 14–25.

Hawal, Qasim. *al-Sinima al-filastiniya*. Beirut, 1979.

"al-Hawiya al-qawmiya fi tadjribat al-sinima al-^carabiya al-suriya." *al-Hayat al-sinima'iya* (Damascus) 30 (1986) 11–22.

Haywood, John A. *Modern Arabic Literature 1800–1970*. London, 1971.

Heath, Stephen. "Film: The Art of the Real." *Cambridge Review* (Oct. 1974): 17–20.

Hennebelle, Guy. "Le cinéma algérien aujourd'hui." *Afrique–Asie* 134, no. 2 (May 1977): 48–50.

———. "Les cinémas africains en 1972." *L'Afrique littéraire et artistique* (Paris) 20 (special issue) 1972.

———. "Cinémas du Maghreb." *CinémAction* (Paris) 14 (1981).

———. "Le cinéma syrien." *L'Afrique littéraire et artistique* (Paris) 36 (1975): 87–98.

———. "Entretien avec Moumen Smihi." *L'Afrique littéraire et artistique* (Paris) 38 (1978): 99–105.

———. "Le premier festival de Damas a confirmé le renouveau des cinémas arabes." *L'Afrique littéraire et artistique* (Paris) 23 (June 1972): 79–86.

Henebelle, Guy, and Khémais Khayati. "Le Palestine et le cinéma." *E. 100*. Paris, 1977.

Henebelle, Monique. "Entretien avec Tewfik Saleh: 'Mes six films sont des fables sur le destin des peuples arabes.'" *L'Afrique littéraire et artistique* (Paris) 26 (Dec. 1972): 89–105.

———. "La nouvelle vague du cinéma tunisien." *L'Afrique littéraire et artistique* (Paris) 25 (Oct. 1972): 67–81.

Hesse, Reinhard. "Adieu Bonaparte." *Die Tageszeitung* (Berlin), 21 May 1985.

Higson, Andrew. *Waving the Flag: Constructing a National Cinema in Britain*. Oxford, 1995.

Hillauer, Rebecca. *Encyclopedia of Arab Women Filmmakers*. Cairo, 2005.

Hoad, Phil. "The Disappearance of *Jinn*, the United Arab Emirates' First Horror Film." *The Guardian* (London), 12 Dec. 2012. http://www.theguardian.com/film/2012/dec/12/disappearance-djinn-uae-horror-movie

Horkheimer, Max, and Theodor W. Adorno. *Dialektik der Aufklärung*. Frankfurt am Main, 1971.

"Ibn al-sabil: ramziyat al-hamish wa-l-daya^c." *al-Hayat al-sinima'iya* (Qunaitara, Morocco) 1 (June 1985): 8–10.

Ibrahim, Bashshar. *Ru'a wa mawaqif fi-l-sinima al-suriya.* Damascus, 1997.

Idris, Ahmad Sidjilmasi. "Filmughrafyat al-sinima al-maghribiya al-aflam al-riwa'iya (1912–1986)." *Dirasat sinima'iya* (Qunaitara, Morocco) 8 (Feb. 1988): 13–19.

Idris, al-Qari. "al-Sinima al-maghribiya bayn ghiyab al-mashru[c] al-idjtima[c]i wa afaq bina' al-maghrib al-[c]arabi." *Dirasat sinima'iya* (Qunaitara, Morocco) 9 (Nov. 1988): 26–29.

_____. "al-Sinima al-maghribiya: nahw mashru[c] muqaraba susiyuludjiya." *Dirasat sinima'iya* (Qunaitara, Morocco) 8 (Feb. 1988): 7–12.

Idtnain, Omar. "Le cinéma Amazigh au Maroc: Eléments d'une naissance artistique." *Africultures* (Les Pilles), 20 Oct. 2008. http://www.africultures.com/php/?nav=article&no=8117

al-[c]Imari, Amir. "al-Sinima al-djaza'iriya." *Dirasat sinima'iya* (Qunaitara, Morocco) 8 (Feb. 1988): 20–39.

Internationales Forum des jungen Films, ed. "La mémoire fertile." Blatt 22 in 31st *Internationale Filmfestspiele Berlin.* Berlin, 1981.

Intidam, Said. "Le cinéma national: Un cinéma régional. A propos du centre et de la périphérie." *Dirasat sinima'iya* (Qunaitara, Morocco) 6 (April 1987): 54–57.

_____. "La marginalité dans le film marocain: Quelques éléments d'analyse." *Dirasat sinima'iya* (Qunaitara, Morocco) 8 (Feb. 1988): 49–52.

[c]Izz al-Din, Hasan. "al-Sinima al-filastiniya." *al-Hayat al-sinima'iya* (Damascus) 19 (Fall 1983): 34–35.

Jaidi, Moulay Driss. *Le cinéma au Maroc.* Rabat, 1991.

Jameson, Frederic. *Das politische Unbewußte.* Reinbek, 1988.

_____. "Third World Literature in the Era of Multinational Capitalism." *Social Text* (USA) 15 (Fall 1986): 65–88.

Jayushi, Salma. *Trends and Movements in Modern Arabic Poetry II.* Leiden, 1977.

Jeaggi, Bruno, and Walter Ruggle, eds. "Nacer Khemir: Das verlorene Halsband der Taube." *Edition Filmbulletin.* Baden (Switzerland), 1992.

Kamil Mursi, Ahmad. *Mu[c]djam al-fann al-sinima'i.* Cairo, 1973.

Kemp, Wolfgang. *Theorie der Fotografie (III).* Munich, 1980.

Kennedy-Day, Kiki. "Cinema in Lebanon, Syria, Iraq, and Kuwait." In O. Leaman, ed., *Encyclopedia of Middle Eastern Cinema*. London, 2001.

Kettelhake, Silke. "Oday Rasheed's 'Underexposure': Blinking Incredulously at the Sun." Qantara.de, 2005. http://www.qantara.de/webcom/show_article.php/_c-310/_nr-214/i.html

Khalil, ᶜAbd al-Nur. "al-Khatt al-bayani li-l-sinima al-misriya hal yas-ᶜad baᶜd al-sittin?" *al-Mussawar* (Cairo), 29 January 1988.

Khatib, Lina. *Lebanese Cinema: Imagining the Civil War and Beyond*. London, 2008.

Khayati, Khémais. *Cinémas arabes: Topographie d'une image éclatée*. Paris, 1996.

———. "Egypte–Tunisie: 'La guerre du cinéma.'" *Arabies* (Paris) 45 (September 1990): 77–80.

———. *Salah Abou Seif, cinéaste égyptien*. Cairo, 1990.

Khayri, Wadjih. "al-Haram wa-l-halal fi-l-sinima." *al-Kawakib* (Cairo), 13 July 1982.

Khelifa, Said Ould. "Abdelatif Ben Amar: Pour une cinématographie dépouillée." *Les 2 écrans* (Algiers) 26 (July 1980): 25–27.

———. "Aziza: Et ma part d'horizon?" *Les 2 écrans* (Algiers) 26 (July 1980): 23–24.

Khlifi, Omar. *L'histoire du cinéma en Tunisie*. Tunis, 1970.

Khoury, Philip S. *Syria and the French Mandate*. Princeton, 1987.

al-Khudari, Khalid. *Mawqiᶜ al-adab al-maghribi fi-l-sinima al-maghribiya*. Rabat, 1989.

———. "al-Riwaya al-ᶜarabiya fi-l-sinima: mas'ala tarikhiya." *Dirasat sinima'iya* (Qunaitara, Morocco) (n.d.): 13–17.

———. "al-Zift bayn al-sinima wa-l-masrah." *Dirasat sinima'iya* (Qunaitara, Morocco) 3 (March 1986): 12–18.

Kilpatrick, Hilary. *The Modern Egyptian Novel*. London, 1974.

Knilli, Friedrich, ed. *Semiotik des Films*. Munich, 1971.

Kobe, Werner. "Néjia Ben Mabrouk." *Journal Film* (Freiburg) 22 (Fall 1990): 17.

———. "Nouri Bouzid." *Journal Film* (Freiburg) 22 (Fall 1990): 19.

Krämer, Gudrun. "Studien zum Minderheitproblem." *Islam 7, Minderheit, Millet, Nation? Die Juden in Ägypten 1914–1952.* Wiesbaden, 1982.

Krichen, Aziz. *Le Syndrome Bourguiba.* Tunis, 1992.

Kurze, Gerhard. *Metapher, Allegorie, Symbol.* Göttingen, 1988.

Landau, Jacob. *Studies in the Arab Theater and Cinema.* Philadelphia, 1958.

Lange, Claudio, and Hans Schiler, eds. *Moderne arabische Literature.* Berlin, 1988.

Lewis, Bernard, ed. *The World of Islam.* London, 1976.

Lovell, Terry. *Pictures of Reality: Aesthetics, Politics and Pleasure.* London, 1980.

Lüders, Michael. "Film und Kino in Ägypten: Eine historische Bestandsaufnahme 1896–1952." M.A. thesis, Freie Universität Berlin, 1986.

———. *Gesellschaftliche Realität im ägyptischen Kinofilm: Von Nasser zu Sadat (1952–1981).* Frankfurt am Main, 1989.

MacCabe, Colin. "Realism and the Cinema." *Screen* 15, no. 2 (1974).

Madanat, ᶜAdnan. "Liqa' maᶜa al-mukhridj al-tunisi Mahmud bin Mahmud." *al-Hayat al-sinima'iya* (Damascus) (n.d.): 27–36.

———. "Zur Geschichte des palästinensischen Films." In *Filmtage der Solidarität mit dem palästinensischen Volk.* Berlin, 1981.

"Madjmuᶜat Talashi al-sinima'iya tusharik fi mihradjan Abu Dhabi al-sinima'i bi-sabᶜat aflam." *Riyadh,* no. 50 (Riyadh), 5 April 2009. http://www.alriyadh.com/420191

Magny, Joël, ed. "Théories du cinéma." *CinémAction* (Paris) 20 (1982).

Maherzi, Lotfi. *Le cinéma algérien.* Algiers, 1980.

Malkmus, Lizbeth, and Roy Armes. *Arab and African Filmmaking.* New Jersey, 1991.

Ma'oz, Moshe, and Avner Yaniv, eds. *Syria under Assad.* London, 1986.

Marks, Laura. "What Is That *and* Between Arab Women and Video?" *Camera Obscura* 54 (18, no. 3): 41–69.

al-Masnaoui, Mustafa. *Abhath fi-l-sinima al-maghribiya.* Rabat, 2001.

Megherbi, Abdelghani. *Les Algériens au miroir du cinéma colonial.* Algiers, 1982.

_____. *Le miroir apprivoisé*. Algiers, 1985.

_____. *Le miroir aux alouettes*. Algiers, 1985.

Mehdaoui, Khaled. "Le retour de manivelle." *Horizons* (Algiers), 2 Oct. 1985.

Mejcher-Atassi, Sonja. "Abounaddara's Take on Images in the Syrian Revolution: A Conversation between Akram Zaatari and Charif Kiwan." In *Jadaliyya*, (Washington DC), 8 July 2014. http://www.jadaliyya.com/pages/index/18433/abounaddara%27s-take-on-images-in-the-syrian-revolut

Merdaci, Djamel Eddine. "Adapter telle est la question." *Les 2 écrans* (Algiers) 52 (Jan. 1983): 20–22.

_____. "Algérie: Cinéma au féminin." *Les 2 écrans* (Algiers) 25 (June 1981): 6–10.

Merolla, Daniela. "Digital Imagination and the 'Landscapes of Group Identities': The Flourishing of Theatre, Video and 'Amazigh Net' in the Maghrib and Berber Diaspora." *The Journal of North African Studies* (London) 7, no. 4 (Winter 2002): 122–31.

Mikhail-Ashrawi, Hanan. *The Contemporary Literature of Palestine*. Ann Arbor, 1983.

Mimoun, Miloud, ed. "France–Algérie: Images d'une guerre." Edition Ciné-IMA (Paris) 1 (June 1992).

Ministry of Culture and Heritage Preservation (Boughedir, Ferid). *Le cinéma en Tunisie/Cinema in Tunisia*. Tunis, 2006.

"Mirzaq ᶜAlwash: hiwar maᶜa al-djumhur al-djaza'iri." *al-Hayat al-sinima'iya* (Damascus) 4 (Oct. 1979): 30–33.

Monaco, James. *Film verstehen*. Reinbek bei Hamburg, 1980.

de la Motte-Haber, Helga. *Filmmusik*. Munich, 1980.

al-Mufradji, Ahmad Fayad. *Fananu al-sinima fi-l-ᶜIraq*. Beirut, 1981.

_____. *Masadir dirasat al-nashat al-sinima'i fi-l-ᶜIraq 1968–1979*. Beirut, 1981.

Mühlböck, Monika. *Die Entwicklung der Massenmedien am Arabischen Golf*. Heidelberg, 1988.

Multaqa al-mar'a wa-l-zakira, ed. *Zaman al-nisa'*. Cairo, 1998.

Mustapha, Raith. "De l'âge d'or à la stagnation." *al-Watan*, 8–9 Oct. 1991.

Mustapha, T. "Illusions." *al-Moudjahid* (Algiers), 7 July 1991.

Naficy, Hamid. "Phobic Spaces and Liminal Panics: Independent Transnational Film Genre." In Ella Shohat and Robert Stam, ed., *Multiculturalism, Postcoloniality, and Transnational Media*. New Brunswick, 2003.

Nagbou, Mustapha. "Le grand problème des petites salles de cinéma." *Le septième art* (Tunis) 72 (Aug. 1991): 12.

al-Naggar, Ahmad al-Sayyid. "Sina‘at al-sinima fi Misr." In Ahmad al-Sayyid al-Naggar, ed., *al-Itidjahat al-iqtisadiya al-istratidjiya 2001*. Al-Ahram Center for Political and Strategic Studies. Cairo, 2002.

al-Nahas, Hashim. *al-Hawiya al-qaumiya fi-l-sinima al-‘arabiya*. Cairo, 1986.

———. *Nagib Mahfuz ‘ala al-shasha*. Cairo, 1975.

al-Nahas, Hashim, ed. *al-Insan al-misri ‘ala al-shasha*. Cairo, 1986.

Najar, Ridha. "Le déséquilibre audiovisuel Nord–Sud." *Colloque international: Création cinématographique du Sud face au marché du Nord. Journées cinématographiques de Carthage, Tunis*. 5–6 Oct. 1992.

Naji, Jamal Eddine. "Le cinéma marocain: Une problématique à poncteur." *Lamalif* (May 1976): 36–39.

Neidhardt, Irit. "Michel Khleifi und Hany Abud Assad im Gespräch mit Irit Niedhardt." In V. Theissl and V. Kull, ed., *Poeten, Chronisten, Rebellen: Internationale Dokumentarfilmemacherinnen im Porträt*. Marburg, 2006.

———. "Palästina im Film: Eine Einführung in das Selbstverständnis und die Geschichte des palästinensischen Kinos." *Palästina-Journal* (Berlin) 3 (June 2000): 266–83.

———. *Untold Stories*. Westminster Papers in Communication and Culture 7, no. 2 (2010). https://www.westminster.ac.uk/__data/assets/pdf_file/0011/79967/004WPCC-Vol7-No2-Irit_Neidhardt.pdf

Nesselson, Lisa. "Review, *Viva Laljérie*." *Variety* (Los Angeles), 11 May 2004. http://variety.com/2004/film/reviews/viva-laldjerie-1200533527/

Nichols, Bill, ed. *Introduction to Documentary*. Bloomington, 2001.

———. *Movies and Methods (I)*. Berkeley, 1976.

Nicholson, Reynold A. *A Literary History of the Arabs*. Cambridge, 1953.

Nicollier, Valerie. "Der offene Bruch: Das Kino der Pieds Noirs." *CICIM* (Munich) 34 (Dec. 1991).

Nouri, Shakir. *A la recherche du cinéma iraqien 1945–1985*. Paris 1986.

Novak, Anneliese. *Die amerikanische Filmfarce*. Munich, 1991.

Onohiolo. "Entretien avec Mohamed Zran." *Le Messager* 1895 (8 June 2005).

Othman, Susan. "Le cinéma marocain et l'authenticité: Discours et image." *Les Cahiers de l'Orient* (Paris) 18 (March 1990): 175–88.

Ouannès, Moncef (Wannas, al-Munsif). *al-Dawla wa-l-mas'ala al-thaqafiya fi-l-djaza'ir*. Tunis, (n.d.).

———. *al-Dawla wa-l-mas'ala al-thaqafiya fi-l-mamlaka al-maghribiya*. Tunis, 1991.

Paech, Joachim. *Literatur und Film*. Stuttgart, 1988.

Pflaum, Hans Gunther. *Film in der Bundesrepublik Deutschland*. Bonn, 1985.

Pines, Jim, and Paul Willemen, eds. *Questions of Third Cinema*. London, 1989.

Prokop, Dieter. *Soziologie des Films*. Frankfurt am Main, 1982.

Prüfer, Curt. *Ein ägyptisches Schattenspiel*. Erlangen, 1906.

Qalyubi, Muhammad Kamil, et al. *al-Sinima al-carabiya wa-l-ifriqiya*. Beirut, 1984.

al-Rabici, Shaukat. *al-Fann al-tashkili al-mucasir fi-l-watan al-carabi*. Cairo, 1988.

Rahat, G. "Quel avenir pour le cinéma algérien? Problème de la langue." *al-Moudjahid* (Algiers) 22 (May 1967).

al-Raci, cAli. *Finun al-kumidiya: min khayal al-zil ila Nagib al-Rihani*. Cairo, 1971.

———. *al-Kumidiya al-murtadjala fi-l-masrah al-misri*. Cairo, 1968.

———. *al-Masrah fi-l-watan al-carabi*. Kuwait, 1980.

Ramzi, Kamal. "Arbac qadaya djadida fi-l-sinima al-misriya." Study for 5th Film Festival. Damascus, 1987.

———. "Asda' al-sabcinat fi rubaciyat Yusuf Shahin." *Sinima 81* (Cairo). al-Thaqafa al-Djamahiriya, 1981.

———. "Liqa' maca Muhammad Khan wa cAtif al-Tayyib." *Sinima* (Cairo) 1. al-Markaz al-Qaumi li-l-Sinima, 1981.

_____. "al-Masadir al-adabiya fi-l-aflam al-misriya." In *2e Biennale des cinémas arabes à Paris*, ed., Institut du Monde Arabe, 122–45. Paris, 1994. French: "Les sources littéraires dans le cinéma égyptien," 111–20.

_____. "Sawwaq al-utubis." *Sinima 83* (Cairo). al-Thaqafa al-Djamahiriya, 1983.

_____. "al-Shakhsiyat al-tarikhiya fi-l-sinima al-ᶜarabiya." *Shu'un ᶜarabiya* (Tunis) 26 (April 1983): 79–97.

Real, Michael R. *Mass-Mediated Culture*. Engelwood Cliffs, 1977.

van Reenen, Dan. "Das Bilderverbot, a New Survey." *Der Islam* (Berlin) 67, no. 1 (1990): 27–77.

Richter, Erika. *Realistischer Film in Ägypten*. Berlin, 1974.

"Rih al-sadd taltahiq bi-riyah al-ridda." *Dirasat sinima'iya* (Qunaitara, Morocco) 5 (Jan. 1987): 22–24.

Ristau, Malte, ed., *Identität durch Geschichte*. Marburg, 1985.

Ritman, Alex. "Whatever Happened to the Qatari Film Industry?" *The Guardian* (London), 6 March 2014. http://www.theguardian.com/film/2014/mar/06/qatari-film-industry-doha-festival-black-gold

Rosant, Lucas. "Census and Analysis of Film and Audiovisual Co-productions in the South Mediterranean Region 2006–2011." *Euromed Audiovisual III CSU*. Strasbourg, 2012.

Rother, Rainer, ed., *Bilder schreiben Geschichte: Der Historiker im Kino*. Berlin, 1991.

al-Roumi, Mayyar, and Dorothée Schmid. "Le cinéma syrien: Du militantisme au mutisme." In R. Wafik, ed., *Cinéma et monde musulman: Cultures et interdits. Euroorient* (Neuilly) 10 (2001): 4–25.

Ruggle, Walter. "Gewalt löst keine Probleme: *Noce en Galilée* von Michel Khleifi/Gespräch mit Michel Khleifi: Ich bin ein Ghetto-Kind." *Filmbulletin* 3/88 (1988): 45–53.

Saᶜd, ᶜAbd al-Munᶜim. *al-Mukhridj Ahmad Badr Khan uslubuh min khilal aflamih*. Cairo, 1975.

Sadoul, Georges, ed. *Cinema in the Arab Countries*. Beirut, 1966.

Said, Edward. *Orientalism*. London, 1991.

Salih, Ahmad Rushdi. *al-Adab al-shaᶜbi*. Cairo, 1971.

Salmane, Hala, Simon Hartog, and David Wilson, eds. *Algerian Cinema.* London: BFI, 1976.

Salti, Rasha, ed. *Insights into Syrian Cinema: Essays and Conversations with Contemporary Filmmakers.* New York, 2006.

Sarmini, Salah. "Malamih al-kumidya fi-l-sinima al-suriya." *Les 2 écrans* (Algiers) 40 (Dec. 1981): 8–11.

Scott, Victoria. "DFI Postpones New Festival after Laying Off Dozens of Employees." *Doha News* (Doha), 12 January 2014. http://dohanews.co/dfi-postpones-new-film-festival-after-laying-off-dozens-of-employees/

Seeßlen, Georg. *Kino der Gefühle.* Hamburg, 1980.

Sermini, Salah. "Cinema in the Arab Mashriq (East)." Filmmuseum Frankfurt. *Panorama of Arab Cinema, 1954–2004.* Frankfurt am Main (2004): 70–74.

Shafik, Viola. "Der belagerte Film oder Europas arabisches Filmschaffen." Landeszentrale für politische Bildung Baden-Württemberg. *Der Bürger im Staat* (Stuttgart) 2 (2006): 131–35.

———. "Egyptian Cinema." In O. Leaman, ed., *Encyclopedia of Middle Eastern Cinema*, 23–129. London, 2001.

———. "Film in Palästina—Palästina im Film." *Die siebten Tage des unabhängigen Films,* ed. Augsburg, 13–17 March 1991.

———. "Mohammed Malas: Traum und Erinnerung." *Journal Film* 22 (Freiburg), Fall 1990.

———. "Palestinian Cinema." In O. Leaman, ed., *Encyclopedia of Middle Eastern Cinema*, 130–49. London, 2001.

———. *Popular Egyptian Cinema: Gender, Class, and Nation.* Cairo, 2007.

———. "Realität und Film im Ägypten der 80er Jahre." M.A. thesis, Universität Hamburg, 1988.

———. "Resisting Pleasure? Performativity and Political Resistance in Arab Cinema." In Karima Laachir and Saeed Talajooy, eds, *Resistance in Contemporary Middle Eastern Cultures,* 121–37. London, 2012.

———. "Youssef Chahine." *Kinemathek* (Berlin) 74 (1989).

———. "Youssef Chahine: Barocke Obsessionen." *Die siebten Tage des unabhängigen Films,* ed. 13–17 March 1991.

———. *Zensierte Träume: 20 Jahre syrischer Film*. Edition Initiative Kommunales Kino Hamburg e.V. Hamburg, 1991.

Shaᶜrawi, ᶜAbd al-Muᶜti. *al-Masrah al-misri al-mu' asir*. Cairo, 1986.

Sharif, Issam A. *Algerien vom Populismus zum Islam*. Wien, 1992.

Shawkat, Reem. "The Struggle of Young Egyptian Artists in Natural Colors." *Menassat* (Beirut), 22 Jan. 2010. http://www.menassat.com/ ?q=en/news-articles/7369-struggle-young-egyptian-artists-natural-colors

Shohat, Ella. "Egypt: Cinema and Revolution." *Critical Arts* (USA) 2, no. 4 (1983): 22–32.

———. "Imagining Terra Incognita: The Disciplinary Gaze of Empire." *Public Culture* (New York) 3, no. 2 (Spring 1991): 41–70.

———. *Israeli Cinema*. Austin, 1989.

———. "Post–Third Worldist Culture: Gender, Nation, and the Cinema." In M. Jacqui Alexander, ed., *Feminist Genealogies, Colonial Legacies, Democratic Futures*. Routledge, 1996.

Shohat, Ella, and Robert Stam. "The Cinema after Babel: Language, Difference, Power." *Screen* (London) 26, no. 3–4 (May–Aug. 1985): 35–58.

———. *Unthinking Eurocentrism: Multiculturalism and the Media*. London, 1994.

Shukair, ᶜAbd al-Karim. "ᶜAra'is min qasab wa-l-naᶜura." *Dirasat sinima'iya* (Qunaitara, Morocco) 3 (March 1986): 7–11.

Shusha, Muhammad al-Sayyid. *Ruwwad wa ra'idat al-sinima al-misriya*. Cairo, 1977.

Soueid, Mohamed (Suwaid, Muhammad). *al-Sinima al-mu'adjala*. Beirut, 1986.

Souiba, Farid, and Fatima Zarha el-Alaoui. *Un Siècle de cinema au Maroc, 1907–1995*. Rabat, 1995.

Stam, Robert. *Subversive Pleasures: Bakhtin, Cultural Criticism and Film*. Baltimore, 1989.

———. "Third World Cinema." *Journal of Film and Video* (USA) 36 (Spring 1984): 50–61.

Stauth, Georg, and Sami Zubaida, eds. *Mass Culture, Popular Culture and Social Life in the Middle East*. Frankfurt, 1987.

Steinbach, Udo. *Politisches Lexikon Nahost*. Munich, 1981.

Stora, Benjam. "Ein dunkler Thriller." *Qantara* (Bonn), 14 Aug. 2013. http://de.qantara.de/inhalt/interview-mit-dem-algerischen-regisseur-nadir-mokneche-ein-dunkler-thriller

Sulaiman, Khalid A. *Palestine and Modern Arab Poetry*. London, 1984.

Sunduq Da^cm al-Sinima, ed. *Banurama al-sinima al-misriya 27–82: dalil al-aflam al-misriya*. Cairo, 1983.

Suwayba, Fu'ad. "al-Sinima al-maghribiya fi-l-thamaninat." In *al-Hayat al-sinima'iya* (Damascus) 21 (Spring 1989): 16–31.

Sweileh, Khalil. "Raymond Boutros: The Last Communist." *Al-Akhbar English* (Beirut), 2 Aug. 2012. http://english.al-akhbar.com/node/10700

Der Tagesspiegel Online. "Ein Berliner Filmclub für Bagdad." 19 August 2004. http://www.tagesspiegel.de/berlin/archiv/19.08.2004/1308120.asp

Tamzali, Wassyla. *En attendant Omar Gatlato*. Algiers, 1979.

———. "La nouba des femmes du Mont Chenoua: Notes prises pendant le tournage, Tipasa, Mars, 1977." *Les 2 écrans* (Algiers) 5 (July 1978): 46.

Tazaroute, Abdelkrim. "CAAIC: Situation alarmante." *al-Moudjahid* (Algiers), 15 May 1992.

———. "Mustapha Azouni, DG du CAAIC." *al-Moudjahid* (Algiers), 25 March 1992.

Thabet, Madkour. "Industrie du film égyptien." In R. Wafik, ed., *Cinéma et monde musulman: Cultures et interdits. Euroorient* (Neuilly) 10 (2001): 26–53.

Thoraval, Ives. *Regards sur le cinéma égyptien*. Beirut, 1975.

Thoraval, Yves. *Les écrans du Croissant Fertile: Irak, Liban, Palestine, Syrie*. Paris, 2003.

Tibi, Bassam. "Von der Selbstverherrlichung zur Selbstkritik." *Die Dritte Welt* (Meisenheim) 1, no. 1 (1972): 158–84.

Torchani, Narjès. "Tunisie: Centre national du cinéma et de l'image—Du retard à rattraper." In *Allafrica* (Cape Town), 20 Nov. 2012. fr.allafrica.com/stories/201211201588.html

Touma, Habib Hassan. *Die Musik der Araber*. Wilhelmshaven, 1989.

Tudor, Andrew. *Image and Influence*. London, 1974.

Tulayma, ᶜAbd al-Munᶜim, ed. *al-Hawiya al-qaumiya fi-l-sinima al-ᶜara-biya*. Beirut, 1986.

"Tunisia." In *The Mediterranean Audiovisual Landscape*. Euromed Audiovisual II, 2008. http://euromedaudiovisuel.net/Files/2013/02/25/1361790429172.pdf?1361800421627

al-ᶜUbaydi, Amal Sulayman Mahmoud. "Cinema in Libya." In O. Leaman, ed., *Encyclopedia of Middle Eastern Cinema*d. 407–19. London, 2001.

Vatikiotis, P.J. *The History of Egypt*. London, 1985.

Wassef, Magda, ed. *Egypte 100 ans de cinéma*. Paris, 1995.

Whittock, Trevor. *Metaphor and Film*. Cambridge, 1990.

Williams, Christopher, ed. *Realism and the Cinema*. London, 1980.

Williams, Raymond. "A Lecture on Realism." *Screen* (London) Spring 1977: 61–74.

Yusuf, Yusuf. *Qadiyat Filastin fi-l-sinima*. Beirut, 1990.

Zaccak, Hady. *Le cinéma libanais: Itinéraire d'un cinéma vers l'inconnu (1929–1996)*. Beirut, 1997.

_____. "Regard sur le cinéma libanais." *Travaux et jours* (Beirut) 69 (2002): 171–91.

Zaptia, Sami. "Libya Movie Awards Come to Successful Conclusion. *Libya Herald* (Tripoli), 10 Nov. 2013. http://euromedaudiovisuel.net/p.aspx?t=news&mid=21&cid=20&l=en&did=1703

Zebari, Ahmed Abdel Hamid. "Iraqi Kurdistan Seeks Cinema Revival." *al-Monitor*, 1 July 2013. http://www.al-monitor.com/pulse/origi-nals/2013/07/iraq-kurdistan-cinema-revival.html

Zerrouki, Yassmine. "From *Casanegra* to *Zero*: A Story of Casablanca." *Morocco World News* (Rabat), 19 Jan. 2012. http://www.moroccoworld-news.com/2013/01/74471/from-casanegra-to-zero-a-story-of-casablanca/

INDEX OF TITLES

INDEX OF NAMES

CPSIA information can be obtained
at www.ICGtesting.com
Printed in the USA
JSHW040346051020
8386JS00002B/2